320

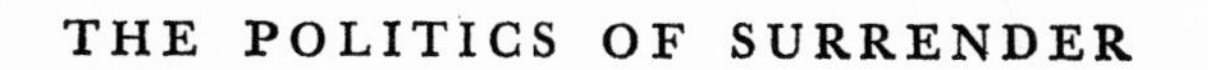

THE POLITICS OF SURRENDER

Books by M. Stanton Evans

REVOLT ON THE CAMPUS
THE LIBERAL ESTABLISHMENT
THE POLITICS OF SURRENDER

THE POLITICS OF SURRENDER

M. Stanton Evans

THE DEVIN-ADAIR COMPANY

New York 1966

Copyright © 1966 by The Devin-Adair Company.
All rights reserved. No portion of this
book may be reproduced in any form without
written permission from the publisher,
The Devin-Adair Co., 23 East 26th Street, New York 10010,
except by a reviewer, who may quote brief passages
in connection with a review.

Canadian Agent: Abelard-Schuman Canada, Ltd, Toronto

Library of Congress Catalog Card Number 66-25294

Manufactured in the United States of America

Acknowledgments

This is a layman's book on an expert's subject, leading from the historical record rather than from the writer's authority. I have therefore been greatly dependent on the advice and counsel of many people.

Among those who have been kind enough to help in tracing down facts and establishing context, I should like especially to thank Allan Ryskind, William Schulz, Antoni Gollan, and Ross Hermann. I also owe a particular debt of gratitude to Ferdinand L. Mayer, whose long experience in the foreign policy field has been invaluable, and to Richard V. Allen, whose encyclopedic knowledge of Communist techniques I have relied upon in several places.

Thanks are also owing to the office staffs of Senator Strom Thurmond and Representatives Richard Roudebush, William Cramer, Howard Robison, and Edward Derwinski, and to Benjamin Mandel. Among members of the journalistic community, I wish to acknowledge the kindness of Walter Trohan of the *Chicago Tribune,* Mrs. Ann Lloyd Merriman of the *Richmond News-Leader,* and Virginia Gill of the Copley News Service and the library staffs of the *New York Herald-Tribune* and the *San Diego Union.* Closer to home, Miss Jo Mohr has once more been unfailing in her assistance and Mr. and Mrs. Lawrence Arany have done their usual superlative job with the index.

Most important, I wish to thank my wife, Sue Ellen, who has worked hard on this volume and deserves billing as its co-author. She correctly observes, however, that responsibility for all opinions and statements contained herein is my own.

SURRENDER. . . . To give up (something) out of one's own possession or power into that of another who has or asserts a claim to it; to yield on demand or compulsion, esp. (Mil.) to give up possession of (a fortress, town, territory, etc.) to an enemy or assailant . . . More widely: To give up, resign, abandon, esp. in favour of or for the sake of another . . . To give oneself up into the power of another, esp. as a prisoner . . . To give oneself up to some influence, course of action, etc.; to abandon oneself to.

—*The Oxford Universal Dictionary*

Contents

Introduction:

THE PROBLEM

We must realize that we cannot coexist eternally, for a long time. One of us must go to the grave. We do not want to go to the grave. They do not want to go to their grave either. So what can be done? We must push them to their grave.

—Nikita Khrushchev

★★ 1. *The Danger Is Internal*

1. *The Purpose of Foreign Policy*

THE FIRST PURPOSE of a nation's foreign policy is to protect the lives and vital interests of its citizens from the hostile initiatives of alien powers.

This definition is in part historical and descriptive—derived from the fact that almost all governors, diplomats and military strategists have, legitimately or not, invoked such motives as the point and justification of their actions. It is also a product of the Western theory of government which says political authority exists to serve the people and to maintain the arena of order within which they may go peacefully about their business. If government is obliged to promote the interests of the governed, then its first and most elementary function is to protect the governed from foreign enemies. To supply such protection was one of the explicit reasons alleged for the formation of the American union.

It is the argument of this book that the usual conception of foreign policy has been abandoned by important elements in American society and that these elements have, over a span of years, succeeded in translating a revolutionary view of the foreign policy function into critical phases of our diplomacy. The net result, we shall argue, is that the United States in its conduct abroad has increasingly defaulted the first purpose of successful governance.

The alteration in principles has not always been explicit, nor has the consequent default of the military-diplomatic function been all of a piece. Our foreign policy of the past generation has been a mixed bag, sometimes relying on the old definitions and old rhetoric, more often abandoning them for something else. It is to trace the lineaments of that something else, and to assay its consequences, that this volume has been written.

The default of American foreign policy proceeds from a number of causes, all of which have been thrown into high relief by the Free World's encounter with international Communism. It embraces certain assumptions about the nature of man, society, and government which differ radically from those on which the American nation was founded. These assumptions, and the foreign policy derived from them, are today generally known by the name of "Liberalism."

The chief characteristic of Liberal foreign policy is a wide-ranging effort to order the actions of our government abroad, not according to available criteria of national interest, but according to certain abstract ideas about the way the world ought to be in some ideal future. By his own accounting, the Liberal has in his head a picture of a sort of tranquil ecumene in which national interests wither quietly away, and he sees the power of the United States government in international dealings as an instrument for bringing this to pass. The essence of the thing is to use American power to contrive the evanescence of American power. It is the diplomacy of the self-denying ordinance.

As one high-ranking official of our government has put it: "It is a legitimate American objective to see removed from all nations—including the United States—the right to use substantial military force to pursue their own interests. Since this residual right is the root of national sovereignty, and the basis for the existence of an international arena of power, it is, therefore, an American interest to see an end to nationhood as it has been historically defined."[1]

How such an other-worldly approach to the conduct of nation-states might have worked out under favorable conditions is difficult to say—although history does not suggest much likelihood of its success. The fact of the case is that the Liberal attitude has become dominant in our affairs at a period when power politics in the world at large have been played with unparalleled intensity and ruthlessness, and when a hostile force has became capable, as never before, of threatening America's national well-being. We have thus tended to abandon the precepts of national-interest diplomacy precisely at a time when we stand most in need of them. Beset by the aggressive dynamism of the Communist world-empire, we have pledged ourselves to national renunciation and honed our foreign policy into an implement of global sanctimony.

The result has been a startling divergence between reigning theory and the shape of reality. As the Communists have prosecuted their various aggressions, we have gone about our business quite as if there were no such thing as a Communist, as if the world were a sort of placid laboratory in which we could undertake all kinds of social and political tinkering without casting up the consequences. Thus we have worked to eliminate Western "colonialism" from Asia and Africa or to pull down military-type anti-Communist regimes because they offend against the ruling abstractions, oblivious of the fact that Communist forces rush into the power vacuums thereby created. We have tried to establish "broadly-based" "coalition" governments that include Communists because the abstractions say such governments are democratic—even though experience shows such governments more often than not are preliminaries to Communist takeover.

It would be difficult to conceive a danger to man or nation greater than this discrepancy between challenge and response. Confronted by some kind of external menace, however great, an intelligent man in possession of his faculties may calculate dangers and opportunities and set about defending himself. But for the man incapable of apprehending his peril or ordering his responses, there is no hope. He is at the mercy of his antagonist and can be rescued only by fate or the opponent's error; he most certainly will not rescued by any purposeful effort of his own.

Given the necessary difference between a single man and the mingling of wills by which a nation is directed, this is more or less the present condition of the United States. We have shown ourselves alternately unwilling or unable to order our responses to suit the nature of our crisis. We have lost the ability to dispose our policies according to a realistic assessment of the world around us. *Instead of defining our policy in terms of the enemy, we have taken to defining the enemy in terms of the policy.* The abstractions set the pace, and our conception of reality comes tagging after.

2. *The Nature of Liberalism*

Liberal assumptions about the nature of the world we live in, the purposes of foreign policy, and the characteristics of Communism read roughly as follows:

The world at large is and should be headed toward a species of welfarist democracy under the aegis of paternalist governments and, at some point in the future, under the aegis of just one such government. The mature societies of the world are advancing into a benevolent paternalism in which government assumes more and more responsibilities for managing the economy; the younger or "underdeveloped" societies are trying to get themselves mobilized to reach the economic "take-off" point. Both kinds of activity demand a good deal of centralized coercive planning. These processes are going to occur willy-nilly, and are at worst merely complicated rather than caused by the intrusions of the Communists. ". . . the real danger from Communism," says one Liberal spokesman, "lies in an unrealistic approach to social revolution in underdeveloped countries and . . . it cannot be combatted by military force, but only by a new attitude toward revolutionary regimes."[2]

Liberalism holds that the purpose of American foreign policy is, among other things, to assist and hasten the coming about of the much talked-of revolution, and to advance as specific policy objectives "social justice," plebiscitary government by majority rule, the abolition of Western colonialism, economic growth in the underdeveloped societies, and—most important of all—Peace. The Liberal is not averse to *all* forms of violence or warfare—e.g., a war waged by "democrats" or agrarian reformers to overthrow a military government, or a war waged by the United Nations to overthrow the government of Katanga. He is opposed, however, to warfare with the Soviet Union or Red China which could lead to "nuclear holocaust." The first and foremost objective of Liberal foreign policy, while all the other things are going on, is therefore to do whatever is necessary to avoid warfare between the United States and these Communist powers. "Our purpose," says State Department officer Harlan Cleveland, ". . . *is to avoid war* while, in more and more corners of the world, the idea of human freedom triumphs over the idea of coercion as the guiding principle in human affairs."[3] (Italics added.)

The Liberal believes Communists are at bottom not too different from ourselves, and that the Cold War is the result of misunderstanding. If the Communists once were dangerous (which the Liberal doubts), they are now "mellowing," and the urgent necessity of the hour is to build bridges of mutual trust and association—to establish contacts between East and West which will dissipate the misunderstanding and make the outbreak of war less likely. The Liberal sees the spread of Bolshevism as evidence, not that Communists are aggressors, but that *we* have failed to satisfy the revolution of rising expectations and have thereby created a natural pull toward the Communist program of social justice, democracy, reform, *etc.*

These ideas are elaborated by some subsidiary points which have been advanced and cherished for so long that—although instrumental in nature—they have assumed the status of major assumptions. Some of these subsidiary ideas include the following:

1. "Nationalism" (except for underdeveloped societies) is *per se* bad and should be submerged in the machinery of a world government.

2. American policy, abjuring "nationalism," should be oriented to "world opinion," as a proper measure of rectitude and a portent of the better day to come.

3. "Neutralism" in the Cold War, generally associated with regimes very much interested in the take-off point and social justice, is preferable to militant anti-Communism, generally associated with "reactionary" regimes.

4. Left-wing governments in general are preferable to right-wing governments, since there is a presumption that the former are somehow "democratic" while the latter are not.

5. Nations conquered by Communism cannot reasonably hope for liberation, because to suggest that we should like to

see a change of regime behind the Iron or Bamboo Curtain could lead to war; nations belonging to the Free World are open to challenge through Communist "wars of liberation," however, because to pronounce a flat prohibition against such wars would be to manifest delusions of "omnipotence" and could lead to nuclear holocaust.

6. The communization of half the world over the past 20 years is nobody's fault in particular and is simply testimony to the fact that the Communists have, so far as the global revolution is concerned, built a better mousetrap.

These ideas, mingling with, interacting upon and reinforcing the basic assumptions of Liberal diplomacy, lead by one route or another to the action programs we have mentioned, which among them aim to advance "social justice" and "ease tensions" between ourselves and the Communists. We cannot discuss all of these here, but most readers will readily recognize the following:

1. Increased trade, negotiations, and exchanges with the Soviet Union and other Communist nations so that the Communists can learn more about us and we about them.

2. Herculean restraint by the United States issuing in various concessions to the Communists, demonstrating that our intentions are peaceful and encouraging them to further mellowness.

3. Constant demonstrations to the world that we want peace and global collectivism quite as much as do the Communists, thus outbidding Moscow and Peking in their appeal to the revolutionary temper of the times.

4. Strenuous efforts to achieve nuclear disarmament as quickly as possible even if this means a certain amount of risk, since no danger is greater than the danger of nuclear holocaust.

5. Less emphasis on military aid and alliances, greater emphasis on economic aid helping nations to achieve take-off, social justice and revolution.

6. All-out support of the United Nations even when it adversely affects our own interests and a constant effort to strengthen it at the expense of national sovereignties.

7. Support for the "democratic left" all over the world, encouragement of neutralism, and overthrow of anti-Communist "right-wing" regimes.

This list might be expanded or reduced; it is, obviously, an arbitrary selection. But it is not, as we shall seek to demonstrate in the succeeding chapters, an inaccurate selection.

3. *A World We Made*

The ideas spelled out above have, off and on, been in charge of American foreign policy since 1945. They are responsible for whatever success, or lack of it, has attended our dealings in the Cold War. It is therefore useful, both to begin our assessment of Liberalism and to establish the general conditions which nowadays confront the makers of American foreign policy, to attempt an overview of what has happened in the decades since 1945.

Several possible measures of our foreign policy during this span come to mind. U.S. diplomatist Harlan Cleveland suggested some of them back in 1962 by telling us the history of the Cold War has been the history of the advancement of liberty, of dawning civilization, of a new compassionate humanity.[4] This is an encouraging sort of retrospect, and we would doubtless all feel better about things if it were true. Unfortunately, there is hardly a particle of evidence in the record to support it.

Has the objective of our foreign policy been the encouragement of "peace"? There has in fact been no peace in the world since 1945; there have been, by authoritative calculation, more than 100 wars of all descriptions, and continuous warfare of one sort or another somewhere in the world.[5] The United States has fought one bloody war in Korea, and at this writing is conducting another one in Viet Nam. Wars and other kinds of violence are repeatedly breaking out in Africa, Latin America, and Asia.

Has the objective of our policy been the advancement of "democracy"? If we look over a map of the countries which we labored so hard to liberate in World War II and in which we have exerted our influence to banish "colonialism," we find nothing approaching personal freedom or popularly-elected government. We find instead military dictatorships, juntas, one-man fiefdoms, oligarchies.

Has the objective of our policy been to spread the values of a humanitarian civilization? Again, the record is unprepossessing. Lord Acton suggested the minimum test of civilization is human life—whether one is willing to take it through murder. The period since 1945 has been replete with killings of every sort. It is probable that more people—30 million at least—have died through various forms of political murder in the two decades 1945-1965 than in any other comparable period of history.

Has the objective of our policy been to spread material well-being? The people of the world had less to eat in 1965 than they did in 1950, since, as James Burnham notes, it is a perverse fact of history that "in the past 15 years the average per capita food consumption has been going down, not up."[6] In certain "underdeveloped" countries, the continuation and intensification of poverty are directly related to the character of our foreign policy.

In none of these categories have the abstractions of Liberal ideology been realized. Envisioning a world without war or want or human misery, we have somehow helped midwife a world where there seems to be a larger quotient of these things than ever before. Thus, taken on its own grounds, Liberal foreign policy has little to show as evidence of success. Even more important, perhaps, the grounds selected tend to miss the point. It is a terrible thing that there are now less amiability and democracy in the world than was the case two decades ago. It would be wonderful if there were more of these things. But neither alternative tells us anything about the rationality of American foreign policy, because neither speaks to the chief problem relevant to the security of the United States, the problem of Communism.

The proper measure of reigning foreign policy assumptions in the Cold War is and must be the balance of strength between the Free World and the Communist one. Our security and survival are bound up with the Free World, and they are threatened by Communism. At a minimum, our foreign policy objective should be, and on several occasions has been stated to be, to keep Free World strength from shrinking and Communist strength from growing. In point of fact, just the opposite has occurred. The perimeters of the Free World have since 1945 contracted alarmingly, while the boundaries of the Communist empire have correspondingly moved forward.

In 1944, world Communism controlled an estimated 170 million people and some 8 million square miles of territory. By 1964 Communism controlled more than 16 million square miles of territory, 18 separate states, and more than 1 billion people. The countries under Communist dominion, outside the USSR itself, included Latvia, Lithuania, Estonia, Poland, Yugoslavia, Czechoslovakia, Bulgaria, Hungary, Rumania, Albania, East Germany, China, Mongolia, Tibet, North Korea, North Viet Nam and Cuba. Communism has additionally established footholds in Laos, Afghanistan, Zanzibar, and Malaysia, and drawn into its orbit a host of "neutrals" too numerous to be listed here.

In those areas where a determined anti-Communist resistance remains, the Communists and their various allies have been relentlessly on the attack. To name the hard anti-Communist nations of the world is to name, with scientific precision, the areas where the prevailing regimes are embattled and of doubtful longevity: Rhodesia, Spain, Portugal, Angola, South Africa, South Viet Nam, Free China. The small and dwindling band is under the same ferocious pressure that in the past was deployed against anti-Communist leaders in Yugoslavia, Poland, Cuba, the Dominican Republic.

Small wonder the Communists proclaim the world strategic situation has undergone a momentous transformation in their favor. In 1938 Stalin said the "socialist" countries were confronted by the menace of "capitalistic encirclement"; in 1956, Nikita Khrushchev proudly told the assembled comrades at the 20th World Congress of the Communist Party that things had been reversed—that the capitalist countries were confronted by "socialist encirclement." He was, for once, telling the truth.

How did these things come to pass? Despite the considerable cleverness and unflagging zeal of the Communists, the story of this astounding reversal was written, not by Communist strength, but by Western weakness. The Communists have not in fact been winning the Cold War so much as we have been losing it. We have, on a variety of pretexts, been steadily surrendering the world to the enemy in the Kremlin. We have been losing the fight because, for the most part, the abstractions of Liberalism keep telling us we aren't in it. So much, at all events, we shall argue in the succeeding pages of this volume.

To suggest that the adverse history of the Cold War is traceable to Free World default rather than Communist strength is to evoke a retort about jingoism or supposed yearnings after American "omnipotence." To suggest that a different policy in Washington or London or Paris could have changed things is, we are told, simplistic and naive. Great tides are sweeping the world. We cannot expect to make the rest of the globe conform to our own ideas. The world is changing and we must change with it.

A glance at the record will suggest these statements are alibis rather than explanations. Quite clearly, the United States is not "omnipotent." It is, however, the strongest nation on earth, and in 1945, when the long decline began, probably came as close to "omnipotence" in world affairs as any nation in the course of modern history. The apposite question is not whether the world's strongest nation is "omnipotent," but why the world's strongest nation has been acting as if it were the weakest.

That we *are* the world's strongest nation, despite some fustian about "missile gaps" and "growth rates" five or six years ago, is nowadays generally conceded. And in 1945 there was of course no need to argue the matter at all. So far as mere questions of physical equipment went, we were the preeminent nation of the world, a state of affairs which, by common consent, existed at least until 1950—a period of some five years. Any advances made by Communism during that period did not result from the military superiority of the Communists, or even from the tactical intricacies fostered by an assumed condition of stalemate. We had unquestioned strategic superiority. Yet it was precisely during that period that we turned over to the Communists the strategic leverage points necessary for the conquest of Eastern Europe and China, brought pressure to bear to topple anti-Communist leaders in Yugoslavia and Poland, observed and cooperated in the fall of mainland China, witnessed the rise of Communist insurrection in Indochina and Korea.

The reasons given for this performance have been various: We had to demonstrate our "good will"; Moscow had a right to "friendly governments" on its borders; the Soviets were historically "suspicious" of the West and only by easing their suspicions could we bring them out of their shell. The logic of these arguments will be examined at various places in the course of this book. The simplest commentary on them is to note that when the objective conditions of foreign policy had transparently altered—when the Communists stood before us in Korea as naked aggressors—these reasons were quietly dropped from sight while the policy remained the same. We still yielded to the Communists, made concessions to them, retreated before their hostile initiatives, exactly as before. Whereas the policy of retreat had previously been justified on the grounds that the Soviets should be handled gently to lull their suspicions, it was now justified on the grounds that Moscow was too powerful to cross. When Soviet weakness would have allowed us to act, we were told they were not hostile; when Soviet hostility made it imperative for us to act, we were told they were too strong. The net result in both cases was that we did not act.

The common element, in 1945 or 1950 or 1966, has been the predominance of Liberal abstraction in the conduct of our foreign policy. Then as now we set out to refashion the world according to the ideological patterns of the Liberal faith rather than to array our strength in defense of our vital interests. Then as now we insisted upon ignoring or conjuring away all those features of Communism which if accurately perceived might have embarrassed the abstractions. Then as now the Bolshevik cadres pressed forward under cover of our confusion to seek new gains and to work new methods for our destruction.

The radical disjunction between Liberal ideology and the shape of the world we live in is the most serious problem confronting the United States today. Because of it, American foreign policy has failed to serve as a shield for our protection. We have been surrendering the globe to an enemy whose true character Liberalism refuses to acknowledge.

★★ 2. *The Face of the Enemy*

ANY DISCUSSION of American foreign policy must begin from some firm understanding about the nature of Communism. The Communist world is the adversary with which our diplomacy must grapple. If we do not understand Communism, then, in today's world, we understand very little.

The relevant questions about Communism which must be answered before we can undertake a proper assessment of American diplomacy are essentially three. The first of these is, quite simply, whether Communism is in fact an "enemy" of the United States and the Free World—whether it is a force committed by ideology, interest, historical performance or any combination of these to aggression against us.

Of all secular questions we might pose to ourselves, this is obviously the most important. We can take no proper steps against an enemy unless we recognize him as such; if he seeks our destruction and we fail to place that fact at the center of our calculations, we shall be running enormous dangers. If he is not so committed, and we assume he is, then we shall be running dangers of an opposite sort. There can, in short, be no fundamental determination about the validity of any given course in the Cold War until the question of Communist intention is settled.

Second, we must inspect the question of whether the Communists, who repeatedly invite us to "ease tensions" or to adjourn the Cold War altogether by negotiation and diplomatic barter, can be counted upon to abide by such agreements; whether, that is, any real prospect exists of ending conflict between the United States and the USSR through the exchange of pledges and understandings. To answer this, we must have some idea of what Communists believe about the validity of agreements, and how they have behaved on other occasions when they have entered negotiations with the West.

Finally, we must inspect the specific question of "peaceful co-existence." Does this phrase, so often heard from spokesmen on both sides of the Iron Curtain, suggest an amicable way out of the Cold War? Does it imply that the Communists—whatever their past record and previous utterances—have come to believe the West is entitled to survive, and that friction between the systems can be abated?

Each of these questions will, in one form or another, subtend every phase of our discussion. It is therefore necessary to seek an answer to each before that discussion can be attempted. What, then, is the relevant evidence?

1. *Communist Aggression*

The researcher seeking to document the record of Soviet aggression suffers from one difficulty only—an embarrassment of riches. It would be simpler to rehearse those few instances in which the Soviet Union has *not* committed aggression or steeped itself in atrocity. To establish the criminal side of the Soviet record, both in theory and in practice, would take more pages than we have in this book.

The implacability of Communism toward the Free World, its commitment to overthrowing non-Communist governments, is boldly asserted by Soviet theoreticians. Lenin was a tireless exponent of the theme. "As long as capitalism and socialism exist," he said, "we cannot live in peace; in the end, one or the other will triumph—a funeral dirge will be sung over the Soviet republic, or over world capitalism."[1]

And: ". . . there is no other alternative: either the Soviet government triumphs in every advanced country in the world, or the most reactionary imperialism triumphs, the most savage imperialism, which is throttling the small and feeble nationalities and reinstating reaction all over the world . . . One or the other. There is no middle course."[2]

And again: ". . . the existence of the Soviet republic side by side with imperialist states for a long time is unthinkable. One or the other must triumph in the end. And before that end supervenes, a series of frightful collisions between the Soviet republic and the bourgeois states will be inevitable."[3]

Lenin made it clear he did not intend the "funeral dirge" to be sung over Communism. "As soon as we are strong enough to defeat capitalism as a whole," he said in 1920, "we shall immediately take it by the scruff of the neck."[4]

Stalin was equally vehement on the subject, declaring that "who will conquer whom" was "the whole question," and that the job of the Soviet Union was to carry the battle to the Free World.[5] "The victory of socialism in one country is not an end in itself," he said; "it must be looked upon as a support, as a means for hastening the proletarian victory in every other land. For the victory of the revolution in one country (in Russia, for the nonce) . . . is likewise the beginning and the continuation of the world revolution."[6]

The Bolshevik triumph in Russia, Stalin proclaimed, "has

ushered in a new era, the era of proletarian revolutions in the countries of imperialism . . . of colonial revolutions which are being conducted in the oppressed countries of the world in alliance with the proletariat and under the leadership of the proletariat."[7] The October rising had given world Communism a firm base and "jeopardized the very existence of world capitalism as a whole."[8] It had created "a powerful and open base for the world revolutionary movement . . . a powerful and open center of the world revolutionary movement . . . around which it now can rally and organize a united revolutionary front of the proletarian and oppressed nations of all countries against imperialism. The revolution is spreading beyond the confines of one country; the period of world revolution has commenced."[9]

Nor was Nikita Khrushchev, Stalin's successor, laggard in stressing the deep hostility of East to West, or the "inevitability" of Communist triumph. "Capitalism is a worn-out old mare," he said, "while socialism is new, young, and full of teeming energy . . . Our firm conviction is that sooner or later capitalism will give way to socialism. No one can halt man's forward movement, just as no one can prevent day from following night . . . Whether you like it or not, history is on our side. We will bury you."[10]

These precepts have been thoroughly enforced by the conduct of Soviet foreign policy. From the beginning, the Soviet regime has striven to "export" its revolution—*i.e.*, to engineer the overthrow of non-Communist governments. It succeeded for a time in Hungary and Bavaria, and in 1920 launched an attack against Poland. At the second meeting of the Comintern, Communists the world over were instructed "to make propaganda within their countries' armed forces, when necessary by secret and illegal means," and to develop in every country a "clandestine organization capable at the decisive moment of fulfilling its duty towards the revolution."[11]

Even during the "united front" heyday of the 30s, the Kremlin was preparing for aggression. On August 23, 1939, Moscow signed a treaty of amity with Hitler—a vulgar prelude to a joint campaign of depredation. "I know how much the German nation loves its Führer," Stalin said. "I should therefore like to drink his health."[12] The two dictators symbolically toasted one another in the blood of Poland. The Soviet-Nazi invasion brought England to the victim's defense, touching off World War II; the "peace-loving" anti-Hitler Communists were thus accomplices in the very act of Nazi aggression which launched history's greatest holocaust.

During this same period, according to their aggressors' pact with Hitler, the Communists also pressed their attack against Latvia, Estonia, Lithuania, and Finland. For its attack on Finland, whose heroic resistance inspired the imagination of the world, the Soviet Union was expelled from the League of Nations.

On June 22, 1941, Hitler violated his agreement with Stalin by invading Russia. The consortium of dictators was broken, and the USSR was by force of circumstance thrust into the arms of the West. Its involvement in the war against Hitler was, therefore, a matter of raw necessity, of defending its own interests against its former partner.*

At war's end, the Communists hardly missed a beat in their continuing history of aggression. They reinvaded Finland and brazenly demanded "war reparations." Earlier, when they drove into Poland, they had provoked the Warsaw rising and allowed Polish resistance leaders to be slaughtered by the Nazis. They absorbed Latvia, Lithuania, and Estonia whole,

* Interestingly enough, when Hitler's troops rolled into Western Russia, they were greeted as liberators by the oppressed Russian populace. This illusion was, however, quickly shattered by the atrocities of Hitler's troops. The two dictatorships thus maintained parity, since Stalin's men had committed their own share of atrocities in Poland, including the infamous massacre of 15,000 Polish officers in the Katyn Forest. In the post-war Nuremberg trials, the Soviets had the *sangfroid* to sit in judgment on their former partners in crime and arraign *them* for the crimes of the Katyn Forest.

and went immediately to work to bring the Balkan states under Communist rule. They provoked new fighting in Greece and began aiding the Chinese Communist effort to conquer the mainland of China.

In the years ahead lay the Berlin blockade, the conquest of China, the establishment of Red regimes in North Korea and Viet Nam, the Korean War, continued campaigns of subversion, *coup d'état* and outright aggression in Cuba, the Congo, Venezuela, Laos, Viet Nam; terrorism, agitation, and revolution at every vantage point in Africa and Latin America; the crushing of Hungary; the invasion of Tibet; the placement of lethal missiles in Cuba; the Berlin Wall and the murder of those who tried to escape across it; the illegal detention of American citizens behind the Iron Curtain; brainwashing and atrocities in Korea; the killing of American servicemen, etc.

The Communists, in addition, plundered American secrets, infiltrated the American government, and attempted to subvert American policy. Harry Dexter White, identified as a Soviet agent by former Attorney General Herbert Brownell, gave the Communists American currency plates. U.S. materials were shipped directly to Moscow. Vital military secrets were stolen. American policy in China was subverted. Fuchs, May, Pontecorvo; Alger Hiss and the Rosenbergs; Burgess and Maclean; Martin and Mitchell—all contributed their mite to Moscow's peace offensive: "Saying, Peace, peace, when there is no peace."

2. *The Broken Agreements*

The record of Communist duplicity from the beginning of the Soviet state is Homeric in dimension. Never has there been a regime in which violation of pledges and general falsehood have been more systematically employed. None of which, of course, should be particularly astonishing, since the

Communist view of morality holds such things not only permissible but mandatory if they advance Communist interests. Marx and Engels preached that there were no fixed standards of morality; all ethical views, they maintained, were the result of economic circumstance. The only real test of right and wrong was what helped or hindered the triumph of Communist revolution.

Although many features of "Marxism-Leninism" have undergone tactical and other alteration, this particular Communist doctrine has been faithfully adhered to. Under its sign, Communists have blandly murdered dissidents, extorted rigged confessions, forged documents, erected slave labor camps, induced famines, exterminated women and children, stolen secrets, subverted policies, lied before tribunals national and international. They have claimed the paternity of every modern invention from the electric light to the airplane, attempted to foist off the hoax of Lysenkoism,* and doctored information on their economic and military performance. And, most relevant to our immediate subject, they have never hesitated to enter any agreement, or to break any, when either of these actions suited their purposes.

"The strictest loyalty to the ideas of Communism," Lenin said, "must be combined with the ability to make all necessary practical compromises, to 'tack,' to make agreements, zigzags, retreats, and so on, in order to accelerate the coming into power . . ."[13] Stalin put it thus: "A diplomat's words must have no relation to action—otherwise what kind of diplomacy is it? Words are one thing, actions another. Good words are a mask for the concealment of bad deeds. Sincere diplomacy is no more possible than dry water or iron wood."[14] In another celebrated dictum, Lenin formulated it succinctly: "Promises are like pie crusts, made to be broken."[15]

* Trofim Lysenko is the Russian biologist who claimed, contrary to the findings of modern genetics, to have demonstrated that acquired characteristics can be inherited.

Lenin's lieutenant, Zinoviev, spelled the matter out even more plainly. "We are willing to sign an unfavorable peace," he said concerning the treaty of Brest-Litovsk. "It would only mean we should put no trust whatever in the piece of paper we should sign. We should use the breathing space so obtained in order to gather our strength so that the mere continued existence of our government would keep up the worldwide propaganda which Soviet Russia has been carrying on for more than a year."[16]

Holding that view of international morality, the Communists have, unsurprisingly, compiled a stunning record of diplomatic falsehood. In 1933, to take but a single example, the Soviet Union and the United States exchanged notes opening channels for diplomatic recognition; Soviet Ambassador Maxim Litvinov signed an agreement pledging the Soviet government "to refrain from interfering in any manner in the internal affairs of the United States . . . To refrain, and to restrain all persons in government service and all organizations of government or under its direct or indirect control . . . from any act . . . liable in any way whatsoever to injure the tranquillity, prosperity, order, or security of the whole or any part of the U.S. Not to permit the formation or residence on its territory . . . and to prevent the activity on its territory of any organization or group . . . which has as an aim . . . the preparation for . . . the bringing about by force of a change in the political or social order of the United States."[17]

Such was the solemn understanding on which our recognition of the Soviet Union was based; the agreement was hailed by spokesmen like Senator William Borah and Senator Hiram Johnson as the precursor of a new era of U.S.-Soviet amity. Needless to remark, Soviet promises and Western expectations were almost immediately shattered. The Moscow government, notes the Senate Internal Security subcommittee, "was violating the very first agreement it signed with the United States at the very moment the Soviet envoy, Litvinov, was putting his signature to the agreement."[18]

The Communist Party of the United States—supposedly prevented "from interfering . . . in the internal affairs of the United States"—boldly announced in the wake of recognition that it would "more than ever strive to win the American workers for the revolutionary way out of the crisis, for the emulation of the Soviet Union and its revolutionary victories."[19] In July 1935, the CPUSA sent representatives to a Moscow meeting to report on revolutionary progress in America. U.S. Ambassador William C. Bullitt, formerly an ardent backer of recognition, denounced the Soviet government for an "act of unparalleled treachery" and called for severance of diplomatic relations.

While benefits supposed to accrue to America from this agreement never came to pass, the benefits to the Soviets were tangible indeed. As both *Pravda* and *The Daily Worker* pointed out, recognition by the United States was a momentous victory for Moscow, signalling a new respectability and prestige for the Bolshevik revolution. "Reversal of U.S. Non-Recognition Policy," said the headline in *The Worker,* "Is Victory for the Workers' Fatherland."[20] Our action, overturning a settled policy of diplomatic aloofness, was interpreted as U.S. approval of Soviet performance. It launched the USSR as a major force in global politics.

Meanwhile, still other violations of Moscow's pledges, to America and to others, followed one another in giddy procession. A 1955 report of the Senate Internal Security subcommittee observes:

> The subcommittee staff studied nearly a thousand treaties and agreements . . . both bilateral and multilateral, which the Soviets have entered into not only with the United States, but with countries all over the world. The staff found that in the 38 short years since the Soviet Union came into existence, its government had broken its word to virtually every country to which it ever gave a signed promise.[21]

The categories in which these violations occurred, the report makes clear, are very much like the categories in which agreements are sought today:

The Soviet government signed treaties of nonaggression with neighboring states and then absorbed those states. It signed agreements, promises to refrain from revolutionary activity inside the countries with which it sought "friendship," and then cynically broke those promises. It broke the promises it made to the Western nations during previous meetings 'at the summit' in Teheran and Yalta. It broke lend-lease agreements offered to it by the United States in order to keep Stalin from surrendering to the Nazis. It violated the charter of the United Nations.[22]

In 1959, Congressman Craig Hosmer (R-Calif.) updated the subcommittee's findings to include agreements reached between 1955 and 1959. Inserting his findings in the *Congressional Record,* Hosmer concluded that: "In its 40-year history the Soviet Union has executed over 2,000 agreements with non-Communist governments. It is safe to say that those remaining unviolated by the Kremlin are only those which it has not yet appeared expedient to break."[23]

In 1964, the Senate subcommittee itself re-examined the subject of Soviet diplomacy, and found almost all major pacts the Kremlin had agreed to since the first accounting had been violated. Noting that Western nations were still trying "to add to the stacks of documents"[24] containing agreements between Moscow and the Free World, the subcommittee found no reason to alter its prior conclusion: So long as the West has no iron-clad method of enforcing agreements with Moscow, "it is futile to direct our efforts toward adding to the accumulation of documents which have already been signed and violated by the USSR and other Communist countries."[25]

This is a lesson which the United States, to its sorrow, has learned time and again. President Kennedy testified to Soviet duplicity in the 1962 missile crisis. Citing the Soviet government's contention that the missiles being transported to Cuba were purely defensive, Kennedy flatly charged "that statement was false." He rendered the same judgment on a subsequent assertion by Soviet foreign minister Gromyko. "Neither the United States of America nor the world community of nations," Kennedy said, "can tolerate deliberate deception and offensive threats on the part of any nation, large or small."[26]

Similar testimony came from a disillusioned President Eisenhower in his 1959 State of the Union Message: "We have learned the bitter lesson that international agreements, historically considered by us as sacred, are regarded in Communist doctrine and in practice to be mere scraps of paper . . . As a consequence, we can have no confidence in any treaty to which the Communists are a party, except where such a treaty provides within itself for self-enforcing mechanisms."[27]

Such were the conclusions of two Presidents who, whatever their differences, were alike in their willingness to extend every conceivable effort to attain a peaceful settlement of our differences with the Soviet Union. Is it still possible, in the face of that testimony and in the teeth of the record, to believe we can repose our faith in the Communists?

3. *Peaceful Coexistence*

Despite this abundant history, many Western observers return continuously to the notion that Communism is "changing," that its aggressiveness has dissipated, that we are entered upon an era in which our differences can be settled by negotiation. While this idea has been brought forward repeatedly over the past generation, it was given new and special impetus in 1956 as a result of Khrushchev's famous "de-Stalinization" speech, in which he denounced his predecessor and declared the Free World and the Communist world had entered into a new epoch of "peaceful competition." The speech was hailed as a momentous breakthrough to peace, and the decade since its delivery has seen American diplomacy built increasingly upon the theory that the Communists have "mellowed."

Such interpretations ignore the fact that "peaceful coexistence" means something quite different to the Communists from what it means to us. To Western theorists, "peaceful coexistence" is a pleasant-sounding phrase which implies living side by side and minding one's own business. To the Communists, it is a strategy designed to secure defeat of the Free World.

The idea that "coexistence" might conduce to Communist purposes was not new to Khrushchev—although he made it, under the circumstances in which he found himself, a leading rather than a subordinate principle of Soviet strategy. Both Lenin and Stalin had suggested that, should the world strategic situation be altered, the doctrine of "peaceful coexistence" would become useful. In the early days of the Soviet revolution, the Communists saw the situation as one of "capitalist encirclement" of their bastion; strategic necessity required a militant stance, in the manner of a combatant who has his back to the wall. He must dig in and fight for his life, calling upon whatever outside help he can get, catch as catch can.

Lenin and Stalin envisioned, however, that the situation might change. Capitalist encirclement of the USSR might give way, in a happy Communist future, to Communist encirclement of capitalism. Under those conditions, the strategic line would be different. Rather than a desperate underdog, Communism would become a winning player who needs only to avoid flagrant error to achieve final victory. World Bolshevism would then seek to avoid any sudden or dramatic reversal of the situation, any single episode which might retransform strategic relationships or galvanize the opposition into fierce and purposeful resistance.

In 1924, Stalin speculated that such a transformation of capitalist-Communist power relationships might occur. "In the remote future," he said, "if the proletariat is victorious in the most important capitalist countries, and if the present capitalist encirclement is replaced by a socialist encirclement, a 'peaceful' path of development is quite possible for certain capitalist countries, whose capitalists, in view of the 'unfavorable' international situation, will consider it expedient 'voluntarily' to make substantial concessions to the proletariat."[28]

The significance of Khrushchev's 1956 speech and the 20th World Congress to which he addressed it was that, in the Communist view, *precisely such a shift in relationships had occurred*—making "peaceful" Communist victory possible. "The situation in the world is fundamentally changed," Khrushchev said. "Capitalist encirclement of our country no longer exists. There are two world social systems: Capitalism which is coming to the end of its days, and socialism in the full flood of its growing forces, on whose side are the sympathies of the working people of all countries." As a result of this transformation, "no shadow of doubt can remain as to the fundamental outcome of the world struggle. In this respect the final victory of socialism is fully and unconditionally assured."[29]

Thus the avowal of "peaceful coexistence" should hardly be cause for rejoicing in the West. From the Communists' point of view, they are pronouncing a judgment of doom. They are saying they have advanced so far in their drive for world conquest they can now mop up the remainder in relatively easy stages. War is to be avoided under circumstances which might upset the Communist progress toward victory. At such times as war is *useful* in that drive to victory, it is of course to be employed. The question is simply one of how best to conquer the Free World, and the strategy of "peaceful coexistence," on the present Soviet view, is the right way of getting the job done. Only the Communists' assessment of the strategic situation—*not* their intentions—has changed. "A fight is in progress," Khrushchev averred, "between these two systems, a life and death combat. But we Communists want to win this struggle with the least losses and there is no doubt whatsoever that we shall win." That, in essence, is the meaning of "peaceful coexistence."[30]*

In addition to signifying the Communists' belief that they are on top and we on the bottom, "peaceful coexistence" is itself *an instrument* for achieving the victory which is the end and object of every Communist stratagem. It is a method for causing the capitalist nations to relax, to open themselves to new but subtle initiatives from the Communist side, to stop resisting the "inevitable" march of Communism toward victory. If the West believes Communism is no longer hostile, it will stop taking measures to resist. "Peaceful coexistence" is a weapon as well as an emblem of Communist triumph.

"The policies of peaceful coexistence," Khrushchev said in 1959, ". . . facilitate the victory of the Communist Party and other progressive organizations of the working class in capitalist countries, make it easier for the peoples to combat aggressive war blocs and foreign military bases, and contribute to national liberation movements."[31] In December, 1960, the World Communist Party similarly asserted that, "In con-

* "De-Stalinization" made equally little difference in the matter of internal police terror, according to former CIA chief Allen Dulles. "This speech not only served to open Khrushchev's attack on Stalinism and the Stalinists still in the regime," Dulles writes, "but was also intended to justify new purges of existing state security organs, which he had to bring under his control in order to strengthen his own position as dictator . . . the press has been full of reports recently that courts in the Soviet Union have been handing down death or long prison sentences for many offenses that in the United States would be only minor crimes or misdemeanors . . . all these shake-ups, purges, and organizational changes have had remarkably little effect on the aims, methods and capabilities of that part of the Soviet security service which interests us most—its foreign arm." *The Craft Of Intelligence* (New York, 1963), pp. 90-91.

ditions of peaceful coexistence favorable opportunities are provided for the development of the class struggle in capitalist countries and the national-liberation movement of the colonial and dependent countries."[32]

"Peaceful coexistence" does not, then, imply a cessation of hostilities. It means, instead, a style of warfare wholly slanted in favor of the Communists—in which they continue to press their attack in new and various ways, while the Western world stops resisting and starts cooperating in its own demise. It is not even, the Communists make clear, the absence of war as such; it is merely the absence of *any particular war in which the Communist empire might be threatened*—most typically, a direct one-to-one confrontation between the Soviet Union and the United States.

"Some try to reduce the notion of peaceful coexistence to the renunciation of war," says Rumanian Communist spokesman H. Dona. "But peace and peaceful coexistence are not one and the same thing."[33] Two Soviet spokesmen, I. Glagolev and V. Larionov, put it that "Peaceful coexistence, which is the general line of the foreign policy of the Soviet Union and other Socialist countries, does not imply a temporary absence of war, or a breathing space between clashes."[34] And Estonian Communist N. Shishlin says:

> In the view of the Communists, peaceful coexistence between the two systems is certainly not a passive process in which there is some sort of parallel development of capitalism and socialism . . . *but an active and intense struggle, in the course of which Socialism irresistibly attacks, while capitalism suffers one defeat after another*. (Italics added.)[35]

"Peaceful coexistence" is peaceful, that is, precisely to the extent the Western powers stop resisting. The Communists, indeed, want "peace"—the peace that results whenever one side gives up the struggle and leaves its opposition victorious. The point is made clear, and Western misreadings of the doctrine corrected, in the 1963 statement of a leading Soviet theoretician, T. T. Timofeyev:

> Many bourgeois and Social-Democratic ideologists take peaceful co-existence to mean a reconciliation of the two warring, irreconcilable classes, the proletariat and the bourgeoisie, and say that it leads to a fade-out of the struggle between the antagonistic class ideologies, the Socialist and the bourgeois.
>
> Marxist-Leninists cannot accept this distorted interpretation . . . of the policy of peaceful coexistence . . . The Communist Party has always acted on the assumption that the peaceful coexistence of the two systems does not exclude but, on the contrary, implies a further development of the working people's class struggle . . . It opens up before all revolutionary forces of our day new prospects for successful advance.[36]

The "new prospects for successful advance" of the Communist empire were spelled out by Khrushchev in his speech to the 20th Congress and are everywhere visible in the world around us. They include new and unconventional methods of waging aggression under assumed conditions of "coexistence" and strategic stalemate: Proxy wars, guerrilla uprisings, *coups d'état,* terrorism, espionage—all under the rubric of "wars of national liberation." As pointed out by Khrushchev, *these* types of warfare are definitely *not* ruled out by "peaceful coexistence," and in fact are part and parcel of the definition of that concept. "The Communists," Khrushchev said, "fully support such just wars and march in the front rank with the peoples waging liberation struggles."[37]

Wars of this type—in Algeria, Viet Nam, the Congo, Laos, Angola—are permissible under "peaceful coexistence"; and, even more important from the Communist point of view, they are *aided by* "peaceful coexistence." Since the doctrine means, in essence, that both sides renounce direct strategic confrontation, the Communists employ the *threat* of such a confrontation to prevent Western resistance to subliminal advances. At any point where the United States might feel impelled to intervene in one of these struggles, the threat is conveyed that such intervention would lead to "nuclear holocaust." "There are only two ways," Khrushchev said in his 1956 speech. "Either peaceful coexistence or the most destructive war in history."[38]

The Communists know that, when Cuba falls to Fidel Castro through internal revolution, war is being waged and that world Communism is winning; the West, defining "war" in the conventional sense of armies marching across borders, seeks its solace in the absence of nuclear exchange. It clings to the notion that, despite the Communist advances, "peace" prevails.*

One of the chief objects of "coexistence" policy is to encourage the development and persistence of precisely these thought patterns in the West. So long as we conceive of war in a narrow sense, and congratulate ourselves on the presence of "peace" when in fact the new style of war is everywhere being waged against us, the West is going to lose. So long as we convince ourselves the Communists really want peace in the same sense we do, so long as we concentrate our efforts on trying to "reason" with the Communists rather than marshalling effective resistance against them, the Communists are going to win.

* ". . . The Communists have acquired a spectrum of weapons much more variegated than that which composes the arsenal of the West. They discern weapons where the West sees only the implements of peaceful international relations. According to the Communist doctrine of protacted conflict, war, politics, diplomacy, law, psychology, science, and economics—all form a continuum and all are closely integrated in the conduct of foreign policy." *Protracted Conflict,* by Robert Strausz-Hupe, *et al.,* (N.Y., 1959) p. 33.

★★ *Part I:*

WHAT LIBERALS THINK

I have just a hunch that Stalin doesn't want anything but security for his country, and I think that if I give him everything I possibly can and ask for nothing from him in return, he won't try to annex anything and will work for a world democracy and peace.

—Franklin D. Roosevelt

★★ 3. *The View from the Top*

1. *Ten Quotations*

AN EPIDEMIC OF CHOLERA is always dangerous, but at some times and places it is more dangerous than at others.

In advanced countries, where cholera is understood to be a malignant disease and is treated as such by science, it can be combatted, controlled, and neutralized. In backward nations where its ravages are viewed as the work of spirits and are treated with spells and incantations, it becomes, not merely a disease, but a plague. It can exterminate whole societies.

With respect to Communism, Liberal orthodoxy today is very much in the position of the backward native confronted by an epidemic of cholera. Oblivious of the true nature of the affliction, he relies on verbal placebos and burnt offerings to appease the baleful spirit. And the disease, unhindered, consumes everything before it.

From our examination of international Bolshevism, three essential points emerged: (1) Doctrinaire Communists are committed to global revolution and therefore to aggression against non-Communist nations; (2) Doctrinaire Communists, in pursuit of revolution, are ready to make, or to break, any agreement that advances their purposes; (3) Doctrinaire Communists are willing, when the occasion requires it, to assume the falseface of conciliation to delude the credulous.

The shifting map of the Cold War is derived from the fact that these propositions have been and continue to be true, while American policy-makers have consistently acted as though they were false or of only conditional relevance. Against the background of the Communists' own unbroken testament and history of aggression, consider the following statements on the subject of the Cold War:

The general trend in the Soviet Union is toward liberalization.[1]

. . . the changes that have recently occurred in Russia . . . represent, I think, the beginning of that mellowing process which overtakes sooner or later all militant movements . . .[2]

[Statements about Communist aggressiveness and brutality] impute to the Soviet leaders a total inhumanity not plausible in nature and out of accord with those humane ideals which we must recognize as lying—together with other elements less admirable in the eyes of some of us—at the origins of European Marxism. I should like, therefore, to end these observations with a plea for something resembling *a new act of faith in the ultimate humanity and sobriety of the people on the other side* . . . (Italics added).[3]

We are . . . prepared to find limited areas of overlapping interest with Communist regimes and work patiently toward the development of the kind of world that we envisage.[4]

. . . the Soviet Union, though still a formidable adversary, has ceased to be totally and implacably hostile to the West. It has shown a new willingness to enter mutually advantageous agreements with the West and, thus far at least, to honor them. It has therefore become possible to . . . deal with the Soviet Union, for certain purposes, as a normal state with normal and traditional interests.[5]

Would the Russians . . . accept an unambiguous opportunity to reduce world tensions? . . . The similarities between us are probably much greater than the differences we stress . . . and they probably would welcome a way out of this mess as much as we would.[6]

Eventually, I am persuaded, [the Communists] must open their society to the overwhelming benefits and requirements of a hopelessly interdependent world.[7]

In short, both the United States and its allies, and the Soviet Union and its allies, have a mutually deep interest in a just and genuine peace and in halting the arms race.[8]

We are going to go down any road that can possibly lead to peace. . . . We will meet the Russians halfway, and even further than halfway, if that is necessary.[9]

When Chancellor Erhard was here I told him: Put yourself in the position of the Russians. Try to understand their feelings. They are worrying about the Germans, and that is understandable.[10]

Many other specimens of Liberal thought, even more emphatically expressed, could be cited. Among various "peace" agitators and left-wing groups, these statements sometimes take the form of espousing the Communist cause against that of the Free World. The Fair Play for Cuba Committee, which began with a number of prominent Liberals on its letterhead, has taken exactly this stance with regard to American policy in the Caribbean. The Viet Nam demonstrators who became so prominent in 1965 in many cases openly declared their sympathies on the side of the Viet Cong. Were we to parade these febrile sentiments before the reader, the effect of our argument would be considerably heightened—and since such efforts have in many cases been countenanced by important elements in the Liberal community, such allusions would not be altogether wide of the mark.

We have chosen, however, to make our case with the specimen statements quoted above—for one simple reason: All of them were made by people either high up in our government or with excellent governmental connections. The sentiments quoted are taken, in order, from Charles E. Bohlen, American ambassador to the USSR and to France, and one of President Kennedy's chief advisers on foreign policy; George F. Kennan, former ambassador to the USSR and to Yugoslavia and a venerated authority on foreign policy subjects (statements two and three); Walt W. Rostow, Chief of Policy Planning for the State Department under both Kennedy and Johnson; Senator J. William Fulbright, D-Ark., chairman of the Senate Foreign Relations Committee; *The Liberal Papers,* a foreign policy anthology edited by United Nations delegate James Roosevelt; Assist. Secretary of State Harlan Cleveland; the late President Kennedy; and President Johnson, from whose public statements both of the last two assertions have been gleaned.

These ten statements, then, represent something very like an official line on the Cold War. Taken together, they suggest the image of Communism with which our leaders have equipped themselves. They conjure up an adversary which is not essentially hostile, which is "mellowing," which down deep is as interested in peace as we are, which indeed is pretty much like us all the way around, and with which we can therefore find areas of "overlapping interest."

None of this, on the evidence, is true. It bears little or no resemblance to the face of the enemy sketched in the preceding chapter, drawn from the enemy's own statements and own performance. It bears no resemblance, in fact, to any kind of "enemy" at all; what emerges from this composite of official opinion is a kind of misunderstood and suspicious neighbor, who quite possibly can, through some Dale Carnegie exertions on our part, be turned into a friend. Liberalism, in short, has mistaken the disease of Communism for a curious and appeasable spirit to be treated with incantations and talismans, rather than with hostility and resolve. And the disease has been rapidly consuming us.

2. *The Kennedy View*

It will perhaps be objected that, in selecting our ten quotations, we have given a stark and truncated view of what Liberals think about the Cold War. Such statements, it may be argued, can only be understood in context, and must be measured against other statements and against the over-all performance of Liberal diplomacy. Fair enough. One cannot, in fact, understand the elements of Liberal foreign policy simply by reading ten quotations. Yet a review of the total context, verbal and axiological, confirms rather than denies our central assertions.

Let us take, for example, the most notably "complex" expositions of Liberal opinion—those emanating from the White House. Presidents do not, of course, utter their official sentiments in flat, unequivocal tones. Their most typical statements are both attenuated and roomy, combining a little toughness with a little flexibility; their fondest imaginings of the peaceable world to be include some element of readiness to resist; their most unequivocal vaunts include certain escape hatches of conciliation.

This being the case, straightforward professions of official belief that the Communists can in some wise be relied upon, that they are people very much like ourselves, that we can do business with them—the profession of such sentiments as these from the White House must be indicative of a rather settled policy. And if we examine the programmatic statements on world affairs issued by both President Kennedy and President

Johnson, we shall find this idea not only present but, looming through some slender filaments of resolve, consistent and predominant. Consider the speech by President Kennedy widely regarded among his admirers as his major statement on the terminal issues of the Cold War—his 1963 address at American University. In this speech, the late President said the following:

> No government or social system is so evil that its people must be considered lacking in virtue. As Americans we find Communism profoundly repugnant as a negation of personal freedom and dignity. But we can still hail the Russian people for their many achievements—in science and space, in economic and industrial growth, in culture and in acts of courage.
>
> Among the many traits the people of our countries have in common, none is stronger than our mutual abhorrence of war . . .
>
> . . . We are both caught up in a vicious and dangerous cycle in which suspicion on one side breeds suspicion on the other and new weapons beget counterweapons.
>
> In short, both the United States and its allies, and the Soviet Union and its allies, have a mutually deep interest in a just and genuine peace and in halting the arms race.[11]

In this celebrated address, the rhetoric is, as usual, mixed—a little toughness in there with the accommodation; but, quite clearly, the toughness is the warm up; the accommodation is the punch line. The net impact of what Kennedy was saying, so understood by all the media of the world and by his friends and critics alike, was that, all being said and done, "peace" is obtainable with the Soviet Union through negotiation, "cooperation," mutual interest—obtainable, that is, precisely on the terms suggested in our ten quotations. And, in so arguing, Kennedy incorporated most of the major propositions suggested by our review of those quotations, or which have been, in the elaboration of Liberal foreign policy, derived from them.

Most strikingly, Kennedy's remarks *identify the people of Russia with the Soviet government.* This is a standard feature of accommodationist policy. On the one hand, he said, we oppose Communism, but we can "still" hail "the Russian people"—as though there were some presumptive identity of interest between the Soviet regime and the people who are its captives. In point of fact, we should "hail" the Russian people, not *in spite of* our opposition to Communism, but because of that opposition; and we should "hail" them, not because of the asserted achievements of the Soviet regime, but because we share with them a common humanity which the Soviet regime has historically sought to extinguish.

Having identified the Soviet regime with the Russian people, the speech confounds confusion by next identifying *our* people with the Russian people, and therefore inferentially identifying our government with the Soviet government. Both the Russian people and the American people, it says, abhor war—and so they do. But since the Russian people with their abhorrence of war are not in charge of Soviet policy, and the Communist Party with its penchant for war *is* in charge of that policy, the statement is worse than irrelevant; it is affirmatively misleading. It suggests a mutuality of interest in "peace" in the United States and the USSR which does not exist.

With the Russian people, the Soviet government, and the United States thus hopelessly intertwined in defiance of all fact, yet another sort of misconception is thrown into the speech: The two substantially equal entities, the United States and the Soviet Union, are depicted as common victims of an external and mechanical force, a "vicious and dangerous cycle" in which groundless suspicions are fomented and an arms race is forced upon equally unwilling votaries of peace. The Cold War is attributed, not to the unflagging thrust of Communist aggression, but to a compound of circumstance in which the Communists are apparently no more to blame than ourselves. We are placed on all fours with the Bolshevik enemy; our "suspicions" of them are equated with their "suspicions" of us; our effort to ward off their aggression is made comparable to the aggression itself.

This ineffable confusion is underlined by the statement that the two sides of the confrontation "have a mutually deep interest in a just and genuine peace and in halting the arms race." As stated, this assertion is palpably false; the merest acquaintance with the history of the Cold War makes it apparent the Communists are *not* interested in a "just and genuine peace." What Kennedy might have said, with some accuracy, is that both sides *should* have such an interest. But that statement, while accurate, would have been operationally meaningless, since it could be realized only by the abdication of the Soviet Communist Party, and by other things which are in no way likely to occur.

A concluding fillip of error is the single phrase joining and equating a "just and genuine peace" with "halting the arms race." If the external-force-vicious-cycle notion of the Cold War were correct, these two things would be equivalent and interchangeable; if the Cold War were *caused* by the arms then halting that race would indeed end the Cold War.* Since the arms race is *not* the cause of the Cold War, however, it is altogether possible that "halting the arms race" would have no connection whatever with a "just and genuine peace."

On the contrary, halting the arms race could very well destroy all hope of such a peace, since the mutual abandonment of strategic weapons systems by the United States and the Soviet Union would, on balance, work in favor of the latter. America's strategic arsenal did not cause the Cold War but has instead been instrumental in restraining the aggres-

* Alternatively, it is true on an entirely different analysis that halting the Cold War would also mean halting the arms race—although this involves considerations hostile to the Kennedy diagnosis and is clearly not what he was talking about.

sive intentions of the Communists. To suggest, as the Kennedy statement does, that our arsenal somehow shares in the guilt for creating the Cold War, and that getting rid of it could somehow contribute to a "just and genuine peace" is the very opposite of the truth.

The "accommodationist" thrust of Kennedy's views is confirmed by the man who, above all others, should know the true direction of the late President's thought. Theodore Sorensen gives us this interesting commentary on the Kennedy approach to the Cold War: "Khrushchev's first private letter compared the world to Noah's Ark, where both the 'clean' and the 'unclean' wanted it to stay afloat, regardless of who listed himself with each group. Kennedy replied that he liked that analogy, that whatever their ideological differences, their collaboration was essential to prevent another war destroying everything."[12] Sorensen repeatedly uses the word "accommodation" to describe Kennedy's major policy line toward Moscow and notes that "from his Inaugural onward, he referred to the Communists not as 'our enemies' but as 'those who would make themselves our adversary.' "[13] (This specific locution, Sorensen also notes, was injected into the Inaugural on the advice of Walter Lippmann, a veteran advocate of accommodating Moscow.)

Such, then, was the programmatic view of the Cold War held by President Kennedy. It is a view, as we shall see, which has been elaborated in some detail by subordinate officials in the American government, and which has, even more importantly, been put into practice in the working policies of the United States. The confusions are not simply rhetorical; they are intellectual, and they are deep-rooted. They are accepted as though they were fact, worked up into policy directives in the State Department, and put into practical operation in various theaters of international conflict.

We have noted that, in most presidential utterances, the

rhetoric of toughness is mixed in with the language of accommodation. If we could penetrate to the arcana where diplomats talk among themselves rather than for public consumption, we would have a firmer idea of which half of this public presentation is the more seriously intended. Such glimpses are offered but rarely. One such was afforded us, however, in the famous controversy over "muzzling" the military, when State Department comments on the general shape of the Cold War, and on State Department understanding of the policy line laid down by President Kennedy, were read into the public records of Congress.

The State Department censors had been eliminating from the remarks of American military men phrases deemed provocative or offensive to Moscow. The notations and memoranda from the censors elicited by congressional investigators showed clearly that the notion of Communist "mellowing" and high-level overtures toward "accommodation" were the central axioms of American policy. Consider the following statements:

> The word victory has a militaristic and aggressive ring less suited than the substituted phrase for describing our national objectives. It also implies an all-or-nothing approach leaving no room for accommodation.

> Re-iterated statements by a military officer concerning the intent of the Soviet Union to militarily attack the United States could have been used to cast doubt on the sincerity and good faith of the President's expressed desire to seek an accommodation with the Soviet Union.

> At a time when the President was speaking in terms of establishing 'a beach-head of cooperation' which might 'push back the jungle of suspicion,' it was considered inappropriate for a high military officer to cast the relation between Communism and the Western civilization in all-or-nothing terms.

It was deemed particularly inappropriate to have a U.S. official make this charge at a time when the new administration was attempting to develop its avenues of communication with Communist governments.

It was the policy during this period to speak civilly in reference to the USSR and Communist China in order to encourage the creation of new avenues of communication.

This speech was to be made shortly after the President's inaugural address and the State of the Union message in which he had stressed need to explore all possible areas of cooperation with the Soviet Union. At such time it was deemed unwise to refer to our competition with the Communist world as a matter of life and death.

The reviewer considered the deleted words provocative and out of keeping with the policy of the administration as expressed in the first State of the Union message that 'this administration intends to explore promptly all possible areas of cooperation with the Soviet Union and other nations to invoke the wonders of science instead of its terrors.'

In this period when the new administration was still feeling its way in our policy toward the Russians, references which might suggest adherence to a policy of liberation of the satellite nations of Eastern Europe were considered inadvisable.[14]

And so forth. Anyone reading these comments and analyzing the nature of the remarks deleted (*e.g.*, "the Communist challenge," changed to "the challenge", *etc.*) can hardly doubt that our working policy toward the global Communist enterprise was, precisely, one of accommodation. Also of interest is the fact that the censors repeatedly tied their comments and the reasons for the deletions to phrases taken here and there from President Kennedy's early addresses; these passages, much less comprehensive than the American University address, were obviously viewed as the key to American policy, while the so-called "tough" verbiage that sometimes accompanied them was ignored.

That the censors had chosen properly—and no doubt in obediance to official instructions—was indicated when Secretary of State Rusk, speaking for the administration, refused to identify the individuals involved and assimilated responsibility for their actions and comments to the government as a whole. In this he was backed up by President Kennedy. It is apparent that the "accommodation" half of the Kennedy presentation, rather than the "tough" part of it, was the part meant to be taken seriously.

3. *The Johnson View*

The view of Communism evinced by the State Department censors was the official view when President Kennedy assumed office and when he spoke at American University, and it remains the official view in Washington at this writing. American diplomacy under Lyndon Johnson is as wedded to the notion of "accommodation" with Moscow as it was under John Kennedy.

Johnson is less a phrasemaker than was Kennedy, and even less given to general, comprehensive statements. He has, however, gone on record, as it were, by degrees. His opinions on one specific occasion or another yield a discernible trend of thought, summed up by one knowledgeable Washington reporter not at all hostile to Johnson as "a readiness to take new initiatives in foreign affairs, exploring new avenues for relaxing tensions with the Soviet Union and moving toward some enforceable disarmament scheme."[15]

Like Kennedy, Johnson usually mixes the "relaxation of tensions" theme with certain allusions to America's steadfastness of purpose in defending its interests. On occasion, as in Johnson's July 1965 speech on Viet Nam (or Kennedy's 1961 speech on Berlin), the militant theme becomes predominant.

The major tendency of Johnson's foreign policy statements has nonetheless been in favor of the accommodationist position, a point established by the presumptively definitive foreign policy discussion in his book, *My Hope For America.* In this volume, Johnson says there are, in essence, six different "paths to peace," as follows:

1. To use "restraint" in the exercise of our military power.
2. To build the "trust" that "comes from a long series of agreements."
3. To dispel the apprehensions of "other nations" who "may honestly fear our intentions or the intentions of our allies."
4. To co-operate in solving "the problems which are greater than immediate conflicts."
5. To adjust disputes "without the use of force."
6. To place "much hope" in the United Nations.[16]

This line of thought, on the face of it, is markedly similar to that of President Kennedy, and—also like that of President Kennedy—markedly unresponsive to the issue of what to do about the surging tide of Soviet aggression. We are to restrain, agree, pacify, negotiate, cooperate, and repose our hopes in the U.N. Just how any of these steps, or all of them taken together, will counter the Soviet program of total subjugation of the Free World is not explained. Johnson's words in expansion of Point No. 2 will serve to illustrate the quality of Cold War thought which now disposes of the national destiny. Discussing ways and means of building "trust" between the United States and the USSR, Johnson says:

"And so, even while we are caught in a conflict in one part of the world [Viet Nam], we labor to build the structure of agreement which can bring peace to the rest of the world. We have signed a treaty ending nuclear tests in the atmosphere. We have cut back our production of atomic fuel and weapons. We have established a hot line between Washington and Moscow. We are meeting with the Soviets to pool our knowledge about making fresh water from the oceans. These agreements, by themselves, have not ended tensions; they have not ended the risks of war. But because of them we have moved closer to peace."[17]

President Johnson's second-in-command, Vice President Hubert Humphrey, has been even more explicit than his chief in spelling out the accommodationist view of the Cold War. Twenty years ago, Humphrey was an aggressive spokesman for American myopia. "We have to keep in mind," Humphrey said, "what Russia wants and needs." What Russia wanted and needed were "border states which are friendly to the Soviet Union and governments in those states which will not serve as agents of anti-Soviet forces. An outlet into the Mediterranean. A rectification of her boundaries with Poland and Rumania. The inclusion of the Baltic states into the Soviet Union."[18]

Which happened, of course, to be the Communist program for taking over Eastern Europe. The "rectification" of boundaries so complacently referred to meant, in the first instance, incorporating half of Poland into the Soviet Union, mass deportations, imprisonments, and murders. Similar consequences flowed from the rest of the Communists' wants and needs. Humphrey found nothing to criticize in this program: "I would say that these are the major demands of the Soviet Union, none of which are in any way impossible of solution, and all of which fit very nicely into a more secure and stable Russia."[19]

As this soothing formula indicates, Humphrey was not particularly concerned about possible dangers from Communism. The real menace, he said, was on the right: "The major political danger arising in Europe is not that of Communism, but is rather the greater danger of the old rightist ruling forces of the past seeking to dam up the change that is certain to sweep the continent."*[20]

* So speaking, Humphrey struck a characteristic note for Liberals in the post-war world. In 1947, in its founding charter, Humphrey's organization,

Over the years, despite certain alterations in the rhetoric, the Humphrey view of the Cold War has not changed appreciably. In general, Humphrey now believes that—contrary to his own 1945 assertions—the USSR was untrustworthy *then,* but has of late become more manageable. The effective policy results are therefore remarkably similar to what they were at the beginning of the Cold War: conciliation of the Communists. In his 1964 campaign book, *The Cause Is Mankind,* Humphrey says:

> Ever since the early post-war years, when Stalin set out deliberately to expand the perimeter of world Communism, we have used our commercial power in the effort to halt the growth of world Communism. *We knew then, on the basis of all our experience, that the Soviet leaders were hopelessly committed to a course of forcible annexation as the only way of demonstrating the inevitability of Communism. . . . Today the situation appears to be quite different.* For one thing, Russia's leaders have apparently learned the hard lesson that a government cannot indefinitely substitute promises for basic needs if it is to endure and gain acceptance . . . Until the American wheat sale to the Soviet Union, our trade policy was based on the most rigid possible concept. It took no account of the changes from Stalin to Khrushchev, of the implications of the Sino-Soviet split, or the lessening of American-Russian tensions.[21] (Italics added.)

In making this retrospectively "tough" analysis of Communism in the early post-war years, Humphrey neglects to note that, while Stalin was setting out "to expand the perimeter of world Communism," and to pursue "a course of forcible annexation," none other than Hubert Humphrey looked favorably on that program and said it fitted "nicely

---

Americans for Democratic Action, had stated: "We firmly believe in the urgent need for breaking out of the vicious circle of mutual distrust between ourselves and Russia. We favor a policy based on an understanding of the legitimate aspirations of the Soviet Union."

into a secure and stable Russia," and averred that "the major political danger arising in Europe is not that of Communism."

While Humphrey '45 and Humphrey '64 are thus poles apart on the nature of Communism at the beginning of the Cold War, they are remarkably similar in one other respect: Both are agreed that, everything else aside, Soviet Communism is not particularly menacing. Humphrey No. 1 said Communism was not a danger in 1945; Humphrey No. 2 says it is not a danger in 1964. The Communism Humphrey now says was menacing in 1945 has "changed" and is not menacing now. The Communists who were not bad in 1945 but became bad retrospectively in 1964 have fortunately passed away and have been replaced by Communists who are not bad in 1964 and will become retrospectively bad, no doubt, in 1984—when they will have been replaced by other Communists who will not be menacing *then.**

While Hubert Humphrey's variations on the theme of not being beastly to the Kremlin would be sufficiently disturbing merely by virtue of Humphrey's position in our government, they become all the more so when they are conjoined to the similar utterances of Presidents Kennedy and Johnson. Such statements, in the 1960s as in the 1940s, have no relation to fact. They are, indeed, the reverse of fact, everywhere rejected by the evidence. They are spun, purely and simply, from the loom of Liberal ideology.

* The change in ADA's view of the situation is roughly the same. Looking back on the post-war years, ADA *now* says that the Communists were aggressive *then,* but that things have improved. In the present age of "lowered tensions," ADA said in 1964, "we must and shall go forward to lay firmer foundations for world peace—moving toward effective and enforced disarmament, building the United Nations, working through trade and aid policies for economic growth for the developing countries, and seeking to broaden areas of cooperation and to contain and ultimately resolve conflicts which constitute a present or potential threat to peace."

★★ 4. *The Rostow Line*

1. *Inside the State Department*

IN THE TWILIGHT WAR WITH COMMUNISM, with its mixture of military, diplomatic, economic and other competitions, the American State Department is our first line of defense. It is the State Department, so the average citizen would assume, which is chiefly responsible for defending and advancing American and Western interests *vis à vis* the Communist enemy.

But, as we have seen in our brief glimpse of high level expertise, the State Department does not itself take such a view of its role. It does not, for one thing, look upon Communism as an "enemy." And it conceives its duties in ways which tend to submerge American interests beneath the vague imperatives of global uplift. The State Department, in fact, is the fountainhead and citadel of the whole "accommodationist" school of thought, and has been such ever since the mid-1940's—that is, since the Cold War began.

This fact is of overwhelming importance. Presidents come and go; the State Department bureaucracy and the professional "experts" go on and on. When a John Foster Dulles is in office, these bureaucrats batten down, muffle initiatives in paperwork and routine, and buck against top-level policy when they can. When an "accommodationist" administration is in the saddle, and a Secretary of State like Dean Rusk comes into office, the career diplomatists surface, and happily carry out to the last extremity every suggestion of *détente* and conciliation issuing from the White House or the Secretary's office.

The capacity of the professional State Department bureaucracy for sheer survival means that, despite the tenure of four different presidents since the inception of the Cold War, essentially the same group of people have been in charge of American policy throughout the entire period. Former Assistant Secretary of State Adolph Berle, himself a fervent Liberal, described the accession of this group to power as follows:

> As I think many people know, in the fall of 1944, there was a difference of opinion in the State Department. I felt that the Russians were not going to be sympathetic and cooperative. Victory was then assured, but not complete, and the intelligence reports which were in my charge, among other things, indicated a very aggressive policy, not at all in line with the kind of cooperation everyone was hoping for, and I was pressing for a pretty clean-cut showdown then when our position was strongest.
>
> The opposite group in the State Department was largely the men—Mr. [Dean] Acheson's group, of course—with Mr. Hiss as a principal assistant in the matter . . . I got trimmed in that fight and, as a result, went to Brazil, and that ended my diplomatic career.[1]

The group thus described by Berle took full possession in 1947, with the ascent of Gen. George Marshall to the Secretaryship, and, with certain exceptions under Dulles, has guided American policy ever since. Even during the Eisenhower years, the Acheson-Marshall group held on. Former Under Secretary of State Robert Murphy relates, for example, the conflict of opinion over "trusting" the Communists that Dulles had with his own subordinates.[2] Former Ambassador to Cuba Earl Smith, describing the policies which brought about the fall of Cuba to Communism, says this event was owing to a "policy of many in critical positions in the State Department" whose test of diplomatic rectitude is "not what is beneficial to the United States but what fits their doctrinaire views of the future world":

> . . . it was impossible for Assistant Secretary of State Roy Rubottom, his associate William Wieland, and the Fourth Floor not to be aware of Fidel Castro's Communist affiliations . . . But I am sure that the Secretary of State, and the Undersecretary of State and the President were not adequately and correctly informed on this subject until it was too late . . . The Secretary of State was preoccupied with Peking, Moscow, and Berlin. The policy decisions on Cuban affairs were determined on the Fourth Floor of the State Department, where influential persons believed in the revolution and hoped for its success . . .
>
> These men are protected by the Foreign Office Service Law, by the Civil Service Law, by the Veterans Administration Law, and by congressional pressure. For all practical purposes, they cannot be dismissed. They protect each other as though they belonged to a fraternity.[3]

Smith's assertions were backed by former Ambassador to Mexico Robert C. Hill, who said reports about Castro's Communist affiliations had not reached the top echelons of our government because they were "sidetracked at the desk level."[4] When Dulles' successor Christian Herter told FBI

Chief J. Edgar Hoover he had received no warning concerning Castro's Communist background, "Hoover informed Herter that the FBI had been sending reports of this nature to the State Department for approximately four years."[5]

With the advent of the Kennedy administration, the State Department professionals no longer had to work around an unsympathetic figure like Dulles. Dean Rusk, the new Secretary, was himself an alumnus of the Acheson-Marshall group, a personal protege of Dean Acheson. With his return to the State Department, the be-kind-to-Moscow school was, for most practical purposes, back on top.

Secretary Rusk, like the authors of our ten quotations, is quite willing to find changes in and mitigation for Communist performance. Concerning the present condition of the Soviet dictatorship, Rusk has expressed the opinion that "a sense of national pride and desire for national independence, yearnings for more freedom for the individual himself, and the desire for higher standards of living and security for family and home have forced certain changes in the monolithic structure of the authoritarian system."[6] He has also stated that "the themes of young writers and poets tell much of the direction societies will take; and in the Soviet Union these writers of the new generation are the beginning of what I believe will be a continuing trend—a slow trend, perhaps, but one leading inexorably toward freedom."[7]*

The notion that the Soviet Union is somehow evolving into a more humane society, obliquely expressed by Rusk, is the chief axiom of the accommodationists. Because the Soviets are supposedly mellowing, it is anticipated they will become increasingly amenable to Western demonstrations of kindness but made suspicious by actions or statements which seem "provocative."

Rusk's second-in-command, Under Secretary George Ball, has also advanced this notion in official correspondence. It

*** A further analysis of Rusk's opinions appears in chapter *19*.**

was Ball who was called upon by the Senate Armed Services Committee to justify the actions of the State Department censors in the "muzzling" controversy. At various points in his testimony, he attempted to disown specific comments by the censors, describing one assertion that the word "victory" has an "aggressive" sound leaving no room for "accommodation" as "fatuous . . . foolish . . . inartistic and inaccurate." Yet Ball himself had submitted to the senators, with a cover letter signed by him, a report which used exactly the same phraseology. "I am enclosing," Ball wrote, "our explanations for deletions or changes in certain speeches by Defense Department personnel." "Our explanations," as submitted by Ball, contained the following statement:

"The word 'victory' has a militaristic and aggressive ring less suited than the substituted phrase to describe our national objectives. It also implies an 'all-or-nothing' approach leaving no room for accommodation."[8]

Another State Department higher-up, Assistant Secretary Harlan Cleveland, has attacked "the illusion that foreign policy issues are comfortably two-sided," and declared that "We see new leaders of Communism facing with realism the fact that their old dream of a Communist one world is an obsolete and perilous delusion."[9]

2. *Walt W. Rostow*

These statements by Rusk, Ball, and Cleveland are merely the occasional utterances of working diplomats. To achieve a full understanding of the official Cold War line, we must go deeper, and examine the views of those State Department officials who are considered experts on the subject. Prominent among these is Walt W. Rostow, Chief of Policy Planing of the State Department under both Kennedy and Johnson, and more recently a White House assistant to the President.

An example of Rostow's thinking appeared in a 1962 interview assertedly spelling out U.S. Cold War strategy. The basic elements of that strategy, Rostow said, were: to "tighten the bonds" between the "developed" nations involved in the defense of the free world; to help the "underdeveloped" nations to "modernize their societies"; to get the developed and the underdeveloped nations together in a "partnership"; and to maintain the military strength of the free world. All of which sounds fine. But since it is purely procedural—a line of action taken in the expectation of reaching some defined objective—it needs a goal to give it meaning, some recognizable purpose involving the Communists. That purpose, according to Rostow, is as follows: "The fifth element of our strategy concerns our posture toward the nations that are now under Communist rule. We see natural forces at work within those nations—a growing nationalism and the natural desires of people everywhere for increased individual liberty—that should tend to produce a more livable world. *We are, therefore, prepared to find limited areas of overlapping interest with Communist regimes and work patiently toward the development of the kind of world that we envisage*—but this kind of slow evolutionary development depends absolutely on building the unity of the free world and protecting it. In short, the fifth point depends on the other four."[10] (Italics added.)

It is interesting to note the verbal sleight-of-hand by which Rostow arrives at the possibility of "overlapping interests" with the Communists. He first cites the popular unrest at work in the Soviet satellites, jumps from this to the statement that the unrest "should tend to produce a more livable world" and proceeds to the assumption that the Communist *regimes* somehow should inherit the sympathy accruing to their restless subjects—which implies that the regimes actually represent the people and are in harmony with their wishes.

Identifying real unrest among the satellite peoples with

imaginary change among their captors is only one step in Rostow's master strategy. He has elaborated a whole theory of the "mellowing" of the Communist bosses which, according to copious evidence, is now the working basis of American foreign policy. His argument, to which other New Frontier officials contributed, was set forward in a 286-page report entitled "Basic National Security Policy." What is known of this document, together with a vast mosaic of collateral data, makes it clear that the idea of seeking "overlapping interests" with the Communists is now the central conception of American diplomacy.

The theme of Rostow's report is that the Soviet Union is changing dramatically for the better, and can be weaned away from aggression by an improvement in American manners. He enjoins the United States to be conciliatory toward Moscow, to insure that nothing in our policy stirs the Soviets to renewed hostility.

Willard Edwards of the *Chicago Tribune* gives the following paraphrase of Rostow's ideas:

> . . . Communist regimes and peoples are to be dealt with in terms of 'overlapping interest,' a phrase which is also popular with Rostow in public statements.
>
> The United States Information Agency must be used abroad to define and dramatize the 'limited but real areas of overlapping interest' between the United States and other governments and peoples, the paper asserts. . . .
>
> One theme is consistent in the proposed strategy plan—continuing communication with Russia, informal and formal, direct and indirect, must be maintained in order to dispel its fears of the United States and give it a clear understanding of our peaceful intentions.
>
> Rising tensions or the pleas of our allies or of the American public must be ignored in any crisis with Russia. The temptation must be avoided to prolong or expand any crisis in an effort to degrade or embarrass the Soviets in the eyes of the world . . .
>
> Gentle treatment of the satellite nations is advocated. No

official attacks should be made against their regimes, whatever the provocation, and even criticism should be softened. Western Europe, at the same time, must be encouraged to closer relationship with the satellites and urged to furnish aid to them.

East Germany, the policy draft says, cannot be forever insulated from dealings with the United States and business must be transacted with them.

Above all, no encouragement or support must be given to armed uprisings in Eastern Europe. . . ."[11]

Subsequent to the embarrassing disclosure of this manifesto, the Kennedy administration claimed it wasn't so. "The State Department," Edwards noted in 1962, "is still advising inquiring members of Congress that the press articles were so inaccurate that it was unlikely that any reporter had actually seen the Rostow document. While there was no citation of a single inaccuracy, the implication seemed to be that the stories were the product of a fevered imagination."[12]

In answer to these allegations, Edwards gave a full rundown on the national beat he scored by unearthing the Rostow paper.

My interest in the Rostow document [Edwards relates] was first aroused on June 7, 1962 when I was covering the appearance of Under Secretary of State George W. Ball before the Senate Armed Services Subcommittee. Ball was almost the final witness in a five-month hearing which had probed military censorship practices and other phases of the administration's cold war strategy. . . .

Senator Strom Thurmond, of South Carolina, wanted to know why administration policy had been based on a theory that the Kremlin could be appeased with soft words and gestures. He asked Mr. Ball if the subcommittee could see a new foreign policy guide which he had heard was in preparation under the supervision of Mr. Rostow.

Ball was astounded. The papers, he said, were not official and had not been approved by the President, Secretary of State, or anyone else. They were an incomplete working draft, representing the views of a number of persons in government, and certainly were in no shape for review by Congress.[13]

Edwards notes there had already been some "leaks" concerning the Rostow documents to "pro-administration publications" (among them, *Newsweek* magazine), but that few details had been given concerning it. He decided to find out about it on his own:

It took a week of digging; patient questioning of many persons in government and in Congress; one of those fortunate "breaks" which occasionally lighten a newspaperman's heart; a solemn pledge to protect a confidential source—and I had a copy of Rostow's document in my hands.

As I flipped it open, one of the first sentences to leap from its pages was this: "The Soviet Union's domestic and foreign policies have mellowed in the post-Stalin period."

The two long stories which I wrote for publication the following week-end were based on typed, verbatim extracts from the volume, totaling some 2,000 words in length. There was some paraphrasing, some comparison with public statements by Mr. Rostow, some injection of critical comment from military and intelligence experts, but the final result was a faithful and accurate account of ideas suggested as a basis for a future United States foreign policy.

As a final precaution, I voluntarily submitted these articles to inspection by an intelligence expert of unassailable position who screened them to insure that no detail, by any stretch of the imagination, would be revealed which might be regarded as a violation of security.[14]

Further evidence that Edwards' version of the Rostow report was accurate is a column by Robert S. Allen, which reported that a "master plan" prepared by Rostow was being circulated "at the highest level in the Kennedy administration for comment from other cabinet members." In general, Allen said, the document "rules out any U.S. military action against the Soviet Union or Communist China unless those nations launch a nuclear attack against the U.S. or Europe," and "calls for the Kennedy administration to adopt a completely defensive containment policy against the spread of international Communism, stating that the ultimate U.S. objective is a peaceful world in which every nation can determine its own destiny."[15]

3. *Charles E. Bohlen*

The notion that Communism is softening with age is not held exclusively by Prof. Rostow. It has other champions high in the ranks of the Establishment—for example, Kennedy adviser Charles E. Bohlen.

Until his appointment as the Kennedy administration's minister to France, a position which at this writing he still holds, Bohlen served as special adviser to the Secretary of State on Soviet affairs. As such, he had ample occasion for wielding influence on U.S. policy. In his present position in one of our most important embassies, he can still wield a great deal.

Bohlen is portrayed by such pillars of the Establishment as the *Washington Post* and *The New York Times* as the State Department's leading authority on everything appertaining to the Soviet Union, and as a "firm" opponent of the Bolsheviki. As one news service put it, back in 1959, Bohlen could claim a "long history of blunt negotiations with the Communists."[16] Daniel Schorr of CBS asserted he was "something of a legend for his verbal duels with Soviet leaders."[17]

Yet an examination of Bohlen's views, and of Soviet attitudes toward him, does not suggest much by way of toughness. When Bohlen was removed from Moscow in 1957, according to Schorr, Premier Bulganin exclaimed: "We do not understand why they are taking you from us." And Khrushchev put it, "We like competent ambassadors who know how to give correct appraisals to their governments." Schorr says Bohlen was not pleased at the prospect of his departure, "nor was anyone else in Moscow."[18]

The reports which Khrushchev apparently considered "correct appraisals" were not similarly viewed by Secretary of State Dulles. By all accounts, Dulles thought Bohlen lacking in firmness toward the Communists. "There was," Schorr says, "the clash of the specialist's view of a Russia in flux and the Secretary's single-minded picture of the external threat of international Communism."[19] Or—to put it in the terms with which we began this discussion—Bohlen's view that Communism was "changing," and Dulles' view that Communism, so long as it remains Communism, does not change in any essential aspect.

Bohlen, as the nation's number one "Soviet expert," might very well be the original author of the thesis that Communism is "mellowing." Schorr, summarizing and quoting Bohlen's views as of 1959, gives us the key phrases: "Ideology is playing a steadily decreasing role in determining Soviet action. When the Communists were fighting for power, ideology was their master. Now it is their servant . . . The general trend in the Soviet Union is toward liberalization. It is a trend occasionally checked by some event such as the Hungarian rebellion, but it was not reversed, nor is there any present evidence that it will be."[20]

More generally, Bohlen would seem entitled to be called the father of Kremlinology—the school of statecraft which seeks to predict "trends" within the Soviet Union by piecing together scraps of minutiae. In this discipline, the tiniest slivers of evidence are built into a vast edifice of theory about the directions in which the Soviets are going to "change":

Whether the "hard" Communists will be cowed by the "moderates," whether the "split" between Red China and Moscow will widen, *etc.* Anything which might suggest the long hoped-for surge of mellowness is seized upon and made the center of an elaborate phantasmagoria. It is noteworthy, in this connection, that among Bohlen's predictions of "liberalization" has been a forecast that the post-Stalin "collective leadership" would endure (wrong), and that among his previsions of "change" has been a forecast that Georgi Malenkov would make a comeback (wrong).

4. *George F. Kennan*

In the pantheon of American Liberalism, "Chip" Bohlen has only one rival as an "expert" on the Soviet Union—George F. Kennan, former Policy Planning Chief of State, former ambassador to the USSR, and President Kennedy's envoy to Yugoslavia. Kennan was one of the promising young men—along with Bohlen—trained in Soviet affairs by the State Department, back in the 1930's, in the confident expectation that the USSR would be recognized. And his attitude on current questions, as the public record abundantly reveals, is substantially the same as that of his colleague.

Six months prior to the Hungarian revolution of 1956, George Kennan was telling the world that:

> Where regimes of this nature have been in power for more than a decade, there can be no question of putting Humpty Dumpty [i.e., a relative condition of freedom] together again and restoring the *status quo ante* . . . there is a finality, for better or worse, about what has now occurred in Eastern Europe . . .[21]

Let us not, he further admonished Americans:

> . . . after having criticized the Russian Communists all these

years for being too totalitarian, pour scorn and ridicule upon them the moment they show signs of becoming anything else.[22]

Because Khrushchev and Bulganin were contrite about Stalin's excesses, Kennan believed, Russia as of 1956 was the scene of "far less terror, internally," "relaxation of restrictions," "greater liberality," "more liberal attitudes," "greater maturity, confidence, and courtesy."[23] (His words made interesting reading, in the autumn of '56, alongside the dispatches which every day poured out of Hungary.) Kennan concluded that the Soviet Union was evolving into "something resembling a traditional authoritarian state, oligarchically governed." And, he asked, *"What more do we want in three-and-half years?"*[24] What, indeed? That question would be easier to answer if there were any reason to believe the "liberalizing" Kennan conjured ever took place. We had only his (and Khrushchev's) word for it—to set over against the bleeding corpse of Budapest and the monstrous barrier of the Wall.

Summing up his view of what had happened in Russia and what Americans should do about it, Kennan said: ". . . the changes that have recently occurred in Russia . . . represent, I think, the beginning of that mellowing process which overtakes sooner or later all militant movements . . ." In the Mellow Era, he added, officious Americans would have to drop their "hazy and exalted dreams of intimacy with other peoples," because "there are ways of looking at things and reacting to things about the Russian people which will always be strange to Americans and will always tend to arouse resentment if we become too closely involved in their affairs."[25]

Similar views have been advanced by Kennan on a number of other occasions. In 1954 he suggested the best interests of the Free World would be served only if "the vital prestige of Soviet power is not too drastically and abruptly engaged" by

U.S. foreign policy. The Communists, he said, will not yield under outside pressure, but from "compulsions resident within the structure of Soviet power itself." He concluded with a parable:

> . . . you will all recall the Aesopian fable about the competition between the Sun and the North Wind to see which of them could make the traveler remove his cloak. Well, the traveler is the phenomenon of Soviet power. The cloak is that zone of inordinate power and influence in Eastern Europe and elsewhere with which it has tried to shelter its own inner sanctum. And you will all recall that it was not by the direct huffing and puffing of the North Wind, but by the gentle indirection of the Sun that the stubborn traveler was at last induced to remove his cloak.[26]

That American sunshine might thaw Soviet hostility was suggested in a 1958 Kennan opus called *Russia and the West.* This book is, for the most part, an excellent historical review of Soviet treachery, brutality, and intransigence. Yet the final chapter attributes all the misdeeds to Lenin and Stalin, and tells us that, under Khrushchev, the Communists have "changed." "I feel it particularly important to stress," Kennan says, "lest it be forgotten, that what I have been describing was the eras of Lenin and of Stalin, and not that of Khrushchev." There are, he says, "relative" but "not unimportant" differences: "The drastic alteration in the role of the police has constituted a basic change in the nature and spirit of Soviet society." There is a movement "away from the horror of unadulterated police intrigue," there is a "rudimentary parliamentarianism," there is a "relaxation" of the Iron Curtain "within modest limits." Moreover, he concludes, "the evil of Communist subversion" is "definitely on the wane." Too many people "seem afraid to admit to themselves or to others that Stalin is really dead."[27]

There is, however, a note of warning. "Neo-Stalinist echelons" lurking within the Khrushchev regime do not like all the "relaxation." These elements, one gathers, will move in if

Khrushchev's position becomes untenable. And, in another paragraph, Kennan suggests that the memory of Stalin's regime is "a reminder of how much worse things could be." In short, Kennan clearly implied, we ought to be pretty thankful that Khrushchev was in charge of things in Moscow. Meanwhile, as we meditate on the virtues of the de-Stalinized USSR, Kennan invites us to a simultaneous consideration of our own faults. "When the ambivalence of one's virtue is recognized, the total iniquity of one's opponent is also irreparably impaired."[28]

In a 1964 effort entitled *On Dealing With The Communist World,* Kennan drops some of the circumlocution and goes all-out for "coexistence." His major themes in this volume are that the Soviets are immensely powerful, unshakable in their grip over those whom they have enslaved, yet ever mellowing, increasingly reasonable, and, all in all, despite some vaguely unpleasant things about which he never gets too specific, a fairly decent bunch with whom we can and must learn to get along. He bitterly chastises those who venture to believe that, on the few occasions when America stood firm and the Soviets backed off, they did so out of fear. Such occasional reversals in the Soviet advance, he says, are merely signs of "prudence" and "moderation."[29]

Among Kennan's other *aperçus* are statements that, should the Communist government in Moscow be overthrown, "I would know of no assurance that whatever might conceivably come in place of what is there now would be any closer to liberal ideals"; that political change in the USSR can come "only on the foundation of and within the framework of the present political system"; that "I can think of nothing more catastrophic than that the policy of our government should be committed to the break-up of the traditional Russian state"; that "the Soviet government is a great power, with a far-flung and complex pattern of international interests, involvements and commitments."[30]

And, on the subject of "change":

"I do not see how anyone can dispute the difference between the weak and isolated Soviet state of the 1920s and the 1930s and the great power we have before us today, with its far-flung interests and involvements, its embarrassments of empire, its obligations of alliance, its new personalities, and its evolving internal problems. This, surely, is something far more like the traditional, established great power of 'Russia' than like the fanatical political personality we faced in the Soviet regime of Lenin's time or nightmarish totalitarian despotism of Stalin."[31]

Which means, to boil it all down, that there is no prospect of beating the Communists, so we must repose our hope for survival in the idea that they have "changed," and, somehow, some way, don't really mean it.

Kennan's method of arguing all this is, to say the least, unusual. He adopts the stance that the idea of *not* trusting the Communists has been tried and found wanting. We must therefore turn, he says, to "coexistence"—and those who resist this are attempting to return to the old errors of the past. He does not tell us exactly how the Litvinov agreement, or the Yalta conference, or the cutoff of aid to Chiang Kai-shek, or the assistance our State Department lent Fidel Castro, or the refusal to intervene in Hungary add up to a policy of militant mistrust. In the Kennan style of argument, one does not try to prove black is white; one takes it as an axiom of the discussion.

So it is, that, in a 1965 address, Kennan provides us with the most abandoned flight of trust-Moscow rhetoric we have yet encountered. ". . . I should like to plead," he said, "for a basic revision of assumptions concerning Soviet intentions, both hypothetical and actual . . . The assumptions commonly made with respect to Soviet military intentions . . . can be reconciled neither with Communist doctrine (which does not envisage the bringing of socialism to peoples exclusively or primarily on the bayonets of foreign armies*), nor with the moral commitments the Soviet leaders have assumed to their own people, nor with the present state of relations between Moscow and the Communist countries of Eastern Europe.

"*They impute to the Soviet leaders a total inhumanity not plausible even in nature and out of accord with those humane ideals which we must recognize as lying—together with other elements less admirable in the eyes of some of us—at the origins of all European Marxism.*

"*I should like, therefore, to end these observations with a plea for something resembling a new act of faith in the ultimate humanity and sobriety of the people on the other side . . .*" (Italics added.)[32]

Such is the considered and unwavering view, after decades of masterminding U.S. strategy, serving as our top Cold War counselor, and representing the United States in key embassies abroad, of the man widely revered as Liberaldom's premier expert on the Cold War. Our own comment on its relationship to the observable facts is implicit in chapter 2, and in the rest of this book. For the moment, it is interesting to note Kennan's own judgment of it, in a passage which he allowed to represent his views as late as 1952:

> When there is something the Russians want from us, one or the other features of their policy may be thrust temporarily into the background; and when that happens, there will always be Americans who will leap forward with gleeful announcements that "the Russians have changed . . ."[33]

* True enough, but, as phrased in Kennan's jigsaw prose, nothing to the purpose. Of course the Soviets don't believe in conquest "exclusively or primarily" by "the bayonets of foreign armies." They employ subversion, *coup d'etat,* guerrilla movements, and general insurrection, *as well as* "foreign bayonets." What point Kennan is trying to make or to give the appearance of making, and what its relevance may be to the real question of Moscow's hostile intentions and Kennan's "act of faith" is a puzzle each reader may ruminate according to his inclinations. The rest of the statement speaks, all too eloquently, for itself.

★★ 5. *The Fulbright Doctrine*

1. *Mythmanship*

"ACCOMMODATIONIST" SENTIMENT in Washington is centered in the State Department. It has, however, its votaries on Capitol Hill as well. Foremost among these is Senator J. William Fulbright (D-Ark.), chairman of the Senate Foreign Relations Committee.

Senator Fulbright is a very powerful man. Both by situation and by ideological affinity, he is the most influential of all American legislators where the American State Department is concerned, occasional disagreements in special cases (most notably Viet Nam) notwithstanding.

A measure of Fulbright's considerable influence may be seen in the so-called "muzzling" controversy of 1961, when the Senator suggested a policy of extended censorship of anti-Communist statements by the military. Fulbright's efforts on this score came to light in the summer of 1961, when Senator Strom Thurmond of South Carolina unearthed the document which has since become known as "the Fulbright Memorandum." The suggestions contained in this memorandum were almost immediately put into effect by the Kennedy administration, which cancelled anti-Communist seminars being co-sponsored by the military and clamped a tight muzzle on military spokesmen.

On the fundamental question of what the Communists are up to and how we should deal with them, Fulbright is in complete accord with the Rostow-Bohlen-Kennan view–the only significant difference, perhaps, being his willingness to go to even greater lengths than they in the vehemence of his assertions and abandon of his proposals. Beyond this, Fulbright has also worked up several major themes of his own, implicit in the nature of Liberal ideology, but identified in public discussion chiefly with him. These are as follows: 1) that Communists, in Moscow or Peking or Havana, are not only people we can live with but, because of their great power, the stability of their governments, and their generally waxing influence, people we had better learn to live with: 2) that the American people are in general too obtuse to understand this wise proposition, preferring to succor on myths and delusions of "omnipotence;" and 3) that in the interest of educating the people to the higher wisdom of Fulbright, military leaders, militant anti-Communists and other primitives must be bludgeoned into quietude.

Fulbright's style of argument is somewhat like George Kennan's. He almost always begins by selecting a controversial point one would expect him to try to prove by argument, and handles it as though it were a self-evident truth. On the matter of trusting the Communists, he does not try to establish that the Communists *can* be trusted, or *should* be trusted. Nor does he tackle any of the vast historical evidence which goes to show they *cannot* be trusted. He simply asserts the point as though it were something known to any intelligent being.

Conjoined to this striking form of discourse is yet another technique which might be called Fulbright's principle of reversal. Professing a view for which there is not a scintilla of proof, and contesting one supported by reams of documentation and contemporary evidence, Fulbright blandly preempts for himself the mantle of "realism" and disparages all contrary argument as "myth." Thus we find him asserting: "The master myth of the Cold war is that the Communist bloc is a monolith composed of governments which are not really governments at all, but organized conspiracies, divided among themselves perhaps in certain matters of tactics, but all equally resolute and implacable in their determination to destroy the free world."[1]

Over against the senator's assertion, we have the weight of recorded history and of Communist utterance suggesting this alleged "myth" is in fact a very accurate summation of just what Communism is. Were that fact to be accepted, however, the whole foreign policy approach favored by Senator Fulbright would fall to the ground; the unpleasant facts about Communism must somehow be disposed of. They are "myth."

For an authority on "reality," Fulbright has demonstrated a remarkable gift for ignoring some very fundamental realities about Communism. In 1946, Fulbright stated his view of the Soviet Union as follows:

> Another powerful prejudice which has affected our policy is our fear of Russia and Communism. This prejudice can vitally affect our future. Until the revolution in Russia, we had always been on friendly terms with that nation. We had never fought her. Yet, after the revolution was established by Lenin, we refused to recognize Russia until 1933, the last of the major nations to do so.[2]

And:

When I hear the unbridled and intemperate attacks upon Russia by some of our own people, I cannot help but be troubled . . .[3]

And:

I do not believe that the Soviets desire to dominate the world as the Germans did. They have given no evidence that they believe they are supermen. Russia, like America, is a nation of many races, and I can see no reason why we cannot get along peaceably . . .[4]

Other early Fulbright utterances, further demonstrating his "realism," include: "The Russian experiment in Socialism is scarcely more radical under modern conditions than the Declaration of Independence was in the days of George III."[5] And, regarding the United Nations Relief and Rehabilitation Administration: "The Russian government has signed this agreement. If Stalin were primarily interested in promoting Communism throughout the world rather than peace, he would have nothing to do with a plan to bring help to the starving and helpless people of Europe."[6]

Similar shrewdness has marked the senator's more recent utterances as well. In 1959, Fulbright expressed the belief that "the public opinion of the world will cause the Russian people to relinquish their control of the once-free peoples of Poland, East Germany, Hungary, Czechoslovakia, Latvia, Estonia, Lithuania, and Bulgaria. . . . We may even hope that, as conditions of life improve in the USSR, . . . the harsh and brutal attitude of the Russians toward their fellow men may be humanized. . . . We ought not to accept the facile axiom that the Russians have no intentions of ever coming to reasonable terms on any matter directly affecting their own interests."[7]

In 1960, when Khrushchev denounced President Eisenhower on the pretext of U-2 flights over the Soviet Union, Fulbright said "it is difficult to see how anyone could have been expected to act substantially different from the way Khrushchev acted under the circumstances which confronted him in Paris." America's attitude of "smug self-righteousness" on the issue, Fulbright averred, "must have been unbearably provocative to the Soviet government and contributed substantially to the violence and intemperate bad manners of Khrushchev in Paris."[8]

In July, 1961, questioned about the exodus of refugees from Communism through West Berlin, Fulbright commented: "We have no right for them [*sic*] to insist that they be allowed to come out. It just happens, it is a circumstance. . . . I don't understand why the East Germans don't close it because I think they have a right to close it."[9] Two weeks later the East Germans, sharing Fulbright's view as to their rights, began construction of the Berlin Wall, sealing up thousands of East Germans in captivity. (As it happened, Fulbright's view of the Communists' "rights" was mistaken: The post-war agreements on Germany guarantee free movement between the various sectors of Berlin.)

In March, 1964, Fulbright delivered himself of a whole gaggle of opinions on Communism and the Cold War. Among other items, he advised Americans to stop worrying about Fidel Castro in Cuba, and to look forward to recognition of Communist China.

On Castro, he said: "I think that we must abandon the myth that Cuban Communism is a transitory menace that is going to collapse or disappear in the immediate future and face up to two basic realities about Cuba: first, that the Castro regime is not on the verge of collapse and is not likely to be overthrown by any policies which we are now pursuing or can reasonably undertake; second, that the continued existence of the Castro regime, though inimical to our interests and policies, is not an insuperable obstacle to the attainment of our objectives, unless we make it so by permitting it to poison our politics at home and to divert us from more important tasks in the hemisphere."[10]*

2. *The Anti-Communist Danger*

Where Communism is concerned, Senator Fulbright is the picture of relaxation. His message is: Stop worrying, stop getting excited, stop being hostile. Communism is not, he has been telling us off and on for 20 years, a danger.

This does not mean, however, that all is right with the world. On the contrary, there is the problem of those people who *do* think Communism is a danger, and these people are a nuisance. More. They are themselves a danger and, the more the keen intelligence of J. W. Fulbright considers the matter, it appears they are just about the most dangerous thing around.

There is, to begin with, the serious business of those delusions of omnipotence which come over Americans every once in a while—delusions which lead them to believe, contrary to the realism of Fulbright, that they can actually do something to combat the Communists. Referring to the failure of the American government to establish a successful economic quarantine of Cuba, Fulbright says:

"The boycott policy has failed because the United States is not omnipotent and cannot be. The basic reality to be faced is that it is simply not within our power to compel our allies to cut off trade with Cuba, unless we are prepared to take drastic sanctions against them, such as closing our own markets to any foreign company that does business in Cuba."[11]

* Castro responded to this speech by saying Fulbright's position was "essentially true" and adding, "Senator Fulbright is not a Christ but it is tragic that in the United States some persons seem to want to crucify him when his only crime was to address himself to the realities of the Cuban situation."

Fulbright thus seeks to suggest the United States has tried with might and main to establish a boycott of Cuba but simply could not get the job done. In point of fact, no such strenuous effort has been attempted; American policy toward allied trade with Cuba has been one of studied lenience, as it perforce must be considering the fact that the United States is engaged in a burgeoning traffic of its own with Communist nations everywhere around the globe. Fulbright himself, interestingly enough, is a vehement advocate of *not* boycotting Cuba and of increased trade with the Communists. Thus Fulbright works to prevent an effective policy of resistance, then cites the results of his own advocacy as proof that resistance is unfeasible.

Distaste for the assertion of American interests and those who advocate such things has been a consistent feature of Fulbright's public career, paralleling his willingness to think well of the Communists. "The professional patriots beat their breasts and wave the flag and shout 'sovereignty,'" he declaimed in 1944. "In the minds of many, the word 'sovereignty' has some mystical connotation in some way associated with divinity."[12] And, on another occasion: "The real danger is the muddle-headed isolationism of pseudo-patriots who think, by appealing to the petty and short-sighted selfishness of human beings, they are preserving a world that has already vanished."[13]

In 1954, in debate over the Bricker Amendment to limit presidential treaty-making prerogatives, Fulbright said Amendment supporters were afflicted with "the swinish blight . . . of anti-intellectualism" and were "boors," "liars," "louts" and anti-democrats into the bargain.[14]

The prevalence of swinishness, myth, and delusions of grandeur in our national politics, converging in the notion that we cannot trust the Communists, have convinced Fulbright the American people stand badly in need of education. As the Fulbright memorandum put it: "In the long run, it is quite possible that the principal problem of leadership will be, if it is not already, to restrain the desire of the people to hit the Communists with everything we've got, particularly if there are more Cubas and Laos [*sic*] . . . Fundamentally, it is believed that the American people have little, if any, need to be alerted to the menace of the Cold War." The memorandum added that "public opinion must be educated if it is to bolster wise and effective national policies.[15]

In 1963, Fulbright returned to the theme of education and expanded on it at some length. In a convocation sponsored by the Fund For the Republic, he argued for a strong presidency to "educate" the people in matters of international politics. The essay was published in a pamphlet entitled, interestingly enough, *The Elite And The Electorate.*[16]

This obsession with "educating" the public, with getting rid of asserted "myths" and delusions, arises from the fact that most ordinary people, not being experts like Fulbright, dull-wittedly believe a long history of aggression, brutality, falsehood, and broken agreements indicates the Communists cannot be relied upon. This makes things difficult for the accommodationists in government, who are forced to go about their business of conciliating Moscow by indirections. It would all be so much easier if the public shared the expert's view of the matter or, failing that, at least learned to keep its nose out of the expert's business.

That this is exactly what Fulbright wants became apparent in July, 1965, when he arose on the Senate floor to excoriate a group of American citizens for their audacity in opposing trade with the Communists. The conservative youth group Young Americans for Freedom had foiled a favorite program of the senator's, and Fulbright was outraged. "It is disturbing," he said, ". . . when private groups or businesses or individuals take it on themselves, by act or omission, to alter or dictate or defeat official policies of the U.S. government. . . . directly and not through our duly constituted governmental agencies such as Congress."[17] Which sounds, on the face of it, as if YAF had somehow been engaged in a violation of the Logan Act. The facts were otherwise.

Early in 1965, the conservative newsletter *Human Events* reported the Firestone Tire and Rubber Company, encouraged by the Johnson administration, was going to build two rubber plants in Communist Rumania. YAF members in Philadelphia read the article, disapproved, and began publicizing Firestone's proposed transaction through leaflets, picketing, etc. Firestone, apparently believing the unfavorable publicity was bad for business, called off the deal.

Fulbright was beside himself. YAF was, he said, an "extremist" and "vigilante" group, interfering with an American policy "of building bridges to the East," which he proclaimed to be "a proven success." He insinuated that YAF was in cahoots with the Goodyear Rubber Co., which had refused to go through with a similar deal, and was the tool of "irresponsible, selfish interests." The result was that "instead of a healthy profit for Firestone, a solid gain for our balance of payments, and a positive step forward in the building of bridges to the East, the United States will have earned a harvest of ill will and a reputation for being quite incapable of executing policies decided upon by the President and the Department of State." Evidently forgetting the U.S. government is not "omnipotent," Fulbright concluded that the episode was "an example of how the constitutional process by which American foreign policy is being made can be defeated and disrupted."[18]

Fulbright thus demonstrated not only his amiability toward Communist regimes and his hostility to anti-Communist activity, but the authoritarian character of his yen to "educate." The actions he disparaged as "disruption" of "constitutional processes" were in fact purely and wholly *private*. YAF protested a proposed transaction by Firestone; consumers apparently agreed with that protest in sufficient numbers to give Firestone second thoughts; Firestone called off the deal. At what point along the way would Fulbright step in to change the process? Would he halt YAF's right to protest? The consumers' right to react? Or Firestone's right to cancel?

"To a certain extent," he says regretfully, "this sort of thing is probably inevitable in a free society. It can, however, be held to a minimum by a strong sense of public responsibility on the part of private individuals and organizations which become involved in foreign policy, combined with forthright and courageous leadership on the part of the foreign policy-making agencies of the U.S. government."[19] It could be held to a minimum best of all, of course, by assigning J. William Fulbright the role he so obviously desires—that of *gauleiter* in charge of silencing anyone who dissents from his program of appeasement.

3. *Mistrusting The Military*

By far Senator Fulbright's most singular contribution to political debate is his attack on the American military. In addition to its specific allegations about Communism and the lack of danger it presents to us, the Fulbright memorandum was a vehement critique of military leaders and the military mind. The chief danger, it suggested, is not the asserted enemy of Communism, but the men who are supposed to be defending us against it.

Describing the allegedly "radical" and menacing content of various anti-Communist seminars being staged with military cooperation, the Fulbright Memorandum makes these highly significant comments:

> There are many indications that the philosophy of the programs is representative of a substantial element of military thought, and has great appeal to the military mind. . . . There is

little in the education, training or experience of most military officers to equip them with the balance of judgment necessary to put their own ultimate solutions—those with which their education, training, and experience are concerned—into proper perspective in the President's total 'strategy for the nuclear age.'[20]

Fulbright adds that "there are no reasons to believe that military personnel generally" can contribute to an understanding of the Cold War, "beyond their specific, technical competence to explain their own role. On the contrary, there are many reasons, and some evidence, for believing that an effort by the military, beyond this limitation, involves considerable danger."[21] The belief that military men "have the necessarily broad background which would enable them to relate the various aspects of the cold war effort one to the other," Fulbright says, is a "basic error."[22]

To these aspersions, Fulbright conjoins an even more startling statement:

Perhaps it is far-fetched to call forth the revolt of the French generals as an example of the ultimate danger. Nevertheless, military officers, French or American, have some common characteristics arising from their profession and there are numerous military 'fingers on the trigger' throughout the world. While this danger may appear very remote, contrary to American tradition, so also is the 'long twilight struggle,' and so also is the very existence of an American military program for educating the public.[23]

In so arguing, Fulbright was putting forward a cherished if subdominant theme of Liberal advocacy, increasingly visible in recent agitation for disarmament. The late C. Wright Mills, unilateral disarmer and appeasement adept, referred to U.S. military men as "war lords," and bemoaned the fact that "everywhere now there are the generals and the captains who, by their presence, create and maintain a militarist atmosphere . . ." They are, he said, "operating a truly enormous public relations and propaganda machinery." He then added, Fulbright-fashion:

> Their careers and their kind of honor are tied up with the war machine. So long as they remain professional soldiers their training and their way of life tend to incapacitate them for transcending the military metaphysic.[24]

Hostility to the military is equally noticeable in a publication called *The Liberal Papers,* which excoriates "blustering generals" and proclaims that "as long as the great nation-states—the democratic no less than the totalitarian, our own no less than the Russian or the Chinese—found their external relations upon the institution of war, they are bound to reap the results, in the form of internal militarization, of fear, of aggression, and of instability, which the war system in the supertechnical age imposes. It is difficult to see how a liberal statesmanship in the modern era can take as its ultimate goal anything less than the abolition of the war system itself."[25]

A similar cry has been sounded, in somewhat more muted tones, by such disarmament advocates as Professor Seymour Melman, who inveighs against "the Cold War institutional machine,"[26] and Senator George McGovern, Liberal Democrat of South Dakota, who says "Americans have always feared that any trend toward militarism was a threat to the quality of our democracy. I believe that is still a legitimate concern."[27] Like utterances can be found heavily sprinkled throughout much contemporary Liberal literature on the Cold War. Animus toward the military has become pronounced in the public media, particularly in novels and movies like *Seven Days in May* and *Dr. Strangelove,* where the Fulbright vision of a military takeover is painted in lurid hues for popular consumption.

So vehement has such propaganda become that Brig. Gen. S.L.A. Marshall, a famous military historian but hardly a militarist, felt called upon to inquire in the *Saturday Evening Post:* "Why Do We Slander Our Military Men?" Commenting on *Seven Days* and *Strangelove,* Marshall said: "They are not sincere warnings . . . but reckless slander, and the effect of the whole is to poison the public mind. Without the trust of the people, the American military character cannot remain steadfast. Keep smearing a profession, and ultimately the stain rubs in."[28]

What *is* behind the smear of our military men? The sources of this propaganda campaign are several, some less reputable than others, and make the task of answering General Marshall's question a little difficult. There are, to begin with, the Communists. The epithet of "militarist" is, of course, a classic term of Marxist disparagement. U.S. Communist Party boss Gus Hall, a few days before the Fulbright Memorandum came to light, stated that the U.S.A. was endangered by "our own 'French generals,' who feel at home in fascist circles, and are ready to lend themselves to their objectives. It is the outgrowth of 20 years of militarization."[29] As William R. Kintner and Joseph Kornfeder observe: "According to Marx, Engels, and Lenin, the first commandment for revolutionary victory is: smash the military and internal security structure of the target government."[30] The derivation of Gus Hall's opinions is therefore apparent.

Liberal attacks on the military spring from less intelligible motives. The stated fear of military coup or takeover, in view of American history, is absurd. Probably closer to the truth is the Liberals' inveterate hostility to anyone who, at least where the emotional and ideological interests of the left are concerned, takes a clear-cut view of international issues.

Senator Fulbright professes the Liberal's delight in Cold War ambivalence when he says that " 'peace and freedom' mean different things to different people, and . . . , however deeply one may believe in one's own version, it is just possible that someone else's version is as good or even better."[31] George Kennan puts it that: "When the ambivalence of one's virtue is recognized, the total iniquity of one's opponent is also irreparably impaired."[32] And another influential counselor of government says: "The citing of a single cause—whether Communism or capitalism—to explain the conflict is becoming less credible to citizens on both sides."[33]

The Establishment view of the Cold War is, in short, highly uncertain. The Liberals repeatedly suggest they are doubtful as to who is *really* at fault. What have we done, they keep asking, to make the Communists suspicious of us? What can we do to reassure them? If we are as much to blame for the Cold War as they, what can we do to show them we are repentant? This ambiguity leads to a kind of pacifism, and to "complex" theories to justify it; it seeks to explain away the aggressions of the Soviet Union and to interpret its hostile initiatives so that the enemy is no longer an enemy.

The thinking of most military men, although hardly like the caricature sketched by Fulbright, is markedly different: While American military men are dedicated to peace, they do not believe it can be purchased with the coin of appeasement. When they see overt aggression committed over a span of years by a hostile power sworn to destroy us, they do not conclude that the victims of the aggression are somehow at fault. No military man trained to defend his country against all comers can hope to acquire the Fulbrightian sophistication to see that, in discussing the Cold War struggle with Communism, "someone else's" notion of "peace and freedom" is possibly "as good as or even better than" our own —particularly since only relevant someone else, the Soviet Union, seeks the defeat and destruction of the United States.

Military leaders are, moreover, the one group in American life holding stern anti-Communist views who as a class are widely respected by the American people. The combination, from the Establishment point of view, is dangerous. Such clarity of vision joined with such public prestige makes the military man the natural and aboriginal enemy of the Fulbright Liberal. So long as the military is respected, and continues to speak out on the issue of Communism, the Fulbright version of the Cold War will be in jeopardy. The military therefore needs to be discredited in the eyes of the American people and, pending that, forestalled from presenting its opinions.

★★ 6. *The Liberal Papers*

1. *The End of Anti-Communism*

CAN A "DECENT AMERICAN" be anti-Communist?

Most people would have small difficulty answering in the affirmative. But to a group of Liberal intellectuals with important connections in Washington, it is a knotty problem to which a "no" answer suggests itself far more readily than "yes."

The question is raised in a book entitled *The Liberal Papers,* a curious volume published in 1962, which evoked cries of wrath from Republicans and sent administration Democrats scurrying for cover. A collection of essays dealing with American foreign policy, the book was the product of a study group established during the 1959-60 session of Congress by a dozen or so Democratic legislators. The essays were written by a group of college teachers and other professional verbalizers called in by the congressmen to get the Liberal position down on paper. The purpose of "the Liberal Project," as set forward in the preface by then-Congressman (now U.N. delegate) James Roosevelt, was "to call on intellectuals whose ideas were uncommon and provocative."[1]

That the ideas were provocative may be granted. In answer to the question posed above, *The Liberal Papers* say the following: ". . . as the cold war continues, it becomes increasingly difficult for decent Americans, humane enough to prefer peace to an egocentric national honor, to be outspokenly and genuinely anti-Communist."[2] This sentiment is fleshed out, in ample detail, by a number of specific proposals.

While they view the Communists through a golden haze of benevolence, *The Liberal Papers* describe anti-Communists with barely-concealed anger and disgust. The villains of the piece are "backwoods reactionaries," "blustering generals",[2] Chiang, Adenauer, Franco, and "cold warriors" in general who would oppose the accommodation of East to West and stir up "their opposite numbers"[3] on the other side of the Iron Curtain—who, unlike the seraphic Khrushchev (then still in power), might be almost as unbearable as are American conservatives.

Sample statements of *The Liberal Papers* outlook include the following:

> In our judgment, one must work simultaneously on both fronts, diplomacy and disarmament, keeping in mind the long-run pacifist goal of a world in which conflict is settled without weapons and without war.[4]
>
> . . . Americans can indeed envy the ease with which Englishmen discuss alternatives to nuclear war, ranging from unilateral disarmament to diplomatic maneuvers aimed at easing particular points of tension in the Cold War.[5]
>
> This "posture" [of "toughness"] which so many people insist upon becomes self-destructive in a world of fantastically rapid change, where survival depends on flexibility and on willingness

to accept some responsibility for what is happening in the world as a whole.[6]

The attempt to contain Communism by surrounding the Sino-Soviet periphery with military bases and alliances . . . deepened the distrust and hostility of the Communist dictatorships and stimulated their own military efforts.[7]

We believe that if the world survives these next critical years and becomes less uncivilized, we shall move away from the anarchy of nationalism, reducing arms to the level of police forces and handling as imaginatively as we can the problem of coping with despotic governments.[8]

It is easier to envisage a diplomatic give-and-take between ourselves and the Soviet Union that (without complete disarmament) would settle outstanding conflicts of interest in Europe and Asia—even though attempts at such a settlement would encounter the opposition of Adenauer and Ulbricht, Chiang and Mao, American cold warriors and their Stalinist opposite numbers in Russia.[9]

The alliance with Chiang Kai-shek, contracted after his flight from the mainland, serves more to provoke than to ward off attack; moreover, it divides the anti-Communist coalition at its core and cements the Sino-Soviet alliance.[10]

We believe that the time has come when the United States should liberalize its restrictive trade policy *vis à vis* the Soviet Union.[11]

The Polish Rapacki plan [for withdrawal from Europe by the United States] appeals to us as a point of departure in shaping a Western proposal for reunifying Germany at the price of its military neutralization.[12]

. . . adoption [of the Rapacki plan] by the United States would offer assurance to the Communist rulers of the Soviet Union and the satellite states that we had abandoned any intention of overthrowing their regimes by subversion or force of arms.[13]

And so forth and so on. There are innumerable other such proposals set forward in *The Liberal Papers,* dealing with recognition of Red China, unilateral disarmament, creation of world government, *etc.* The quotations above are taken from only three of the dozen articles which make up this odd anthology. The book as a whole is a complete agenda for American backdown, pullout, and conciliation in every known category of foreign policy and national defense. The essays, in order, contain the following suggestions:

1. David Riesman and Michael Maccoby: America, purging itself of "fantasies of omnipotence and virulent nationalism," should realize that peace-lovers can no longer be anti-Communist, and resign from the Cold War.[14]

2. James Warburg: The ultimate aim of U.S. foreign policy should be "universal disarmament under adequately enforced world law."[15]

3. Walter Millis: "A rational disarmament policy might concentrate not on abolishing the nuclear arsenals, but on keeping them in reasonable deterrent balance."[16]

4. Arthur Waskow: Get rid of U.S. weapons "provocative" to Moscow, form a "Peace Agency," and stop nuclear tests.[17]

5. Charles E. Osgood: Our fear of Communist aggression is merely a projection of our own anxieties, so let's take unilateral steps toward disarmament.[18]

6. Emile Benoit: A discussion of how to make disarmament economically feasible in a society geared to defense production.[19]

7. Vera Micheles Dean: The U.S. "might make a powerful impression" on Asian countries by "declaring that it would be ready to give aid to Communist China, which now relies almost exclusively on aid from the Soviet bloc, once Peking has been admitted to represent China in the United Nations."[20]

8. Frank Tannenbaum: America's anti-Communist campaign in Latin America has been "a poor investment. It has aligned the dictators on our side and permitted them to persecute good, decent democrats who opposed tyranny on the grounds that these democrats were Communists."[21]

9. Allen S. Whiting: "There is no question" about Red China's "title over the offshore islands" of Quemoy and Matsu.

"Small wonder, therefore, that Peking feels both politically compelled and legally justified in asserting its claim by force."[22]

10. H. Stuart Hughes: America should pull out of Europe, as proposed in the Communist Rapacki plan, and neutralize Germany, granting recognition to the Communist Ulbricht regime.[23]

11. Quincy Wright: Admit Red China to the United Nations, have the U.N. supervise a vote on Formosa to see if Free Chinese want to be part of Red China.*[24]

Among the essays containing these varied proposals, perhaps the most "uncommon and provocative" is that by Charles E. Osgood, a professor at the University of Illinois. Osgood's contribution to *The Liberal Papers,* entitled "Reciprocal Initiative," is astonishing for its specific policy proposals but more important in terms of our present discussion for the ideological assumptions which underlie the proposals and lead Osgood to believe in their feasibility.

"Reciprocal initiative"—elsewhere referred to by the impish Osgood as "GRIT" ("Graduated Reciprocation In Tension-reduction")[25]—is a program wherein the United States makes a number of unilateral moves toward disarmament, pullback, and conciliation, in the hope of eliciting a like response from the Soviet Union. In Osgood's metaphor, the U.S. and USSR are two men on a teeter-totter, each of whom wants to get back to the center of gravity. Why shouldn't one of these men (us) take a small step back toward the center, Osgood argues, informing his opposite number of what he is doing and suggesting "reciprocation"?

This happy simile does not altogether apply, of course, since the men on the teeter-totter are fully visible to each other and the man taking the first step can immediately tell whether his opposite number has properly "reciprocated." The same is not true in matters of Soviet defense, weaponry, and nuclear materials, which are mantled in obscurity. No

* The twelfth essay, by Prof. Kingsley Davis, is a fairly straightforward and non-ideological discussion of population trends.

matter. Osgood says we should undertake things like unilateral cessation of nuclear tests anyway, to show the Soviets our sincerity. When concessions of this sort start piling up and getting more and more one-sided, the Soviets will become embarrassed, and hasten to make concessions of their own.

Osgood provides a full-scale "hypothetical program" by which this scheme might be carried out. Among his suggestions is a U.S. announcement that "all discriminatory trade and travel restrictions with respect to Communist China will be lifted"; after this has had a chance to sink in, "we announce a unilateral test-ban that will be continued indefinitely and invite reciprocal announcement from Russia, England and France." A week or so after this, "we announce that at the next convening of the General Assembly of the U.N. . . . *we will move the seating of Communist China.*" (Italics added.) In another two weeks we announce the denuclearization of one of our overseas bases in Japan. Then we fluster the Soviets with our triumphant announcement that "the DEW line (early warning system) will be made bidirectional (warning of our flights toward Russia as well as vice versa), and *we invite the Soviets to 'plug in'.*"[26] (Italics added.) Prof. Osgood seems unaware of any possible effect of his program except "embarrassment" to the Communists when they see us racking up so many concessions and themselves without a concession to their name.

If we do not know the Soviets are in fact following our lead in all this unilateral "tension-reduction," won't we be opening ourselves to Communist attack? Not at all, says Osgood, because the Soviets aren't like that. He affects bemused indulgence for anyone naive enough to believe the Communists are aggressors. People who think this way, he says, are suffering from "psycho-logic," projecting their own confused thinking onto the world situation.[27] There is no more reason to believe the Soviet Union would attack *us* if we were totally defenseless than to believe we would similarly attack *them.*

Osgood brings none other than Socrates in from the wings to remark that "you apparently wish me to conclude that Russian man is intrinsically different from American man. But can you support your opinion with reasons?"[28] You can't, Osgood says, because "I can show how such bogyman conceptions of the enemy develop naturally out of the dynamics of human thinking."[29]

The fact of the matter, of course, is that Professor Osgood's much-cherished "Russian man," or the average Muscovite in the street, is not in charge of Soviet policy; "Communist man," or the Soviet Communist Party, is. And "Communist man," who has repeatedly demonstrated his willingness to do everything Professor Osgood presumes to believe Russian man would not do, is a far cry from "American man" and "Russian man" alike. From Osgood's perspective, however, Communist man is nothing to the purpose. Communist aggression and the Cold War are, apparently, figments of our fevered imaginations; all we have to do is plunge headlong into GRIT, grasp the essential truth that the Communists are not aggressors, and cleanse ourselves of "psycho-logic." Appeasement and unilateral disarmament are, in fact, nothing more than an exercise in good mental health.

Since he nowhere mentions them in his discussion, Osgood evidently believes Moscow's history of aggression, the broken treaties, the slaughter of Hungary, the estimated 12 to 20 million people in slave labor camps are hallucination. By way of contrast, the official record, the newspaper morgues, and every known authority of whatever persuasion testify that all these things *are* real and *did* happen. The reader may determine whether it is the disbeliever in Soviet beneficence or Professor Osgood himself who is ready for the rubber room.

2. *Far Out—But 'In'*

The normal assumption of anyone reading *The Liberal Papers* once over lightly would be that such a surrealistic manifesto could under no circumstances have any connection with or influence on the policies of the American government. The normal assumption would be sadly mistaken. On at least three different levels, *The Liberal Papers* are intimately connected with the official Establishment in Washington:

I. *Sponsorship.* Needless to remark, news that a book like *The Liberal Papers* had emerged from a "study" initiated by Democratic Congressmen provided a potent source of campaign ammunition for Republicans. In a 1962 letter to Republican leaders around the country, GOP chairman William Miller said: "Those Democratic incumbents identified with the Liberal Project should be pressed to the wall to defend or repudiate their book during their re-election campaigns . . . All Democratic incumbents should be forced to state whether they are among the 22 'secret' Liberal Project members and whether they defend or repudiate the Democratic book."[30]

No sooner had Miller spoken than the rush to repudiate was on. Democrats reportedly associated with the project fell over themselves saying they had nothing to do with it. One congressman named as a sponsor threatened to sue Republicans who so identified him. Another alleged sponsor, Congressman James O'Hara of Michigan, was quoted as saying: "I never met with the group and discussed policy. Never. Never. Never. Never. Never."[31] And then-congressman Roosevelt, editor of the anthology, asserted that "no congressman endorsed or had anything to do with the papers in any way."[32] On this showing, nobody in Congress had anything to do with *The Liberal Papers* at all; yet it is clear from the public record and the internal evidence of the book that the case is decidedly otherwise.

There is, to begin with, the item of Roosevelt's own connection with the volume, in itself a refutation of his statement. And the fact that Roosevelt has since graduated from the House of Representatives—where he was a key legislative lieutenant of both Kennedy and Johnson—to diplomatic status at the U.N. in no way lessens the uneasiness which the connection inspires concerning the mental processes of our governors.

Others publicly identified as sponsors of the volume are former Representative and Kennedy-Johnson diplomat Chester Bowles; Representative Robert Kastenmeier (D-Wis.), former Representative Charles O. Porter (D-Ore.), Representatives Frank Thompson (D-N.J.), William Moorehead (D-Pa.), and the late Clem Miller (D-Calif.), and former Representatives Byron Johnson (D-Colo.), Leonard Wolf (D-Ia.), William Meyer (D-Vt.), and George Kasem (D-Calif.). Along with Representative O'Hara, Miller and Thompson rushed to disavow the Liberal Project and its issue, as any sensible office holder might.

While the project sponsors for the most part kept themselves discreetly anonymous, the authors of the book say a "dozen or so congressmen" were in on it. Among the Democratic officeholders and ex-officeholders named in the book are Bowles, Kastenmeier ("Chairman of the Liberal Project"), Porter and Meyer. Moreover, Roosevelt's statement that no congressman "had anything to do with the papers in any way" is flatly contradicted in the first chapter of the book. Authors Riesman and Maccoby tell us:

"The essay that follows was prepared for the Liberal Project and *reflects the concern of the congressmen* with an American political climate that makes it difficult for them to develop a coherent program. *It was discussed in June 1960 with the congressmen, their staff assistants (one of whom, Marcus Raskin, has taken a leading role in the development of the Liberal Project)*, and a few newspapermen"[33] (Italics added).

The "essay that follows" is the essay containing the statement that "decent Americans" find it "difficult" to be "outspokenly and genuinely anti-Communist."

The invaluable Marcus Raskin, at the time the study was initiated, served as an aide to Congressman Kastenmeier. Far from suffering demotion after taking his "leading role" in the project, Raskin was promoted to the special staff of the National Security Council—our government's highest policy-making body. Project sponsors Wolf and Johnson, both retired from Congress in the 1960 elections, were appointed to the Agency for International Development, and ex-Representative Meyer was named a "consultant" to the Department of the Interior.

Nor is that all. Allen S. Whiting, the contributor who thinks it "small wonder . . . that Peking feels both politically compelled and legally justified in asserting its claim (to Quemoy and Matsu) by force," was on the staff of the Rand Corporation, think-factory of the Air Force. Professor Osgood has served, according to Congressman John Rhodes of Arizona, as a special disarmament consultant to the government. Arthur Waskow, who formerly served on Kastenmeier's staff, has composed study papers for the U.S. Disarmament Agency. Etc. It becomes clear that, however loud the disavowals, *The Liberal Papers* are not without credentials in the official circles of the Democratic regime.

II. *Policy Assumptions.* Even more important than the personal and political connections of *The Liberal Papers* to the official Estabishment, however, is their intellectual connection. The enormities of Rep. Roosevelt's project stem from the belief that, despite the evidence of history and the testimony of Communist theory, the Soviet Union is not committed to our destruction. As Quincy Wright says, "it appears that today tensions between the great political blocs exist, less because of expansionist or crusading policies, than because of mutual fears which are not justified by anything known of the intentions of the governments at opposing sides of the Iron Curtain."[34]

There is an occasional suggestion that the Communists may not, in all times and in all places, have been quite so reasonable as they are now pictured; but this merely heightens the urgency of accepting their present benevolence. As Prof. H. Stuart Hughes puts it, "liberal tendencies" are at work behind the Iron Curtain—tendencies we should, by heroic conciliations, encourage.[35]

From this set of unwarranted premises flow all the curiosities of the Roosevelt anthology: Prof. Osgood's elaborate design for capitulation; Prof. Whiting's scrupulous effort to see the Chinese Communists' side of things; Prof. Hughes' advocacy of pullback in Europe. Such proposals are the logical result of assuming the Communists have no irreducible antagonisms toward us, and that they are, like ourselves, accessible to the lure of "reason," peace, and international uplift. If the Communists are like that, it follows that we must assure them of our own good intentions, and they will join with us in finding areas of accommodation. As Osgood puts it, with characteristic candor and naivete, his stupendous program of concessions *"indicates that we believe [Soviet] motives parallel, if not identical, to ours."*[36]

The belief that Communists are "reasonable" men or becoming such finds acceptance, as we have seen, at the top echelons of the incumbent administration. It is manifest in the pronouncements of Fulbright, Rostow, Bohlen, Kennan, Secretary of State Rusk himself. Like the authors of *The Liberal Papers,* our high officials frequently discuss the problem of "Russia" as they would the problem of "France"—*i.e.,* as if the phenomenon of Communism, with all its ideological and historical baggage, did not exist.

The most typical example is the tendency to view the USSR as though it were a parliamentary democracy—as though the Communist regime represented, and was responsible to, the people it has enslaved. It is upon this essential confusion between the people living under Communist dictatorships and the people who have brutalized them that Osgood's whole fantastic edifice of unilateral "initatives" is constructed. And while his confusion is of the most elementary sort, it is wholly of a piece with the chief policy axioms of the American government. Osgood's assumptions about "Russian man" and "American man" are quite similar to the ideas of Prof. Rostow and George Kennan and virtually identical, as we have seen, to the formulation used by President Kennedy in his American University address.

III. *Specific proposals.* As the administration program resembles *The Liberal Papers* in its fundamental approach to the Cold War, it also resembles it in an astonishingly large number of specific proposals. The major difference being that, whereas Rep. Roosevelt's wordy myrmidons unabashedly carry their misconceptions through to the logical destination of appeasement, most government officials cannot be quite so unrestrained. Under constant pressure from Congress at large and from the American public, they move more slowly, stay behind a thicket of obscurity and double-talk, and tend to pull up short when challenged. They are nevertheless heading, with relentless certainty, in the same direction.

Among the suggestions from *The Liberal Papers* which have been put into effect by the Kennedy-Johnson administration, or have been given careful high-level consideration, are the following: Halt nuclear tests; establish a "Peace Agency"; set universal disarmament under the United Nations as official American policy; undertake a series of unilateral steps toward disarmament in the hope that Moscow will follow suit; insure that American and Soviet strategic arsenals are "in balance"—*i.e.,* that our arsenal is not bigger and more powerful than theirs; get rid of weapons deemed "provocative" to the Soviet Union; seek recognition of and

U.N. membership for Communist China; channel our foreign aid to economic rather than military purposes, preferably through the U.N.; give our support to the democratic left in Latin America; seek the creation of what would in effect be a world government.

Every one of these proposals—and some others even more difficult to believe—is today part of the official policy apparatus of the United States government, either as an accomplished program or else as a projected one to be put into effect as soon as it appears feasible. Even Prof. Osgood's recipe for "reciprocal initiative" is now officially accepted at the echelons where high policy is made—as we shall observe in subsequent portions of this essay.

Finally, there is one specific suggestion in *The Liberal Papers* which is so bizarre that even the authors put it in rather tentative fashion—but which nevertheless has become official policy.

The Liberal Papers tell us that, among other things, the United States should take the Soviet Union under its wing, and help the Communists achieve prosperity. ". . . our relationship with Russia is similar to that of a big brother who is obsessed with fear that his little brother will overtake him." This is unfortunate, say the authors, because "we are missing a chance to provide a better goal for Soviet growth. We may hope that the Russians will get rich enough to be preoccupied with the problems of national purpose which currently plague us; and in the American-like desires of the Soviet Union, we find signs of this development."[37]

On reading and re-reading this passage, one can only conclude that it means Soviet "growth," if properly directed, is a good thing, because it will make the Communists forget about external matters and cause them to become concerned with the moral and social perplexities of affluence. Therefore? Therefore—one hesitates to state it—the United States should help its little brother achieve affluence. Is that the message the authors seek to impart? Is that the program ascendant in Establishment circles?

There is considerable evidence that American assistance to the Soviet Union is indeed the policy line of the current administration. The evidence is found, in its most concentrated form, in something called "The Phoenix Papers."

★★ 7. *The Phoenix Papers*

1. *Merging With Moscow*

SITUATED IN A SUITE of offices at 1666 Connecticut Ave. N.W. in Washington, D.C. is an organization called The Institute for Defense Analysis. Although unknown to the vast majority of the American people, IDA wields an immense influence on the policies of the United States.

Established with a half-million dollar grant from the Ford Foundation, the IDA subsists on some $10 million in annual contracts from the United States government. The Defense Department, the Arms Control and Disarmament Agency, and other government bureaus contract with IDA, at very handsome prices, to work up "studies" on various aspects of Cold War defense policy.

Public interest in this organization flickered briefly in 1963 when it was learned that an IDA document called "Study

Phoenix" was being circulated in and around the high echelons of the government. "Phoenix" was prepared by a man named Vincent P. Rock, billed as a "Senior Research Analyst" at IDA.

Although the IDA is understandably reluctant to have its views and its proposals broadcast to the world at large, the Rock study was discovered by *U.S. News and World Report* and summarized by that magazine in its issue of November 18, 1963. The paper, said *U.S. News,* urged that the United States become "interdependent" with the USSR. Its central theme, according to this and other journalistic reports, was "the possibility of creating a substantial cross-nation diffusion of interest" in an era when "material progress brings diversity and with it new possibilities for weaving a web of interdependence across national lines."[1]

To achieve this "interdependence," the paper proposed increased cultural exchange programs, U.S.-Soviet cooperation in space and other scientific ventures, sale of American industrial equipment and farm surpluses to the Soviets to help them out of their agricultural difficulties, and augmented trade with the Communists of Eastern Europe.

In the words of the Arms Control and Disarmament Agency, "the report recommended the United States seek Soviet cooperation in future Soviet space efforts . . . that the United States consider assisting Soviet agriculture . . . reducing restrictions on trade with the Soviet Union . . . and increased scientific cooperation with the Soviet Union . . ."[2]

Rock flatly uses the term "collaboration" to describe this approach to the Soviet Union. *"The United States should accept the need for a dual policy of collaboration and conflict,"* he is quoted, *"as a significant improvement over unmitigated conflict."*[3] In other words, we should consider it a step forward when we are both helping and fighting the Communists, rather than merely fighting them. Other terms in the Rock vocabulary are *"détente,"* "relaxation," and "diversity."[4]

That these summaries were all too accurate was confirmed in 1964 when Rock published a book entitled *A Strategy of Interdependence.* The thesis of this volume is that the United States and the Soviet Union are in many ways essentially alike. Each, Rock writes straight-facedly, has its "vision of unity"[5] for the world, which is all to the good (he neglects to point out the detail that Moscow's "vision of unity" is that of a monolithic slave society). He asserts that, on certain essential matters, the United States and the Soviet Union are as alike as two peas in a pod:

> Each saw the common interests of mankind in peace and well-being. Each noted imperfections in the present order. Neither was entirely clear how they could best be overcome. Each, however, envisioned a world community, of men or nations, a new *communitas* to give expression to their ideal of unity.[6]

Thus, on Rock's analysis, the Communists in Moscow are devoted to "peace and well-being," correction of existing wrongs, and *communitas*—a shrewd insight that would no doubt be comforting to, say, the Hungarian freedom fighters ground into the pavements of Budapest in the interest of Communist "peace and well-being."

"Each side," Rock states, "is attempting to work toward world unity in the long run . . . each side is concerned with its power and influence in third areas . . . each society has innumerable internal tasks which it seeks to accomplish . . ."[7] On Rock's view, America is tweedledum to Moscow's tweedledee. We are, after all, concerned about our mass transit systems—while they are concerned about tending to the several millions of people they have locked up in slave labor camps. We both have internal tasks to accomplish.

While the United States and the Soviet Union are alike in their good traits and their generous aspirations for "unity," they are also alike in their faults. Both tend to be suspicious, Rock thinks, and to rely on nuclear weapons, which is very bad: "The United States, scarcely less than the Soviet Union, is prone to rely excessively on force."[8] Worst of all, these two look-alikes have concentrated their energies on competing with, rather than on helping, each other. When two nations are as similar as America and the USSR, what could be more natural than a little mutual assistance?

> There remains the possibility of creating a substantial cross-national diffusion of interest and ultimately of power which would enhance restraint and contribute to the growth of a sense of community . . . Despite fundamental limitations the idea of coexistence represents a movement in the right direction toward facing the consequences of the nuclear armed world . . . A strategy of interdependence envisages a step-by-step approach, but on a broad front, to the creation of conditions in which the United States and the Soviet Union will find it in their self-evident interest to work together both constructively and in the restraint of the use of force . . .[9]

The web of interdependence can be woven, Rock says, by a series of joint U.S.-Soviet undertakings which "contribute to the convergence of values and purposes in the two societies."[10] These might start with increased traffic between private citizens in the U.S. and the USSR, thus creating a "structure" of confidence between the two sides which can be translated into the behavior of their governments. Precisely how private citizens in the USSR are to inject their notions of confidence into the performance of their government Rock does not say.

Among the projects Rock urges to build "interdependence" between Good Nation A (the United States) and Good Nation B (the Soviet Union) are increased trade, cultural exchanges, joint scientific ventures, etc. "This will require," he notes, "a major shift in the present policies of the United States in the field of trade and in Soviet policies in equally important areas."[11] But, most of all, the building of interdependence will require the United States to take as a task in its own interest the building up of the Soviet economy.

Rock says "it could be of great material importance"—which indeed it could—"if the United States were willing to help and the Soviet Union were willing to accept help."[12] He explains this observation by remarking:

> The commitment to development must in the end include both common enterprises in the international sphere and a reasonable concern for the internal health of the antagonist's economy. The Soviet Union has begun to show interest in the prosperity of the West, but the contribution of Western economic progress to stability and thus to the security of the Soviet Union has not been fully accepted . . . the Western attitude toward the economic progress of the Soviet Union remains ambiguous [despite the fact that] . . . each side has an interest in the orderly development of the other.[13]

If we help the Soviets build up their agricultural economy with our aid and know-how, Rock reasons, we will help usher them into prosperity, thus demonstrating our good will and reducing Moscow's "temptation" to "external" adventure. In return, we can get some Soviet assistance with our electric power system. We shall then be ready for disarmament and *communitas.* All shall be first and all shall have prizes.

Like *The Liberal Papers,* Rock's fantasy is premised on the idea that the Soviet Union, to the extent it may have been a bit authoritarian in the past, is now "mellowing." He never comes right out and says, of course, that there was anything seriously wrong with the Soviet regime before, either in its program of internal terror or in its program of external global revolution. He couches mention of such things in double-talk like: "The state may by coercion and investment play a predominant and even effective role in putting in place the major foundations of society, although many in the

West judge the human cost too high"[14]—an apparent reference to the fact that in imposing collectivist slavery on Russia, Communism has killed and imprisoned several millions of human beings. Even graceful allusions like these, however, are immediately countered by superlatively favorable comments about such things as "Lenin's bold achievement." Rock gives us this imaginative description of the way things are going in the USSR:

> . . . the increasing achievement of the goals of Communist society, such as improved educational opportunities and industrialization, has provided careers for the brighter sons and daughters of the Soviet Union . . . as the society modernizes, man's capacity for expressing his individuality in a growing variety of ways as artist, scientist, tourist, merchandiser, and consumer seeks to assert itself. These capacities need an increasing range of associations through which they may find expression. The needs of the community must reassert themselves even if in no other way than under the aegis of the state.[15]

The success of Communism in creating material progress has, in other words, brought about a climate of well-being in which the whole system becomes more Western and less Communist in outlook. "Communist ideology may be adequate for the 'take-off,' in Walt W. Rostow's phrase, but its content must undergo substantial change as the peaks of affluence are approached."[16]

Thus while Rock is vague in suggesting what might have been wrong with Communism in the past, he is most explicit about saying what is *right* with it now. Heading for "the peaks of affluence," it is ready, able, and all-but-willing (thanks to that inspiriting "vision of unity" so comparable to our own) to merge with the United States in *communitas,* if only we will give out with trade, aid, and unilateral initiatives toward disarmament.

It is unfortunate we did not have Rock around in the late

1930s to explain to us Hitler's "vision of unity" and "Schacht's bold achievement" in Germany, which would have made it possible for the United States to have cultural exchanges, increased trade, and outright aid programs with the Nazis. Such a program of "convergence of values" and "interdependence" might well have prevented World War II, and insured the merger of America and Germany into a new *communitas.* That the *communitas* would most probably have meant enslavement by Hitler would, of course, have been an insignificant detail, hardly worth mentioning—just as Rock nowhere dilates upon the Communist program of global conquest.

2. *It's Official*

Is it conceivable the views set forward by Vincent Rock are prevalent in the American government? Is it possible the Phoenix papers' vision of U.S. "interdependence" with Moscow, aid to the Soviet economy, and benevolence toward Communism as a brotherly force for *communitas* has been translated into the official policy of the United States?

When news of Rock's "collaboration" proposals leaked out, there was a small official effort to suggest he was speaking only for himself, in a purely "private" capacity. The foreword to the Phoenix papers, however, makes the opposite point. "Study Phoenix," it says, "was initiated with support from the United States Disarmament administration, of the Department of State, under contract No. SCC 28270, date February 24, 1961 . . ."[17] And the Disarmament Agency says the project "was contracted for by the United States Disarmament Administration before the Arms Control and Disarmament Agency came into existence."[18] Like other IDA studies, "Phoenix" was in fact a government-financed project. Some 300 copies of the document were printed up, at a cost to the taxpayers of $78,600.[19]

That the Rock report was prepared under government auspices is apparent. Equally apparent is the fact that Rock's ideas are reflected in the reigning policy of the present administration. The Disarmament Agency observes with apparent pride that Rock's program for aiding the Communists had been implemented by the government before his report was prepared. "Many of Rock's ideas," the agency states, "were advanced long before the publication of the Phoenix report even though they were not approached from the standpoint of their relationship to arms control. The implementation of some of these long-standing ideas did take place after the publication of the Rock report. This was, however, coincidental. *The fact is that the implementation of some of these ideas was related to an improved atmosphere in our relations with the Soviet Union.*"[20]

Concerning Rock's recommendation that "the United States consider assisting Soviet agriculture," the background paper notes, as though by way of rebuttal: "The expansion of farm exports was recommended by President Kennedy in his February, 1961, Special Message to Congress on Gold and the Balance of Payments Deficit, more than two years prior to the Rock report."[21]

The point the Disarmament Agency seems anxious to make is that the government had not adopted a be-nice-to-Moscow policy because of the Rock report, but independently of it. This is, however, not a rebuttal but a confirmation. Whoever influenced whom, the ideas expressed in the Rock report are also the ruling ideas of our government—so much we have on the government's own authority.

The similarity of Rock's ideas and official policy was further established by *U.S. News,* which noted that "high officials in the administration are known to have given careful reading to the paper."[22] Describing the document as "a blueprint for the latest American strategy in the field of diplomacy," *U.S. News* adds that "special attention is given to the Rock study because of two recent speeches by President Kennedy—one at the University in Washington, D.C., on June 10. In these speeches, and in other statements, President Kennedy appears to have followed closely the policy line suggested by the new paper on control of conflict."[23]

U.S. News summarized the program of the Kennedy regime as "blueprinted" by Rock:

Strategy of the U.S. in dealing with Soviet Russia is in process of sharp change. This change is toward more contact and dealings with the Russians. It is away from the old objectives of the Cold War.

At the heart of the new strategy is this plan: Seek a *détente*—a period relaxation or informal truce—during which an "interdependence" between the U.S. and the Soviet Union can be established.

There is to be emphasis on "shared experiences." There will be more effort to do business, to carry on joint ventures, to seek areas of cooperation, to come less in conflict.

The new policy might best be summarized as a "togetherness" in world affairs.[24]

Steps in this direction, said the magazine, were the test-ban treaty, emphasis on increased trade, the "hot line" between Moscow and Washington, increased contacts between Khrushchev and Kennedy, and a "trade" for the mutual pullback of missiles. Kennedy's proposal at the U.N. that the Soviets join us in a venture to the moon was an "interdependence" initiative which the Communists did not take up. *U.S. News* adds:

Under the new strategy, the Communists in Cuba obviously will not be pushed out by force. The Wall in Berlin and Soviet control over East Europe are no longer to be stressed. While removal of such "irritants" is to be sought, their existence is not to preclude moving ahead with the new plan.[25]

Among the specific objectives to be sought in the quest for interdependence, *U.S. News* cites the following:

"Cultural exchange programs will be increased and broadened.

"Additional offers of cooperation in space and other scientific ventures will be made.

"Fertilizer-making equipment, as well as farm surpluses, will be sold to the Russians to help bail them out in their farm crisis.

"Trade with the Communist bloc in Eastern Europe will be encouraged."[26]

All items, of course, prescribed by Rock.

Further indication that the Phoenix papers do in fact represent the high strategy of our government is the consistent advocacy of Rock's program by various important Liberal spokesmen. Vice President Humphrey, for one, has favored us with a statement which might have been lifted wholesale from the Phoenix papers. "We need to keep in close contact with all elements of Soviet society," Humphrey says. "We need to increase suitable programs of cultural exchange. And we need, above all, to review our policy of trade with the Communist world, for such trade has vast significance and many ramifications . . . if we move carefully in the direction of a more permissive trade policy with Eastern Europe, we shall be putting Soviet intentions in the field of international cooperation to a genuine test . . . Increased trade would have the important by-product of increased contact—and contact could eventually lead to greater understanding. This is the premise for our program of cultural exchange; it is equally valid for extension of trade to the East European nations."[27]

Humphrey's organization, Americans for Democratic Action, went on record in 1964 in much the same fashion. Using language similar to Humphrey's and to the Rock report, ADA urged "immediate steps to improve American contacts and understanding with the Soviet Union and the Eastern European nations," as follows:

A vigorous expansion of trade in non-strategic goods, on reasonable rather than unduly restrictive credit terms.

A steady and substantial increase in the present programs for cultural and technical exchange and the mutual removal of restrictions on the entry of books, magazines, and newspapers.

Stepped-up cooperation in research and development in non-military fields, such as space communication and exploration, medical research, meteorology and geophysics.

Expansion in the exchange of visits by private citizens, up to and including the topmost levels of government.*[28]

In various of his 1963 speeches, President Kennedy himself leaned heavily on the Phoenix papers vocabulary of "interdependence." Rock says we need "interdependence" and a "convergence of values" with the Soviet Union; in his American University address, Kennedy urged that we "re-examine our attitude toward the Soviet Union" and "direct attention to our common interests and to the means by which [our] differences can be resolved."[29]

Rock also says there is nothing inconsistent about simultaneously competing and "collaborating" with Moscow; in a 1963 speech at the University of Maine, Kennedy declared there was "nothing inconsistent with signing an atmospheric-nuclear test-ban on the one hand and testing underground on the other; about being willing to sell to the Soviets our sur-

* In urging these steps, ADA said: "In the face of a military stalemate between East and West, the first in the Sino-Soviet bloc and the emergence of polycentrism in world Communism, a totally new situation confronts us, with new challenges and opportunities. Our policies toward the various and increasingly individual Communist nations should embody concepts of defense without provocation and conciliation without the sacrifice of essential principle and interests. As these nations evolve toward diverse behavior and goals, American policy should be pragmatic and flexible, welcoming and reciprocating any movements in these nations toward the normalization of their relations with the United States and with their non-Communist neighbors." This is precisely the argument of the Rock report.

plus wheat while refusing to sell strategic items; about probing their interest in a joint lunar landing while making a major effort to master this new environment; or about exploring the possibilities of disarmament while maintaining our stockpile of arms."[30]

With the way already paved by Rostow, Fulbright, and the authors of *The Liberal Papers,* the "Phoenix" mentality invested the higher echelons of the Kennedy administration. The New Frontier, under cover of ambiguous rhetoric but with tell-tale streamers flying, set sail toward *détente* with Moscow.

★★ *Part II:*

WHAT LIBERALS DO

There is plenty of room for doubt about the wisdom of the U.N's action, but no room for hesitancy in backing it up in an open-eyed way, doubts and all. Once the U.N. has decided, wrongly or rightly, that a certain political solution is necessary for peace, it seems to me it must be imposed.

—Max Lerner

★★ 8. *The War for Men's Minds*

1. *World Opinion*

WHILE THE QUEST for a good Communist is the central and controlling premise of Liberal foreign policy, it is not the only one. Mixed in with this recurrent notion are various other Liberal themes, complementing and reinforcing the basic strategy of accommodation. The most important of these is the Liberal's long-term fondness for internationalism.

"Internationalism" means, among other things, disparagement of American sovereignty and distaste for patriotic ardor ("jingoism"); a yearning toward international or supranational institutions; and a profound reverence, in the current jargon, for something called "world opinion." These tendencies, founded in Liberal ideology itself, ante-date the Cold War and the U.S.-Soviet confrontation. But the various ways in which they can meld with and reinforce the Liberal yen to curl up with Moscow are readily apparent.

Consider, for example, the sovereign potency of "world opinion." We are informed that the United States must do something, or refrain from doing something else, because the exigencies of "world opinion" require it. Most characteristically we are told some hard initiative against the Communists is unfeasible because it would inflame and alienate "world opinion," than which there is no greater enormity.

References to "world opinion" or something of the sort run like a *leit-motif* throughout Liberal discussions of foreign policy—*e.g.*, Theodore Sorensen's chronicle of the Kennedy regime. One Liberal spokesman gives us this assertion of the absolute efficacy of "world opinion": "There is no force on earth capable of making a power give up what it regards as legal rights, unless it may be the force of world opinion . . . The fearful heat of world moral judgment is proved by the desperate efforts of those who are in the wrong to defend themselves by arguments which they hope will cover them."[1]

Whether the force of "world opinion" can cause the generality of nations to back away from their rights or interests may be doubted; but that it can make the United States wilt in utter confusion is demonstrated fact. The classic instance of this sort was, of course, the 1961 fiasco in the Bay of Pigs, in which our government took a whole series of actions, culminating in the denial of promised air support to the Cuban exile invaders, aimed at conciliating "world opinion," and thereby doomed the expedition to failure. Other such episodes include our refusal to continue atomic tests in the atmosphere, our hesitation in the Cuban missile crisis of 1962, and our participation in the overthrow of President Ngo Dinh Diem of Viet Nam—three instances, as our officials have conceded, in which we acted in accordance with what "world opinion" *thought* were the merits of the case, rather than on what we ourselves knew to be the merits of the case.

Here is the way reporters Thomas Ross and David Wise sum up high-level U.S. thinking in the Bay of Pigs episode: ". . . political and foreign policy considerations began to outweigh the tactical plan. . . . Could the president permit another B-26 strike on Monday and still convince the world that somehow a new covey of Castro pilots had defected from the Cuban Air Force? The President decided he could not . . . President Kennedy personally approved the change [of the landing-site]. The CIA believed that this was a political and foreign-policy decision by the president, prompted by concern over potential world reaction."[2]

Precisely what "world opinion" is, and who formulates it and measures it, is difficult to say. As conveyed to us by the world press and by the respected journals of the Establishment, the anointed spokesmen for world opinion appear to be people like Sukarno of Indonesia, Touré of Guinea, or Nasser of Egypt. Why the United States should be guided by the "world opinion" these rulers represent, or even by the opinions of a whole synod of such rulers, is never made very clear. The usual answer is that we are engaged in a "war for men's minds," and that we must be hyper-sensitive to every nuance of mood these leaders exhibit. "The third world," as journalist C. L. Sulzberger puts it, is burning with "the fever of nationalism, of economic ambition, of great expectations," and the United States must learn "to adjust itself to this flame."[3]

Presumably, "the war for men's minds" is a contest between the Free World and the Communists in which each side tries to persuade the human race its system has the superior merit—a sort of popularity sweepstakes in which X number of leaders speaking for Y millions of people view the performance of the Communists on the one hand and ourselves on the other, then cast their ballots on the basis of amiability and international etiquette. Whoever gets the most votes "wins."

It is clear, however, that the Cold War cannot be decided

simply by convincing a majority of humanity of the fact that freedom is better than Soviet domination. The people of Hungary and East Germany, for example, have already demonstrated that they are convinced of this fact. Which would mean, on the "world opinion" analysis, that we have "won" the Cold War in Hungary and East Germany. But since no action has been taken to give the Hungarians or Germans the freedom they want, we have in fact "won" nothing.

The success of this policy in dealing with "The Third World" is equally in question. Whether we are in fact conforming to "world opinion" when we accede to the clatter of an Nkrumah or a Nasser is more than any mortal man has yet determined. Most of these "neutralists" are dictators who reign by force (and who are subject at any moment to being deposed by it) and who at best speak with intelligible certainty only for the claques of retainers who help them keep their power. Whether the teeming millions they allegedly represent hold similar opinions on a given subject, or any opinion at all on the subject, are matters open to serious doubt.

Almost all of these leaders are, moreover, products of Marxist or parallel forms of revolutionary development, with a partiality for Marxist techniques and a tendency to side with Moscow or Peking in matters of foreign policy. This being so, our effort to bend our policies to their biases must inevitably produce a movement in world politics the reverse of what is intended. The stated objective of "the war for men's minds" is to draw these people *away* from Communism and toward us. Yet by consistently yielding our interpretation of events to theirs, we quite obviously get the opposite result. They do not move closer to us; we move closer to them.

That this is so may be readily noted from the leftward drift of our policy. Our original Cold War design was to create a network of pro-Western states. Under the Kennedy regime, our objective increasingly became one of embracing "neutralism" as our best hope of averting Communist advance. Now, in the pronouncements of people like Vincent Rock and Senator Fulbright, we find a rising tendency to seek satisfaction in the appearance of so-called "independent Communists." In step with this alteration in our thought, the number of nations in the Communist, pro-Communist, and "neutralist" camps has increased markedly, while the ranks of the pro-Western nations have been correspondingly reduced.

That transformation suggests continued obeisance to "world opinion" is losing rather than winning "the war for men's minds." And it suggests, even more fundamentally, that what Liberalism means by this ritual phrase is a make-believe contest by its nature detrimental to the Western position. If there is one motive which could convince the practiced oligarchs of Asia and Africa they should throw in with the West, it would be a conviction that the West is going to win. But when they view the transformation of strategic relationships that has occurred over the past 20 years, these men must be hard-pressed to draw such a conclusion. The fundamental shift in power relationships is obvious to them, even if it is not obvious to Americans for Democratic Action. As Henry Kissinger has put it: "If the West can be humiliated over a period of time, the new nations, whatever their moral preference, will consider Communism the wave of the future . . . No amount of economic assistance will avail against the conviction that the West is doomed."[4]

The Cold War is indeed a "struggle for men's minds." But the locus of that struggle is not in Cairo, or Accra, or Jakarta; it is in Washington. The thought processes of the so-called uncommitted leaders indeed have a certain secondary importance; but at the first and most important level, it is *our* mind, the mind of the Western leadership, which is at stake. To the extent that mind is befuddled and without discernible purpose, the Bolshevik cadres will continue their triumphal progress, and the "uncommitted" will increasingly bestow their commitments to the East.

2. *Foreign Aid*

The "world opinion" syndrome leads to certain long-term programs by the United States aimed at institutionalizing the merits of internationalism. One of these is foreign aid—an attempt to formalize, through the medium of hard cash, the virtue of not being jingoist and Liberalism's principal surrogate for purposeful Cold War action.

There are essentially two types of foreign aid: Military aid, given to various nations in the expectation that they will use it in defense of their territory against Communist aggression; and economic aid, distributed on the premise that it will strengthen the economies of the recipient countries.

Concerning the first of these, there cannot be much quarrel—provided the military gear in question can be suitably employed for its stated purpose, and is actually going to nations which will use it against the Communists and not against us. The economic aid, however, is more troublesome. It is, we are told, a matter of hard-headed practical policy—one of our "most needed" weapons, as President Kennedy put it, in the struggle "against the spread of Communism." The most successful "counter-guerrilla efforts," Kennedy averred, "cannot succeed where the local population is too caught up in its own misery to be concerned about the advance of Communism."[5] Foreign aid, he suggested, will alleviate the misery.

Secretary of Defense Robert McNamara has given this "poverty" analysis of Cold War problems what is perhaps its most systematic high-level statement to date. "There can . . . be no question," he says, "that there is an irrefutable relationship between violence and economic backwardness. . . . Our role must be precisely this: To help provide security to those developing nations which genuinely need and request our help . . . Development means economic, social and political progress. It means a reasonable standard of living. . . . As development progresses . . . their resistance to disorder and violence will be enormously increased." The United States can forestall the social upheaval which provides Communism its entree into underdeveloped societies, McNamara concludes, by a program of foreign economic aid, dealing "directly with the roots of underdevelopment and not merely attempt[ing] to alleviate the symptoms."[6] Thus do we head off the progress of Communism.

This formulation, on a quick review of the record, is suspect. The fact that the United States has expended more than $100 billion in foreign aid precisely during the period that Communism has made the most staggering gains ever recorded by any aggressor in the history of the human race does not on the face of it suggest foreign aid, as a venture in anti-Communism, has been very successful. On the other hand, it is conceivable that without the aid things would have been worse—Communism might have conquered three-quarters of the world rather than half of it. Something of the sort is the argument generally advanced in favor of aid (or of any other cherished project) by Liberal spokesmen. To test the validity of that notion, let us examine the particulars of the program a bit further.

Can foreign aid cure poverty, and by so doing make the recipient nations less vulnerable to Bolshevik intrigue? The evidence suggests it cannot. Such aid is given to governments, which means it has a built-in bias toward an uneconomic collectivism rather than private enterprise. That bias has been heavily reinforced by the explicit demands of the Kennedy-Johnson regime that aid recipients use the resources we bestow upon them for programs of top-down government planning and "land reform."

How this has worked in practice is demonstrated by Prof.

Peter T. Bauer of Cambridge University in his study of U.S. aid to India. Under India's Second Five Year Plan, Bauer notes:

> There are the severe restrictions, or complete bans on the supply of both imported and even locally produced consumer goods . . . restrictions on the extension of efficient industrial capacity . . . official restrictions on the establishment of road transport enterprises, and on the movement of agricultural products . . . severe restrictions on the establishment of all enterprises . . .

These rigidities were imposed by the Indian "plan" despite a manifest need for more consumer goods, higher living standards, industrial progress, increased flow of commerce, and better utilization of resources. Bauer notes that such measures "not only affect adversely the standard of living, but also restrict further any economic demand there might be for the output of the capacity created under the heavy industry program."

None of this has relieved India of poverty, or made it a free society; but it has gone a long way toward achieving what the Indian authorities desire—"the adoption of the Socialist pattern of society as the national objective." Foreign aid has sustained and encouraged this tendency, making it possible for India to follow the uneconomic vagaries of Brahmin collectivism. Such aid, Bauer concludes, is "much more likely to retard the rise of general living standards in India than to accelerate it, and to obstruct rather than promote the emergence of a society resistant to totalitarian appeal."[7]

An intensive survey by Sen. Ernest Gruening (D.-Alaska), resulted in the charge that like results were being subsidized by American aid to Chile. Our subsidies, Gruening said, "erode Chile's incentive to undertake the necessary steps to formulate its investment program on a rational basis."

Similarly with "land reform," a euphemism for taking property away from one owner and distributing it among a lot of other owners. This procedure not only violates private property; it also puts power over the most important resource of any nation, and particularly of an agrarian nation, in the hands of government, and makes both the original large landholder and the subsequent small one subservient to the state. It is, moreover, uneconomic on the face of it.

Professor Karl Brandt of Stanford University observes:

> The destruction of the large and efficiently operating private farm enterprises and their parceling is precisely the recipe prescribed by Stalin in his book *Lessons in Leninism,* namely, the first necessary stage of the Communist revolution, which, according to party doctrine, must precede the second stage of collectivization. Political hostility to plantations has ruined the world's former leading natural rubber and cane-sugar industries in Java, and it impedes a potentially prosperous agricultural development of tea, cocoa, oil palm, and banana culture in many tropical zone countries.[8]

Under the Eisenhower administration, U.S. aid was often conditioned on some effort in the recipient country to move toward private enterprise. Under the Kennedy-Johnson regime, this policy has been exactly reversed. Consider, to take the most prominent recent example, the Alliance for Progress, allegedly exporting prosperity to the nations of Latin America, and forestalling the advance of Communism.

The Kennedy Task Force which did the blueprints for the Alliance said U.S. policy in Latin America must be directed toward "coordinating and supporting the widespread democratic-progressive movements . . . pledged to representative government, social and economic reform (including agrarian reform), and resistance to entrance of undemocratic forces from outside the hemisphere."[9] Arthur Schlesinger, who by his own account played a substantive role in the conduct of New Frontier policy in Latin America and who authored the regime's "white paper" on Cuba attributing its communization to the stress of poverty, speaks with undisguised contempt for the Eisenhower bias toward free enterprise, and glowingly of Latin Socialists.[10]

In his statement announcing the Alliance, President Kennedy proposed "a vast new Ten-Year Plan for the Americas," in which the Latin nations "can mobilize their resources, enlist the energies of their people, and modify their social patterns so that all, and not just a privileged few, share in the fruits of growth."[11]

In a second statement, Kennedy said the effectiveness of the plan "depends on the willingness of each recipient nation to improve its own institutions, make necessary modifications in its own social patterns, and mobilize its own domestic resources for a program of development. . . . such measures will be a condition of assistance from the social fund . . ."[12] This is repeated in the rules of the Alliance itself, which make a "plan" for such collectivist forward-leaping a precondition of getting aid. As professor Milton Friedman drily notes, the prosperous United States could not qualify under these stipulations—but the chronically impoverished nations behind the Iron Curtain could. In the long run, Friedman says, the effect of the aid program is simply "to promote centralized planning and socialist methods of control."[13]

Even if foreign aid did eliminate poverty, there is no reason to believe it would by virtue of the fact be an impediment to Communism. That there is no necessary correlation between the incidence of "poverty" and the advance of Bolshevism may be discerned from the fact that some of the poorest countries in the Western world—Spain, Portugal, and Ireland—have the smallest internal Communist parties; whereas some of the wealthiest—Italy and France—have the largest.

Perhaps the most telling example in this category is Cuba. On the Liberal logic, Cuba, as the first Latin nation to go Communist, should have also been the poorest. It was in fact one of the richest. Former ambassador Earl Smith, who witnessed Cuban economic conditions from close range, makes this point emphatically. "There was a general misconception," Smith says, "that the events in Cuba were brought about by low standards of living and social inequalities. The facts belie this." Smith adds:

> The best economic year in Cuba's history was 1957. For twenty-five years. . . . Cuba's standard of living rose to a place among the highest in Latin America. . . . In 1957, Cuba's national income was $2.397 million. The population was approximately 6,500,-000.[14]

How this compared with other Latin American nations was summed up by the Department of Commerce in 1956, when it observed that "subsistence living, so prevalent in many areas of Latin America, is not characteristic of Cuba. . . . Cuban national income has reached levels which give the Cuban people one of the highest standards of living in Latin America."[15]

A parallel judgment was offered in a 1962 report of the U.S. Department of Agriculture:

> . . . when the present government assumed power the Cubans were among the better fed people of the world. . . . Farm output in the late 1950s was twice the 1935-39 level with an average annual growth of 3.5 per cent over the two decades, significantly higher than the average population growth of about 2.3 per cent for the same period. Furthermore, production for both domestic consumption and export was accelerating just prior to the Castro takeover.[16]

The International Commission of Jurists remarks . . . "despite the fact that Cuba is the youngest Latin American republic, a comparative analysis of the economic development of the Latin American countries shows that it has become one of the most advanced. . . . It is a fact that, in recent years, before the Castro revolution, foreign capital was being gradually but steadily replaced by Cuban capital."[17]

Cuba at the time of Castro's triumph held first place among Latin countries in number of TV sets per 1,000 of population, second place in foreign trade per capita, third in medical care, newspaper circulation, telephone units per inhabitants and automobiles per 1,000 of population. The average daily wage of the Cuban agricultural worker in 1958 was $3, higher than the amount paid comparable wage-earners in West Germany, Belgium, Denmark, and France.

The Cuban example suggests there may in fact be some kind of correlation, in "underdeveloped" nations, between economic advance and susceptibility to Communist or other subversive agitation, rather than the other way around. As Harvard's Edward Banfield notes, "economic development, by hastening the decay of tradition and other forms of authority, will create ferment and disorder . . . In India, Asia, Africa, and Latin America the more economically developed regions have been more prone to violence than the less developed ones."[18] This likelihood, interestingly enough, is alluded to (and welcomed) by Professor Rostow and his coadjutor Max Millikan, who note that, *e.g.*, the spread of reading skills makes people more open to the possibilities of subversion.

Since the "aid" program is not in fact advancing prosperity very noticeably, this possible reverse-English effect need not be of major concern. The systemic planning and revolution our "aid" has subsidized contribute, however, to the same demoralizing result. The disruption of national life, sweeping centralization of power, and breakdown of traditional institutions implicit in the various "Five Year Plans" we are sustaining have in at least some instances made conditions more favorable for Communist advance, rather than less. A classic example is the total statism imposed on Bolivia, made possible by American aid. Former Bolivian official Alberto Ostria Gutierrez observed, prior to the ouster of dictator Paz Estenssoro: "The Communist objective has been attained in Bolivia to a greater extent than in any other Latin American republic. The Army has been destroyed, the workers and peasants are organized in armed militias, private property is no longer respected, the institutions of democratic government have disappeared, the independence of the judiciary has been abolished, the labor unions are indirectly subject to Communist control—in short, totalitarianism has already triumphed."[19]

Secretary McNamara's contrary argument that there is an "irrefutable relationship" between poverty and social disorder paving the way to Communism is founded in a statistical survey showing that, since 1958, almost all the major violence in the world has occurred in the "very poor" and "poor" nations of the Southern Hemisphere. McNamara neglects to add, however, that these nations are precisely those areas of the world (a) thrown open to violence by the abrupt withdrawal of Western power in obedience to Liberal hostility to "colonialism" and (b) relentlessly subjected to the exhortations of revolutionary leaders trained by the West, sustained by American aid, and assisted in Marxist adventure by the kind of "development" programs McNamara advocates. The correlation between upheaval and poverty is not nearly so impressive as the correlation between upheaval and the sway of Liberal doctrine.

3. *The Ultimate Test*

The ultimate test of foreign economic aid, of course, is simply to match its record of performance against the claims of its sponsors. Dispensation of U.S. tax dollars for economic and social "reform" in Africa, Asia, and Latin America will, we are told, nurture democratic and anti-Communist governments—a community of nations whose Cold War stance will increasingly diverge from that of Moscow and Peking. On the record, however, nothing of the sort has happened. Consider, to take a single but eloquent example, the matter of the 47 countries which voted in 1965 against the United States position on seating Communist China in the United Nations. All but two of the states which went directly counter to our policy to stand with the Communist nations on this crucial question had been recipients of our aid. The list, with aid stipends to 1964, is as follows:[20]

Afghanistan	$ 281,000,000
Albania	20,400,000
Algeria	149,000,000
Burma	110,000,000
Cambodia	376,000,000
Central African Republic	2,000,000
Ceylon	92,000,000
Congo (Brazzaville)	5,000,000
Cuba	52,000,000
Czechoslovakia	189,000,000
Denmark	953,000,000
Ethiopa	231,000,000
Finland	57,000,000
France	9,477,000,000
Ghana	163,000,000
Guinea	49,000,000
Hungary	19,000,000
India	5,622,000,000
Iraq	94,000,000
Kenya	28,000,000
Mali	14,000,000
Mauritania	3,000,000
Morocco	466,000,000
Nepal	59,000,000

Nigeria	131,000,000
Norway	1,267,000,000
Pakistan	2,629,000,000
Poland	548,000,000
Sierre Leone	21,000,000
Somali	42,000,000
Sudan	84,000,000
Sweden	109,000,000
Syria	99,000,000
Tanzania	29,000,000
Uganda	15,000,000
USSR	186,000,000
United Arab Republic	952,000,000
United Kingdom	8,712,000,000
Yemen	33,000,000
Yugoslavia	2,586,000,000
Zambia	1,000,000

The root fallacy of the foreign-aid approach to global problems is that it seeks, in company with other Liberal nostrums, to cure the ills of mankind by tinkering with the environment. Yet the evidence is impressive that Communism is not a product of material forces but a disease of the heart and intellect. The advance of Communism, from Marx and Engels to Castro and Cheddi Jagan, has been the handiwork of intellectuals, men well enough off materially but infected by the characteristically intellectual virus of plotting compulsory utopias. The belief of the Marxists that they can mould mankind by moulding its institutions has particular appeal, not for the poor and downtrodden, but for the self-styled maker and destroyer of worlds weaned on the materialist doctrines of the 20th-century enlightenment. A list of Marxist leaders in the modern world reads like a who's who of intellectuals in politics: Mao Tse-tung, Castro, Ho Chi Minh, Jagan, Nkrumah, Paz Estenssoro, Betancourt, Bosch. Similarly with the

Free World's most famous defectors to Communism—Alger Hiss, the Rosenbergs, Klaus Fuchs, Allen Nunn May, Bruno Pontecorvo, Martin and Mitchell, Burgess and Maclean. These were people of substantial background, well-fed and well-educated. Far from being products of a penurious environment, they were intellectuals who were drawn to *the doctrine of environmentalism*—precisely the doctrine expounded by Secretary McNamara.

Despite the fact that foreign aid does not seem to be getting discernible results—or, worse, results counter to what was originally projected for it—there has been no abatement of Liberal enthusiasm for it. As its failure becomes increasingly apparent, Liberal theorists devise new ways of rendering it less effective still. Having discovered foreign aid is not a very reliable means of producing anti-Communist sentiment, they conclude that the thing to do is to keep the aid but drop the anti-Communism.

Nothing could better illustrate the fact that foreign aid is ineffective in halting the advance of Communism than the type of rhetoric our leaders have taken to using in justifying it. The aid program has always contained an element of pure globalism—helping other nations "because it is right." Increasingly, this element in the Liberal presentation has become predominant (except, perhaps, when aid officials are testifying before Congress about the need for further appropriations), and the anti-Communist angle has been shuffled over in embarrassed haste. Thus Secretary Rusk proclaimed that "foreign aid has more solemn purposes"[21] than combatting Communism, and President Kennedy put it that the fundamental task of our aid program "is not negatively to fight Communism," but to demonstrate that "economic growth and political democracy can develop hand in hand."[22]

Increasingly, also, suggestions are made that our aid program should move away from anti-Communist military aid toward greater emphasis on economic aid to "neutralists," and, equally significant, should be divorced as much as possible from the crass pursuit of American Cold War interests by channeling its distribution through the United Nations. The foreseeable result of this departure will be the next object of our consideration.

★★ 9. *The United Nations*

1. *The Future of an Illusion*

LIBERALISM'S FAVORITE SECULAR INSTITUTION is the United Nations. Few programs or organizations have been so lavishly praised or accorded such unstinting support by the American government. According to our policy-makers, the U.N. is the light and hope of the world, and, most important, the chief guiding influence in the conduct of American diplomacy.

President Kennedy, for his part, described support of the U.N. as "the cornerstone of American foreign policy."[1] Adlai Stevenson called the world body "the center and principal forum of our foreign relations."[2] Secretary Rusk, "the symbol and the primary substance of the kind of world which the United States seeks to build."[3] And President Johnson, "the best instrument yet designed to promote the peace of the world and to promote the well-being of mankind."[4]

The sources of this high enthusiasm are readily apparent. The U.N. is, in theory at least, an ideal meeting-place for U.S.-Soviet negotiations, common action, "fruitful dialogue," and all the other items on the agenda of accommodation. It also provides an arena, amplifier and scoreboard for the "world opinion" tournament, in which all the nations down to the merest Dahomey or Upper Volta can say what they think and have their votes counted up. In addition, the U.N. is perfectly constituted to assuage such contributory Liberal passions as the squelching of "jingiosm," the elevation of welfarist pursuits over military ones, and the dissemination of U.S. aid dollars separated from suggestions of American national interest.

The U.N. is, in other words, an elaborate consummation of everything the Liberal believes—a laboratory experiment in the workability of Liberal doctrine, with all the favorite shibboleths set up and functioning, staffed by secretariats, committees and bureaucracies, lavishly financed by the American taxpayer. Its record of performance therefore provides a perfect opportunity for determining how well Liberal presuppositions fit the facts of international life.

The principal purpose of the U.N. when it was launched back in 1945 was clearly set forth in the Charter, Article I, Section I: "To maintain international peace and security, and to that end: To take effective collective measures for the prevention and removal of threats to peace, and for the suppression of acts of aggression or other breaches of the peace."[5] This job was entrusted to the Security Council, where the so-called "Big Five," including America and the USSR, were empowered with the right of veto. The U.N.'s hope of stopping aggression, therefore, was based squarely on the belief that none of the world's major powers would be a party to aggression.

Considering the fallible history of man, this would have been a vain enough hope even if the Soviet Union as we know it had never existed. But when applied to the Soviet Union, whose record of bad faith and imperialistic tendency were and are notorious, it was an act of faith which would have shamed the most ardent of medieval theologians. There was no reason, beyond the parameters of Liberal illusion, to suppose any such arrangement including the Soviet Union would work; and work, as everyone now acknowledges, it did not.

Liberal affection for the U.N. has not, however, diminished. On the contrary, enthusiasm for the world body has appeared to wax in direct proportion as its influence and substantive performance have waned. The U.N. cannot function as originally intended? So much the better, say the Liberal spokesmen; we have other and nobler tasks for it. Professor Quincy Wright of *The Liberal Papers,* for example, says the assumption of "unity" among the Big Five was a "political error . . . accentuated by incorporation in the Charter of the concept that the United Nations should be composed only of 'peace-loving' states. . . ." But, happily, all this is now behind us:

> In principle, the United Nations has committed itself to the proposition that all sovereign states should be members. The wisdom of this position has been increasingly recognized. It has become clear that the United Nations should not be a club, membership in which is a privilege, but a reflector of world public opinion as it actually is, an interpreter of the basic obligations of all states, set forth in the Charter, and a procedure for maintaining the responsibility and enforcing the obligations of its members.[6]

Which is to say: The idea of the U.N.'s combining to stop the chief aggressors of the world is out; the aggressors themselves are in. The criminal is put on the police force, there to help "interpret the basic obligations" of the community, and to participate in "enforcing" those obligations on the populace. Precisely who will enforce the obligations of the criminal himself is a quibble which no one interested in having a "reflector of world public opinion as it actually is" wants to discuss.

Pressed to detail just how the criminal can be restrained when he is given a badge and a night stick—plus veto power over the rest of the police force—U.N. supporters drift uncertainly back toward "world opinion." Senator Fulbright informs us that "the United Nations has become a focus for the peaceful yearnings of an entire generation," and thus has "a power of persuasion that, in this divided world, far surpasses the power of coercion that an international army might exercise."[7]

Yet even Fulbright in effect admits this miraculous power does not work with respect to the Soviet Union. The U.N.'s effectiveness, he says, is limited to "the prevention of wars in areas where the great powers do not directly clash."[8] In other words, where Soviet ambitions impinge directly on the Free World, the U.N. cannot be expected to do anything about it; it is a most excellent machine for preventing aggressions—with the single exception of those committed by history's foremost aggressor.

In neither of its incarnations, then, has the U.N. been capable of blunting the Communist advance. The 20 years of the U.N.'s existence have seen Bolshevik aggression proceeding at a redoubled pace, with the United Nations standing by as a sort of Greek chorus—loquacious but impotent. As Communist onslaughts and barbarities have been piled one upon the other, the U.N.'s characteristic response has been to debate about it, perhaps to suggest it ought to be stopped, and to move on to the next piece of business.*

* In 1958, the U.N. did send a team of observers to Laos to investigate complaints of Communist aggression from neighboring North Viet Nam. The observers concluded there was nothing to worry about.

The sole exception in the U.N.'s history of talkative desuetude was Korea, where the Security Council backed America's initiative in combatting the Communist aggression of June, 1950—a move made possible only by the unexplained absence of the Soviet delegate. Yet this also ended in confusing rather than strengthening Free World resistance. Although supplying only token percentages of men and financial support, the U.N. exerted a powerful influence on Korean policy, and used that influence to press for an accommodationist line allowing the Communists "privileged sanctuary" north of the Yalu River. This policy prevented bombardment of staging points for Communist armies, of bridges they used to launch their attacks, of facilities in North Korea which provided power to the Communists in China and the USSR, and of an ammunition depot where the Soviets landed supplies. The same pressures, combined with the predispositions of our own government, prevented use of Nationalist Chinese troops and employment of nuclear weapons against the Communists' massively superior numbers.[9] (See pp. 200, 301-303)

The U.N.'s inability to halt aggression is not limited to the actions of the Communists. When the aggressors have been merely pro-Communist or "neutralist" the world body has also been remarkably feckless. In Kashmir, held illicitly since 1948 by the force of Indian arms and in violation of Premier Nehru's own pronouncements when the troops went in, the U.N. sputtered for almost two decades without securing compliance, through moral force or otherwise, in its request for a plebiscite. When India invaded the 450-year-old Portugese enclave of Goa, the Soviets vetoed a resolution of condemnation in the Security Council, the General Assembly would not act, and the U.N. did nothing. And when Indonesia's Sukarno began mounting preparations for an attack on Dutch New Guinea, the U.N. bent its energies—not against Sukarno—but in an effort to get the Dutch to hand over the disputed territory without a struggle.*

2. *Why We Can't Win*

This is not to say the U.N. has failed to do anything. When we look at the other side of the ledger, we find the world body has been very active indeed. Although it will not take action against Communist or "neutralist" aggression, it *will* take action against the internal policies of anti-Communist states. It waged a bloody and expensive war against the anti-Communist state of Katanga. It voted sanctions against anti-Communist Portugal. It voted sanctions against anti-Communist South Africa. And it voted sanctions against anti-Communist Rhodesia.

There should be nothing very mysterious about the one-sidedness of this performance. That the net advantage of U.N. activity should accrue over the long pull to the Soviets and not to the West is implicit in the structure of the organization—or, more exactly, in the complex interaction of Liberal policies, Communist intransigence, and the U.N. machinery.

In the first phase of projected U.N. action to maintain peace, the world body could not take substantive measures against the interests of a Big Five member willing to use the veto power. Since the Soviet Union was quite ready to use the veto power, the U.N. could not, *ipso facto,* take substantive action contrary to the interests of the Soviet Union.

Our own officials, however, are extremely reluctant to use the veto, even when the most crucial issues are raised. This

* Britain's Lord Home commented on the Goa invasion that when "we have reached a stage when a large part of the organization which is dedicated to peace openly condones aggression; when an organization which was founded to sustain law and order encourages policies which must endanger it; or when a refusal by many to carry out their share of the costs brings a prospect of power without responsibility, it is an understatement to say that there is cause for anxiety."

means the Security Council can and does take actions counter to our national interests and the interests of the anti-Communist nations we are supposedly leading and defending, even as it is forestalled from taking similar action against Moscow and the Communist bloc. So much for phase I.

In the second or "town meeting" phase, the differing tempers of the Soviet and American governments have yielded equally lugubrious results. The idea that votes in the General Assembly will somehow shame or persuade recalcitrant nations into compliance through the potencies of "moral force" ignores the fact that the Soviet Union is blandly impervious to "world opinion" and "moral force" alike. It has never abandoned a project of aggression simply because other nations, whatever their number, disapproved of it. Only if such disapproval indicated willingness to *act* against Soviet aggression would a vote in the General Assembly have a deterrent effect on Soviet ambitions. Since no such willingness has been manifest, the Soviets ignore such occasional muted rebukes as the U.N. has felt called upon to deliver.

To take but one particularly vivid example: In October, 1961, the U.N. General Assembly voted its disapproval of a Soviet decision to set off a nuclear blast in the atmosphere. The vote of protest, expressing the bent of "world opinion" on this subject, was 87-11.[10] Shortly after this vote was taken, Moscow set off the blast in question. Nothing further was said about it, and the Cold War continued precisely as it had before.

Our government, on the other hand, is perpetually exercised over what other nations think of us; whole lines of American policy are laid down with this consideration alone in mind. In Cuba, in Viet Nam, in our nuclear test program, we have shown ourselves paralyzed by the thought that other nations may disapprove of what we are doing. In neither phase of its existence, therefore, has the U.N. been capable of acting against the Soviet Union; but it can and does act effectively against the interests of the Free World.*

The situation inevitably becomes worse as time goes on, and the Communist onslaught by degrees transforms an increasing number of nations into satellites or fellow-travellers. Many nations formerly represented in the U.N. by anti-Communist governments—Cuba, for example—are now represented by Communist ones. Other nations, newly formed or previously represented by anti-Communist governments, are now in thrall to revolutionary, pro-Communist regimes. Still others in which no essential change of government has occurred are either impressed or frightened by the Communist advance, and have veered away from the West.

The result is that, within a framework already hostile to our interests, the voting balance has shifted steadily toward the Communists. Indeed, the more than 50 members of the Afro-Asian bloc, plus the Communist nations, now make up an actual majority of the U.N. Senator Dodd notes:

> There are few conceivable issues on which the Communist nations could not rally enough support to prevent the two-thirds majority vote required to override a Soviet veto. And when the 11 Communist nations—including Cuba—can persuade the . . . Afro-Asian nations to vote with them, they have a simple majority required for their own way in procedural matters. If another 20 nations were to enter the United Nations, the day may not be too far distant when the Soviets will be able to muster in the Assembly the two-thirds majority necessary to override a Western veto.[11]

The general outlook which has now come to prevail in the

* The classic case in point was the divergent U.N. response in the fall of 1956 to the twin crises in Hungary and Suez. The world body was able to do nothing about the Soviet invasion of Hungary; but it did secure—through the force of "world opinion" and the pressures of the United States—an end to the Anglo-French invasion of Egypt. See *The New United Nations,* by George E. Taylor and Ben Cashman (Washington, 1965), p. 29.

U.N. is suggested by the fact that Secretary General U Thant, advertised as "our man" in opposition to the Soviet Union's troika scheme, is a devout "neutralist" who has spoken in the most compassionate and respectful terms toward the Soviet Union. In 1962, U Thant said "Russia's obsessive fear of encirclement" was comparable to America's apprehensions in the aftermath of Pearl Harbor, that the U.S. and Moscow were equally guilty of "preoccupation with ideology and dogma," and that the Cold War was the result of "mistrust and fear"—making it quite clear that Communist aggression, in his opinion, had nothing to do with it.[12] If this is *our* man, then we are indeed losing the struggle for men's minds with a vengeance.

It is characteristic of our distress that this fading of American influence is greeted with pleasure by certain Liberal spokesmen. *The New York Times,* for example, rejoices that votes in the General Assembly have been going increasingly against us: "The role of this deliberative body, in a world that must be made safe for diversity, is precisely to express the diverse views of its 117 members and the interest groups to which they adhere. The United States itself is well rid of the illusion of omnipotence and universal popularity with which it sometimes bemused itself in the days of automatic Western majorities." We are indeed fortunate, in this view, that matters are going so badly for us.

The truly remarkable thing about all this is that none of it could happen without our consent. The U.N. was created and nourished by the American government; it receives the bulk of its financial support (an estimated 40 per cent) from the American government; its aggression against Katanga was financed and supplied by the American government; and when that aggression led it to the verge of bankruptcy, it was bailed out by American support for its so-called "bond issue" of 1962. No matter how far afield the U.N. ranges, American Liberals seem ready to support it.

The "bond issue" is a notable illustration: It demonstrates the willingness of American Liberals to support the U.N. under almost any conceivable circumstances and to change premises in mid-flight while doing so—even as it confirms the inability of the U.N. to demand minimum standards of international performance from the Communists.

Because the "bond issue" was highly controversial, President Kennedy took pains to assure opponents the device provided a golden opportunity for chastising the Soviet Union, thus invoking anti-Communist motives to secure backing for the U.N. "These bonds will be repaid with interest at the rate of approximately $10 million a year," Kennedy told Congress, "as part of the regular assessment. *Every nation—including the Soviet Union—will thus be required to pay its fair share or lose its vote.*"[13] These representations helped assure passage of the measure in Congress, and although there was some question concerning the validity of the President's argument, a subsequent ruling by the World Court decreed that, under the U.N. charter, such penalties could in fact be imposed.

America purchased $100 million worth of U.N. "bonds." The Soviet Union, along with France, refused to follow suit. The stage was therefore set to deal the indicated rebuke to Moscow. But when the time came to enforce the penalty, when the showdown arrived, the United States backed off. The reason, according to U.N. Ambassador Arthur Goldberg, was that only thus could we save the U.N.—a declaration widely acclaimed by the very people who had promoted the "bond issue" in the first place. Typical of Liberal enthusiasm was the commentary offered by the U.N. correspondent of the *St. Louis Post-Dispatch:*

It was clear that only disaster lay ahead if the United States continued to insist that France and the Soviet Union be deprived of their votes in the General Assembly for refusing to pay for peacekeeping operations with which they were in disagreement

. . . This change of policy cost the United States nothing . . . The Assembly . . . is now able to go forward in its work on a normal, voting basis. The air is cleared. The controversy has been defused. Negotiations become possible.[14]

Goldberg himself had attempted to justify his action on still other grounds: In point of fact, he had said, we backed down because we had to; we could not muster the votes to impose the requisite penalty on the Soviet Union.[15] In other words, *it was impossible to get a majority in the United Nations to impose the terms of its own charter, as construed by its own judicial agency, against the Communists.*

3. *The U.N.'s 'Achievements'*

Exactly what benefits are supposed to accrue to the United States or to mankind at large from all of this is never made clear. The main point seems to be that our only alternative is "war." A scanning of pro-U.N. literature reveals nothing very much in the way of comprehensive rational argument on this score, since the proponents are more given to emotional apostrophe than systematic statement. In general, however, the pro-U.N. argument seems to consist of these points:

1) That the U.N., by embarking on various missions of aid, technological assistance, and improved education, is building the pre-conditions of a "peaceful and stable world"; 2) That the U.N., by providing machinery for intervening in various global trouble spots, has "prevented little wars from developing into big ones"; 3) That the U.N. has provided a kind of buffer which heads off "great-power confrontations" between the United States and the Soviet Union, and thus diminishes the danger of nuclear war; 4) That the U.N., by providing a forum where nations can "talk out their differences," has created a kind of safety valve releasing emo-

tions without overt conflict; and 5) That there has not been a nuclear war yet, so the U.N. must have prevented it.

On the first of these points, we have already examined the question of whether aid and technical assistance missions in fact make for a "stable and peaceful world." There is little to support such an assumption, even less to support the idea that such things are in any way relevant to the fundamental issues which divide East and West, and no reason at all to suppose that, assuming the desirability of such things, the U.N. with all of its vast machinery concerning everything else under the sun is necessary to do them.

The notion that the U.N. has prevented small encounters from developing into big ones is equally dubious. In many instances "small" disputes and "big" ones alike have been *created* by the U.N. In Angola, South Africa, Rhodesia, and Katanga, the U.N. has intruded itself without legitimate authority into chiefly local matters, creating an international incident out of something that should have been settled by the people directly involved. In each of these cases, it was precisely the intrusion of the U.N. which escalated a parochial controversy into a global one.*

On the other hand, there have been several encounters between East and West in which the United Nations has played only a marginal role or none at all which have *not* escalated beyond the boundaries of the immediate situation. The Berlin airlift, the Truman Doctrine for Greece and Turkey, Quemoy and Matsu, Lebanon, Viet Nam, the Cuban missile crisis of 1962: In all of these, the United States stood face to face with one or another of the chief Communist powers. None of them generated a nuclear holocaust. Where the United States has acted firmly and on its own recognizance (Quemoy and Matsu being the clearest example),

* The Congo is alleged as an exception; but the fact is that, without the United Nations, the central Congolese government could not have moved against the recalcitrant state of Katanga. For background on U.N. actions in this controversy, see chapter 27.

the crises tend to get themselves shut down rather quickly; where the United Nations takes over (the Congo being the clearest example of this), things tend to drag on and the Western world finds itself progressively enfeebled.

The argument that the U.N. is a "safety valve" which allows passions to cool and prevents certain types of conflict is in a sense true—but the truth it conveys is hardly reassuring to the West. The U.N., indeed, *is* a safety-valve; it is a place to go *to talk instead of taking action.* And, through talk, it both assuages and dissipates the desire for action. In the 1956 Hungarian crisis, the American people were deeply moved by the agony of the freedom-fighters. But instead of attempting to help the Hungarians, the United States took the matter to the U.N., where it was, as a matter of course, talked to death. The endless debates created the false impression something was being done. And when the fact that nothing was being done at last became clear, the rape of Hungary was a *fait accompli,* Free World passions had diminished, and it was over. The "safety valve" had worked, and Moscow had won.

The Hungarian episode illustrates as well the partial but unfortunate truth of the assertion that "when we are talking, at least we aren't fighting." It is true that when *we* are talking *we* aren't fighting; but the same is not true of the Communists. Negotiations or U.N. debates are for them merely convenient rest periods in which they recoup their strength, or else an even more convenient cover under which they continue battling while we lie doggo.

Finally, the statement that the U.N. has somehow prevented nuclear war, premised on the fact that it has existed for 20 years in which there has been no nuclear war, is supportable neither in logic nor on the historical record. The mere fact of the U.N.'s existence during a period of nuclear restraint does not establish any kind of causal connection; this is the crudest sort of *post hoc* fallacy—a fact which has not, however, prevented the U.N. itself from relentlessly employing it. One could as easily argue that the American Prohibitionist Party, the Chicago *Tribune,* or the annual performance of the World Series were responsible for the absence of nuclear war since 1945, since all of them have been in existence during the identical span of time.

On the factual merits of the case, there is nothing to suggest the U.N. has prevented nuclear war. To the extent that the Soviet Union has been forestalled from launching a strategic blow at the West, or unleashing a massive attack on Western Europe—the two events most widely recognized as containing the likelihood of nuclear war—the United Nations has manifestly had nothing to do with it. Those two dangerous initiatives have been deterred by the nuclear arsenal and delivery capability of the United States Strategic Air Command, and by the defense commitments of the United States —arrived at, significantly, outside the machinery of the U.N. —to nations threatened by Soviet attack.

The U.N.'s contribution to these deterrent factors has been zero; indeed, to the extent it has affected the strategic situation, the U.N.'s actions weakening the West and thereby encouraging Communist adventure have made war of all kinds, including nuclear war, more likely rather than less. Had the history of the Cold War been run without America's strategic power, but with the U.N. in full working order, there is every reason to suppose the Soviet Union would have long since invaded Western Europe. Had the same history been run with American strategic power, and without the U.N., there is no reason to suppose the Soviet onslaught would be any further advanced than it is now.

In all its phases and modulations, then, the U.N. is necessarily hostile to the Free World. As a mechanism for "enforcing obligations," either through military action or "persuasion," it is ineffective against the Communists, but effective against the West. As a buffer, safety-valve, and talk shop, it is suited to Communist purposes, but ill-suited to our own. It is something like a ratchet: It runs smoothly as long as it is moving against anti-Communist governments, against the free world, against the United States. But if an attempt is made to reverse direction—to move against the murder of Hungary, the communization of Cuba, Soviet violation of a test-ban—the machinery locks.

It would be wrong to conclude, however, that the U.N. is responsible for what has happened to the United States. Quite the contrary. It has influence over our actions only to the extent we grant it such influence. Indeed, it has no power of any kind except to the extent that the West, and the United States in particular, is willing to back it up, yield to it, and support it financially. The failure we have been discussing is not, strictly speaking, a failure of the U.N. It is a failure of the fundamental policy assumptions of which the U.N. is the expression and the servant, of the notion that the civilizational crisis of our time will yield to the remonstrances of conversation, of the idea that Communists can be "accommodated," or that "world opinion" is a sovereign remedy for all our ills.

★★ 10. *Aiding the Enemy*

1. *The Wheat Deal*

AMONG THE MOST STARTLING of the proposals we have reviewed is the notion that America should consider "assisting" the Soviet Union. Even in the councils of conciliation and *détente,* the idea that we should actually *aid* the Communists has a certain breathtaking quality about it. Yet evidence that such a policy line has gained favor in Liberal circles, reaching into the government itself, is abundant. There are "Study Phoenix" and the echoes thereof in the utterances of many public officials. There are *The Liberal Papers,* with their explicit suggestion that aid be given Red China and their broad hint that it be proffered to Moscow as well. And there are increasingly blatant efforts to promote such ideas in the arena of public controversy.

In the last-named category, a man named Louis Bohmrich,

former administrative chief of America's delegation to the U.N., has in recent months been travelling about the country delivering lectures to private groups on U.S. foreign policy and the Cold War. In one 1966 session, Bohmrich blandly urged a "Marshall Plan" for Red China, with the United States and other nations contributing some $20 billion to Peking over a five-year period. "Every effort must be made to help China evolve," Bohmrich declared. ". . . We must guarantee that China does not have to fight for food. It must be assured." A development fund for China, the former U.S. official added, should be administered through the United Nations, dispensing funds to the Communist regime into the indefinite future. "Maybe UNESCO* will come in with a teacher-training institute," he said. "I hope one of the early loans of the World Bank will go for education in China."[1]

Bohmrich's statements suggest the advocates of direct aid to the Communists—who in previous efforts have confined their proposals chiefly to esoteric reading for the in-group—now feel confident enough to test their "provocative" opinions in the waters of public discourse. And if such things are being discussed openly by Liberals in public, we may be certain they are also being promoted within the insulated corridors of the American State Department and elsewhere in government. As noted, the Disarmament Agency has complacently attested that to extend aid to the Soviet Union is already the official policy of the American government. The Disarmament Agency, indeed, might have been even more emphatic. For our government is aiding the global Communist enterprise in a large number of other ways as well.

Consider the wheat deal with the Soviet Union. This was, supposedly, a straight matter of "trade." It was in fact an instance of subsidy to the Soviet Union, extended by the

* The United Nations Educational, Scientific, and Cultural Organization—a semi-autonomous offshoot of the world body.

United States government and paid for by the American taxpayer.

In 1963, when Moscow let it be known that the latest Soviet food shortage was acute, the Kennedy administration agreed to sell the Communists $200 million worth of American wheat; and to get the deal consummated, our government went a good deal further than half way. As Senator Thomas Dodd noted: "The wheat was sold not at the price which the government had paid the American farmer, but at the artificially low world price; so that the American government, in effect, was subsidizing the Soviet Union. Concessions were also made on freight rates and on credit. The sale was made without conditions of any kind."[2]

When the deal was first announced, it was advertised as a transaction on "normal commercial terms." But, as *U.S. News and World Report* observed, "the government has been involved . . . at every step of the way."[3] The involvement became particularly noticeable when private bankers refused to guarantee credit to exporters doing business with Moscow. President Johnson thereupon forced through Congress—by the expedient of having the leadership hold the legislators in session up through Christmas, 1963—authorization for the Export-Import Bank, a government agency, to guarantee the Communists' credit, in effect pledging the American government to back up the Kremlin's good faith.

When the Continental Grain Co. subsequently agreed to sell $78.5 million worth of wheat to Moscow, the Johnson regime paid almost one-third the price—$24 million—through an export subsidy. The effect of this action was to make American wheat available to the Russians at a lower price than that at which we sold it to friendly nations, with the U.S. taxpayer picking up the difference. U.S. policy, commented Rep. Bob Dole (R-Kan.), seemed to be "to get the best price you can from the Free-World countries and give the Russians a bargain."[4] Shortly thereafter the performance was repeated when Cargill, Inc., a Minneapolis firm, agreed to sell the Soviets $53 million worth of wheat, and the U.S. government picked up $18 million of the bill. Thus, in these two transactions alone, the American taxpayer subsidized the Communists to the tune of $42 million.

The wheat deal dramatized the general effort of the Kennedy-Johnson regime to extend aid to the Communists in the guise of trading with them. Representative Glenard Lipscomb (R-Calif.) notes that, in its efforts to encourage trade with the East the administration has "apparently liberalized the previously established policy of not guaranteeing commercial credits by the Export-Import Bank for more than five years on sales to the bloc. In the case of the sale of the petroleum refining unit to Rumania, the Export-Import Bank guaranteed credit for a total of five years beginning 30 months after the date of the contract . . ." Lipscomb summarized the massive credit guarantees given Communist nations with U.S. tax dollars as follows:

> Through July 31, 1965, the Export-Import Bank has authorized 83 guarantees to Communist bloc nations totalling $66,743,-300. This includes 21 guarantees for machinery and equipment to Yugoslavia, totalling $18,224,600; 29 guarantees to Hungary for what is described by the Export-Import Bank only as commodities, totalling $24,373,000; 32 guarantees to Poland for commodities, totalling $4,150,700; and the one guarantee to Rumania for the petroleum refining unit at approximately $20 million.[5]

2. *You Paid For It*

Nor is this the only method by which U.S. tax money has been put to use, by indirections, to aid and support Communist nations. Through the United Nations, America paid 40% of the bill for an agricultural experimental station in Communist Cuba, as well as for a number of projects abetting other Communist nations. In the first instance the American managing director of the U.N. Special Fund, Paul Hoffman, protested that no American dollars were being used to pay for Castro's aid project; yet American tax dollars pay 40% of the fund's operation, which means any project it undertakes, whatever the particular dollars used, is necessarily subsidized by us at our pro rata share of 40 per cent. U.S. officials protested this grant verbally, but took no other action.

In early 1966 it was revealed that our government, by the same circuitous route, was helping to finance the Cuban missile threat against the United States. Through its 40 per cent contribution to the United Nations Economic and Social Council, the U.S. has been footing a substantial part of the bill for a subsidy to the University of Havana. This school graduates some 1500 advanced electronics majors each year, a majority of whom proceed to the USSR for training in missile technology, then return to Cuba. As the Republican Congressional Committee newsletter comments, "unless plans are rescinded, Americans could well be helping train men who some day will aim missiles at them."[6]

A third instance of U.N. aid and comfort for Moscow was revealed in a 1963 United Press International dispatch which reported the United Nations Educational, Scientific, and Cultural Organization (UNESCO), a U.N. appendage, had released a booklet attacking Western nations for "colonialist oppression" and describing the Soviet Union as a "brotherhood of free and equal peoples." The pamphlet, written by two Russians, said "it was the Communist Party which showed the peoples of Russia the true way to free themselves from social and national oppression."[7]

In case there is anyone who hasn't guessed, the largest contributor to the organization which published these tidings is none other than the United States. The U.S. picks up one-third of the bill for UNESCO, which reciprocates by allowing straight Communist propaganda to be published under its auspices.

These are not the only examples of American tax funds

paying the tariff for the Communists. Two other instances, involving similar transfers of funds, came to light in 1962. In August of that year, as the Soviet Union stuffed Cuba with missiles and soldiers the Kennedy administration said weren't there, it was disclosed that "the United States will continue to supply Communist Cuba with funds through the Pan American Health Organization." A motion was before the health group, meeting in Minneapolis, Minnesota, to expel Cuba. UPI reported that "delegation chiefs, including U.S. Surgeon General Luther Terry," struck this "controversial topic" from the agenda. The wire service concluded that "the result is that Cuba will continue to receive PAHO funds, 66% of which are provided by the United States."[8]

At about the same time, Congressman E. Ross Adair (R-Ind.) revealed that the Kennedy administration had used American foreign aid money to pay up the assessments of various nations including Cuba and several other Red satellites for the U.N. action in the Congo. The New Frontier, Adair disclosed, had handed over a "voluntary contribution" to the U.N. to help pay for the Congo operation. The U.N. then turned around and reduced the assessments of some 78 nations by sums totalling the same amount.

Adair noted that, "as of June 30, 1962, U.S. contributions to UNEF amounted to $23 million. These voluntary contributions made it possible for the U.N. to reduce substantially the assessments of other countries—including Communist and Communist-dominated countries—for the financing of these U.N. activities . . . For the period November 1961 to June 1962, U.S. voluntary contributions to the U.N. military operations in the Congo amounted to $11.4 million. During the same period, the assessments of 78 countries including those of Albania, Bulgaria, Poland, Cuba, and Yugoslavia—were reduced by $11.4 million . . ."[9]

The breakdown on the assessments for these Communist nations: Albania (owed $32,000; we paid $25,600); Bulgaria (owed $160,000; we paid $128,000); Cuba (owed $176,000; we paid $140,800); Poland (owed $1,024,000; we paid $512,000); Yugoslavia (owed $304,000; we paid $243,-200). Thus the American taxpayer paid of the bulk of these Communist nations' Congo assessments, allowing them to keep their good standing in the world organization.

Thanks to the proliferation of U.N. aid projects heavily supported by American money, instances of U.S. tax dollars being funneled to the Communists by this route have become the rule rather than the exception.

Representative Durward Hall (R-Mo.) noted in 1963 that "the United States has donated $100 million to the United Nations Special Fund. We have donated nearly $200 million to the [Expanded Technical Assistance Program] since 1951. That's the 40 per cent of the Special Fund budget and an even larger percentage of ETAP's budget . . . The Communist bloc has given only token funds and has increased donations by less than five per cent in the last five years."[10]

While America was doing most of the paying for these and other U.N. projects, Hall said, the Communist nations were doing most of the receiving: "I find that Communist Cuba alone is receiving United Nations aid for no less than 16 separate projects . . . Communist Poland has contributed $625,000 to the Special Fund. It has received U.N. aid valued at nearly $2 million. Communist Yugoslavia . . . has donated less than $1 million to the Special Fund. It has gotten back projects worth two-and-one-half times that much—one of them for nuclear research involving radioactive isotopes . . .

"We're paying to help a Red expert devise textbooks for Fidel Castro's schools . . . We're paying so that Cuban officials can learn to fly and to service airplanes at a U.N. training center in Mexico City . . . We're helping provide a fishery study for Castro that involves improving his fishing fleet—a fleet equally adept at running guns to Central America—and that also involves improving Cuban ports which may well wind up servicing Red submarines."[11]

Additional helpings of American tax dollars have found their way to Communist governments through still other special activities of the U.N. One of the U.N.'s affiliated organizations, the United Nations Children Fund, has routinely supplied dollars provided from American tax revenues (and from annual "trick or treating" by American children at Halloween) to Communist governments. Challenged on this score, UNICEF officials reply that the dollars they distribute go to "buy milk for hungry children" and that, anyway, the percentage of funds going to Communist governments is small. They also contend that no major transfusions of UNICEF dollars have gone to the Communist bloc since the early 1950s. The fact is, however, that UNICEF's own statement of "Allocations, Expenditures, and Balances of Allocations" for 1959 shows an allocation of $1.5 million for Communist China, that millions of UNICEF dollars in the post-war era went into the Communist governments of Eastern Europe, and that Communist regimes in Poland, Yugoslavia, and Cuba have received UNICEF grants right up through the 1960's.[12] To suppose that resources thus placed in the hands of Communist governments aid "hungry children," when the governments themselves have charge of distribution, is to suppose more than has ever been true of any Communist government to date. Of additional interest on this score was the revelation, early in 1966, that a UNICEF official named Vadim Asikov, drawing $16,000 a year as procurement officer for the organization, had been serving as an agent for Soviet intelligence.[13]

In more direct fashion, our government has permitted American materials to be used in the construction of a Soviet showplace hospital in Cambodia; and when the Soviet power plant proved inadequate for the hospital's needs, U.S. aid also remedied that. A House subcommittee headed by

Representative Porter Hardy (D-Va.), commented that foreign aid officials in Cambodia made "a deliberate and premeditated determination to finance and construct two radio stations which, when completed, became an adjunct to a Chinese Communist gift to the Cambodian government of a radio broadcasting complex."[14]

When a foreign aid investigator discovered this misuse of American tax money, he immediately reported it to his superiors. He noted that steel rods, cement bags, and a tractor being used in constructing the Russian showplace hospital bore United States emblems and commented drily that "the U.S. foreign aid program does not, of course, have as its objectives the fostering and implementing of Soviet economic aid projects."[15] For his audacity in bringing this matter up, the protesting investigator was subsequently fired. The official who okayed the use of our aid materials in the Communist project was promoted.

With respect to the power plant for the hospital, the Hardy subcommittee concluded: "This transformer and connecting cable were purchased with [$520,000] U.S. foreign aid dollars, but . . . I.C.A. [the foreign aid agency] . . . and the Department of State were unaware of their use for the Russian project for approximately one year. No evidence was produced to show that the people of Cambodia were ever informed that it was U.S. aid that enabled the hospital to function."[16]

In similar vein, the National Science Foundation granted $4,350 to Soviet scientists for a tour of American research centers in 1961. Shortly thereafter the New Frontier used $5,675 for an exchange of U.S. and Soviet scientists, and made two grants, of $61,000 and $373,000, to the Nolit Publishing House in Belgrade, Yugoslavia. In 1962, it was revealed that the National Science Foundation had arranged a financial grant of nearly a million dollars—$901,100—to a Polish printing house for translating and publishing scientific and technical material in English. "Nearly a million dollars in tax money," said Congressman Richard Roudebush (R-Ind.), "seems an extremely high price for the work. If it is absolutely necessary to our survival that we have these foreign language journals translated and printed, I suggest a more economical means would be through our embassy. I am quite sure we could employ competent translators and bring their work back home for printing at considerably less than $1 million."[17]

Continuing his researches in 1965, Roudebush discovered the Johnson administration was spending almost $100,000 on a projected tour of U.S. scientific facilities by representatives of the Iron Curtain countries. The scientists in question were to come from Poland, Yugoslavia, Rumania, Hungary and Czechoslovakia. Purpose of the visit was to have the Communist representatives "lecture, conduct seminars, survey our current research, take field trips in the U.S., and conduct research of their own."[18]

Roudebush revealed that the visiting scientists, thanks to the National Science Foundation, the National Academy of Sciences, and the State Department, would be travelling first class: "American taxpayers will provide travel, lodging, food, medical costs and even pay the scientists from the Communist countries a salary while they are here. If they plan to stay five months or longer, U.S. taxpayers will have the added burden of financing the visiting scientists' families who will also be allowed to come to the United States. Accommodations will be first class, with the taxpayer providing 'housing appropriate to the visitor's professional status and also his family.' "[19]

On the occasion of a previous similar visit by Communist scientists, Roudebush had observed that a member of the delegation was in fact the Communist Party's top commissar in charge of keeping scientists regimented. That discovery suggested to him that, from the Communist point of view, the purpose of this "exchange" might be more aggressive than peaceful.

"Our officials," he concluded, "have even agreed to supply the visitors with information about our scientific laboratories in order that they may select the ones of most interest. The American taxpayer not only must pay for the $3.3 billion in foreign aid every year, but now is being called upon to foot the bill for Communist scientists to junket to the United States for a look around our scientific laboratories.

"Scientific research in the Communist nations is rigidly supervised and highly centralized. We must assume that those persons involved in this work behind the Iron Curtain are tightly disciplined and regimented by the Communist political bosses. Aside from the $99,400 total cost of this program, which I question at this time of national danger, I do not see the advantage of this program from the security viewpoint."[20]

3. *Those 'Independent' Communists*

The stipends directed to Poland and Yugoslavia for printing are, of course, only a small part of the aid given these two Communist nations. As of June 30, 1964, Poland had receive no less than $548 million in U.S. aid, while Yugoslavia had garnered some $2.4 billion.

The stated purpose of grants to such Communist nations is to enable them to achieve "independence" from Moscow. The idea, according to Liberal theorists, is to help these regimes achieve a "certain measure of autonomy," even though they remain within the Communist bloc. There is no evidence, however, that any of these nations has deviated substantially from the Kremlin line in the Cold War, or that our aid has brought about any increase in political freedom for their subjects—the two results we are assertedly trying to achieve. On the contrary, the evidence indicates our dollars have served to strengthen the Communist governments, simultaneously relieving Moscow of the need to assist them and tightening their hold on their subject peoples.

A study released by the Senate Internal Security subcommittee discloses, for example, that the trend of events in Poland has been just the reverse of what "accommodationist" theoreticians project: "It is a grim, ironic fact that, as U.S. props have increasingly fortified his internal position, Gomulka has whittled down the liberties won by Polish courage in 1956. Polish foreign policy is an extension or echo of Soviet foreign policy. Mass resistance spirit against Communism has dropped to near nil, partly because the U.S. seems to be on Communism's side . . ."[21]

The authoritative Assembly of Captive European Nations came to a similar conclusion about Poland, reporting that the intellectual freedom supposedly nourished by our aid money is nonexistent. One Polish intellectual, Melchior Wankowicz, was sentenced to an 18-month jail term for criticizing government persecution of intellectuals. Another writer received the same sentence in September 1965 when he declared "there is no freedom of speech or thought, or of the press in Poland."[22]

Further reflecting on Poland's asserted independence in the Cold War are the revelations of former Polish Communist official Powàl Monat, who describes in considerable detail the errands he was required to perform—including extensive espionage—for his Soviet superiors. ". . . They were running the show," Monat says, "and as our senior partners . . . worked hard . . . to coordinate our efforts to their own ends."[23]

In Rumania, which has been a particular favorite of the Johnson administration, the results have been no better —despite the claim of Senator Fulbright that "Rumania has demonstrated its interest in improving relations with the United States" and that the Red regime there is one of those "which abstain from hostile activities against non-Communist countries." As Senator Strom Thurmond points out, on the day previous to Fulbright's remarks, the Communist government in Rumania declared its solidarity with the international Communist line on Viet Nam, where Red guerrillas were busily engaged in shooting and killing American soldiers.

"Yesterday in Bucharest," Thurmond observed, "the Rumanian Communist Congress, meeting with representatives of Red China and Soviet Russia, passed a resolution condemning the United States 'acts of open war' in Viet Nam. Furthermore, the new general secretary of Rumania stated that the only legitimate representative of the people of South Viet Nam is the National Liberation Front—that is, the Viet Cong, who constitute the Communist invaders from the north."[24]

In the matter of internal freedom, the ACEN survey showed personal liberty was no more prevalent in Rumania than in Poland. The report disclosed that religious leaders Ion Baldauser and Alexander Todea were in Communist prison camps there, and noted that a governmental decree had lately given the state the power to have committed to a mental institution anyone whose activities tended to "disturb the working conditions of others"[25]—a classic measure of indiscriminate totalitarianism.

Our continued beneficence to Communist Yugoslavia affords a particularly good case study in the merits of giving aid to Communist nations. U.S. aid to Tito, according to a 1961 assertion by State Department information officer Lincoln White, is based on the theory that "Yugoslavia has remained independent, and has not participated in policies or programs to bring about the overthrow or subversion of legitimate governments by world Communism."[26] The record from the inception of the Cold War does not support this.

At the end of World War II, U.S. aid helped Tito to oust his anti-Communist opponent, Draja Mihailovich, and to overcome the ravages of the war. He received some $429 million worth of UNRRA supplies, 73 per cent of which was provided by the United States. According to U.S. Foreign

Service Officer Eric Pridonoff, who served as economic analyst for the American Embassy in Belgrade, Tito used this aid to build the strength of his Communist faction against the anti-Communists. He concealed its Free World origin and sold most of it to get foreign exchange while his people were starving. He confiscated American property, shot down two American aircraft, killed American servicemen and burned their bodies, ordered American personnel to leave Yugoslavia, placed American diplomatic officials under constant surveillance, and impeded passage of supplies to the American Embassy. Simultaneously, he lavished praise on the Soviet Union, and told the Yugoslav people the UNRRA aid they received was a gift from Moscow.

In the intervening years, nothing much has changed. Tito's much-publicized "break" with Moscow in 1948 (when he was excommunicated from the Cominform, not separated by his own free will) produced little to alter the pattern. In September, 1961, after receiving a shipment of jet fighter planes from the United States, and having had the pilots for them trained in America, Tito responded by announcing his support for the Soviet position in Germany.*

The Liberal theory is that Tito's "independence" will lead him to use the arms we supply him on our side in any European conflict. Yet Germany is precisely the spot where such a conflict is most likely to occur, and Tito has made it clear his support in such an event would go to the Kremlin. He has exuberantly praised East Germany and attacked the

* Some other items from the more recent past:

On June 11, 1956, Tito proclaimed: "Yugoslavia, *in time of war,* as well as in time of peace, marches shoulder to shoulder with the Soviet people toward the same goal—victory over the enemies of Socialism."

In April, 1958, Tito charged that NATO was an instrument of aggression, and denounced the Western trade embargo against the Soviet Union.

Also in 1958, Tito, whose peculiar virtue is supposed to be the advocacy of a pacific "national Communism," proclaimed himself a votary of "proletarian internationalism"—which translates into global assault by Communism against all free societies.

free government in Bonn as a system "pregnant with interwoven remnants of fascist and revenge conceptions and tendencies." Which would suggest that, in any war over Germany, those American jets and American-trained pilots would be used, not to defend Tito's western benefactors, but to kill them.

Further examples of American subvention to the Communist empire might be added at length were it not for the danger of fatiguing the reader. Enough evidence has been posted, we believe, to show that such aid is being extended, either directly or indirectly, in substantial quantities. The natural question is: Why? What, exactly, do our diplomats think they are doing? To the extent that any rational answer is available, it seems clear the logic of these transactions is precisely the logic of the Phoenix Papers. By doing all of these things we are "building bridges" of understanding to the Communists; we are attempting to weave Professor Rock's web of "interdependence" with our enemies—even as we fight them in Viet Nam. It is noteworthy that Secretary McNamara, discussing the prospects of Cold War *détente* in 1966, lapsed into Phoenix Papers jargon similar to that we have already quoted from the speeches of the late President Kennedy. Explaining the course of American policy under the Johnson administration, McNamara stated:

"There are many ways in which we can build bridges toward nations who would cut themselves off from meaningful contact with us. We can do so with properly balanced trade relations, diplomatic contacts, and in, some cases, even by exchanges of military observers . . . President Johnson has put the matter squarely. By building bridges to those who make themselves our adversaries, 'we can help gradually to create a community of interest, a community of trust and a community of effort.' . . .

"Mutual interest, mutual trust, mutual effort—those are the goals. Can we achieve those goals with the Soviet Union, and with Communist China? Can they achieve them with one another? The answer to these questions lies in the answer to an even more fundamental question. Who is man? Is he a rational animal? If he is, then the goals can ultimately be achieved. If he is not, there is little point in making the effort . . . I, for one, would not count a global free society out."[27]

This is indeed the language, and the practice, of the Phoenix Papers. We shall find more of both as we explore our subject further.

★★ 11. *East-West Trade*

1. *The Ball Report*

WHILE THE EXTENSION of direct subsidy to the Communists is the most flamboyant of Liberal foreign policy initiatives, it is probably surpassed in substantive impact by the results of increased commercial traffic with Iron Curtain countries.

Accelerated American trade with Communist nations is a long-term objective of the State Department bureaucracy come to fruition under Kennedy and Johnson. Over the past five years, the Liberal regime in Washington has negotiated trade deals with Moscow, issued countless export licenses, guaranteed Communist credit, subsidized the Eastern end of the transaction, and kept pressure on businessmen to traffic with the enemy as a matter of patriotic duty.

The first explicit effort to justify increased trade with the Communist nations was the so-called "Ball Report" of 1960, prepared by a task force under the leadership of Under Secretary of State-to-be George Ball. The net impact of the report, as paraphrased by *The New York Times,* was that increased trade with the Communist bloc nations was "inevitable," and that the United States had better knuckle under and go along. The key paragraph of *The Times* story says:

"A complete alteration of United States policy on trade with the Soviet bloc countries was recommended by the task force. It held this to be imperative not only because the present policy is outmoded but also because it had begun to affect our relations with other industrialized countries as well as with the underdeveloped areas. The problem will not go away because Americans consider trade with Communist countries to be immoral, dangerous and of doubtful economic benefit, said the group. It said such trade would become vastly more important in this decade than in the last because other Western countries had found such trade to be advantageous. As a result, said the report, our allies have refused to follow docilely the tariff discriminations and export limitations on Communist trade imposed by U.S. law. Meanwhile, because the United States has refused to face the issue, trade between the Soviet bloc and Western Europe has been developing largely on Soviet terms, the group said. It said that the time has come for the United States to give direction to this inevitable development."[1]

Other voices calling for increased trade with the Communists and an alternation of U.S. law to achieve it include Walt Rostow, the Phoenix Papers, Vice President Humphrey, Senator Fulbright, and Secretary Rusk. "Peaceful trade" with the USSR, as Rusk put it, "may erode gradually the concept that conflict between us is inevitable and replace it with some recognition of the mutual advantage of closer economic relations."[2] And: "I do not believe that we ought to close up all channels of trade" with the Communists because "there is an impetus toward stability and peace in the growing consumer demands of the Soviet Union."[3]

Various elements in the State Department had long been in agreement with these sophisticated notions and had worked to do something about them—despite the existence of statutes intended to prevent such things. The principal act of Congress aimed at cutting down Free World trade with the Communist bloc is the so-called Battle Act of 1951, which calls for a cut-off of aid to nations that knowingly send strategic items to Communist countries. It is perhaps the most punchless decree of Congress since the Volstead Act. Back in 1956, the Senate Permanent Subcommittee on Investigations came to these conclusions:

"The subcommittee believes the executive branch of the government has violated the spirit, if not also the letter, of that act since its enactment in 1951. It appears that in this matter the executive branch has disregarded the clear intent of Congress.

"The wholesale revision of the Battle Act list in 1954, together with the corresponding removal of 200 items from the international list, demonstrates that there has been no attempt to enforce the penalty provisions of the Battle Act. On the contrary, Mr. Harold E. Stassen, as Battle Act administrator, in effect circumvented the Battle Act by determining that items of manifest strategic significance, and which had been so regarded prior to the 1954 revision, were not strategic for purposes of allied trade with the Communist bloc."[4]

The subcommittee found, as other investigators have found before and since, that it was difficult to get a straight story from the State Department about just how much loosening up there had been in the matter of trading with the Communists. The senators charged that:

"The Battle Act administrator, Mr. Stassen, in 1954 misstated the facts in his Fifth Battle Act Report . . . when he reported: 'Minerals and metals of basic importance to the

Soviet military power, such as aluminum, cooper, nickel, molybdenum, cobalt, magnesium, tungsten, and titanium remain on the embargo list.'

"In this and other portions of the Fifth Battle Act Report, Mr. Stassen misrepresented facts, which thus misled the Congress and the American people. Moreover, when he testified before this subcommittee, Mr. Stassen appeared to be an arrogant, evasive, and uncandid witness. The subcommittee feels that Mr. Stassen is to be severely criticized for his conduct in this matter."[5]

As a result of this performance, the subcommittee concluded, the Soviet war machine had been greatly enhanced: "The United States government, by revising the Battle Act list, and by agreeing to the downward revisions of the international strategic list, has thereby enabled our allies (principally the NATO countries) to ship to the Communist bloc in Europe such highly strategic materials as copper, machine tools, electric generating equipment, electronic devices usable in the atomic-energy and guided-missile fields, as well as numerous other materials of critical importance to the Communist war machine, with complete immunity from the Battle Act's penal provisions."[6]

2. *The Hard Sell*

When the Kennedy regime took office, efforts in this direction were vastly accelerated—both in the State Department and on Capitol Hill. The ideas spelled out in the Rostow report and the Ball report were put energetically into effect. The congressional leader in this enterprise was Senator Fulbright, who proposed that the Battle Act be weakened still further, and that the President be allowed at his option to step up commercial exchanges with Communist nations and to permit foreign countries receiving U.S. aid to do the same.

Early in 1961 the Kennedy administration approved for export to Russia precision machine tools designated as "clearly of military value" by the Defense Department. When Rep. Glenard Lipscomb (R-Calif.) began inquiring into the matter, the Pentagon suddenly decided to "withdraw" its objections to the transaction.[7]

In August 1961, Rep. John Ashbrook (R-Ohio) revealed that exports to Communist nations were, under the Kennedy stewardship, zooming upward. "The Department of Commerce licenses to those who trade with the Reds," Ashbrook said, "show that in the three weeks preceding July 25 . . . U.S. goods licensed for shipment to Communist countries had a total value of $750,196, while in the three weeks after July 25, exports jumped 800 per cent or $6,278,566 . . ." Among the products the Commerce Department found appropriate for export to the Communists were rail equipment, synthetic rubber, industrial equipment, coal tar products, carbon black, industrial and specialty channels and pipe valves. "Eight million tons of scrap iron have been loaded at Houston, Texas," Ashbrook noted, "for shipment to Czechoslovakia."[8]

On October 25, 1961, Secretary of Commerce Luther Hodges confirmed Ashbrook's alarum. "There has been," Hodges said, "a substantial increase in the dollar value rate of exports to the Soviet bloc under general licenses . . . in the first half of 1961 as compared with previous years."[9]

In 1962 the Kennedy regime began a campaign to convince American businessmen they should trade with Moscow. The Baltimore *Sun* reported "the government is quietly encouraging American businessmen to expand their trade with the Soviet bloc," quoted one high official on the virtues of commerce with the enemy, and reported President Kennedy's rebuke to American citizens who protested such trade (they could better fight Communism, Kennedy said, by joining the Peace Corps).[10]

Two years later, the policy of promoting private trade behind the Iron Curtain had become more systematic. Journalists Robert Allen and Paul Scott got hold of a report on trade with the Soviets, prepared by an international business research agency and circulated among U.S. businessmen with the cooperation of the Johnson administration. The report set forward, in detail, ways and means of landing contracts in Moscow. In the weeks succeeding the 1964 election, "more than 200 U.S. businessmen . . . made the journey to Moscow," and "a few U.S. firms, with a big assist from the State and Commerce Departments, [were] sending representatives for extended stays of one to three months."[11]

Meanwhile, the government's own involvement in trading with the enemy proceeded at a quickening tempo. In February, 1963, the State Department announced it was selling $51.6 million worth of surplus farm commodities to Communist Poland, to be paid for in Polish zlotys (acceptable only in Poland) at long-term credit rates. This brought to $477.3 million, by official calculation, the amount of U.S. trade with Poland.

In June, 1964, the administration signed an agreement with Communist Rumania, paving the way for trade deals involving "oil refineries, industrial plants, possibly even a nuclear reactor or two."[12] And as noted in Chapter 5, it persuaded the Firestone Tire and Rubber Co. it would be a good idea to build rubber plants in Rumania.

In 1965, the Johnson regime extended the policy of doing business with the Communists still further by paving the way for trade with East Germany. The North American Newspaper Alliance reported: "Now, U.S. business firms are being advised American trade with East Germany will be encouraged on approximately the same basis as with other Western [*sic*] countries, primarily West Germany and Britain."[13]

In May 1965, Representative Howard W. Robison (R-N.Y.) revealed that there were nine organizations being allowed to function in the United States as agents of Communist governments, through which Americans can purchase "gift certificates" on stores in the Communist countries, supposedly to aid friends or relatives behind the Iron Curtain. This was, Robison noted, "an effective device whereby Communist nations may build up not inconsiderable dollar credits."[14]

In July, 1965, Representative Edward Derwinski (R-Ill.) charged that "for more than a year the State Department has carried on secretive trade discussions with the Communist governments of Eastern Europe and the Soviet Union itself. . . . It is not the intention of the administration merely to permit expanded trade agreements with Communist governments, but it is the specific intention to subsidize that trade."[15]

Finally, in September, 1965, Congressman Lipscomb undertook an exhaustive survey of the type and quantity of goods licensed for export to the Soviet Union and other Communist nations—goods employed in the manufacture of any number of militarily useful products. Among these were materials involved in the manufacture of tires, precision parts for automobile engines, oil, synthetic fibers, containers for explosives, synthetic rubber, copper, tin, steel, electronic parts, aircraft components, and literally dozens of other items of great potential value in military development.[16]

These examples indicate the 1963 wheat deal was not a special or unusual case, but part of a settled and determined policy.

To achieve these results, Liberal diplomatists have had to put a rather sizeable dent in the law. As Senator Dodd pointed out when the wheat deal was first announced: "Without any approval from Congress, in fact in the face of expressed congressional disapproval, our government is to sell to Russia subsidized wheat at a price substantially below that paid for it by the American taxpayer. . . . Only a few weeks ago this would have been unthinkable, as it was in 1961 when Congress passed Public-Law 87-128 which states the sense of Congress that subsidized agricultural commodities should not be made available to the Soviet Union or to countries dominated by the USSR. But this morning's press [October 1, 1963] states that 'official sources are not too impressed with Congress' restrictions against selling subsidized grain to unfriendly nations.' "[17]

Nor, as noted, have State Department bureaucrats been particularly "impressed" by the strictures of the Battle Act and other acts of Congress decreeing that U.S. foreign aid should not go to countries involved in strategic trade with the Communists. An authoritative survey on this subject, *East-West Trade: Its Strategic Implications,* gives this summary:

> . . . free world exports to the Communist nations have increased substantially every year since 1954, and by 1962 had increased threefold over the 1954.
>
> The reports [of the Battle Act administrator] and the accompanying statistical data demonstrate the failure of the United States to persuade its allies to adopt security controls on trade with the Communist nations comparable to its own.
>
> The penalty provided in the Act (termination of U.S. aid) was never imposed. In 86 cases, from January 24, 1952, when the act became fully operative, through 1963, there was a presidential determination, as provided in the act, that continuance of aid was in the interest of national security.
>
> On February 18, 1964, the United States curtailed military aid to Great Britain, France, and Yugoslavia, estimated to amounts in 1964 of only $100,000 each. It was also announced that no new commitments would be made to Spain and Morocco until it is known what steps they are taking to halt shipments to Cuba. In 1963 military aid to Spain amounted to a little over $30 million and economic aid to Morocco to $20 million. No action was taken with respect to 14 other countries who were considered to have taken appropriate steps to halt shipping to Cuba.[18]

The volume of East-West trade, thanks to the practice of the Kennedy-Johnson regime, has increased even more markedly since 1962. In that year, the total amount of Free World trade with the Communists totalled $50 million. In 1963, it zoomed up to $139 million; and in 1964, year of the wheat deal, to more than $400 million.

3. *Has It Worked?*

Rock, Humphrey, Ball, and other advocates of trading and aiding the Communists into affability claim their policy will bring about a "thaw" in East-West relations. The historical record suggests, however, that the Soviets have not responded very kindly to our pacific overtures. While the wheat deal was moving toward completion, indeed, Communist acts of hostility seemed if anything to increase. Senator Dodd noted:

First, on October 22, the very anniversary of the Cuban missile crisis, Soviet MIG fighters, operating out of Cuba and more than likely manned by Soviet crews, attacked an American-owned freighter on the high seas.

Second, there was a series of harassments in October, 1963, of American and British convoys on the Berlin Autobahn.

Third, in the month of October, 1963, an official Soviet delegation in Hanoi, the capital of North Viet Nam, broadcast a call for the overthrow of the Diem government and for the expulsion of the "American imperalists" from South Viet Nam.

Fourth, the Soviets, again during the month of October, 1963, further inflamed the highly dangerous situation in North Africa by sending arms and equipment to the Ben Bella government in large quantities, and by openly inciting the Algerians against the Moroccans.

In the month of November, 1963, the Congolese government was compelled to expel the entire Soviet mission when members of the mission were caught red-handed in a left-wing plot to overthrow the Congo government.

In January, 1964, there were the Panama riots, which were

organized and led by identified Castro agitators and which were supported to the hilt by the entire Soviet propaganda apparatus.[19]*

In a general sense, it is obvious any aid we extend to the Communists will be used against us, since to the extent that we alleviate agricultural shortages in the USSR we strengthen their hold on their subjects and release resources for other uses. And to supply precision machine tools, rubber factories, oil refineries, motor vehicles and other such items is, of course, to stoke the Communist war machine in very obvious ways.

Some curious facets of our trade include, moreover, the 1966 sale to Moscow of technical data for the construction of three large fertilizer plants (one of the items recommended in the Phoenix report), while the Soviets were in turn supplying North Viet Nam with upwards of 150,000 tons of fertilizer. We have sold $660,000 worth of platinum pellets, useful in the manufacture of high octane gasoline, to Bulgaria. And we have supplied Rumania with electronic equipment to be used in airplanes obtained from the Soviets.

Many U.S. sales to the Communist countries, Congressman Lipscomb noted, were obviously "prototypes"—instruments or designs which the Communists could readily copy and manufacture in large numbers once they had obtained a specimen or blueprint of the original. This is in direct defiance of a finding by a select House committee on Export Control which declared:

It makes no more sense to strengthen the economic potential of

* The Communists in Germany not only interfered with autobahn traffic but molested U.S. flights. Rep. Paul Findley, (R-Ill.) commented: "I hope the Johnson administration doesn't try to justify its Russian wheat sale to the families of U.S. airmen killed when the Communists shot down their unarmed airplane in East Germany." As it happened, the Johnson administration went Findley one better. Rather than setting about to justify trade with Russia after these East German atrocities, it simply initiated trade with East Germany itself.

our cold war Communist enemies than to arm them; and yet the select committee has found glaring instances where we have economically strengthened countries in the Soviet bloc . . .

Immediate steps should be taken to more effectively control the exports of technical data. The furnishing of plans, specifications, and production details of strategic items to the Soviet bloc in many instances has given as much or more advantage to those countries as the shipment of the commodities themselves. . . .

The select committee urges that our government take a firm position with our allies to extend and make more effective international control of export of strategic commodities to Communist countries, including Cuba. Similarly, the select committee recommends tight control over export of prototypes of single units to Communist countries.[20]

Communist use of materials we supply to advance Cold War policy objectives was revealed in August, 1964, when Lipscomb discovered that wheat purchased by the USSR, far from feeding starving Russians, was being trans-shipped to Rumania—to strengthen the Soviet grip on that satellite nation. This at the same time that we were plying Rumania with trade of our own, in order to woo it away from Moscow. Rep. Ed Gurney (R-Fla.) similarly found the Soviets were shipping wheat purchased in Canada to Cuba—thus using aid given them by the Canadians to shore up their threat to America in this hemisphere.

These trans-shipment episodes gave a special piquancy to the disclosure that the Continental Grain Co. was following up its wheat sale to Moscow with a shipment of rice. Rice is not a high-consumption item in the USSR. It is, of course, in the Orient, where Chinese, Korean, and Vietnamese Communists are as much in need of provender as are Cubans and Rumanians. It is altogether possible, therefore, that American tax dollars, which subsidized the rice sale just as they did the wheat sale, went to feed the Viet Cong terrorists shooting at American soldiers in Viet Nam.

Lipscomb noted the irony of U.S. trade flowing into Communist lands to strengthen their war potential even as they backed the Vietnamese aggressions. Who knows, he asked, where Rumanian oil produced with our assistance will finally wind up? And who knows what ultimate use will be made of the copper products we are helping Yugoslavia to manufacture? As for our policy of building up the Soviet Union itself:

The USSR is heavily committed to helping North Viet Nam in its aggressive designs against South Viet Nam. A recent report indicates that Soviet railroad equipment is to be furnished to North Viet Nam. Their railroads, of course, are one of the targets of our bombings. There is another report that the Soviet Union has trained North Vietnamese pilots to fly the MIG-21 Russian jet fighter, the latest version of the MIG jet. Russian trawlers are reported to be located off Guam to provide early warnings of B-52 strikes on Viet Cong concentrations in South Viet Nam. And, of course, there are the surface-to-air missiles and missile launchers in North Viet Nam undoubtedly placed there by the USSR.

And yet we go blithely ahead selling things to the Red bloc which may very well end up being used in support of the Communist aggressors in Viet Nam. Does it make sense to help equip and feed the Soviets who are helping the aggressors kill our soldiers in Viet Nam?[21]

Equally important, the fact that the United States is trading with the Soviet Union itself makes impossible any serious effort by our government to deter our allies from trading with the Communists in Viet Nam, Cuba or anywhere else. And while the Johnson administration has gone through the motions of trying to prevent such trade, it has apparently recognized the absurdity of the situation, and yielded to the acceleration of free world commerce with Hanoi and Havana.

Appearing before the Senate Foreign Relations Committee, Secretary of State Rusk alleged that the United States was consulting with Free World nations engaged in trade with Hanoi—principally Great Britain—and that, as a result, "we . . . have succeeded in reducing it very sharply."[22] These assertions were seemingly supported by the release of figures showing only 16 Free World ships had called at the North Vietnamese port of Haiphong in the first three-quarters of 1965, and that only 21 had called there in the last quarter. Later inquiries by Congressman Charles Chamberlain, (R-Mich.), revealed, however, that the number of ships was in fact a good deal larger: There were in truth 36 ships visiting Haiphong in the first three quarters of 1965, and 21 in the last quarter. Moreover, in one six-month period, no less than 64 British vessels called at North Vietnamese ports.[23] In short, Free World trade with the Communist Vietnamese, far from being reduced, was both substantial in volume and steadily increasing. And, since we have set the example ourselves, we could hardly expect it to be otherwise.

★★ 12. *Cultural Exchanges*

1. *Plus and Minus*

YET ANOTHER DEPARTMENT of "sophisticated" cold war theory involves cultural exchanges. The argument advanced in support of increased swapping of athletes, singers, artists, and whatnot is that such contact between "our people and theirs" cannot help but serve the cause of peace. This is one of the means by which the break in "communications," assertedly at the root of the Cold War, can be mended.

The theory is vulnerable on the face of it, for at least two reasons. First, since the Cold War is not caused by a breakdown in communications, even the most extravagantly successful program of "contacts" could not bring it to an end. Second, the highest possible level of improved understanding with the Russian people could not ameliorate Cold War conditions, because the Russian *people* are not in charge of Soviet policy.

There is, however, still a third reason why "cultural exchanges" cannot do the job suggested for them, which would doom the enterprise even if these considerations did not prevail. Because the Soviets never enter into any mutual exchange in good faith, the "exchanges" are not authentic contacts, on either end of the transaction. Americans who go to the USSR are shown exactly what the Soviet regime intends for them to see. Soviet nationals who come to the United States are, by party decree, either Communist functionaries or else tightly controlled by them.

In some instances, of course, these conditions do not obtain with perfect rigor. An occasional American can find out certain things inside the USSR, even on a severely limited itinerary; and now and again a Soviet diplomat or athlete will break out of his ambulatory confinement and bring us some valued information and a propaganda victory vis-à-vis the Communists. These are plus items in the "exchange" ledger.

They are not, however, the "plus" items the exchange advocates tell us we ought to expect, and, indeed, arise from circumstances which belie the assumptions of the program. Cultural exchange is not supposed to benefit us because some American reporter evades his surveillance; it is supposed to benefit us by making us realize how much better things are getting in the USSR and how much like Americans the Russian people are. It is not supposed to benefit us because a fugitive violinist or shot-putter slips his secret police guard and defects to the West; it is supposed to show the "Russian people," *sans* all mention of secret police, how ready we are to like them (and the system they are escaping).

The unhappy truth is that the USSR views the whole "cultural exchange" idea as it views everything else, as another device for penetrating and harrying the West. Consider these statements from the Senate Internal Security subcommittee:

. . . Every form of exchange between Communist and other countries, whether diplomatic, cultural, commercial, technical or athletic, is conceived and worked out with propaganda in mind. Not, of course, open propaganda for Communism, but propaganda of an indirect, enveloping underhanded kind for pro-Soviet views . . . The notion prevalent in the West that contacts with them may "widen their horizons and humanize their views" is absurd, for these are not men who can give free rein to their inclinations, but docile tools by means of family hostages whom they have left behind in their country . . . When the West puts a man in the exchange institute it is for carrying out exchanges. When the Soviets do so it is for subversion.[1]

And:

Every member of a Soviet cultural mission is an observer for military intelligence.

Each such member is screened to assure political reliability.

Each such member is duty bound to use every contact with the American public to acquire information which may be useful to the Soviet government.

Each such mission includes at least one official representative of Soviet intelligence. . . .

Benefits to the United States from such missions are meager at best. No Soviet citizen, no matter what he would have observed in this country, would dare to question the propaganda which the Soviet serves to its people, and there are very, very few defectors.[2]

And:

Soviet visits to the United States are an element of Soviet tactics of the "peaceful coexistence" period . . . Soviet visits to the United States serve these purposes:

1. Obtaining information ranging from the study of American conditions, collection of technical data and verification of previously obtained data, to direct espionage and the establishment of contact.

2. Engaging in propaganda, both: (a.) pro-Soviet in the United States where it is aimed at misinforming American society on the objectives and possibilities open to the USSR and Communism, and at demobilizing American public opinion, and (b.) pro-Soviet in the USSR and other so-called Socialist countries where it is aimed at confirming [the] Soviet thesis concerning the superiority of the Soviet system over the capitalist and the inevitable destruction of capitalism, and at presenting documentary proof of the prestige enjoyed by the USSR and Communism, as well as Soviet political leaders in the Free World.[3]

That such "exchanges" are indeed part of the "peaceful coexistence" tactic which has as its objective the psychological disarmament of the West has been attested by no less an authority than Khrushchev himself. In the very de-Stalinization speech which spelled out the strategy of "coexistence," Khrushchev made specific reference to the utility of exchanges, saying "the expansion of business and cultural contacts is of great importance for the further improvement of relations between countries. On its part, the Soviet government is doing everything possible for the all-round development of these ties." As noted in chapter 2, the explicit purpose of such "coexistence" overtures is that "in conditions of peaceful coexistence favorable opportunities are provided for the development of the class struggle and the national-liberation movement of the colonial and dependent countries."[4]

No Soviet citizen can go abroad, of course, without the permission of the Communist authorities. To get that permission, the Internal Security subcommittee notes, certain rigid requirements must be surmounted:

1. That the person has excellent or positive "characteristics" in the Communist Party and the government.

2. That he is a member of the Communist Party or the Young Communist League. A non-Communist may go if he can obtain permission to make the trip and if his record is satisfactory.

3. That the person does not have any relatives abroad.[5]

These conclusions are based on the testimony of defectors from the Soviet Union, analysis of the personnel in Soviet "exchange" delegations, and the witness of numerous authorities who have lived in the Soviet Union and know how it operates. Eugene Lyons writes that "the assumed reciprocity in the exchange deal is largely fraudulent. Where ideas are concerned, no fair exchange is permissible or possible when the other party is a police state. Moscow selects its authorized tourists with extreme care. It plants dependable secret agents in every group to supervise its political morals. It holds hostages as insurance against defections while outside the homeland . . . Whether the Soviet exchange contingents are dancers or athletes, professors or priests, this police ingredient in its makeup can be taken for granted."[6]

2. *The Visiting Churchmen*

How these conditions work out in specific circumstances may be gathered by examining a particular "exchange" program—one which occurred under the most pious and venerated auspices. In 1963, a delegation of Soviet clergymen headed by Archbishop Nikodim came to the United States, sponsored by the National Council of Churches. These men were greeted as representatives of the Christian faith and welcomed with open arms by American clergymen—an episode which obviously served to confirm the impression that there were autonomous practicing Christian churches in the USSR, that the Soviet government was in some part congenial to the free play of religious sentiment, and that therefore things could not be quite so bad in the USSR as we had previously been led to believe—all ideas congenial to the strategy of "coexistence."

According to expert authority, this portrait of the Soviet clergymen is a long way from the truth. Here is the 1956 testimony of former Soviet agent Yuri Rastvorov before the Senate Internal Security subcommittee:

> As you know, the church in the Soviet Union is not independent, as, at the present time, the Soviet government is trying to prove. It is completely dependent on the state, and the state conducts all activities of the church in the Soviet Union.[7]

Rastvorov went on to say that when the Russian Orthodox Church set about to organize seminaries, Soviet secret police agents were sent to the seminaries as students: "They sent officers, counterintelligence officers to these seminaries, and later they became bishops in many churches in the Soviet Union."[8]

Concerning Metropolitan Nikolai, a high officer of the Russian Church, another former Soviet operative gave similar testimony. Peter Deriabin, one-time Communist secret police agent, testified before the House Committee on Un-American Activities:

> Another example was in 1956, when the Soviet religious delegation was here, the Soviet Orthodox Church. The chief of that was Metropolitan Nikolai. He is not a member of the KGB [the Soviet secret police], but he is an agent of the KGB since World War II, who gives information to KGB. KGB is asking him and he is giving information. He is actually an agent.[9]

If such things are true concerning Soviet clergymen, we can imagine what the case is concerning other less sacred occupations like ballet dancers and distance runners. On this score, Deriabin gave further instructive testimony. ". . . when the Soviet delegation is going abroad," he said, "it always includes some intelligence or counterintelligence officers. For instance, in 1957 there was a Soviet delegation, a construction delegation in the United States, which includes one Soviet intelligence officer whose name is Major Zagorsky, who was a member of that Soviet delegation.

"When the Moiseyev dancers were here, Lt. Col. Aleksandr Aleksandrovich Kudriavtsev was a member of the Moiseyev dancers who is working for Soviet intelligence for many years, and he is a colonel. Both of them were working with me in Moscow when I was there."[10]

Congressman Roudebush, contesting a tour of U.S. research centers by Soviet scientists, pointed out that one of these emissaries of better understanding was Aleksandr V. Topchiev, "political watchdog and commissar in behalf of the ruling Communist Party" in the USSR, and "the man chiefly responsible for regimentation and discipline of Soviet scientists." Topchiev's official title is Vice President of the USSR Academy of Sciences, an organization characterized by the Internal Security subcommittee as "the scientific arm of the Soviet government and a political tool of the Soviet Union." When he was chosen to his high position with "the Academy," Topchiev declared "that he was primarily a dedicated Communist and only secondarily a scientist."

"Enough of our secrets have reached Russia through other means," Roudebush commented, "without opening the doors of our universities and laboratories to allow our dedicated enemy to investigate and recruit followers at our expense . . . I do not feel that the American taxpayer should be required to pay for travel of Russian scientists to look over our installations and learn our techniques."[11]

One motive behind the exchanges is the hope that Soviet visitors, having got a look at our country and the things we have here, will go home and tell their fellow Muscovites about it, spreading good will for the United States. Even assuming some of the visitors would like to do so, they would be extremely foolhardy to follow the impulse; that, quite obviously, is not what the Soviet government has in mind. An intensive survey by the Internal Security subcommittee shows that articles and statements by returning exchangees are uniformly slanted to discredit the United States, to play up real or imagined blemishes in our society, and to omit mention of anything which might reflect credit on us. "No tourist," the committee notes, "would dare to submit to the totalitarian press of the USSR a description of the United States contrary to the official propaganda line."[12]

FBI Chief J. Edgar Hoover says exchange programs are highly useful to the Soviets in obtaining technical information. All scientific delegations, he notes, have members among them who carry special assignments from the KGB and at least one and sometimes more KGB officers in charge of the visitors. "Upon returning," Hoover says, "Soviet scientists who have visited the United States under the exchange program are required by the KGB to submit comprehensive reports on the technical aspects of their trip, including descriptions of installations visited, research being conducted, and the status of particular projects. They must also submit reports concerning Americans contacted for possible future use by the KGB." Hoover estimates that 20 per cent of the "students" sent to the U.S. from the Soviet Union are KGB or other similar agents.[13]

3. *Exchanging Diplomats*

The Soviet Union and other Communist nations, then, employ the functionaries they send to Western countries as intelligence agents and worse. Wherever Communist diplomatic or exchange missions congregate, there is sure to be a heavy traffic in Cold War intrigue, including everything from theft of secrets to policy subversion to acts of terror. The United Nations, where Communist diplomats are able to foregather on American soil, is a striking case in point.

Among its several other attributes, the U.N. is the chief outpost of Communist terror and espionage in the Free

World. From the Soviet point of view, it is almost perfect in this respect, since its precincts on 42nd St. are immune from every form of U.S. authority. If a spy or terrorist can make his way to the U.N. grounds, he is safe from American police. Pierre J. Huss and George Carpozi Jr., discussing cases of Soviet terror and espionage, note that "all of these plots . . . were initiated in one central location—the so-called Moscow 'high command post,' centered in a busy house not many blocks away from the United Nations: the Soviet Mission to the United Nations. Soviet nationals at the U.N. and staff employees from Iron Curtain satellites are part and parcel of this 'high command post' . . . It is the nerve center on this side of the Atlantic Ocean for almost every phase of the Kremlin's subversive activities in North and South America."[14]

In addition to their own delegations, the Communists have succeeded in planting a number of employees on the staff of the U.N. itself. The Central Intelligence Agency, looking into the matter at the request of Senate investigators, gave this breakdown of a list of 100 U.N. employees from Communist-controlled nations:

a) Thirty-two of the employees were engaged in active work for the intelligence agencies of their respective countries.

b) Twenty-nine others were high-ranking Communist Party officials. . .

c) Twenty-one more were engaged in active Communist organization work of an underground or subversive nature outside their native homelands.

d) Fifteen others were not in the CIA's "derogatory information file."

e) The remaining three had definite pro-American sympathies or had shown disaffection with Communist ideology.[15]

In other words, 82 out of the 100 employees were actively working in behalf of Communism. In addition, the committee found the U.N. was a haven for American subversives and security risks. In a statement issued January 28, 1953, the committee said "nearly a score of the Americans employed by the U.N. refused to testify before the subcommittee as to whether they are involved with the Communist Party or not, and some even declined to say whether they ever had engaged in espionage against the United States." Senator Pat McCarran (D-Nev.), chairman of the subcommittee, commented: "I realize that the United Nations secretariat cannot recognize Communist affiliations as a bar to employment of persons who are citizens of a Communist state, but that is no excuse for allowing one disloyal person to contaminate the American group or misrepresent our ideals."[16]

The net conclusion of Huss and Carpozi is that "Communist terrorists, wholesale killers, spies, and subversive agents did, in fact, hold jobs with the United Nations and its subsidiary organizations."[17]

The U.N. example suggests the unfortunate results which flow from the most massive of all East-West exchanges—the Free World's exchange of diplomats with the USSR and other Communist states. Despite such premonitions, however, the Johnson regime has been seeking to expand this particular exchange by a treaty to swap consulates with the USSR—setting up Soviet diplomatic offices, enjoying immunity from American law, in the major communities of the United States. Reciprocal privileges would be granted us, assertedly, inside the USSR.

The exchange is advertised as a great boon to peace and improved understanding between the U.S. and the USSR. One Liberal Democrat says: "It is important to remember that all provisions of the treaty are reciprocal—neither nation will be given any advantage over the other. There is some reason to believe that this convention could be an important step forward in trying to improve the relations between the United States and the USSR."[18]

FBI Director Hoover, the nation's premier expert on

Communism, views the proposal with less enthusiasm. He describes the step applauded by Liberal spokesmen as "a cherished goal of Soviet intelligence." The FBI chief has testified that "one Soviet intelligence officer in commenting on the agreement spoke of the wonderful opportunity this presented his service and that it would enable the Soviets to enhance their intelligence operations."[19]

That this is self-evidently true may be discovered by noting that the bulk of existing Soviet embassies and consulates, like the U.N., are established focal points of espionage, subversion, and political agitation. In a 1960 report on Communist espionage, Hoover observed that Moscow's "primary intelligence activities . . . against the United States" are directed from "Soviet embassies, consulates, trade delegations, news media, the United Nations, and the Amtorg Trading Corporation."[20]

A former Soviet intelligence agent, Hoover continued, "has estimated that from 70% to 80% of the Soviet officials in the United States have some kind of intelligence assignment."[21]

Under the exchange-of-consulates proposal, this percentage would no doubt be increased—since the treaty would give the Soviets absolute immunity for all crimes including espionage. This is the first time in history that the U.S. has entered into a treaty conferring such sweeping immunity.

Senator Jack Miller (R-Iowa) observed that we have in the past granted immunity for minor offenses, but "for murder, for espionage, there is no immunity that has ever been granted." Even without immunity, he noted, Communist representatives in this country had engaged rather extensively in espionage. With immunity, the imagination boggles at the scope of activity which would be opened up to the more than 800 Communist functionaries now stationed on American soil.[22]

In describing the exchange-of-consulates idea with such

glowing enthusiasm, Liberal spokesmen usually make no reference to these important facts. When Hoover's statements are brought to their attention, they counter with the suggestion that our own intelligence operatives can get the same kind of results from our embassies and consulates behind the Iron Curtain.

For the moment, we may pass over the curious reasoning which views an exchange of espionage outposts as a step toward "better understanding." The apposite point is that, contrary to Liberal assertion, our own intelligence operatives do not and cannot derive the same benefits from our installations in Russia as do Communist operatives from their installations here.

In the first place, the USSR is a closed society, while ours is an open one. Communist officials can secure voluminous information about us from phone books, the public media, the patent office and other government agencies, etc.—simply by being here. Our own diplomats in Moscow, where there is not even a public phone book, cannot obtain critical information with similar ease.

In the second place, it is impossible for us to make intelligence and espionage a function of our embassies in Communist lands after the fashion of the Communist practice described by Hoover. It is well-known that the Communists so thoroughly penetrate diplomatic outposts in their countries, staffing them with Red agents and bugging them with electronic listening devices, that we could not derive comparable benefits from these installations even if we wanted to.

Our diplomats have apparently forgotten that memorable day at the United Nations when Ambassador Henry Cabot Lodge displayed the eagle presented to us as a token of friendship by the Soviets—complete with concealed microphone. They also must have forgotten that Lodge and Rear Admiral Leslie Stevens have testified that, when conversing in the U.S.

embassy in Moscow, they invariably spoke "for the mike," because they knew the Soviets were listening.[23]

It seems highly doubtful that parallel arrangements can be made by our government at Soviet installations in America. All personnel in Communist offices in the United States are Soviet citizens, loyal to the Communist government; whereas many clerical, maintenance and other personnel in U.S. offices behind the Iron Curtain are also Soviets, loyal to the Communist government. As of 1960, there were 195 Americans and 93 Soviets in the U.S. embassy in Moscow; there were 271 Russians and zero Americans in the Russian embassy in Washington.[24]

The "reciprocal" advantage derived from these installations is, therefore, of a very peculiar kind: the Soviets gain from their embassies and consulates in the United States, and the Soviets gain from our embassy and consulates in Russia. The proposed exchange is indeed a two-way street—but both ends of the street empty into the porticos of the Soviet secret police.

★★ *Part III:*

THE DISARMAMENT LOBBY

. . . acceptance of any precipitate program of disarmament . . . would constitute for the West a strategic defeat of enormous magnitude, leaving an irresolute Western world only the recourse of seeking accommodation with an aggressive movement which is dedicated to achieving mastery of the globe.

—Report of the Senate Internal Security Subcommittee

★★ 13. *Is There a Stalemate?*

1. *The Balance of Terror*

WE TURN NOW to Establishment doctrine in the crucial area of defense. To do so, we must first examine the doctrine of "the stalemate." All official theorizing about military defense against Communism takes place against the backdrop of "stalemate"—or, as it is sometimes phrased, "the balance of terror"—an assumed standoff in which the United States and the Soviet Union each has the capability of destroying the other, and neither can successfully defend its people against the terrors of nuclear exchange.

Here, for example, is the statement of one influential spokesman: "That military superiority is no longer purchasable *at any price* is a conclusion Americans are finding very hard to take . . . [The] change of advantage in favor of the offensive in nuclear war marks the termination of meaningful military advantage among nations, each of whom is equipped with major nuclear offensive capability . . . Each side [can] destroy the other, and neither side [can] defend itself against attack by the other . . ."[1]

A similar utterance comes from a high-level study subsidized by the Department of Defense:

> The United States has lived in recent years with a strategic 'balance of terror,' and there has been much discussion about how delicate the balance is . . . Because of . . . trends in weapons, effective retaliation against surprise attack in either direction is increasingly guaranteed . . . This 'stability,' associated essentially with the notion of certain strategic retaliation, is not likely to be upset by new strategic developments.[2]

These assertions, or something like them, could be crystallized out of almost every major policy statement of our defense and foreign policy specialists. The image of a standoff between giants, each capable of obliterating the other with nuclear-tipped missiles, controls the diplomacy of the State Department, holds a squirming populace in line when called on to accept national indignities, is cited by fierce anti-Communists demanding a greater sense of free world urgency, underlies most sophisticated works of military theory.

With belief in a nuclear impasse so widespread and such important consequences depending from it, we must have at hand a solid body of information showing what kind of nuclear hardware the Soviet Union possesses, and some degree of certainty about the delivery systems by which they are assertedly able to rain destruction on our cities. We must—or more exactly, we should; but in point of fact we don't.

It is perhaps the most curious feature of a curious policy, but the truth is that those who seek to limit and direct our national behavior by the frustrating imperatives of "the stalemate" have paid slight attention to the question of whether the Soviet Union has *in fact* reached a level of military strength equivalent to our own. Even the most thoughtful students of national policy are, it appears, willing to accept this crucial point with only perfunctory attention to the particulars in the case, and with a great deal of reliance on Soviet assertion.

What, after all, do we *know* about Communist military strength? We know, to begin with, that the Soviets have large land armies, tanks, MIG fighter planes, and so forth. We know this because countless Western observers have seen these things during World War II, in Korean combat, in Eastern Europe, in the Soviet Union itself. We know additionally that the Soviet Union can set off large nuclear explosions of some sort because we have radiological evidence in substantiation of this. And we know the Communists have a number of short-range and intermediate range ballistic missiles, because we have seen these in Cuba and Viet Nam, and have tracked missile tests of some sort on our radar screens in Turkey.

That knowledge adds up to a formidable military establishment of a kind. But it does not add up to anything like the defense arsenal of the United States as of, say, 1960, when we had 1,700 long-range bombers capable of delivering 36 megatons of destructive power in a few hours' time to any spot on the globe. In particular, it does not add up to a defensive arsenal which could inflict immensely damaging blows on the United States equivalent to the damage we could inflict on the USSR.

If the public evidence does not validate the balance of terror, what does? There are four principal answers to this question: (1) Soviet assertion—Moscow *says* it has nuclear and delivery capabilities equal to, or better than, our own; (2) Soviet space performance—the sputniks and cosmonauts of the Communists allegedly prove Moscow has a missile delivery capability which can bombard the United States;

(3) official intelligence about Soviet space and missile capabilities not available to the public; and (4) Western assumption—the idea that, whatever the state of our information, we would do well to assume Moscow's power equivalent to our own, in order to avoid underestimating our enemy.

Of these four sources of authority on the stalemate, the first need concern us for the shortest span of time. Moscow's assertions are, notoriously, the least reliable evidence in the world. The Soviets have a long and notable history of deceit and falsification of data—including everything from ersatz peasant villages masking slave labor camps to the long-exploded hoax of Lysenkoism. There is small reason to assume the government which has falsified in other areas would not falsify in this one.

Concerning Moscow's alleged feats in space, suffice it to say we know very little indeed. Every Soviet space assertion—from the weight of the first sputniks to the "lunik" photographs of the moon to the adventures of the cosmonauts—has been shrouded in secrecy and confusion. Confirmation of critically relevant data in each case usually comes back to accepting what the Soviets tell us; and, as this writer has had reason to discover in some eight years of checking Soviet space claims with governmental officials and scientific authorities, the job of arriving at such confirmation has been accomplished by ignoring various oddities and discrepancies in the Soviet presentation. We are left with something we do not know very much about as "proof" of something else we do not know very much about; indeed, we know a good deal less about the proof than we do about the matter it is supposed to settle.

Let us, however, simply grant what has yet to be established—that all or most of the doubts about Soviet space performance can be resolved in favor of Moscow; the principal issue remains. The space controversy is important chiefly as a source of inference about Soviet nuclear and missile capabilities. And what do we really know about those capabilities?

Does the Soviet Union have an Air Force comparable to our own? An industrial base capable of fueling a military machine comparable to our own? An ICBM force?

The "stalemate" argument has repeatedly told us it does—and at this stage relies on "intelligence" to prove its point. As one prominent aviation writer has put it, the notion of vast Soviet military power is affirmed by "intelligence reports on Soviet rocket development," the fact that "our intelligence services accumulated overwhelming evidence of startling Russian advances in ballistic missiles," "our own intelligence reports on Russian ballistic missiles progress," "secret testimony before congressional committees"—and so forth.[3] Assertions like these have been constantly employed to suggest the Kremlin is making vast strides in nuclear technology, industrial growth, airplane development, ballistic missiles.

This presentation, unless American officials have perjured themselves on the subject, is untrue. Responsible authorities have repeatedly confessed that, by and large, we really *don't* know such things. In 1957, when it was being widely asserted that "intelligence" showed the Soviets were ahead of us in missiles development, Secretary of Defense Neil McElroy testified "it is not clear to me that we are behind the Russians in the overall missile development . . . I don't believe we have positive knowledge as to whether we are behind, and I am quite sure we don't have positive knowledge as to whether we are ahead. . . . I have no assurance that they are ahead of us."[4]

In 1959, Hanson Baldwin, military editor of *The New York Times,* reported: "Despite the repeated alarms in Washington, hard evidence of Soviet capability of launching long-range missiles is still absent. No verification has reached this country of numerous reports still published here and abroad of the identification of ballistic missile launching pads. Several such reports have been investigated and found to be erroneous."[5]

2. *Those Missing 'Gaps'*

There have been at least four major instances in which important industrial-defense capability has been attributed to the Soviet Union on the strength of "intelligence" or Soviet assertion, only to prove out as illusion. In each of these, Moscow claimed and Western spokesmen acknowledged vast Soviet attainments. Yet we now know the things so freely granted on the basis of assumed "intelligence" information or otherwise were not true and should not have been granted.

The first of these instances occurred during the Korean War, when the concept of "stalemate" was employed to prevent resolute Western response to Communist aggression. We could not afford to hit Chinese Communist staging points to the north and west of the Yalu River, it was asserted, because such action might escalate into a nuclear war, involving the Soviet Union and its supposed atomic capability. This argument was based on the rather scanty evidence that the Soviets had set off some kind of nuclear explosion in 1949—from which it was reasoned by stalemate theorists that Moscow had achieved a nuclear arsenal comparable to our own. It was determined by the Rand Corporation in 1957 and is now universally acknowledged, however, that the Soviets in fact had no such nuclear arsenal at the time of the Korean conflict; the 1950 "stalemate" which prevented decisive action by the U.S. was a hobgoblin based on Soviet bravado and Western concession.[6]

The second instance was the so-called "bomber gap," allegedly discovered in 1955 and cried up by such Democratic spokesmen as Senator Stuart Symington of Missouri. In 1956, Symington asserted that "if you add together their modern long-range bombers, the Bison, and the Bear, they will have a substantial quantity margin over us as far in the future as we have estimates."[7] This assessment, widely trumpeted at the time and employed to sustain the image of "stalemate," is now also universally conceded to have been false. As Baldwin notes: "An important reassessment of Soviet bomber strength indicates that the production of the Russian long-range bombers—the Bison and the Bear—has been far less than was expected. . . . There is not much doubt that there are far more United States Boeing B-52 jet bombers in operation than there are Soviet Bisons, and the turbo-prop Bear seems to have been built only in small quantities."[8] Similar testimony has come from numerous other authorities and today is contested by no one.

A third instance concerned the matter of the Soviets' economic "growth rate." This is an important indicator in any assessment of "stalemate," since an advanced industrial base would be necessary to support a military system even remotely comparable to the gigantic establishment of the United States. If the Soviet Union really *was* enjoying a fabulous splurge of productivity and industrial advance, that would argue in favor of the stalemate. If it were not enjoying such an advance, that would do the reverse.

That the splurge was on, and that the Soviet Union was experiencing an economic renaissance of epic dimension, was a favored argument of presidential candidate John Kennedy back in 1960. We were, Kennedy said, falling dangerously behind the Kremlin in the matter of industrial growth, and this constituted one of the chief reasons why we had to "get this country moving again." Like the nuclear capability of 1950 and the bomber gap of 1956, however, this asserted excess of economic vigor wasn't so. The careful inquiries of economists Colin Clark and G. Warren Nutter showed, contrary to claims being advanced by and for Moscow, that the Soviets were a rather primitive industrial society with, for their station in life, a very bad growth rate indeed.[9] Today, after Moscow has staggered through subsequent agricultural and other economic crises, that point of view is more generally accepted. Very little is nowadays heard about the fabulous "growth rate" of the Soviet economy.

Which brings us to "the missile gap."

The years 1957-60 saw the United States terrorized by the idea that the Soviet Union had taken the lead over us in military rocketry. This so-called "missile gap" had been conjured up by the assertions of the Soviets about their space performance and their arsenal of ICBMs, and by the emotional response of many Western spokesmen including, most prominently, Senators Kennedy and Lyndon B. Johnson, who decried the "missile gap" and the consequent existence of nuclear stalemate or worse from every available forum. Kennedy stressed this theme early in his campaign and never relinquished it. On August 26, 1960, he said: "The facts of the matter are that we are falling behind in our rate of growth. The missile lag looms large." On October 1, he derided the Republican Party as the "party which gave us the missile gap." On October 4, he said "we do not have a defense second to none, and we are not in the lead in missiles . . ." On November 4, he put it that "we are now entering the age of the missile gap."[10] Similar utterances were proffered by Johnson.*

By 1959 or 1960, most Liberal spokesmen and military people—who had had different motives for crying up the nonexistent "bomber gap"—admitted no such thing had transpired. The Soviets, it was acknowledged, didn't have the kind of air force attributed to them; it had all been a mistake.

* In view of this performance, it is interesting to note the construction Kennedy gave to the "missile gap" myth his own words had created in his defense message to Congress in 1961. "It has been publicly acknowledged for several years," he said, "that the United States has not led the world in missile strength"—failing to point out that it had principally been "acknowledged" by himself while he was in the Senate and during the 1960 campaign; and also failing to point out that what had thus been "acknowledged"—as admitted by the Kennedy regime itself before Kennedy made this 1961 speech—was false.

Westerners who played up the Soviets' supposed might in this sphere had, not to put too fine a point on it, been taken. That fact suggested to prudent minds a certain degree of caution in assessing Moscow's new claims to wondrous achievements in missiles. To the Establishment mind, however, it suggested the opposite.

". . . there are many well-informed individuals in intelligence circles," wrote missile-gapper James Gavin, "who doubt that the Soviets have huge fleets of manned bomber aircraft. Instead, they believe that the Soviets achieved a significant lead over us by jumping ahead to missiles quite a few years ago, while at the same time they led us to believe that the bomber threat was the most serious."[11] In other words, the fact that Moscow fooled us with respect to airplanes was construed as evidence that they were *not* fooling us with respect to missiles. The non-existence of the bomber gap was proof positive of the missile gap.

But, as it turned out, the missile gap was false, too. Secretary of Defense McNamara confessed, in a February 1961 news briefing, that there wasn't any such thing after all; subsequent acknowledgments of the same sort came from Deputy Defense Secretary Roswell Gilpatric, and, somewhat elliptically, from Kennedy himself;* the non-existence of the missile gap at last became fully certified when *The New York Times* commented that "the same forces and the same congressional and journalistic mouthpieces who manufactured

* McNamara subsequently backed and filled about whether or not he had said the missile gap was non-existent, although reporters on the scene agreed this was precisely what he had conveyed to them. In the interest of face-saving, the New Frontier apparently sought to have the information about the "gap" come forward in trickles, giving the impression that the administration *had* found a gap and had rapidly filled it. In an article for *Look,* obviously based on extensive New Frontier briefing, Theodore White sets the time at which the gap was authoritatively disposed of as September, 1961; the McNamara disclosure, however, was in February, when the new regime had been in office only 18 days and had barely had time to inventory the materials passed on to it by the Eisenhower regime.

an alleged bomber gap in the 1950s sponsored, and invented, the alleged missile gap in the 1960s. . . ."**[12]

In his book on the Kennedy regime, Theodore Sorensen describes the outcry over the nonexistent "gap" as "honest error by both military and civilian officers," and states that "Kennedy's error in 1960 on the 'missile gap' had been the result of the public's being informed too little and too late . . ."[13] That is as it may be. The relevant point is that, for the fourth time in as many turns at bat, the heralds of Soviet strength and global stalemate had ignominiously struck out.

Just as the missile-gappers learned nothing from the bomb-gappers, so have the "balance of terror" theorists learned nothing from any of the episodes we have examined. That there was in fact no "balance" to speak of in 1950, or 1955, or 1960 is now apparent—even though we were in each of these years led to assume precisely the opposite. Yet even as past errors are grudgingly acknowledged, new ones are formulated to be put in their place, and the "stalemate" idea plugs along as durably as ever. Thus, one high-level study prepared by a government-supported agency notes the Cold War tendency to "overestimate the opponent's strength," and says: "The data obtained [from U-2 flights over the Soviet Union] indicated that the Soviet Union had not made significant progress in building a strategic force able to threaten American invulnerability."[14] The U-2 flights in question occurred in 1960, at the height of the "missile-gap" furore. At that time, America had an immense Strategic Air Command capable of obliterating any target in the USSR; if the Soviets

** Even Arthur Schlesinger Jr. concedes the awful truth of the matter, reflecting that inspection within the Soviet Union might "expose the myth of the 'missile gap,' which had become so politically beneficial to them, and reveal Soviet missile sites as low in number and high in vulnerability." Schlesinger does not acknowledge that the myth of the missile gap, so beneficial to the Soviets, was spread far and wide by his chosen presidential candidate and subsequent employer.

did not have "a strategic force able to threaten American invulnerability," then there was no balance, no stalemate, no stability. Yet the paper making this very point about 1960 takes the existence and frustrations of the "balance" as the central uncontested premise from which all its theories are derived.

3. *The Safe Assumption*

We come now to the ultimate source of authority for "the stalemate"—the idea that, whatever the real strength of the Soviet Union, it is prudent to accept Moscow's claims at face value. At this point we leave the realm of evidence for the world of policy, and approach, by virtue of that translation, the real reason for Liberal insistence upon "stalemate." The notion of equivalent nuclear arsenals on either side of the Iron Curtain is not, from the Liberal point of view, a matter to be decided by so vulgar a procedure as weighing the evidence; it is a necessary axiom from which the desired foreign policy can be suspended, and without which the policy can neither be made to work nor granted public acceptance.

That the stalemate idea is crucial to Liberal strategy has been partially obscured by the fact that a number of "hard" anti-Communists and military men have convinced themselves the idea is also useful from their point of view. This unanimity on the subject has insured that, despite the poverty of the evidence, the Kremlin's asserted might has achieved wide acceptance among the American people and in the free world generally.

The point of the "safe assumption" in hard anti-Communist theory is that the American people are too "complacent" about what is going on in the world, and—in a sort of Machiavellian conspiracy against them—it is up to those who are aware of the nation's peril to play along with Soviet claims as a means of waking everybody up. Unfortunately, this shock treatment has not had quite the therapeutic effect its advocates suppose. Consider, to take a prosaic example, the matter of inducing better output in our own missile project—a prime objective of the "safe assumption" tactic. The form in which America's corporate apathy normally finds expression, in the safe assumption view, is a failure to appropriate enough money for missiles. Yet responsible authorities connected with our program of military rocketry have testified that the program, prior to the rise of the safe assumption, had not been limited by lack of funds. Lt. Gen. Bernard Schriever, head of long-range missile development, repeatedly said our program was proceeding at optimum rates and could not be speeded simply by pumping in more money.

At the mechanical level, the "safe assumption" often tended to make things worse instead of better. Asked to explain a number of early failures in the testing schedule of the Atlas, DOD research chief Herbert York replied: "We have gotten somewhat frantic about catching up with the Russians. Most of our failures have been due to somebody taking a gamble, or not being able to think things through, or trying to save a month or two and taking a chance that something would work."[15]

Similar difficulties afflicted America's much-maligned Project Vanguard, originally scheduled for launching in mid-March, 1958. Under the lash of those convinced the Soviets' first two sputniks had put them years ahead in the race for space, the Vanguard technicians rushed to try a premature launching in December, 1957. The result—still vivid in memory—was a dismal burst of flame and flying debris. Six more such "failures" followed, all well-publicized, and the Vanguard was "at last" launched on March 17, 1958—exactly according to its original schedule. All its alleged failures, and all the stunning blows to American spirit and prestige, had been induced by our panicky belief that we were falling behind the Soviets.

The mechanical fallacies of the safe assumption, however, are relatively unimportant. Its essential error consists precisely in its obsessive concern with mechanical effects, and in its suggestion that the struggle against Communism can be won simply by producing quantities of arms.

Even sophisticated students of the world struggle like Edward Teller and Oskar Morgenstern have fallen into the habit of viewing the matter in these terms. In deciding to accept the safe assumption in his own thinking, Morgenstern writes, "I have been guided by the fact that if the enemy's strength is overrated *we are merely wasting our treasure and effort,* but if we underestimate him, we are forsaking our lives and the life of our country."[16] (Italics added.) It is of course true that to underestimate the enemy could prove to be a fatal error; but, precisely because the matter is not simply a mechanical equation, a gross *over*estimation can prove to be no less fatal—with consequences far beyond "merely wasting our treasure and effort."

To determine whether our problem is merely one of increasing the quantity of our armaments, or even of achieving the most radical of technological breakthroughs—as important as that is—we need only note that from 1945 to 1955, at a minimum, the United States was unquestionably the preeminent military power of the world. Yet in that same decade Communism scored repeated victories. We had the physical means of stopping the Communists; but we did not have the will to use them or the bargaining strength afforded by them. By accepting the Kremlin's portrait of itself as a missile-bearing colossus, we aggravate the deficiency chiefly responsible for our previous defeats. We weaken the will of the non-Communist world to resist the Communist advance.

During the furor that followed the announcement of Sputnik I, Scripps-Howard correspondent Ludwell Denny filed a dispatch from Europe suggesting the true psychological impact of what we have been assuming. "Russia's fantastically rapid rise," Denny wrote, "has created a kind of prestige which is unlikely to suffer from moral, political and diplomatic defeats of the type which now afflict the United States." He added that if the USSR "treated Poland to the Budapest butchery tomorrow, it would not diminish but add to the fear prestige which the conquest of outer space has given her."[17] When sentiments like these are abroad in the world, can it seriously be maintained that the "assumption" of Soviet might is a service to the cause of anti-Communism?

Through the paralysis of mind it induces, the fear psychology also brings us full circle and promotes a renewed belief in Soviet good will. Why has the West, after Hungary and all the other infamies in the Soviet record, shown such an elastic willingness to accept at face value any show of amity from Moscow? In part because the mind falters in disbelief before the idea of transcendent evil armed with transcendent power. George Kennan makes this clear when he states that "in the predication of only the worst motives on the adversary's part there lies, today, no hope at all."[18] Because we cannot live without hope, and because we have forbidden ourselves to gainsay Soviet power, we keep returning to the notion that someday, somehow, the Communists will stop being Communists, and we will be released from our sojourn in hell.

The safe assumption additionally misconceives the nature of Soviet strategy and frustrates our own. To understand the full intellectual calamity of what we have assumed, one must first understand the concept of "deterrence." The point of deterrence is to scare the enemy into abstaining from activities you don't like. A nation operating in terms of it builds up a stockpile of weapons, not with the intention of using them, but to let the enemy know the wherewithal exists to survive any possible attack and destroy him. *The main point of "deterrence," therefore, is the mental image the enemy has of your capabilities.* By convincing ourselves the Soviets have sufficient striking power to obliterate us, we are yielding them the object of the deterrence game at the outset. We spend $50 billion annually to deter them—and then deter ourselves with one quick assumption!

But that is not all. Given the flexibility of Soviet techniques of aggression—including subversion, revolution, and local hostilities by proxy regimes—the stalemate is really no stalemate at all. As Raymond Garthoff has put it, "the employment of nuclear and thermonuclear weapons is necessary in the United States concept, but not in the Soviet one . . . *If a genuine stalemate in intercontinental capabilities is achieved in a pre-hostilities period, the United States might be endangered by the neutralization of its entire strategy, and hence of its ability to act, whereas the Soviet strategy would be served by this development.*"[19] (Italics added.)

This is precisely what has happened, with the difference that the "stalemate" has been achieved, not by demonstrable Soviet performance, but by our own assumption. In the name of prudence we have deliberately fettered ourselves and freed the Soviets to go about their work of global revolution. The stalemate grants to the Communists a zone of absolute immunity from our policy (because excursions into Eastern Europe or beyond the Yalu or wherever would "escalate" us into nuclear war); relative freedom from the nuclear power which is America's main strength to employ the conventional, guerrilla, and proxy warfare techniques which are Communism's main strength; and, most important of all, a prolonged "pause" of indefinite duration in which the struggle is joined only when and where the Communists want it to be joined, and they have precisely as much or as little time as they want to develop their own strategic defenses.

The nature of the stalemate assumption is such, finally, that it tends to be self-perpetuating. It causes us to attribute to the Soviets every new gain that we achieve, so that our part in the "arms race" becomes very much like that of the dog who chases his tail. In order to be "safe," we assume Soviet capabilities to be at least equivalent to our own and goad ourselves into more energetic work. But if and when that work pays dividends, we find we have really achieved nothing at all, strategically speaking, because the safe assumption requires that we *again* assume Moscow's forces to be equivalent to our own. The chief result of pushing our own work harder is to endow the Soviets with all our hard-won capabilities, and to project to our own people an ever-growing image of Soviet might.

There is, of course, no intrinsic reason why Moscow could not at some future date catch up with or surpass the United States in nuclear armaments and delivery systems—particularly if we grant them all the time in the world to achieve such things while simultaneously cutting back our own work in these fields. A sustained program of technological advance by the Communists, and a long-term contraction of our own arms program, could ultimately produce a situation in which the two curves meet and cross, with the Communists emerging on top.

It is the crowning irony of the "safe assumption" that it has conjured up a world in which precisely these two lines of development—or, in our case, non-development—are being pursued. In the name of safely assuming Moscow to have immense power relative to our own, we may well be on our way to making precisely such a transformation of strategic relationships a reality.

★★ 14. *The Nuclear Terror*

1. *Our Atomic Shield*

"IT IS CERTAIN that Europe would have been Communized like Czechoslovakia, and London under bombardment some time ago, but for the deterrent of the atomic bomb in the hands of the U.S."[1]

When Winston Churchill uttered those words in 1949, he was stating an obvious but neglected truth: The Free World, to the extent it has remained free, has done so because the Soviet Union fears the nuclear arsenal of the United States. He was also expressing America's own assessment of its strategic potential. The defenses of the United States are, in a word, atomic. This was true when Churchill spoke; it is doubly true today. All of our important weapons systems, down to the battlefield weapons of our ground forces in Europe, are geared to the employment of nuclear energy. Subtract the nuclear element and we would be without strategic defenses.

This being so, our atomic weapons have not surprisingly been an object of great concern on the other side of the Iron Curtain. Since the inception of the Cold War, the Communists have waged an unremitting propaganda attack against our nuclear arsenal. As the official platform of the Communist Party of the USSR puts it: "The peoples must concentrate their efforts on curbing the imperialists in good time and preventing them from making use of lethal weapons."[2] In the early post-war years, this campaign took the form of bitter diatribes about the "immorality" of nuclear weapons; to Moscow, they were "immoral" for the simple reason that we had them and the Communists didn't.

In the late 1950's the Communists altered their attack to focus on a hitherto unexploited propaganda bonus. By crying up the dangers of radioactive fallout, they sought to suggest nuclear weapons were dangerous to their owners physically as well as morally. Not only were atomic testers enmeshed in "sin," they were also in danger of contracting cancer and of transmitting it to their children. This program of terror was complemented by Moscow's claims of nuclear, aerial, and missile power equal or superior to that of the United States. In the 1960s, as a result, universal fear became the ambiance in which all discussions of nuclear weapons and foreign policy were suspended. In any given crisis, the Communists could be counted on to rattle their supposed arsenal of ICBMs, neutral nations to inveigh against all resort to atomic weaponry, and Western statesmen to involve themselves in endless speculation as to whether this or that course of action would lead to nuclear oblivion.

Communist motives in inducing this state of affairs were obvious: Fear of nuclear weapons helps achieve Free World backdown in the crisis at hand; it neutralizes the one force in the hands of the West which, above all others, has thwarted

Communist objectives; and, to the extent it can be brought to panic proportions, it tends to divert global anxieties from Communist aggression to the defenses America has arrayed to forestall that aggression.

While Communist objectives in the nuclear controversy are rather clear, the motives of Western spokesmen in co-operating with Soviet propaganda initiatives are less apparent. At every phase of the Kremlin's anti-nuclear offensive, various elements in the West have thrown themselves exultantly into the fray. When the Communists preached nuclear guilt, various physicists and others dutifully felt "guilt." When the Communists cried up the danger of fallout, numerous Westerners immediately became frantic over fallout.

The most apparent motive for all this is the immense destructive power of atomic weapons. Should a total nuclear blow-up occur, millions of people would be killed. This supplies an obvious reason for wanting to avoid such a blow-up, and Western anxieties on this general score, even some of the more irrational ones, are therefore comprehensible. Less comprehensible are the inconsistencies of many bomb-banners and nuclear disarmers in more particular phases of nuclear controversy.

It is interesting to note, for example, that many of the Liberals who today inveigh against nuclear weapons were quite satisfied with mass civilian bombings in World War II. And it was these very tactics which led, in the assaults on Dresden, February 13, 1944, to the death of 100,000 Germans and war refugees—the latter referred to, in one British press report, as an unexpected "bonus."[3] Why are we invited to feel guilt for having killed 70,000 people in Hiroshima but not invited to feel guilt for having killed 100,000 people in Dresden?

One answer is that nobody is trying to *make* us feel guilty about Dresden, while a number of people are trying very hard indeed to make us feel guilty about Hiroshima. Dresden was bombed with conventional weapons, which are not the object of an intensive propaganda campaign; Hiroshima was bombed with atomic weapons, which are the object of an intensive propaganda campaign. We do not feel guilty about the first; we do feel guilty about the second.*

In the second place, the casualty ratios resulting from the advance of Communism itself are well within the range of those envisioned in nuclear battle. Exact estimates as to the number of people killed by the Communists in the past 50 years are hard to come by, but the total number is not improbably something like 40 million. Should the Communists be allowed to conquer the rest of the world, as they would were we to lay down our arms, the number exterminated in the United States alone would probably reach something like 50 million. The number throughout the rest of the world might be as high. In addition, there are quite possibly as many as 30 million people in slave labor camps now behind the Iron and Bamboo Curtains. In a predictably recalcitrant nation like the United States, the figure would be easily as high, with an equal number in other nations of the Free World. The total number of those to be killed and imprisoned by the Communists could be reasonably estimated at upwards of 200 million.

Stefan Possony, a noted authority on Communism, writes: "The Bolshevik revolution has exacted a blood and demographic toll of the peoples within the Soviet Union which ranges anywhere from 15 to 25 per cent . . . If the U.S. were to suffer a fate similar to that of Russia, the human toll of our nation would reach about 45 million . . . worldwide, with the

* An additional distinction between the two episodes: Dresden was full of refugees fleeing from the Soviet advance into Germany; the bombing stopped them and made the Soviet mopping-up operation that much easier. The bombing of Hiroshima brought the Pacific War to a sudden conclusion, thwarting Soviet efforts to jump into the fray and to deal themselves in on the occupation of Japan. Dresden served Soviet strategy; Hiroshima frustrated it.

old safety valve of emigration blocked, the blood toll would reach into the hundreds of millions."[4]

These figures are, of course, guesses; but so are the figures employed by the chroniclers of nuclear hysteria. Yet the statistics on Communist slaughter, many of them already a matter of record, are totally ignored—while the statistics on nuclear death, almost all of them a matter of futuristic speculation, are trumpeted endlessly.

The consistency of the bomb-banners comes further into question when we ruminate their willingness to fall in with anti-nuclear campaigns when the question of strategic exchange and "megadeaths" is in no way involved, and when the campaigns are premised in demonstrable falsehood. The anti-nuclear contingent has shown itself more than willing to propagate false information about atomic weaponry—covering such matters as fallout, the detectability of tests, "accidental war," and so forth—quite anterior to and separate from the question of "holocaust" which ordinarily concerns them; which, indeed, by leading the United States to grave miscalculations about the performance of these weapons and the behavior of the enemy could make such a holocaust more likely, rather than less.

It is on these subsidiary points that nuclear confusion has become rife, and it is these points which have, one by one, caused the United States to back away from its nuclear defenses.

2. *Facts On Fallout*

The agitation about fallout is perhaps the most celebrated of all nuclear themes—and perhaps the most successful campaign of alarmism ever foisted on the American people. The fact is that radiation from atmospheric nuclear tests poses no danger to the health of this generation, or of those to come, comparable to the influences under which all of us already live out our everyday lives.

The natural background radiation of the earth is up to 60 times more intense than the radioactivity from atomic tests. Irradiation experienced by people living in brick houses or at high altitudes, wearing luminous dial wristwatches or taking an occasional X-ray for medical reasons is also much greater than that from tests. Dr. Willard Libby has observed that "persons living at high altitudes on granite rocks always have received extra radiation many times greater than is contained in radioactive fallout from the testing of nuclear weapons, and . . . even those living on certain sedimentary rocks at sea level always have received ten to twenty times the present fallout dose."[5]

After a two-year study, a special scientific committee of the United Nations concluded that 100 years of continued atmospheric testing would yield only four per cent of the radiation mankind receives from natural sources. And findings issued by the Swiss Academy of Medical Sciences similarly inform us that "the present increase in atmospheric radioactivity and in radioactive precipitation plays no essential part and has no practical importance compared with natural radiation. The values which have been recorded do not, in any case, constitute a danger to the health of mankind."[6]

In 1960, the Federal Radiation Council similarly found in a comparison of radiation from tests with natural background radiation that "the average exposure to the U.S. population from activities of the nuclear energy industry, under current practices, is less than that from background by a substantial factor." The report further noted, despite the constant influence of background radiation and the great variations in it between one place and the next, "any differences in effects that may result have not been sufficiently great to lead to attempts to control background radiation or to select environment with background radiation in mind."[7]

Dr. Shields Warren, an acknowledged authority on this subject, points out that there are people in India who have lived for centuries in a monazite rock area where background radiation is 5 to 20 times the average level. There is no evidence that these people have experienced any deleterious results. Dr. Edward Teller and Dr. Albert Latter similarly note that "the difference between living in a brick house and living in a wood house could give rise to ten times as much radiation as we are currently getting from fallout."[8]

Earl H. Voss, in his comprehensive book, *Nuclear Ambush,* sums up the comparison this way: "Man's natural environment gives him a 70-year dose of radiation 17 to 35 times greater than he will receive from fallout from all tests by all countries of the world up to 1961 . . . The doses men receive from radioactive fallout are far too small for their effects to be noticed. At the peak exposure in May 1959, people in Illinois are estimated to have been absorbing a dose rate of eight-millionths of a roentgen per hour or one-fifteenth roentgen per year, had the peak dose persisted. [The minimum danger level is 25 roentgens.] The average annual dose from natural background radiation in the United States is one-tenth roentgen . . . Fallout radioactivity would have to deliver doses hundreds of times greater than the present dose to produce detectable results."[9]

One of the alleged dangers of testing is an increased incidence in leukemia through the accumulation of Strontium 90. This lament ignores the fact, disclosed by a team of British scientists, that the ordinary diet of the average Briton includes radioactive substances equivalent to about 300 times the maximum fallout dose of Strontium 90. It also ignores the report of the American Cancer Society that there is no provable connection between fallout and leukemia. Dr. C. L. Dunham, Director of the AEC's Division of Biology and Medicine, points out that the estimated impact of nuclear tests on leukemia and bone cancer are statistically negligible, involving a risk to the individual of 1/100,000 and 1/300,-000, respectively.

The Federal Radiation Council states that "We have no documented evidence that bone depositions of strontium have produced leukemia. Statements that radiostrontium is leukemogenic are based solely on studies of mice. Since leukemia is a common disease spontaneously occurring in certain strains of mice, one cannot accept this observation as necessarily applicable to man."[10]

Concerning somatic effects resulting from projected atmospheric tests over the next 70 years, Dr. Dunham comes to this conclusion:

> In the same 70-year period we can confidently expect 2,800,000 deaths from automobiles unless something is done about it. In my own opinion, a much more useful purpose would be served by strict enforcement of a no-driving-after-drinking law such as they have in Norway and Sweden than by tampering with the diets of infants and children in an endeavor to produce a fraction decrease in Strontium-90 burden as has been advocated by some persons.[11]

Dr. Dunham also observed in 1963 that, owing to the small amount of radiation emitted from U.S. nuclear testing, the resulting exposure levels had "been well below accepted levels for normal peacetime activities."[12] Even after the Soviet Union's relatively "dirty" tests of 1962, congressional authorities Chet Holifield (D-Calif.) and Melvin Price (D-Ill.) found resulting radioactivity levels "apparently within the current acceptable limits."[13] These and other conclusions about the biological effects of radiation caused the Northwestern National Life Insurance Company, looking into the matter from a businessman's point of view, to conclude:

"Based on even the 'scare' estimates, dangers to human life and health from [nuclear weapons] testing are far too slight to be considered in insurance rate calculations. The hazard from test fallout is found statistically comparable to the risk run by the average American that he will drown in a bathtub."[14]

In sum, there is no scientific evidence that the level of natural background radiation—relatively low although immense compared to fallout from nuclear tests—is harmful. There is even evidence that small amounts of radiation extend the life span. Against those conclusions, the radiation level attained by nuclear fallout—estimated at about one-ten-thousandth of the minimum danger level—can hardly be accounted a menace justifying the paralysis of our strategic arsenal.

It is sometimes argued that, whatever the immediate effects of nuclear fallout, the genetic effects will be something else again—leading to mutations and increased incidence of leukemia and other diseases in generations to come. This is even less supported by evidence than are arguments about somatic effects. Thorough documentation on this subject has been compiled by Drs. J. V. Neel and W. J. Schull, University of Michigan geneticists who analyzed the radiation results of the World War II A-bomb explosions in Japan. Although fallout exposure there was far more direct and intense than would be anything released by current nuclear devices, these experts found no significant genetic differences due to radiation. "Analysis of the frequency of malformed infants by city and parental exposure," they concluded, "reveals no significant consistent effect of parental exposure."[15]

Dr. Stafford Warren of the UCLA medical school similarly noted of the Hiroshima and Nagasaki results that "there have been no obvious genetic effects that could be assigned to radiation as a result of the atomic bomb drops of World War II."[16] And Dr. Marshall Brucer of Oak Ridge states in the *Journal of the American Medical Association* that "the radiation from the Hiroshima bomb beyond 2,000 yards did not produce any additional leukemia. We have positive evidence that there have been no more genetic abnormalities among the children of the exposed Japanese than among the non-exposed . . ."[17]

All of which indicates the hysteria stirred up about fallout was without foundation. One interesting measure of this fact is provided by the city of Denver, Colorado. Because of its high altitude, citizens of Denver are exposed to more radiation than are the citizens of, say, New Orleans or San Francisco. The radiation received from cosmic rays by the average American is about one-thirtieth of a roentgen. But in Denver it is about half again as much—still well below the minimum danger level. This small difference is vastly larger than the amount of radiation received from atomic tests. The extra annual dosage of radiation in Denver (about one-sixtieth of a roentgen) is many times greater than the annual effects of fall-out radiation at their peak (about one-three-hundredth of a roentgen).

Thus, if the opponents of nuclear testing were truly concerned about what "may" happen as a result of *any* increased radiation, they could better have spent their time and energy promoting a bill in Congress to have the citizens of Denver evacuated to New Orleans or San Francisco. There would have been, however, one catch even to that plan: Contrary to the allegedly fatal effects of *any* increased radiation, bone cancer and leukemia rates are considerably lower in Denver than in the other two cities.

3. *The Test-Ban Trap*

Despite all of this, the continued litany of dismay over the dangers of "fallout" pressed the United States relentlessly toward a cessation of its nuclear test program. In service to reigning misconceptions about fallout, a whole series of new misconceptions were devised about the feasibility of a test-ban with the Soviet Union. These became particularly dominant in 1961, when President Kennedy sent his team of negotiators to Geneva to meet with the Communists. The result was a staggering series of Western concessions.

It had been the American position during previous negotiations that achievement of a treaty depended upon "adequate inspection." To this end our negotiators had urged a picket line of 200 seismic wave detection stations around the world, which could record tremors from possible nuclear explosions. The Air Force's Rand Corporation, however, had found that underground explosions, properly contrived, could not be recorded by these inspection devices. And it was established that underground blasts frequently simulate earthquakes—a point proponents of the ban once attempted to deny. All of which meant we could not be certain whether the Soviet Union was testing nuclear weapons.*

Such facts meant all hopes for policing a treaty on general test suspension were doomed to disappointment. It was scientifically impossible for the Geneva negotiations to establish procedures insuring Moscow would not test atomic weapons in secret while we stopped testing. Logically, therefore, the general test-ban negotiations should at this point have been cancelled. When we discover a given set of methods to be unworkable, the rational course is to abandon them. The anti-nuclear school however, prefers to hang on to the methods while altering the objective. Those who had been saying

* Dr. Harold Brown of the Lawrence Radiation Laboratory was questioned by Senator Bourke Hickenlooper: "Would you not say that the probabilities of locating almost any size of underground atomic explosion where there was a determined effort at concealment of the location . . . is practically nil?" Dr. Brown's answer: "I think it is very small. For practical purposes I think it may be quite close to zero." Similarly, John McCone, former Chairman of the Atomic Energy Commission, said we had no instruments capable of monitoring nuclear tests within the vast expanse of the Soviet Union. All these findings confirmed the 1958 judgment of Dr. Edward Teller, that "a nuclear explosion is a violent event, but in the great expanses of our globe such tests can be effectively hidden if appropriate care is taken to hide them. There can be no doubt that this is possible."

we could and must have "adequate inspection" of a test ban admitted they were wrong, that we were unable to know what the Soviets were up to. But rather than reverse their performance, they simply shifted their premises: Negotiate a treaty anyway, they urged, and trust the Soviets to live up to it. Or, as the Associated Press put it: "The more the problem of detecting underground explosions is studied, the more it becomes apparent that some element of trust will have to be built into the treaty."[18]

American negotiators, acting on this premise, proceeded to grant one point after another to their Communist counterparts. In the words of Senator Thomas Dodd, "the dreary sequence of Western concessions followed by increased Soviet intransigence, followed by further Western concessions, has repeated itself like a cracked phonograph record."[19] Precisely as the AP's suggestion had indicated, our negotiators had been so eager to disarm they had reduced us to favoring an unenforceable general ban on nuclear testing—a ban which would depend upon the "good faith" of the participants.

Senator Dodd recited a list of 13 concessions our government had made in the course of these negotiations. The most striking had to do with the use of detection systems to discover cheating. To prevent secret testing, our government in 1958 had called for a global network of more than 600 monitoring stations. This position was later compromised to 180 monitoring stations world-wide, 21 of them in the Soviet Union. In August, 1962, we compromised with our compromise, reducing the requested number of global stations to 80.

As if this were not enough, we also backed off on the question of on-site inspections. As noted, monitoring stations sometimes cannot distinguish nuclear explosions from earthquakes. Therefore, on-site inspections would be necessary in any test ban to determine whether certain types of "seismic event" were in fact atomic tests. Originally, our negotiators demanded on-site inspection of all such disturbances above the level of five kilotons, and of 20% of those below that size. In 1961, this demand was reduced to 20 on-site inspections annually. In 1962, it was reduced to 12 inspections, then to "eight or ten" a year. In 1963, it was reduced to seven.

To top it all off, we actually proposed that the monitoring stations "shall be maintained and manned by the nations of the states in whose territory such station is located."[20] As Senator Dodd observed: "If this principle is ever translated into reality, it will be tantamount to creating a situation in which the Russians are charged with the responsibility of deciding whether or not they are cheating and whether or not to convey this information to us . . . It is as ridiculous as trusting gangsters to police themselves and faithfully report on their own misdoings."[21]

The attitude of our government on this subject was perhaps expressed best by Dr. Hans Bethe, who has made it clear he looks with favor on the prospects of trusting Moscow. Bethe had been part of an American team, back during the Eisenhower administration, charged with making sure no test-ban was arrived at which would allow the Soviets to cheat. He was involved in the demonstration that testing underground, with proper precautions, could be concealed. Far from being proud of this service to his country, however, Bethe feels only embarrassment. He makes this comment:

"I had the doubtful honor of presenting the theory of the big hole to the Russians at Geneva in November 1959. I felt deeply embarrassed in so doing, because it implied that we considered the Russians capable of cheating on a massive scale. I think that they would have been quite justified if they had considered this an insult and had walked out of the negotiations in disgust . . . We have been commended in the American press for this feat of theoretical physics. I am not proud of it."[22]

Dr. Bethe has served as one of the present administration's

top advisers on nuclear affairs. Considering his attitude on the shamefulness of suspecting the Soviets, it is hardly surprising that the administration backed its way by degrees into a situation where its "safeguards" against nuclear deception were not safeguards at all. The end result was that we wound up stipulating guidelines to prevent cheating which would actually have made cheating easier. As Henry Kissinger commented, "in some ways the control system might actually facilitate evasions by furnishing 'proof' of compliance even when secret testing was taking place."[23]

The evolution of safeguards which were not safeguards reached some sort of climax in 1962 when President Kennedy announced the United States had perfected its seismic detection system to enable it to distinguish a nuclear test anywhere in the world. Congressman Chet Holifield (D-Calif.) chairman of the Joint Atomic Energy Committee, thought otherwise. "I doubt very much if we are in a position as yet," Holifield said, "to detect all the explosions in any part of the world. Various explosions register differently in different types of earth. There are means of suppressing explosions, and while I supported the program . . . which is spending several million dollars in the attempt to prove our seismic detection capability, I believe that there is still a long way to go."[24]

In like manner, Congressman Craig Hosmer said that available scientific data "simply do not support the new position of the administration on the Geneva test ban. They are attempting to support a political decision by technical facts which do not exist."[25] As in the preceding negotiations, political preconceptions led the way, and "science" was cut to fit the ideological cloth. The Kennedy regime, it became clear, was determined to get an agreement on ending tests whatever the scientific evidence.

Such was the nature of the test-ban trap which the United States constructed for itself. In 1963, prodded by a new burst of hysteria over fallout, our government jumped in and pulled the lid shut.

★★ 15. *The Great Reversal*

1. *The Moscow Treaty*

WHEN SENATOR DODD SPOKE early in 1963, the Moscow test-ban treaty was already germinating toward reality. In July President Kennedy delivered a major address urging its passage, and in so doing abandoned the fruitless effort to match inspection stations with the Soviet Union, forgot about tests underground, and sought a "self-enforcing," uninspected ban on tests in the atmosphere and under water. In so doing, he conveyed to the nation a highly misleading impression of our ability to monitor nuclear events in the Soviet Union.

"A ban on nuclear tests," Kennedy said *". . . . required on-the-spot inspection only for underground tests.* This nation now possesses a variety of techniques to detect the nuclear tests of other nations which are conducted in the air or under water. For such tests produce unmistakable signs which our modern instruments can pick up."[1] (Italics added.)

From that statement, one would imagine the Soviet Union could not "cheat" on the Moscow agreement by conducting clandestine atmospheric or under-water tests. But the truth is otherwise. There are a number of ways to conduct both kinds of tests in secret—a form of behavior in which the Communists, whatever their other inadequacies, excel. *There is nothing to prevent clandestine tests under the Moscow treaty but the honor of the participating nations.*

There are four principal ways of detecting nuclear tests without rigorous on-site inspection: Fallout analysis, measurement of acoustic waves, seismographic readings, and monitoring radio signals generated by tests. Each of these methods except the second is useful in detecting atmospheric tests, and all four, plus some others, can be used to monitor tests under water. Unfortunately, each method has its weakness, which we may be sure the Soviets will not, should it suit their purposes, hesitate to exploit.

Fallout analysis is the most obvious means of determining whether or not a nuclear explosion has taken place. But suppose a test is conducted over the ocean, or in some uncharted territory like Antarctica? Fallout stored in the troposphere cannot be detected for weeks or months after the event, in which time the testing apparatus could be dismantled and moved. How then do we determine responsibility for the test? Conversely, fallout often stays in the stratosphere for years; what is to prevent the radioactive debris of some bygone test from being interpreted as a violation of the agreement? And when it is detected, how do we construct its meterological history with enough precision to fix its origin?

Equally in defiance of Kennedy's assurance, it is possible to stage low-yield nuclear tests in a thunder storm, so that radioactive materials are immediately "washed out." In this case, only the nearby area would be radioactive, and only the responsible nation would have access to the radiochemical evidence.

Similar considerations affect all the other "unmistakable signs" to which Kennedy referred. We have already commented on the fallibility of the seismographic evidence. In like fashion, acoustic waves can be altered and obscured by meteorological disturbances. And there are so many radio signals bouncing about in space that the job of picking out those caused by nuclear tests would be staggeringly complex.

These and other problems of nuclear detection have been spelled out in detail by such authorities as Dr. Teller, Admiral Lewis Strauss, Dr. John A. Wheeler, Congressman Craig Hosmer, and Earl H. Voss. During the 1958-61 moratorium on U.S. tests, these authorities suggest, the Soviets were in all probability continuing with their own program. Yet test-ban advocates then argued we should not resume our own program, *because we did not know for certain the Soviets were testing*. How, then, can it be argued that we shall now have reasonably accurate knowledge of the event if the Soviets are violating the Moscow treaty?

Even if all these objections could be satisfied, the test-ban treaty was and is a diplomatic Pearl Harbor for America. Because Communist China is not a signatory, nuclear tests inside its boundaries are not construed as violations of the agreement. What is to prevent the Soviet Union from conducting all the tests it wants in China? Such a maneuver would be conveniently covered by the "split" between Moscow and Peking and the mounting propaganda about China's alleged readiness to launch a nuclear program of its own. Having officially affirmed both of these items, the U.S. government is in no position to question a Kremlin disclaimer concerning "Chinese" tests.

The nuclear explosion which took place in Sinkiang Province in China in September, 1964 could easily have been a Soviet test. Sinkiang borders on the USSR, and is much closer to the Soviet military centers of Alma Ata and Tashkent than it is to any similar installations of the Chinese. For all we know, this nuclear event may well have been a Soviet violation of the test ban. But since China is not a signatory, Moscow could continue this kind of testing with impunity while we continued to abide by the treaty. Of similar disturbing potential were the mysterious explosions which occurred in Antarctica in 1963, almost at the precise moment that the test-ban treaty was moving toward ratification. Official confirmation of the polar explosions did not come until after the test-ban had been ratified in the Senate. According to Washington news man Hugh Fleming, "the official who disclosed the shot to the press related that the information had been withheld until the Senate had approved the treaty. The force of the explosion was estimated at 500 kilotons, or 25 times more powerful than the bomb which destroyed Hiroshima." A Washington newspaper quoted officials as saying "the blast could not have been man-made unless it was nuclear."[2]

It is argued by some test-ban advocates that, should Moscow want to break the agreement, it would be more likely to do so openly than secretly. But in that case, too, we lose important ground. Kennedy's 1963 suggestion that we can keep our scientists in constant readiness against a sudden violation does not square with his own previous statements. "We cannot keep top-flight scientists concentrating on the preparation of an experiment which may or may not take place on an uncertain date in the future," he said in March, 1962. "Nor can a large technical laboratory be kept fully alert on a standby basis waiting for some other nation to break an agreement. *This is not merely difficult or inconvenient—we have explored this alternative thoroughly, and found it impossible of execution . . .*

". . . the basic lesson of some three years and 353 negotiating sessions at Geneva is this—that the Soviets will not agree to an effective ban on nuclear tests as long as a new series of offers and prolonged negotiations, or a new un-inspected moratorium, or a new agreement without controls, would enable them once again to prevent the West from testing while they prepared in secret . . ."[3]

The 1963 treaty gave the Soviets exactly what Kennedy warned against: "a new agreement without controls," which will "enable them once again to prevent the West from testing while they prepared in secret."

In his speech urging enactment of the Moscow treaty, Kennedy described it as "a first step." Anyone examining the document and the arguments used in its behalf would certainly concur. The treaty is indeed a "first step." The question is—a step to where? Here are a few signposts:

1. The treaty is badly drafted. Its terms, on the face of it, commit the United States to abstain from using nuclear weapons in the face of a massive conventional attack by the Soviet Union in Europe. Precisely such a commitment has been the goal of Communist policy for years. This question was raised by Congress, and evoked assurances from the President. But, on the public record, no similar assurance was given that this was the understanding of the Soviet Union. If we cannot depend upon the language of the treaty itself, scant enough protection when dealing with Moscow, then surely the treaty is a poorly contrived piece of business.

2. Because it prevents the full development of any new weapons system requiring the use of nuclear warheads, the test-ban treaty tends to freeze the technological level of American defenses. In particular, it prevents us from running complete tests on the workability of our intercontinental ballistic missiles, upon which our strategic deterrent has come increasingly to depend. It prevents us from proceeding effectively with the development of an anti-missile defense system. And it prevents us from testing to perfect tactical atomic weapons.

3. Soviet preponderance in conventional forces—plus their proficiency in subversion, proxy warfare, guerrilla action and

internal revolution—means they do not need *superiority* in nuclear weapons. A nuclear *stalemate* fully serves their purposes. *If they can simply neutralize our atomic arsenal, then all of their techniques of global takeover can work unimpeded.* Even if the treaty is observed in every detail, it would therefore amount to a net loss for America since it would serve to hold all nuclear development at a standstill. If nuclear "stalemate" is achieved, "the United States might be endangered by the neutralization of its entire strategy, and hence of its ability to act, whereas the Soviet strategy would be served by this development."

4. The treaty, contrary to the original understanding, has interfered not only with our atmospheric tests but with underground tests as well. In September, 1963, it was discovered certain underground tests in Nevada had resulted in "venting"—escape of radioactive debris. This phenomenon makes the test-ban treaty doubly damaging. As the *Wall Street Journal* reported, "U.S. atomic weapons testers will have to take unusual and expensive precautions to prevent accidental venting of underground nuclear blasts so they won't give the Soviets grounds for charging that the new nuclear test ban treaty is being violated."[4] Conversely, the "venting" development gives the Soviet Union, for its part, a handy explanation for any fallout we detect wafting from behind the Iron Curtain: It's simply an accident, resulting from an underground test. Precisely this alibi was used to explain fallout from a Soviet test detected early in 1965.

5. Perhaps most important of all, the treaty is viewed as a "first step" toward "complete and general disarmament"—a program to which the United States is explicitly committed by the preamble. The document expresses the obligations formally assumed by the United States as ". . . the speediest possible achievement of an agreement on general and complete disarmament under strict international control in accordance with the objectives of the United Nations, which

would put an end to the armaments race and eliminate the incentive to the production and testing of all kinds of weapons, including nuclear weapons . . . the discontinuance of all test explosions of nuclear weapons for all time. . . ."[5]

The treaty, in sum, amounts to an official sanctification for the rhetoric of nuclear terror in the service of disarmament. That this language is more than idle prosing we shall have occasion to note in the following chapter.

2. *The 1964 Campaign*

The presidential campaign of 1964 saw the transformation of America's nuclear attitudes made virtually complete. Symbol of this transformation was a television commercial sponsored by the Democratic National Committee which showed a little girl picking daisies against the background of a simulated missile countdown, the whole dissolving in an explosion. The import of this commercial was that Republican nominee Barry Goldwater would, in some undefined manner, get the United States into a nuclear war; the premise behind it was that the American people were so afraid of nuclear weapons that this vague but terrible aspersion would infallibly predispose them against his candidacy.

The height of consternation in Republican circles was reached when Goldwater raised the question of how well our forces in Europe could respond to a massive Soviet ground attack. To forestall such an attack, Goldwater said, the Supreme Commander of NATO should have authority to use tactical nuclear weapons against Soviet armies. "The NATO commander," he asserted, "should not be required to wait until the White House calls a conference to decide whether these weapons should be used."[6]

Democratic orators leaped on this suggestion with both feet, and ran for all they were worth on a straight-out program of nuclear terror. Democratic convention keynoter Senator John Pastore said that "on the question of whose finger should be on the trigger of the atomic bomb, that power today rests solely with the President of the United States. That is exactly where it should remain; and we Democrats mean to keep it there . . . I am disturbed when I hear anyone speak so glibly and loosely on the use of these weapons and who should make the decisions to use them."[7]

Vice-presidential candidate Hubert Humphrey put it that "the question before the electorate is simple, prophetic, profound—which of these men, Lyndon Johnson or Barry Goldwater, do you want to have his hand on the nuclear trigger?"[8]

Johnson himself pulled all the stops in depicting the repulsive character of our defenses. "In the first nuclear exchange," he told a Labor Day audience in Detroit, "100 million Americans and more than 100 million Russians would be dead. And when it was over, our great cities would be in ashes, and our fields would be barren, and our industry would be destroyed, and our American dreams would have vanished."[9]

It would appear that no one could have stated the propaganda case against the weapons upon which our strategy depends in more lurid or frightening tones. In a later address, however, Johnson trumped himself by raising the ante to 300 million dead, not to mention "unborn generations forever maimed."[10]

The Democratic presentation, and Johnson's remarks in particular, raised a number of important questions. After all, our hope of deterring aggression depends, rather urgently, on Moscow's belief that we *would* under certain circumstances hazard a "nuclear exchange" to prevent Communist advance. Johnson's words could only lead the Communists to believe that we would not in fact employ our monstrous defenses: the Communists therefore have reason to believe, should they attack, that our response might be fatally delayed or inhibited and be encouraged to new aggressions.

Also harmful was the impact of this campaign on our own thought processes. The thrill of horror generated by the idea of the NATO commander's having authority to respond to Communist attack with battlefield nuclear weapons could only reinforce the idea, already abroad in the land, that the real menace in the Cold War is not the Kremlin, but the Pentagon. What *the Communists* might be able to do in the absence of effective retaliation was not, in the Democratic campaign oratory, so much as mentioned; what the terrible consequences might be should *our own commanders* have the power to retaliate was discussed at great and lurid length. The net effect was to accelerate the transfer of public anxiety from the Communist enemy to our own weapons and military men.

3. *Can We Strike Back?*

The 1964 campaign brought from the Johnson administration such strong protests that it would never allow an automatic response to Soviet aggression that it raised a further question crucial to American defenses: If the Communists launch a massive ground offensive in Europe, can we hit them quickly enough and hard enough to repel the invasion? Suppose the NATO commander in Europe cannot get hold of the President? What then? "A delay in responding to this attack with battlefield atomic weapons," former Vice President Nixon observed, "of even a few minutes, let alone hours, might result not only in losing the war but would endanger the lives of 250,000 American fighting men stationed in Europe."

Just what would happen under such circumstances has been left in doubt. A number of reports were developed to the effect that arrangements of the sort Goldwater was suggesting had already been made. *Time* magazine asserted:

Goldwater insists that the President should delegate such authority. Johnson lets on that he can't and won't. The fact is that he already does, as did Presidents Eisenhower and Kennedy before him. In 1957, the congressional Joint Committee on Atomic Energy received written notification that plans were being developed to give NATO's supreme commander in Europe the right to use nuclear weapons in certain contingencies—such as the incapacity of the President or the breakdown of communications between Europe and the U.S.[11]

Those plans, *Time* continued, "are now in operation," some written, some relayed by word-of-mouth. The magazine said former NATO commander Lauris Norstad, for example, was never in doubt about his authority to use tactical nuclear weapons in the event of a Red attack in Europe during the 1962 Cuban missile crisis.[12]

Similar intelligence appeared in *U.S. News and World Report,* which said that "even now, the understanding is widespread among NATO allies that U.S. commanders in Europe already have orders, issued in advance, to use nuclear weapons in certain emergencies with no further instructions from Washington."[13] The magazine also noted reports that "the administration itself was considering a move away" from the President-only authority over tactical nuclear weapons "before it became a domestic political issue. It is reported that intensive studies were under way in Washington about relaxing the U.S. 'veto' over use of certain nuclear weapons now shared by the allies of the North Atlantic Treaty Organization."[14]

It remained for former Vice President Nixon to supply the most informed estimate of our NATO defense system. President Eisenhower, Nixon said, had "provided that if a Communist attack occurred and the President was unable to issue the order for response with battlefield atomic weapons because of a communications breakdown, illness, or other reasons, that power under certain carefully defined circumstances could be exercised by the NATO commander."[15] Eisenhower felt strongly on this point, Nixon said, because his own three illnesses would have prevented him from issuing the necessary orders.

"The Eisenhower policy," Nixon asserted, "was continued by President Kennedy. Senator Goldwater has called for a reaffirmation of the Eisenhower policy so that the time will never come when because of a communications breakdown or other mishap our American forces in Europe would be at the mercy of a massive Communist attack and would not be able to respond with the battlefield atomic weapons without which the numerical superiority of the Communist forces is overwhelming."[16]

Was President Johnson saying, Nixon asked, that America's men at arms in Europe would, in such circumstances, be left to the mercy of the Communist war machine? The former Vice President posed six questions to the Johnson regime:

1. Has [President Johnson] revoked the Eisenhower procedure which gave the NATO commander authorization to use battlefield atomic weapons to respond to a Communist attack when a communications breakdown makes it impossible for the President to give this order?

2. If he has revoked the Eisenhower policy, what substitute procedure has he adopted, if any, to protect the security of American and other NATO forces in the event of such attack?

3. Is it not true that the entire NATO defense concept is dependent upon the use of America's nuclear power to repulse an attack?

4. It is not true that this NATO defense system will be gutted if the NATO commander is forbidden to react to an attack with battlefield atomic weapons unless and until the President alone, whether or not he happens to be available at the time, authorizes their use?

5. Is it not true that the whole grandiose electronic nuclear control machine President Johnson referred to on September 16 in Seattle will collapse completely if the indispensable communications system should fail?

6. Is it not true also that any aggressor against the United States would strike at those communications coincident with his nuclear attack which, if successful, would consign our whole retaliatory strike into the trash heap until and unless someone could let our NATO commanders know that the President would like them to start shooting back?[17]

It appears, in sum, that an arrangement like that suggested by Goldwater *had* existed (without bringing down on the heads of those responsible cries of "war-monger"), but that somewhere along the way it had been altered by the Johnson administration. Precisely when and precisely how it had been changed, and how much power if any had been left to the NATO commander, were still in question.

The campaign controversy, and Nixon's questions in particular, focused attention on an ominous possibility: We may have devised so many impediments to the employment of our strength that, in the event of a Soviet aggressions, we would not be able to use it. This is, in a way, the supreme irony of our situation. Precisely when it is suggested that some implausible accident might trigger the use of our weapons, the real dangers confronting us are of exactly the opposite kind. We should in fact be seriously examining the likelihood that we might not be able to use our atomic arsenal at all.

The controversy between Goldwater and Johnson concerned tactical weapons, not the strategic weapons which are our ultimate deterrent against Communist aggression. But these, too, are mantled in controls. In order for any one of these to be launched toward Moscow, either via plane or by intercontinental missile, a fantastically complicated series of steps has to be performed on explicit orders from the President.

In the case of our ICBMs, this authorization is received in code by the head of the Strategic Air Command, who must authenticate the message he has received. He must then send launching orders, again in code, to the missile command posts. When the command is received at all these individual posts, it must again be authenticated in terms of the code. The nuclear device within the warhead must then be armed. Even at this point, the missile crews cannot launch the missiles. The missiles can be launched only by electronic devices, to be triggered by "launch-enabling" signals transmitted from SAC headquarters. If any one of these things goes awry, no launch will occur.*

With manned aircraft, the procedure is equally complicated. As with the missiles, the bombers can be sent toward their targets only on presidential order. If there is reason to suspect an enemy attack, our bombers go to their "fail-safe" points and await further instructions. They proceed toward target only if they receive positive oral orders to do so, which also must be authenticated. If they receive no such orders, they return to base.

Like the warheads in the ICBMs, the bombs carried by our airplanes are in fact weapons systems. Even after the go-ahead signal is received and authenticated, these systems must be assembled by a number of crewmen. No single crewman can do the job, and no single crewman can arm one of these bombs or drop it by accident. Should the improbable combination of an insane pilot and an insane crewman disregard fail-safe procedure and try to arm the warhead, other crew

* Authority Lloyd Mallan describes the system as follows: "This launch-or-no-launch aspect of Missile Positive Control can be likened to a chain of almost numberless invisible electronic keys, each of which fits into a special electronic lock. Unless the right key is mated with its proper lock, the 'door' will not open to allow other doors to be opened with succeeding keys. Coupled with the swift opening of electronic doors, all missile-launch personnel must work separately and individually in the most accurate of split-second coordination to fire a single ICBM."

members are equipped with sidearms with which they are instructed to shoot the recalcitrants.

How many precautions can we take? Small wonder Professor Sidney Hook observes: ". . . the existing United States defense control procedures show that far from being trigger-happy or indifferent to the possibility of accident, the government has developed cautions against accident to a point where some persons speculate whether it would not be more justifiable to charge that too many safeguards have been introduced rather than too few."[18] The point is well speculated. It is apparent that such a system of tight, interlocking controls means any failure in communication at any point along the way would render our arsenal useless.

Thus we have proceeded from the "safe assumption" of nuclear stalemate to: (1) Neutralization of our deterrent strategy and heightening of Communist strategy; (2) Widespread nuclear jitters and fear of our own arsenal; (3) A test-ban treaty which prevents us from developing our own defenses; (4) Impediments to the effective use of our battlefield atomic weapons in the event of massive Soviet ground attack in Europe; (5) A lock system on the use of our strategic weapons which in the event of mechanical failure could result in our being unable to use them even if we wanted to.

As fruits of the "safe assumption," these five items would in themselves be bad enough. But there is more.

★★ 16. *The Disarmament Lobby*

1. *The Sanes Go Marching In*

THE IDEAS we have reviewed converge, in Establishment doctrine, in the grand climactic theme of disarmament. Among all projects attractive to the Liberal intelligence, disarmament is the most durable and hypnotic in its fascination, absorbing and harmonizing the impulses of the globalist and pacifist temper.

If we are to strike agreements with the Communists, suppress our military leaders, inhibit American sovereignty and advance toward world government, what could be more ideal than an all-embracing pact with Moscow in which we throw down our arms and consign our fate to the mercies of a global police force? Every fiber of the Liberal being must vibrate in harmony with that mighty chord. Compared to this, assisting Soviet agriculture or funneling a few jet planes to Tito are but the feeblest overtures.

As the theme of disarmament draws the threads of our narrative into a single center, so does it assemble, from their various redoubts in and about the government, our *dramatis personnae*. Almost all our leading characters have, at one time or another, felt themselves attracted to this exalted conception: Here we find Walt Rostow and the interlocking brainpans of *The Liberal Papers,* George F. Kennan and "Chip" Bohlen, Hubert Humphrey and the ADA, Vincent P. Rock and the Phoenix Study, the anti-nuclear claque and the anonymous bureaucrats of Foggy Bottom. Nor are these authorities alone. In their effort to shepherd America down the road to armslessness, they are assisted by a coterie of "experts," little known to the public but immensely influential, who devote long hours of meditation to the dual problems of achieving disarmament and making the result palatable to the American people.

In its most exposed and recognizable form, the disarmament lobby is represented by the Sane Nuclear Policy Committee, a far left group which includes among its sponsors Fair Play for Cuba Committee backers (James Baldwin, Donald Harrington), avowed Socialists (Norman Thomas, Gunnar Myrdal), British eccentric Bertrand Russell and pro-Castro publicist Hugh Hester, mixed in with some less flamboyant Liberals like entertainer Steve Allen.* Its chief themes are a *concordat* with the Communists and hostility to American sovereignty.

The SANE ideology holds that the outstanding danger in the world today is not Communist aggression, but the threat

* Other outposts of the disarmament lobby in the private sector include the Center for the Study of Democratic Institutions (an offshoot of the Fund for the Republic), a group which calls itself the Council for a Liveable World and which works for disarmament-oriented candidates in the political arena, and the magazine *Foreign Affairs,* published by the influential Council on Foreign Relations. One of the most successful undertakings of the lobby is an annual gathering known as the Pugwash Conference, a meeting of Eastern and Western scientists originally sponsored by leftist millionaire Cyrus Eaton.

of nuclear war. SANE believes that, in some never very clearly defined fashion, the Communists can be relied upon to arrive at and honor agreements averting this danger. And it believes such agreements should be administered by some supranational body, arising from the United Nations, in which the sovereignty of the United States will be, and should be, submerged.

The nature of SANE's opinions may be gathered by inspecting the programmatic utterances of its co-founder and most persistent spokesman, Norman Cousins, who has expressed his faith in disarmament through the editorial columns of the *Saturday Review,* which he edits, through countless speeches, and in various books.

On the feasibility of reaching an agreement with the Communists and trusting them to live up to it, Cousins is optimistic. After all, he says, "Mr. Khrushchev declared it was possible to seek and achieve peaceful relations with capitalist nations," an observation which leads Cousins to believe the Soviet Union will "give up . . . the ability to wage nuclear war and surprise attack." Since the alternative "is likely to be no world at all—for the Soviet Union or anyone else—there is a reasonable prospect that a disarmament proposal will be seriously considered."[1]

What about American sovereignty under a global disarmament agency? In our mid-twentieth century world, Cousins says, "the overriding danger to life comes from the absence of authority over the nation itself." He adds that "the fully sovereign nation has become separated from its historic reason for being . . . it has actually become inimical to life and creative freedom." If incursions against freedom are "what total sovereignty has come to mean," he concludes, "then it is a monstrous thing and man has the duty to replace it with the higher and saner forms that conflict neither with himself nor his own natural rights."[2]

The project in whose service these insights are marshaled is a grand enlargement of the United Nations. We must, Cousins argues, invest the United Nations with "the general powers of world law." By this he means the nations of the world should relinquish their weapons and give the U.N. a nuclear monopoly. We should approach this desired goal, first, by conferring on the U.N. military forces three times the size of its contingent in Korea ("about one million men under arms"); second, by calling on all nations to repose their hope for peace in the U.N. force; and third, by turning the U.N. into a world government, acting toward the former "nations" of the world, including ours, as does our own Federal government toward the states.[3]

It will perhaps be objected that, by citing Mr. Cousins' opinions, we have ranged far afield. His view of the Cold War, it may be argued, is so fatuous it could not represent any major tendency in the high councils of the nation. The first part of this argument is of course correct; but the second part is not—for Cousins' views are something very like a working outline of the policy to which the United States government has officially committed itself.

While SANE is the most exposed salient of the disarmament lobby, other members enjoy positions in government or in agencies plying the government with allegedly sophisticated Cold War doctrine. They are ensconced, it goes without saying, in the State Department. They have their very own bureau, the Arms Control and Disarmament Agency. They are under contract to organizations, like the Institute for Defense Analysis, which supply the government with reams of expertise. And they have, in several instances, direct access to the White House itself.

The nation's chief disarmament advocates include such prominent citizens as former presidential adviser McGeorge Bundy, his deputy Carl Kaysen, the bulk of *The Liberal Papers* contingent—particularly Walter Millis, Arthur Waskow and James Warburg—Phoenix Papers' author Vincent Rock, Dr. Jerome Wiesner, Prof. Seymour Melman, former Under Secretary of Defense Roswell Gilpatric, Navy Secretary Paul Nitze and many others. These are merely the names that have got themselves mentioned in the public media. Beneath the surface, their similars are positioned everywhere in and around the government. As the Gilpatric example suggests, they have penetrated even the Defense Department and have, according to sympathetic commentary, enlisted no less a coadjutor than Defense Secretary Robert McNamara himself.*

The impact of the disarmament lobby on official policy has been immense. Referring to one official statement concerning the possibility of unilateral moves toward disarmament by the United States, *U.S. News and World Report* observed: "Essentially the same view is held by other top civilian advisers. Among them are several key members of Mr. McNamara's team of 'whiz kids' at the Pentagon, as well as Jerome B. Wiesner, presidential science adviser; Carl Kaysen, White House arms control expert; and Walt Whitman Rostow, policy planner at the State Department. These men are sometimes called 'peace strategists.' Outside the government, physicist Hans Bethe of Cornell is credited with being the most influential strategist for peace."[4]

In his chronicle of the Kennedy administration, Theodore Sorensen describes the influence of the disarmament lobby—ranging all the way over to Norman Cousins—on President Kennedy's 1963 address at American University. Casting about for material for that speech, Sorensen says, Kennedy expressed admiration for "an April 30 letter from Norman Cousins," urging "the exposition of a peaceful posture," as-

* Says *Newsweek:* "McNamara's insistence on the application of logic . . . has made of him a vigorous advocate of disarmament—gradual, carefully controlled and cautious. Thus McNamara presents the paradox of a defense chief who spends 60 per cent of his regular 75-hour week working on the war in Viet Nam, but never misses an opportunity to make a sensible move or suggestion toward disarmament."

sertedly to defuse Soviet charges against America. In preparing the speech, Sorensen says, "I obtained material from Cousins, Bundy, Kaysen, my brother Tom and others." The President, Sorensen concludes, "was determined to put forward a fundamentally new emphasis on the peaceful and the positive in our relations with the Soviets. He did not want the new policy diluted by the usual threats of destruction, boasts of nuclear stockpiles, and lectures on Soviet treachery."[5]

SANE's cousinly influence has carried over into the Johnson administration as well. When Vice President Humphrey took off for Asia on a late 1965 good will tour, Cousins accompanied him as one of his chief advisers. Other key disarmament lobbyists have, as we shall see, also made the transition from New Frontier to Great Society with scarcely a break in stride.

2. *Messrs. Melman and Wiesner*

While it is not possible here to explore all the various strands of disarmament thought, or to examine the views of all disarmament lobby personnel, an idea of what these people are up to can be conveyed by rehearsing the views of certain key spokesmen. We shall select for examination two gentlemen who have on the record wielded great influence on American Cold War policy: Dr. Seymour Melman of Columbia University, and Dr. Jerome B. Wiesner of Massachusetts Institute of Technology.

Dr. Melman, who in addition to his duties at Columbia is a member of SANE, has devised an approach to disarmament which might be paraphrased as "disarmament by budget-cutting." His theory is that we are spending billions of dollars on "overkill"—nuclear weapons and delivery systems beyond anything we would possibly require to destroy the Soviet Union—while neglecting such domestic needs as polluted streams, bad highways, and the like. What could be more logical, he asks, than to take all the billions being spent for overkill and divert them to domestic needs? Melman extends this reasoning to encompass military aid to various nations allied to the United States as well. Maintaining large military establishments, he says, diverts funds from needed social and economic development in these countries. One of the examples he cites is Viet Nam, where he makes it clear he considers our military aid detrimental. Just what he would have the Saigon government and our own do about the Viet Cong does not emerge very clearly.

All such considerations are casually dismissed, however, in Dr. Melman's analysis. Assuming we can divert no less than $22 billion from current military expenditures, Melman paints this picture of prospective disarmament:

> The single most important move the United States could make to facilitate economic development for the impoverished two thirds of humanity would be to encourage the reduction of armed forces and military spending everywhere. This could be done only if the major powers set an example by carrying out, on their own account, a major change in the use of their own resources accompanied by internationally agreed upon and controlled disarmament treaties.[6]

Anyone who has come this far will perceive that Melman's style of reasoning meshes very well with the "expert" views we have previously examined. The constant reader will perhaps not be astounded, therefore, to learn Prof. Melman is consulted by the administration, and is assertedly a favored theorist of the President himself.

At his first press conference in December, 1963, Johnson announced that Melman had been among his callers. Chalmers Roberts of the Washington *Post* reported that Melman was "cordially received by four new Johnson White House aides"—much more cordially, Roberts added, than he had been received under Kennedy.[7] And, referring to the Johnson defense budget, Jack Raymond of *The New York Times* reported: "The administration is cutting back the pace of this country's build-up of strategic weapons. The move is viewed as a significant concession to the controversial 'overkill' theory (a belief America has more weapons than necessary to wipe out the Sino-Soviet bloc). Many supporters of the 'overkill' argument have based their views on a privately prepared report, under the leadership of Prof. Seymour Melman of Columbia University."[8]

That Raymond's assertion is essentially correct is affirmed by the great popularity of the "overkill" theory in official circles, and by the course of action being followed by Defense Secretary McNamara. In essence, the Melman formula is one of less guns and more butter. By propagating and popularizing this theory, Melman has obviously helped point the Johnson regime to a fortuitous policy combining the joys of "economy" with the pleasures of augmented spending for domestic welfarism.

While Melman's services in rationalizing disarmament-by-economy are thus considerable, he has an additional relevance to disarmament philosophy which deserves our closest examination: The peculiar logic by which he arrives at his conception of "overkill." The defense dollars Melman says are spent for "overkill" are, for the most part, dollars going for research and development. They are expended—not, as he implies, to buy more and more of the existing weapons systems—but to develop *new* weapons systems surpassing the old; they are spent in quest of technological breakthroughs to improve our defenses. A close reading of Melman's text reveals it is this idea of *breakthrough,* of improving American defenses, which is the true object of disparagement.

Melman is at great pains, for example, to deny that either a civil defense shelter program or an anti-ballistic missile defense system (ABM) is possible of development. "Antimissile weapon systems," he says flatly, "would be doomed to ineffectiveness for technical reasons."[9] Defense technology has gone as far as it can go; nothing new or decisive can be achieved by spending research and development money. So let's forget about searching for breakthroughs.

At first glance, Melman's assertions on this score seem merely to be a repetition of the error committed by the admirals who told Billy Mitchell nothing could sink a battleship, or the defense experts who told Wernher Von Braun extensive space flight was impossible. But further inquiry in the wider context of disarmament ideology reveals this animus toward breakthrough is more than casual error; it is in fact a point of doctrine.

The truth is that the disarmament lobbyists don't *want* technological breakthroughs—particularly breakthroughs which have the effect of protecting the lives of American citizens and strengthening the United States. Such steps to defend America, they believe, would be very bad. *It is essential, in their view, that the United States should not be superior in military strength to the Soviet Union.* To explore the background of this peculiar notion, let us turn to Dr. Wiesner.

Jerome Wiesner has had even more direct and ready access to the White House than has Dr. Melman. Wiesner served as President Kennedy's Special Assistant for Science and Technology for three years, from 1961 to 1964, before returning to MIT as Dean of the School of Science. He was, according to *The New York Times,* "the top planner, arbitrator, and counselor of scientific policy" in the Kennedy administration.[10] In 1965, he served as chairman of an advisory group on arms control reporting to President Johnson.

Wiesner's general outlook is indicated by the report of the *Saturday Review* that he "looks upon arms control as almost a crusade," and wants to put "peace explorers in the White House, in the State Department, in the Pentagon, in the

Atomic Energy Commission" and "elsewhere at key points";[11] and by the *Times'* further commentary that "before joining the administration, Wiesner made no secret of his belief that the United States at times had been almost as much to blame as the Soviet Union for blocking arms-control measures . . ."

The *Times* adds that: "One of the principal obstacles standing in the way of disarmament, in Wiesner's opinion, is a 'communications block' between the two sides . . . It was largely because of his desire to break down the 'communications block' that Wiesner last fall [1960] took the potentially impolitic step of going to Moscow to attend a non-governmental conference of East-West scientists on disarmament."[12]

Wiesner makes, in his own fashion, essentially the same point as does Melman: It is not "technically" possible, he argues, to break the nuclear stalemate in our favor. In his book *Where Science and Politics Meet,* he runs through a rather confusing argument to establish that it is unfeasible to produce a satisfactory anti-missile defense. This is a theme to which he has addressed himself on countless occasions. Dr. Wiesner seems, indeed, to be almost fanatically committed to the idea that an ABM program is impossible, unrealistic, unworkable.

What Dr. Wiesner and Prof. Melman are really saying, under cover of arguing that an anti-missile breakthrough is "impossible," is that such a breakthrough is *undesirable.* The disarmament lobbyists are opposed to any such development because it would upset the "stalemate" which is their psychological and political trump card in the crusade for "accommodation." This is the real point.

Professor Rock, for example, states that "ironically, since the balance of terror denies the achievement of victory by violence, it provides the fundamental source of frustration which may be required to turn the two societies to new creative efforts. Thus, premature attempts to uproot and remove this source of frustration should be shunned."[13]

The utility of the "balance" in seeking disarmament was similarly stressed by Dr. Wiesner on his trip to Moscow. "While a system of mutual deterrence is less attractive in many ways than properly safeguarded disarmament," he said, "it may be somewhat easier to achieve and could be regarded as a transient phase on the way to total disarmament . . . If a system of stable deterrents can be used to establish a condition of military security during which military forces and weapons can be cut back, international tensions reduced, and a period of cooperation and mutual confidence achieved, total nuclear disarmament with or without an internation security force may be much more easily agreed upon."[14]

Wiesner subsequently pointed this logic directly at the anti-missile defense system. "Paradoxically," he says, "one of the potential destabilizing elements in the present nuclear stand-off is the possibility that one of the rival powers might develop a successful anti-missile defense. Such a system, truly airtight and in the exclusive possession of one of the powers, would effectively nullify the deterrent force of the other, exposing the latter to a first strike attack against which it could not retaliate."[15]*

To the ordinary citizen, this fact seems to suggest the desirability of developing such a system; if we get it and the Soviets don't, we win; if the Soviets get it and we don't, we lose. But Wiesner and his friends are not, of course, ordinary citizens. The fact that an ABM system could render us invulnerable to Soviet attack and thus upset the assumed "balance" in our favor makes it, in their eyes, *un*desirable.

With the balance thus destroyed, "the source of frustration" pushing the U.S. and the USSR toward accommodation

* Dr. Edward Teller offers the same analysis from another perspective, stating that "an effective defense against ballistic missiles is one of the developments which can upset the strategic balance between the United States and the Soviet Union."

would be gone. As the Institute for Defense Analysis puts it: *"Potential breakthroughs, as a result of military research and development, represent one of the most serious continuing obstacles to stability and still further disarmament."*[16] And: "Whenever a military weapons development seems seriously to impair second strike invulnerability or to create opportunities for counterforce strategies [i.e., to upset the balance], *it seems stabilizing to inhibit its production.* One effective way to assure non-production is to restrict development at the testing stage."[17] (Italics added.) In English, the latter statement means any weapons system which can upset the "stalemate" should be stopped dead before it can get started.

Wiesner made the identical point when he addressed the Moscow Pugwash conference in November, 1960. "It is important to note," he said, "that a missile deterrent system would be unbalanced by the development of a highly effective anti-missile defense system, *and if it appears possible to develop one, the agreements should explicitly prohibit the development and deployment of such systems."*[18] In 1963, Wiesner reiterated this theme in advices to the American government, counselling President Kennedy: "Don't deploy Nike-Zeus . . . Keep it in research and development."[19] Again, in November, 1965, a presidential advisory panel headed by Wiesner (and including Kaysen and Gilpatric among its members) recommended, among other things, a three-year moratorium on developing an ABM system.

The report of this panel contains the following statements about the undesirability of ABM deployment:

> This committee does not believe the time is appropriate for a decision to deploy. First of all, there remains the basic question of the military value of the system . . . Beyond the technical and military-economic questions, the Panel believes that the United States has not given the political consequences of the ABM de-

ployment sufficient thought and certainly has not yet explored the ways in which the U.S. and the USSR could avoid unintended effects of the systems on the other's deterrent force . . .

We also believe that the political posture of the Soviet Union is delicately poised at the moment; it is very clearly in the U.S. interest to avoid such actions as might deflect the Soviet government from a course of improving its relations with the West . . .

[An agreement to "freeze" weapons systems] would not be possible during the construction of ballistic missile defenses; because it seems technically difficult to design a proposal that would freeze a dynamic contest between deployed ballistic missile defenses and the weapons designed to surmount them; and because it may be more difficult, though this is somewhat more controversial, to reach an agreement on a freeze of offensive weapons while the defenses that neutralize them were uncontrolled.

These considerations argue against ballistic-missile defenses . . .[20]

Which is to say: *The anti-missile system which could make the United States invulnerable to Soviet attack and win the Cold War for our side should not be constructed because it might keep the Soviets from "mellowing" and would interfere with disarmament.*

These several acts of *advocacy* on the part of Dr. Wiesner make it apparent that his arguments about the "impossibility" of an ABM defense are tendentious; quite clearly, the professor and his fellow disarmament lobbyists, for the reasons noted, don't *want* an ABM.

Writing in *The Liberal Papers,* disarmament lobbyist Walter Millis extends the logic of the Wiesner position a step further. He tosses out the idea "that a genuinely deterrent policy would require the United States *to co-operate with the Soviet Union in insuring that their retaliatory force was as invulnerable as ours and that our population was equally exposed to attack with theirs.*" The idea, he notes, seems "fantastic," but is nevertheless "the end toward which" U.S.-Soviet policies "have been tending."[21] (Italics added.)

That Millis' analysis is correct, at least with respect to U.S. policy, we have just observed. The desire of the disarmament lobby in opposing the development of an ABM (and, with equal vehemence, a shelter program) is precisely to insure "that our population [is] equally exposed to attack with theirs," in order to maintain the cherished assumption of balance. And there is equal evidence to suggest, after the fashion intimated by Millis, that we are "co-operating" with Moscow to make sure *their* retaliatory force is invulnerable to *our* attack.

Again Dr. Wiesner is our prime example. On that "impolitic" journey to Russia with Prof. Rostow back in 1960, Wiesner discoursed at length, just a few weeks before he became one of our government's key officials, on defense systems which could absorb a "surprise attack," and gave his listeners information useful in the hardening of missle sites.

Of similar tendency is "peace strategist" (and SANE member) Hans Bethe's comment concerning Soviet nuclear tests. "The recent Russian test series included many tests in the range from one to five megatons," Bethe said in 1960. "This is just the range which might be suitable for a Russian solid-fuel missile similar to our Minuteman which could be placed in hardened sites. I hope this is the right interpretation, and that the Russians will also aim for a secure second-strike force."[22]

Finally, lest there by any doubt about the popularity of this novel theory in the administration, it should be noted that Secretary of Defense Robert McNamara also subscribes to it. In an interview with Stewart Alsop of the *Saturday Evening Post,* McNamara suggested America would *benefit from an increase in Soviet nuclear capabilities.* The Defense Secretary, according to Alsop, regretted the fact that the Soviet forces were so "soft" that America could wipe them out in a single blow. McNamara hoped the Communists would acquire a "sure second strike capability," and, Alsop said, McNamara meant "the sooner the better." ". . . a nuclear exchange confined to military targets," McNamara explained, "seems more possible, not less, when both sides have a sure second strike capability. Then you might have a more stable balance of terror."[23]

The "technical" objections of Profs. Wiesner and Melman to the anti-missile defense thus fall into place; the problem is not "technical" at all; it is that a successful United States breakthrough in missile defenses would upset the "stalemate," dashing the hopes of the disarmament lobby. As Oscar Handlin has observed, "every bureaucracy . . . protects its interests by framing all questions as if the issues were technical."[24] That is precisely what the disarmament advocates have done in seeking abandonment of a defense system crucial to the survival of the United States.

3. *Toward World Government*

If disarmament thus satisfies the trust-and-assist element it also satisfies that school of thought which exalts the United Nations and disparages American sovereignty. Most hard-core lobbyists, indeed, are virtuosos on the subject of attaining disarmament through a world super-state.

Liberal Papers contributor James Warburg, for example, suggests as foremost among the "ultimate aims" of U.S. foreign policy "the achievement of universal security against military aggression through universal disarmament under world law." Warburg explains further, in his own italics, that *"the United States should unequivocally declare that its goal is universal national disarmament down to the level of lightly armed police forces; that such disarmament must be enforced under world law; and that the enforcement of such world law must be provided by universal agreement to endow a supra-*

national world organization to maintain peace, and, if necessary, to use armed force in order to prevent violation."[25]

A similar exhortation is offered by Warburg's fellow contributor to *The Liberal Papers,* Arthur I. Waskow. In a book called *The Limits of Defense* (which features an introduction by *Liberal Papers* colleague Riesman), Waskow proposes something he calls "disarmament-plus," described as follows:

"The goal of American policy should be the adoption by joint consent of all nations of a world law against the making, possession, or use by any individual of any weapon above the level of small arms . . . American policy should . . . concentrate on the achieveable goal of total disarmament, enforced by the processes of a court and a police designed solely for that purpose . . . Normal police powers would be granted [the world disarmament authority] to investigate and publicize any instance in which the disarmament law was being broken, and *to arrest and bring to trial* any individuals who violated it. *The police force should be extremely mobile and should possess the world's only meaningful weapons.*"[26]

This proposal comes from a man who has served as administrative assistant to a United States Congressman, has been a consultant to the American government writing out disarmament plans, and, according to disarmament consultant Carl Kaysen, has provided "useful" information for official planners.

That the Warburg-Waskow view is in harmony with high doctrine is suggested by statements of the influential Americans for Democratic Action, which Vice President Humphrey served as chairman and vice-chairman. In its founding statement, ADA declared that "the establishment of a world government with powers adequate to prevent war must be an objective of the United States foreign policy to be achieved at the earliest possible date."[27] In a 1964 set of recommendations to the Democratic platform committee, ADA said: "We reaffirm the commitment of the United States to the ultimate achievement of general and complete disarmament, subject to effective inspection and control with national armed forces reduced to the levels agreed to be necessary for internal security."[28] And: "As we move toward disarmament, we must work to strengthen the United Nations, and to build up its peace-keeping capacity by establishing a U.N. police force composed of contingents from the small countries committed for fixed periods."[29]

In the ranks of the Democratic administration itself, we find the Cousins-ADA-*Liberal Papers* animus toward national sovereignty voiced in a previously quoted statement by U.S. official Walt Rostow. "It is a legitimate American national objective," Rostow says, "to see removed from all nations—including the United States—the right to use substantial military force to pursue their own interests. . . . it is, therefore, an American interest to see an end to nationhood as it has been historically defined."[30]

These intimations of a supranational disarmament authority have been moved from the abstract to the specific by yet another administration official, former Assistant Secretary of Defense and Secretary of the Navy Paul Nitze. In 1960, Nitze journeyed to Asilomar, California, to speak to military and civilian personnel about the intricacies of American defense. In that speech, Nitze suggested America should not strive for nuclear superiority over the Soviet Union, a status which Nitze called a "Class A" capability. Instead, he proposed, the United States should aim for a "secure second-strike capability." Nitze expanded on his theme as follows:

"The actions I propose are . . . That we multilateralize the command of our retaliatory systems by *making SAC a NATO command;* and . . . *that we inform the United Nations that NATO will turn over ultimate power of decision on the use of these systems to the General Assembly of the United Nations subject to the following conditions:* (a) That we and our allies will assume continuing responsibility for manning, maintaining and improving these systems. (b) That U.N. inspectors would be invited to inspect and satisfy themselves that these are the *only* nuclear systems we are maintaining; (c) *That a U.N. order to use them will be honored only in the event some nation has initiated the use of nuclear weapons other than on or over its own territory in self-defense against military aggression . . .*"[31]

Which means, in effect, that America's defense capability would be in the hands of the United Nations, and that even the United Nations would not be able to employ that nuclear capability against massive conventional attack by the Communists; a formula, in short, for divesting America both of control over and the advantage of (even whatever advantage it might hope to possess through the United Nations) its nuclear deterrent against Soviet conventional aggression.

As it happens, something like the suggestions tossed out by Nitze, in keeping with the theorems of the SANE-*Liberal Papers*-ADA axis, has already been translated into official policy. By act of Congress and by executive commitment, the United States is pledged to strengthen the United Nations into just such an institution as that suggested by Cousins, Warburg and Waskow. The groundwork for this plan was laid in President Kennedy's speech to the United Nations in September, 1961, and in the collateral enactment by Congress of a law creating the U.S. Disarmament Agency, the fruit of which endeavor was subsequently laid before the Geneva Disarmament Conference.

In his speech to the U.N., Kennedy exhorted his audience to "join in dismantling the national capacity to wage war . . ." "The weapons of war," he said, "must be abolished before they abolish us . . . The risks inherent in disarament pale in comparison to the risks inherent in an unlimited arms race . . ." The American program for "general and complete disarmament," he added, "would achieve, under the eye of an international disarmament organization, a steady reduction in forces, both nuclear and conventional, until it had abolished all armies and all weapons except those needed for internal order and a new United Nations Peace Force." He concluded that "we must create" "world-wide law and law enforcement as we outlaw world-wide war and weapons."[32]

Exactly what Kennedy meant by these phrases was spelled out by the U.S. proposal at Geneva, which suggests, Cousins-like, a three-stage move toward disarmament, which would establish a "United Nations Peace Force." Ultimately, says the program, "the parties would progressively strengthen the United Nations peace force established in Stage II, until it had sufficient armed services and armaments *so that no state could challenge it.*" (Italics added.)[33]

The resemblance to Sane Nuclear Policy Committee and Warburg-Waskow doctrines is evident. Some informed and sympathetic journalistic commentary, however, should put the matter beyond all possible doubt. In March, 1962, the Los Angeles *Times* carried, under the headline, "U.S. to Propose End of National Armies—U.N. Peace Force Would Keep Global Peace," a UPI dispatch which began: "The United States will submit to the Geneva disarmament conference a plan calling for *the elimination of national armies* within nine years, and their replacement by a United Nations force, reliable sources said Friday."[34]

Of similar import was a dispatch by R.H. Shackford of the Scripps-Howard newspapers which spelled out the ideological framework of the proposal in some detail. In the President's view, Shackford said, the draft treaty meant:

"A revolutionary change in the political structure of the world.

"Creation of a radically new international system.

"Abandonment of most of the old concepts of national states . . .

"In addition, the treaty specified some of the drastic changes that would have to occur, such as:

"Development of international institutions that would encourage nations to give up much of their national sovereignty.

"Acceptance without reservation of the jurisdiction of international court.

"Approval of supranational inspection and verification.

"Willingness to depend for national security on an international peace force under an immensely changed and strengthened United Nations."[35]

Shackford concludes that the American proposal adds up to this:

"There must be developed, simultaneously with the reduction of armaments, what would amount to a world government with comprehensive authority for inspection to guarantee compliance with the disarmament treaty . . . No one here in Washington expects this millennium to occur overnight. The delegates in Geneva have not even agreed yet on how to talk about this problem. But it is a goal—and it is a high one toward which President Kennedy believes the world must start working if a nuclear holocaust is to be avoided."[36] (Italics added)

The United Press and Shackford interpretations suggest that, not only does the disarmament proposal read in critical eyes like a reprise of the Warburg manifesto, but that its own sponsors viewed it in precisely that same light. The ideology of SANE and the *Liberal Papers* has, in short, been converted into the official policy of the United States government.

★★ 17. *Easing Soviet Anxieties*

1. *It's Unilateral*

WHEN SUCH MATTERS as the State Department's disarmament plan are brought up by people alarmed about possible damage to American security, various spokesmen are quick to pour soothing syrup on the protestors. That high American officials would seriously entertain the notion of putting a disarmed United States under the control of a world government is, we are told, absurd. When the particulars are specified, the disarmament program is described as silly, but too visionary to be taken seriously. So why get exercised about it?

The truth is that the American people have good reason to get exercised about the proposals we have reviewed, on at least three different counts:

First, it is an odd form of consolation which suggests we

need not worry about the proposals of our government because they are too preposterous to be enacted;

Second, while the ideological framework of our official policy may or may not seem serviceable *in toto,* that framework obviously controls the direction in which practical results are sought;

Third, and most important, the program we have been discussing, and many of the specific steps which go into it, *are* being put into practice.

How far official thought and action have moved under the impulse of the disarmament lobby may be gathered by inspecting the curious notion of "unilateralism." As applied to disarmament, "unilateralism" simply means the United States gets rid of its weapons and the Soviet Union doesn't. In the advocacy of various disarmament lobbyists, this idea comes in differing shapes and sizes. There are extreme unilateralists who suggest we simply ought to chuck the whole business, renounce our arms, and take the consequences. And there are "moderate" unilateralists who believe that, by laying down this or that piece of hardware which Moscow finds upsetting, we can persuade the Communists of our peaceful intentions and get them to follow suit.

An extreme case of unilateralism is C. Wright Mills, whose opinions on the military we have previously reviewed. Mills' suggestions for a "peace" policy include statements that "the U.S. government should at once and unilaterally cease all further production of 'extermination' weapons," abandon all military bases "outside the continental domain of the United States," immediately recognize Red China, invite the Russians to join with us in programs of global uplift, *etc.* "The U.S. government should announce some such program to the world unilaterally, one big item every other day." It should also realize that "the continued attempt by the U.S.A. to defend the economic and political status quo of the world today will end in war."[1] And since war is verboten, no such attempt should be made.

Yet another disarmament lobbyist speaking in favorable terms of unilateral disarmament is *The Liberal Papers'* Walter Millis, who says concerning proposals of the Mills variety:

> Curiously enough, this looks as though it really might work. Assuming a Soviet Union armed to the teeth with nuclear weapons and confronting a Western and neutralist world that had divested itself of such 'power,' what could the Soviet Union actually do with its armament? It could, of course, make demands and threats on pain of nuclear exterminination. But if the demands were simply rejected, could the power of extermination help them at all?[2]

While these two views are of course more abandoned than official or semi-official utterance, the unilateralism they profess is also popular with their more cautious brothers. We earlier noted the proposals of Professor Osgood in *The Liberal Papers,* which include such items as plugging Moscow in on our distant early warning system. When *The Liberal Papers* first appeared, Osgood's program for "reciprocal initiative" might reasonably have been voted least likely to succeed as a working policy of the American government. Yet there is evidence that a program almost exactly like that spelled out by Osgood—and not too dissimilar from Wright Mills' proposal that we pull in our horns "unilaterally, one big item every other day"—is now official policy.

A first definite clue as to what was afoot was provided by the Moscow sojourn of Professors Wiesner and Rostow back in November, 1960. On that trip, according to reporter Thomas Ross of the Chicago *Sun-Times,* Professor Rostow paid a visit to Soviet Deputy Foreign Minister Vasily V. Kuznetsov, "to get a reading on the current Russian attitude on disarmament and defense and report back to Mr. Kennedy." In essence, Kuznetsov said the Soviets found U.S. planes and advanced missile bases worrisome, and wished the United States would get rid of them:

Rostow reported Kuznetsov had expressed doubt that U.S. military men honestly supported disarmament, and had voiced fears about the aggressive appearance of U.S. forces surrounding the Soviet Union.

In military jargon, Kuznetsov was complaining that U.S. bombers and missiles in Europe and Asia looked like a "first-strike capability"—that is, they were too vulnerable to destruction by a sneak Russian rocket attack to be of much use in a counter-punch.

Therefore, Kuznetsov implied, they were designed to be used against the Soviet Union in a "first strike."

Without endorsing Kuznetsov's reasoning, Rostow replied that he believed the United States "should create quickly at whatever expense might be necessary a second-strike capability as well as a highly mobile deterrent against limited war."

A second-strike capability would comprise missiles, such as the Polaris submarine rocket, which are so invulnerable to sneak destruction that any enemy could have no genuine fears they were designed for a first strike.[3]

Of particular interest in Ross' account is the effect of this parley on Rostow's thought processes.

"A second-strike capability would ease American anxieties," he reports Rostow saying, "make hair-trigger reaction to radar and other danger signals less necessary, and ease Soviet anxieties—if they existed—that might arise from the fact that U.S. strategic forces looked like first-strike capabilities."[4]

Rostow advised Kennedy to get a reliable second-strike capability and mobility for our conventional forces as quickly as possible. "It is my assessment," he said, "that in the end, they will respect us for doing this—even if we enlarge the military budget—so long as our moves are not designed to increase our first-strike capability."

"Striking echoes of Rostow's report," as Ross puts it, appeared in the President's defense message. "We are not creating forces for a first-strike against any other nation," Kennedy said. ". . . As a power which will never strike first, our hopes for anything close to an absolute deterrent must rest on weapons which come from hidden, moving or invulnerable bases which will not be wiped out in a surprise attack."[5]

Sorensen, a prominent participant in all this, manages to skip over mention of these particular doings in his long memoir on the late President. He does give us, however, a passage about Kennedy's defense message which confirms the thrust of Ross' report. Secretary McNamara and the President, Sorensen says, agreed that to "seek a 'first-strike' capability . . . was not only unnecessarily expensive and provocative but not really feasible."[6]

Arthur Schlesinger similarly asserts that Kennedy "had a profound aversion to weapons which could be used effectively only in a first strike and which might invite a preemptive strike from the other side," and notes, as does Ross, that this preference was reflected in the 1961 defense budget. "Both the securing of a second-strike capacity and the diversification of the defense establishment," Schlesinger adds, "seemed to [Kennedy] . . . vital parts of the strategy of deterrence and arms control."[7]

Kennedy himself repeatedly referred to the necessity of avoiding "provocation" of the USSR through our weaponry, in precisely the formula indicated by Rostow. We were not creating forces for a "first strike", he said in his 1961 defense address, adding that "we shall never threaten, provoke, or initiate aggression."[8] In his 1963 address at American University, he declared that "America's weapons are nonprovocative, carefully controlled, designed to deter and capable of selective use."[9]

As one military man has put it: "In two years, there has emerged in this country a military philosophy developed by civilians that predicts a nuclear stand off—with both U.S. and Russia possessing absolute ability to destroy the other. Arms controllers think the risk of war can be lessened by making our forces 'nonprovocative.' Hardened missiles, to be used only in retaliation, are non-provocative. But antimissiles are not to be pushed hard because they could only serve to provoke the arms race. Space weapons are very provocative. And bombers must be abandoned because they are good only as a 'first-strike' weapons and are therefore extremely provocative."[10]

Further evidence on the popularity of one-sided disarmament among Washington theorists is provided by a curious set of documents published in 1963 by the Institute for Defense Analysis. These papers, entitled "Study FAIR" (which stands for "Focus on Arms Information and Reassurance") were subsidized by the Arms Control and Disarmament Agency and by the Defense Department. They explicitly state the need for unilateral disarmament initiatives, and tie these, Rostow-fashion, to a cutback on "first-strike" weapons.

"Study FAIR" says, among many other things, that "it appears that unilateral arms control initiatives by the United States may be quite useful over the next few years," and that "many small but significant, more or less unilateral, first steps in the direction of more effective arms control can be made with currently available information sources."[11]

The reason for the unilateralism is that "formal treaties tend to imply entanglements as well as assurances." Therefore "if the United States wants to determine whether a given limited arms control measure, which involves some risk, will be on balance advantageous or will elicit a favorable response, it may be easier *and* less risky to try it out unilaterally than to embody it in a formal agreement. It should generally be possible, of course, to try the measure in a small or experimental way and to explore the possibility of a desired Soviet response before it is fully implemented."[12]

This is, of course, almost exactly the kind of approach spelled out by *The Liberal Papers'* Osgood, with his two frightened men on the teeter-totter, supposedly edging closer to each other in their quest for mutual safety. It is also, with a few variations, the approach suggested by Vincent Rock, of Phoenix papers celebrity. The principal theme of Rock's "strategy of interdependence" is precisely that a disarmament accord with Moscow can be achieved piecemeal, without benefit of treaties, public debate, or other forms of popular assent, through a series of unilateral initiatives.

A formal treaty on disarmament reductions, Rock believes, would enable "the political opposition" to "make capital of the weakness of the administration."[13] This can be avoided by simply deciding to take some unilateral step toward disarmament and then waiting to see if the Soviet Union follows suit. The effect of such action, Rock says, would be "the creation of conditions in which the United States and the Soviet Union will find it in their self evident interest to work together both constructively and in the restraint of the use of force." This process he calls the "cumulative creation of structure."[14]

2. *Disarmament by 'Economy'*

If we compare these "unilateralist" ideas to the statements and actions of our government, we shall find the resemblance striking. Theodore Sorensen depicts U.S. policy in 1963 as a kind of elaborate effort to impart "signals" to Khrushchev, in precisely the manner suggested by Rock and Osgood. The American University address was one such "signal," as had been the 1961 defense speech. The state of mind which prevailed in the administration is best suggested by the following passages from Sorensen:

> The Soviet chairman, in talks with Harold Wilson and Paul Spaak, and in his letters to Kennedy, seemed to be looking for a chance to live in peace, for a meaningful breakthrough on nu-

clear arms, for a breathing spell to focus on goulash and housing and ballet instead of weapons . . . Khrushchev, in a later conversation with [Averell] Harriman, called [the American University speech] "the best speech by any President since Roosevelt" . . . The "signal" the Soviet chairman had awaited was loud and clear. . . . [Kennedy] welcomed any opportunity to demonstrate to the Soviet leaders that the improved climate of agreement could serve the interests of both nations . . . The breathing spell had became a pause, the pause was becoming a *détente* and no one could foresee what further changes lay ahead.[15]

Schlesinger provides us with a similar picture, discoursing on efforts of the Kennedy regime to "communicate" to and "signal" Khrushchev our intentions concerning disarmament and arms control. Schlesinger cites as his premier authority in clarification of all this disarmament expert Thomas C. Schelling of the Rand Corporation, referring to and endorsing an article which analyzes U.S. defense policy almost entirely in terms of such "signals."[16]*

Schlesinger also says that, "next to the president, [Defense Secretary] McNamara, with the able backing of John McNaughton, probably did more than anyone else to sustain the disarmament drive . . . he forever sought new ways of controlling the arms race."[17] The reference to McNamara is revealing. But so is the reference to McNaughton, then general counsel of the Defense Department. For on the subject of unilateralism and signaling Moscow, McNaughton is on record in a fashion which, with no alteration whatever, might just as easily have issued from Messrs. Rock or Osgood. *U.S. News* tells us: "John T. McNaughton, general counsel of the Department of Defense, and an arms-control expert, says that 'arms control' measures need not necessarily be negotiated

* *E.g.:* "Possibly inadvertently through the test ban, but deliberately through various kinds of pronouncements, we have been signaling to the Soviet Union that we consider nuclear weapons to constitute a special category of weapons, that there is a major threshold between them and high explosives," *etc.*

and based on formal treaties. He feels that arms control can be achieved by starting with 'unilateral acts'—one country taking the lead. Essentially the same views are shared by other top civilian advisers."[18] Among these latter, says the magazine, "are several key members of Mr. McNamara's team of whiz kids," and disarmament lobbyists Wiesner, Kaysen, Rostow, and Bethe.[19] The importance of these advisers and the consistency of their yearning for disarmament are also indicated by Schlesinger.

Vincent Rock himself obviously views the Kennedy regime's performance as a kind of fulfilment of his unilateralist vision of "interdependence." Rock cites the test-ban treaty, the concordat banning weapons from outer space, and stepped-up East-West trade with great approval. "In the last months of 1963," he says with evident satisfaction, "progress was made in a number of areas of East-West relations . . . In the West the feeling grew that the Soviet Union was seriously seeking a *détente*."[20]

In yet another aspect of defense policy Rock's projected "structure"-building has been realized with notable directness. Rock has elevated Prof. Melman's notion of "disarmament-by-economy" into something of a science. If we want to "signal" Moscow, Rock reasons, what better way than through our defense budget? Since the Soviets obviously study this document with care, we can show them we are unilaterally backing off in one area or another simply by slashing appropriations. Moreover, this approach provides a convenient and politically beneficial gimmick. Instead of being put before the American public and Congress as a move toward disarmament, the budget slashes can be justified in the name of "economy."

Thus Study Phoenix asserts that the President "might advocate a further United States tax cut, thereby encouraging the economy-minded to seek a cut in defense expenditures—the obvious candidate for decreases. Then military analysis could establish the mix of expenditures at the lower level. The Soviets would be given unpublicized opportunities to indicate their response, and thereby encourage or discourage the President's proposed plan of action."[21]

Rock's book similarly argues that action toward disarmament "might begin, not with emphasis on the intention to disarm, or even to cut expenditures, but on the value of a further tax cut. The obvious advantage of this approach is that in any society, but particularly in a democracy, few measures are likely to find such widespread public support." Once the tax cut is achieved, and "the gap between expenditures and revenues" is increased, the need for reducing our defenses can be brought forward as an answer. The military establishment, Rock concludes, would be "an unavoidable candidate" for cutbacks.[22]

The bearing of this proposal on the defense budget is confirmed by Schlesinger, who says "the administration, as time went on, began to draw a significant conclusion: That the defense budget itself might be used as an instrument of arms limitation. *For it was evident that the budget was the most effective means of signaling the Soviet Union our intentions, whether defensive or first-strike, as well as the kinds of weapons and strategies which might be mutually advantageous and the kinds of limitation that might be mutually possible.*"[23] (Italics added.) The identical point is made by Schlesinger's mentor on this point, Schelling, who asserts that "the arms budget is a diplomatic tool, a way of influencing the Soviet Union, a technique of communication."[24]

Further confirmation that the defense budget has been used to "signal" our beneficent intentions to Moscow may be seen in the final outcome of Professor Rostow's trip to the Kremlin. As reporter Ross notes, the Kennedy defense message of 1961 was contrived, in certain instances, for the ears of Communist leaders:

The similarities in the statements of Rostow and Mr. Kennedy were no coincidence. *It is known that large sections of the President's defense message were written explicitly for the consumption of top Russian officials.*

Moreover, on the recommendation of Charles E. Bohlen, the State Department's leading expert on Russia, certain Communist phraseology was inserted in the message. Such an example was the word "dialectical" . . .

That much of the defense message was directed to the Soviet leaders is evident in the fact that Llewellyn E. Thompson, Jr., Ambassador to Russia, was given a special briefing on it at the Pentagon on a visit here last month.

The message will now be forwarded to him in Moscow *so he can reassure Soviet officials that the United States is taking care not to produce a first-strike capability.* (Italics added.) [25]

3. *Study FAIR Looks Ahead*

Although the preceding discussion indicates "unilateralism" has already made considerable headway as official American policy, there are indications that even more startling renunciations are in the planning stage. Study FAIR, for example, extends the concept of one-sided U.S. "initiatives" to include the question of intelligence. The document seriously proposes that it is in the interest of the United States *not* to have full information on what the Soviets are doing.

Because certain types of information about Soviet missile movements might seem alarming and provoke us into launching a "first strike," it is considered bad for us to get such information (after all, the intent of the Soviets *may* be perfectly innocent). Study FAIR therefore proposes we take steps to minimize the inflow of such "destabilizing" information, and concentrate on getting "reassuring" information, including, according to one suggestion, "inaccurate" information. The report states:

> . . . one's "best guess" may have been that one had a very powerful first-strike force, but confidence in this estimate was low so that one was not tempted to act on it. *Confirmation of this strength would be destabilizing.* And, of course, information which enhances the first strike forces by pinpointing targets or kinds of weapons suitable to destroying certain targets *must be minimized.* (Italics added.) [26]

That is: It is undesirable for America to know it is strong enough in "first-strike" weapons (bombers and advanced missile bases) to defeat the Soviet Union, or to know the location of potential targets in the Soviet Union which could be hit by such weapons. Such information is "destabilizing" to the "balance," and therefore unseemly.

Again, Study FAIR says:

> . . . Data which merely indicate strength or weakness raise the probability of war to the degree that they encourage belief in first strike rather than second strike capability . . . deployment information showing that the enemy has moved his forces to advance bases would be far more dangerous than that which showed that while the movements have enhanced his ability to mount a surprise attack, they also have made his forces less vulnerable.[27]

In other words, we should *not* want to know that the enemy has moved his forces to advance bases, but *should* want to know (because we would be reassured by it) that his forces were both more capable of hitting us and less capable of being hit by us. Clear?

Study FAIR also says "inaccurate information which indicated that the opponent does not have or seek a first-strike capability would be stabilizing up to a point." Thus, even if the Soviets *are* increasing their arsenal of aggressive weapons, it is good, "up to a point," for us not to know this; because, if we did know it, we might be tempted to build up our own arsenal of aggressive weapons, and that would be "destabilizing." Such is the incisive logic of the high-level brains now charting our national destiny.

Having laid this groundwork, Study FAIR suggests means by which we can cut down on our information about what the Soviets are doing. One particular problem concerns the photographs taken by observation satellites. How, the authors wonder, can we eliminate information we are receiving from these sources? Some suggested solutions:

> . . . an observation satellite which carries infrared detection equipment for the detection of rocket fumes, but has no image-producing equipment. In practice, of course, it will not always be easy to design equipment which is degraded to just the right extent—providing enough information but not too much.
>
> . . . observation satellites which record images on film that must be recovered and processed before the information can become available. This insures that no data, for example, are provided on the current location of mobile missiles, something which might be done by satellites equipped for television transmission.[28]

During some particularly severe crisis between the U.S. and the USSR when the danger of Communist attack seems highest, these satellites may still provide us with too much information. In this event, Study FAIR says, "it might be desirable to be able to turn the cameras off by mutual consent, reactivating them only after the crisis had passed."[29]

So much for efforts to prevent ourselves from finding out what the Communists are doing. There remains the problem of conveying to them information about what we are doing. On this point, Study FAIR suggests "it might be desirable to reassure the Soviets that no Polaris submarines were within firing range of the Soviet Union, and yet the United States would be unwilling to pinpoint the location of all of them. One proposed solution is for the Soviets to be allowed to demand that a few submarines, of their choosing, surface and make their position known."[30] Another possibility is to place Soviet observers on our subs.

The idea behind all this is to prevent ourselves from getting knowledge indicating the Communists are acting in a hostile way, while providing them with knowledge that we are acting in a peaceful way. Under these circumstances, according to the logic of Study FAIR, peace will be assured. Neither side will have reason to doubt the intentions of the other. The balance will have been saved from "destabilizing" increments of knowledge.

Thus does the disarmament lobby come full circle in its reasoning. It is well-established, by the lobbyists' own admission (the quote on page 204 on this score is taken from Study FAIR), that we really do *not* know how strong the Soviets are, and that we have been overestimating their strength. The concept of the "stalemate" is a co-efficient of ignorance. Now it is made the occasion for insuring that we continue to be ignorant. Because we don't know very much about the Soviet Union's strategic arsenal, it is desirable to assume a "balance"; because there is a "balance," it is desirable to be ignorant of the Soviet Union's strategic arsenal. Q.E.D.

Among other Study FAIR ideas to prevent "destabilization" of the assumed balance are such things as increased communication between heads of government, advance notification about missile and plane movements, and an item called "exchange of military missions." The authors do not believe this would do a great deal of good, since in a crisis "the personnel" would probably not be able "to make available the type of information which would be most useful." They nevertheless feel "such missions could help to serve an educative function . . . and this might be a worthwhile aim in itself."[31]

Study FAIR's notion of a U.S.-Soviet exchange of military missions is additionally interesting because the idea popped up again, in 1965, in yet another document spun out of the entrails of the disarmament lobby.* The document in question was prepared for the Air Force by the North American Aviation Company. Entitled "Factors Operative in a Post-Arms Control Situation," it outlines a three-phase plan (the disarmament lobby seems enamored of doing these things in thirds) culminating in global disarmament. The first phase is establishment of a "nuclear free zone" in Europe (a favored theme of *The Liberal Papers*); the second is "exchange of military missions" with the USSR; and the third is "general and complete disarmament." While the specific contents of this paper are not particularly original, the document is important for the way in which it assembles them all into a total programme linked to the final objective of disarmament, and for the way in which it came to be drawn up.

The method of the NAA paper is to suggest futuristic "scenarios" and "chronologies" for U.S. Cold War policy over the coming decade. These hypothetical encounters reaffirm and elaborate almost every accommodationist axiom reviewed in the earlier segments of this book. Among the various actions envisioned for the United States as it moves through the indicated phases:

"More liberal economic policies between East and West become effective . . . U.S. and USSR curtail fissonable [*sic*] materials . . . increased cooperation at Geneva conference . . . bilateral U.S.-USSR agreement for destruction of obsolete bomber aircraft . . . destruction of bombers completed . . . nuclear-free zone treaty signed . . . U.S. government ratifies central European nuclear-free zone treaty . . .

"East-West tensions are eased . . . bilateral U.S.-USSR agreement for exchange of military missions is signed . . . increased cooperation in arms control . . . Communist China admitted to the U.N. . . . U.S.-USSR bilateral agreement

* Also because it has been seconded, as we have seen in chapter 11, by Defense Secretary McNamara.

halting all production of FMW [fissionable material weapons] . . . East-West tensions reducing world-wide; international relations improving in general . . . negotiations in progress for agreement for partial armament reduction in all categories. Verification to be by U.N.-controlled commission . . . General disarmament in phased reduction in all categories. Verification to be by U.N.-controlled commission . . . General disarmament in phased reductions as provided for in two treaties . . ."[32]

It is not altogether clear that either North American Aviation or the Air Force thinks all of this is a good idea, or believes the reasoning sound; North American's assignment seems to have been, given certain assumptions about the course of American policy, to project the plausible consequences. The relevant point is the nature of the assumptions, specified to North American by the Air Force *as the reigning policy of the American government.* In other words, belief that the Soviet Union can be conciliated, that we should have "general and complete disarmament" under the United Nations and quite possibly under a world government, and all of the particular proposals in between, were handed North American by the government as its recognized policy.

Air Force Secretary Eugene Zuckert made this clear in a letter to Congressman Glenard Lipscomb (R-Calif.) "The U.S. policy goals to which reference is made," Zuckert said, "were supplied to the contractor in the contract. *They were gleaned from public speeches and writings of U.S. national leaders as being representative policy goals for the purpose of this study* . . . The arms control measures to be considered in the study were described in the contract and constitute those major proposals which have been placed before the United Nations or the United Nations Eighteen Nation Disarmament Committee, *or have been otherwise given serious consideration by responsible political authority*"[33] (Italics added.)

★★ 18. *A Realistic Plan*

1. *Banning The Bombers*

IN HIS SEPTEMBER 1961 SPEECH to the United Nations, President Kennedy said his program for general and complete disarmament was not a mere slogan, but "a realistic plan." It would, he said, inaugurate "a steady reduction of forces" which would proceed "until it had abolished all armies and all weapons except those needed for internal order and a new United Nations peace force. And it starts that process now, today, even as the talks begin."[1]

To understand the full truth of Kennedy's assertions, it is first necessary to wade through some countervailing statements occasionally thrown out by certain Liberal publicists. Although making it clear in their more esoteric pronouncements that they are steering a course toward disarmament, they like to maintain, for obvious reasons, a somewhat different public image. Thus we find Theodore Sorensen referring to "Kennedy's build-up of the most powerful military force in human history—the largest and swiftest build-up in this country's history"[2] and *Newsweek* contending that present policies have "brought clear benefits to the nation . . . chief among them . . . the enormous improvement that has been registered in the single most vital, life-and-death area of the defense establishment—the nation's nuclear deterrent power and its careful coordination with foreign policy."[3]

The truth is that our nuclear deterrent power under the Kennedy-Johnson dispensation is drastically smaller than the force created by the Eisenhower administration. Under the Eisenhower program, according to the estimate of *U.S. News and World Report,* America's arsenal of the '60's would have been capable of delivering the equivalent of up to 40 billion tons of TNT; the Kennedy-Johnson arsenal, as projected for 1971, the equivalent of somewhere between 2 and 12 billion.[4]

These journalistic assertions were in the main confirmed by McNamara's own testimony before the Senate Armed Services Committee. Reporters Allen and Scott disclosed in September 1964 that "since McNamara became civilian head of the Pentagon in 1961, this country's all-important nuclear weapons stockpile has steadily decreased every year . . . Under policies initiated and forcefully pursued by McNamara, with the full knowledge and approval of the late President Kennedy and President Johnson, the deliverable strategic megatonnage of the U.S., which in 1961 exceeded 36,000 megatons, is declining to the extent that by early 1970 the total will have sunk to around 5,250 megatons."[5]

To fathom the extent to which we have set about disarming ourselves, we need only consider the fate of America's manned bomber force, which in 1961 was a formidable instrument capable of delivering those 36 billion tons of explosive power to any spot in the world, and which by 1970 will be but a shadow of its former self. The bomber cutback pursued by Presidents Kennedy and Johnson, and by Secretary of Defense McNamara in their behalf, has been justified on grounds of expense, shifting technology, sophisticated ideas of deterrence. But the real point of the reduction, made clear by the pronouncements of the disarmament lobby and by the protests and researches of U.S. military men and military authorities on Capitol Hill, is to reassure Moscow, to maintain the all-conquering "balance," and to move toward disarmament.

Secretary MacNamara's stated objective is to produce an American arsenal which consists of intercontinental ballistic missiles in "hardened" sites and Polaris submarines—plus large quantities of "conventional" hardware and personnel for fighting brushfire wars. Since the Polaris cannot strike with sufficient accuracy, distance, or force to threaten central targets in the USSR, this program means our strategic defense boils down to reliance upon ICBMs. McNamara's justification for this policy is three-fold: That the bombers cannot reach their targets as quickly as can missiles; that the bombers are more vulnerable at their above-ground bases than missiles in their silos or Polaris subs under water; and that bombers are more liable than missiles to be shot down by Soviet defenses.

Air power advocates, General Curtis LeMay foremost among them, admit the missiles have certain advantages, but counter that bombers also have their good points—including, pre-eminently, the fact that we know they will work. LeMay and other military men argue that we should try to derive full benefits from both weapons systems by maintaining a "mix." ICBMs, they point out, have never been used under combat conditions; failures, as in the misfire of the Agena-Atlas combination in a projected 1965 space launch, are still a necessary evil; missiles are peculiarly inflexible weapons systems; they have never been tested together with their warheads; and—under the 1963 test-ban treaty—cannot be so tested. As former Strategic Air Command chief General Thomas Power observes: "This is the first time in our history that much or even most of the nation's striking power is to be entrusted to weapons that have never been tested operationally."[6]

The impact of the test-ban was emphatically pointed out by both LeMay and Power in testimony before the Senate Preparedness subcommittee. Power said our missiles could not be considered dependable until we conducted high megaton tests in the atmosphere to discover what such explosions would do to communications and guidance systems. LeMay said: "We are never going to know about missile reliability with the same degree of assurance we have on the manned systems, because we are never going to be able to get the broad basis of experience that we can get with manned airplanes. . . . When we do fire missiles, we are not really firing them under operational conditions because we cannot fire from the actual wartime position of the missiles. They have to be taken out and set up on the range and fired from there. That is not a true operational test. Further, we are not allowed to fire the warheads and the missiles together."[7]

It is sometimes suggested the LeMay-Power view is Air Force parochialism weaned on "nostalgia" and the desire of this service to maintain its own systems. Yet there is no reason the Air Force should object to increased emphasis on ICBMs as such, since these weapons are also in its province. Moreover, the other services have uniformly backed the Air Force position on the need for manned bombers.

Both the Army and the Navy strongly seconded LeMay's opposition to the phase-out of manned aircraft. Gen. Earl G. Wheeler, then Army Chief of Staff, told Congress in 1963 he favored development of the B-70 superbomber. Adm. George W. Anderson, then Chief of Naval Operations, similarly supported the continuation of manned aircraft and development of the Army's Nike-Zeus antimissile defenses. He favored extending the life of bombers, Anderson explained, because "I do not have the same confidence in any of the missile systems as do some of the technicians who attest to the performance of the missiles."[8]

The virtually unanimous opinion of the military has proved more persuasive to congressmen then have McNamara's arguments. Among those who have battled against the McNamara view are Senator Richard Russell (D-Ga.), Chairman of the Senate Armed Services Committee, Senator Henry Jackson (D-Wash.), former Senator Barry Goldwater (R-Ariz.), former Congressman Carl Vinson (D-Ga.) and Rep. Leslie Arends (R-Ill.), GOP whip in the House. After weighing the testimony of McNamara and the military, the legislators have repeatedly affirmed their desire to maintain a manned bomber fleet—to no avail.

In 1963, during discussion of the nuclear test-ban treaty, Senator John Stennis (D-Miss.), chairman of the Preparedness subcommittee, said "the United States is not able to verify the ability of its hardened underground missile systems to survive close-in high-yield explosions . . . We do not know how they will work with a nuclear explosion somewhere near them . . . They have not been tested under those conditions."[9]

Senator Russell Long (D-La.) held a like opinion. "Not only do we not know the information we should have if we are to be secure in our defense," he said, ". . . we do not know whether the overwhelming majority of the missiles will actually work, because they have never been tested under conditions under which they would be fired at a target."[10]

House Armed Services Committee Chairman Vinson summed up the prevailing congressional view when he said America could not afford to put all its eggs in the missile basket. "There is no bomber anywhere near production," he said. "In fact, there is no bomber even designed at this time, and as you all know, design to delivery on a complicated bomber is six to eight years. The time is going to come when there will be no bombers if we do not get started on a bomber today. The B-52s and B-58s will simply wear out. *And should this happen, we will be in the position of depending entirely on missiles, a thing that none of us wants to do.*"[11] (Emphasis added.)

LeMay's argument on flexibility has also proved convincing to congressmen. The missile, LeMay says, "goes where you say it should go when you launch it. You cannot change your mind and bring it back. . . . Manned systems can use judgment, can find targets you know are in the area, but you do not know exactly where until you go and look." Even if the missiles were fully tested and in perfect working order, LeMay says, "I still say you are in a muscle-bound position. . . . You only have two choices. You are either off the button and at peace, or you are on the button and at war."[12]

By way of contrast, a manned bomber fleet makes it possible to employ a show of force, to send planes up on a stand-by basis, and to recall them if the crisis is resolved. During the Cuban missile dispute, as the *Saturday Evening Post* observes, SAC was ready to go "and the Russians knew it." Manned aircraft afford a flexible means of showing the enemy we mean business without launching all-out war. "How are you going to impress them with a missile?" the *Post* quotes one Air Force officer as saying. "Hold your thumb a half-inch nearer the button?"[13]

Ballistic missiles, on this analysis, are our weapons of *last* resort, the defense we would use if there were clearly no alternative but total nuclear war. Manned bombers are, or should be, our weapon of *first* resort. Their greater flexibility, their ability to be sent aloft on standby basis, to maneuver, to be called back if necessary, to decoy enemy defenses through the use of penetration aids, make them far more useful than missiles under conditions of marginal or ambiguous confrontation.*

On several occasions Congress has backed its sentiments on this question with strong votes in favor of bomber development—votes which McNamara has simply refused to honor. In 1961, Congress voted $525 million for an additional wing of B-52s which McNamara declined to purchase. In 1962, the House Armed Services Committee voted $491 million for development of the B-70, and said the Defense Secretary was "directed, ordered, mandated and required" to spend the money for the plane. McNamara also ignored this. In 1964, the House tried again, voting 121 to 29 to authorize $92 million for research on new bombers and interceptors. This too was ignored.

When the 1965 cutbacks aroused still further outcry, McNamara countered with a suggestion that the controversial TFX fighter plane be converted to strategic uses. This proposal met with little enthusiasm, either from the military or from congressmen. "The TFX is not really the solution," LeMay said. "It could be used, but it lacks size, range, and weight-carrying capacity to do the long-range job. We may be caught and have to use this aircraft as a poor substitute, for we are long past the time when we should have started production of a new and advanced system."[14]

* Ballistic missiles, says Congressman Arends, are fine weapons, but essentially untried: "We have not fired them carrying a nuclear warhead. Their behavior mechanically is not one of absolutes—will every one go aloft, will it reach the target, and will it detonate when it lands? We are reasonably sure but not wholly sure.

"A bomber, on the other hand, is a tried and proven weapon. We know what it can do and it cannot do. It can go, stop, and change direction, being at all times completely under manned control. It is a weapon carrying nuclear destruction upon which we can rely, adjustable to fluid warfare conditions.

"The manned bombers should supplement our missions, to give our defense the necessary flexibility and reliability. We presently have on hand such bombers. But we have no bomber program for the future."

Moreover, it was reported that the TFX—now designated as the F-111—was in deep trouble along the production lines. Marked by controversy from the beginning when McNamara over military objection awarded the contract to General Dynamics, the plane was experiencing design problems which evoked a threat of cancellation to the contractor. Again Congress protested, again to no avail.

A subcommittee of the House Armed Services Committee took a long close look at the F-111 and observed that, despite McNamara's assertions, the plane is "an interim aircraft, and not a completely acceptable substitute for the B-52 aircraft now in the SAC inventory." The congressmen noted, among other things, that the F-111 could carry an ordnance load only half that of the B-52, with a much smaller megatonnage range, and was severely limited in performing conventional bombing missions. Moreover, because of range limitations, it could reach only 70 per cent of the targets assigned to SAC. In essence, the F-111 is a fighter plane thrown into the breach by McNamara to quiet congressional outcries over the reduction in our bomber force. After wrestling at length with McNamara's obscure justifications in its behalf, the congressmen concluded that "the F-111 was not designed for or intended to be a bomber. It merely happened to be available at a time when there was nothing else to take the place of the B-52s. Taking credit for having something usable under these circumstances is substituting foresight and planning for what was pure luck."[15]

2. *The Reason Why*

The legislators do not find McNamara's public arguments convincing, and seem puzzled that he persists in his chosen course despite the overwhelming weight of military and congressional opinion.

Repeatedly they grapple with his complex objections to

their proposals for a new manned bomber. The B-70, he says, won't work properly; there is something wrong with the fuel system; the proposed AMSA attack ship has bugs in it; and so forth. The legislators wrestle with these difficulties, perplexed, only to find McNamara suggesting new ones when they have finished.

Some of the mystery surrounding this odd controversy dissipates if we shift our attention away from McNamara's parade of technical objections and note that the public arguments about manned aircraft do not correspond to the private ones. The relative merits of manned bombers and ICBMs as weapons systems in fact have very little to do with it; the relative merits of the two instruments as "provocations" to Moscow or "destabilizing" elements have everything to do with it. The manned bomber "provokes"; the ICBM does not. That is the point.[16] Congressmen and military leaders may argue forever that bombers will make the United States stronger, and they will not budge the disarmament lobby an inch—because the disarmament lobby is not interested in making the United States stronger. It is interested in disarming.

The essence of the matter is that our bombers, along with a good deal of other military hardware, are being dismantled as part of our over-all program of accommodating the Soviet Union. If our previous discussion leaves any lingering doubt on this score, the authors of Study FAIR have been kind enough to make the matter explicit. Among its varied proposals for unilateral arms control initiatives, the document contains the following suggestions:

> It seems feasible in the next few years to withdraw strategic forces from overseas bases. . . . Almost certainly obsolescent SAC bombers of medium range can be withdrawn first. But for overseas base reductions to have maximum usefulness as a demonstration of restraint and stabilizing effort. . . . to be

perceived by the Soviets as one hopes they will be, the United States will be obliged to affirm clearly that its moves are made to create a more stable military situation and to demonstrate the nonaggressive aims of the U.S. policy.[17]

Significantly, the authors conclude that American policy is already settled in the proper groove: A proper understanding of the "balance" is indicated by "contemplated gradual reductions in the relatively vulnerable bomber force accompanied by an increase in hardened Minutemen and mobile Polaris forces," and by the fact that "present U.S. weapons planning does not seem to point toward indefinite increases in Minutemen and Polaris forces, although qualitative improvements and various changes in strategic weapons may of course be expected."[18] They are also gratified to note that neither anti-missile defenses nor shelter programs can "affect the qualitative deterrent balance."[19]

Also significant is the fact that these defense cutbacks have been justified in precisely the kind of rhetoric urged by disarmament lobbyists Melman and Rock. We have had, of course, the tax cut advocated by Rock. We have had the vast increase in domestic welfarism advocated by Melman. And we have had much simultaneous talk of "economy" in the Defense Department during the phase-out of critical weapons systems.

McNamara tied this whole package neatly together in December, 1965, when he announced the shutdown and consolidation of some 149 U.S. military bases and a further reduction of our manned bomber force over the succeeding five years. The jointly-announced cutbacks were justified on the grounds of "economy," with public attention directed toward an estimated savings of $410 million annually from the base shutdown.

In point of fact, "economy" had nothing to do with it, a conclusion which emerges readily from a survey of the relevant figures. The same administration thus supposedly practicing frugality toward our armaments was simultaneously spending more than $50 billion a year—or more than 100 times the asserted savings from the McNamara cutback—on domestic welfare outlays. The military "savings" could have been subtracted from the "war on poverty" or surplus foreign aid dollars in the pipeline and not even have been noticed.

Perhaps the most conclusive evidence that the unilateralist view has fully penetrated our defense establishment is McNamara's settled hostility toward an anti-missile defense. The Defense Secretary has rung the changes in his opposition to development of an ABM, from technical unfeasibility to the imperatives of "economy." The 1965 Wiesner panel approvingly quotes him on the hazards of deploying an ABM, very much in the language of Wiesner himself. "Although the Nike X development is progressing satisfactorily," McNamara stated, "there are many technical problems to be solved, and I believe it is still premature to make any commitment to production and deployment at this time." Among other problems, McNamara noted that of "the nature and effect of an opponent's possible reaction to our Nike X deployment."[20]

The ABM slowdown is justifiable on one set of premises only: The Wiesner-Rock view that development of such a weapon would unbalance the Cold War and thwart efforts toward disarmament. Under no circumstances can an ABM system be described as "offensive"; its sole purpose is to defend Americans from possible Communist attack. Yet it is viewed in official circles as a "provocative" or "first-strike" weapon—an evaluation which can be derived only from the proposition that the "balance" is good and anything which upsets it is bad.

When Wiesner and Rostow returned from the USSR in 1960, America's projected ABM system was, significantly enough, one of the principal casualties. It was killed, Thomas Ross reports, because it was viewed as a "first-strike" weapon:

Three weapons with powerful congressional and industrial support are the B-70 superbomber, the Titan ICBM, and *the Nike-Zeus antimissile missile.* Tens of billions of dollars would be involved in their production and several localities would benefit greatly thereby from defense contracts.

But for varying reasons all three are viewed *as first-strike weapons.* Accordingly, Kennedy defense officials recommended a reduction for the B-70 and a cutback in production of the Titan. The Nike-Zeus, nevertheless, was at first approved for limited production.

The final "hard decisions," of course, had to be made by the President. And the matter was still up in the air when he started to get dressed the night of March 11 for the Gridiron dinner, the annual spoof of high Washington officialdom by top Capital newspapermen.

Sorensen was in the room, briefing the President on the latest thinking on the defense message. Mr. Kennedy struggled with his boiled shirt and white tie, engrossed in his thoughts. *Finally, he turned to Sorensen and directed him to cut out all three first-strike weapons.* (Italics added.)[21]

3. *The Structure of Agreement*

Indications that the present administration has embraced unilateralism are not limited to bombers and ABMs. The whole "reciprocal initiative" program of disarmament by budget-cutting and secret signals to the Kremlin has been put into sweeping effect. The weapons cutbacks noted by Thomas Ross were followed by a number of others, including:

1. Cutback on production of the Atlas ICBM.
2. Phase-out of the B-47, B-52, and B-58 long-range bombers.
3. Sharp reduction in plans for construction of 2,000 Minuteman missiles by 1968.

4. Withdrawal of Thor and Jupiter intermediate range missiles in Greece, Turkey, and Great Britain.
5. Cancellation of the Skybolt missile program which would have given our air force and that of Great Britain a 1,000-mile firing range.
6. A presidential order drastically reducing the production of fissionable nuclear materials and shutting down nuclear reactors.
7. Shelving of plans for additional nuclear aircraft carriers.
8. The 1962 Antarctica treaty supposedly prohibiting nuclear activity in the polar region.
9. The 1963 nuclear test-ban treaty.

Together with the three cutbacks ordered by Kennedy in March, 1961, this makes a round dozen steps taken by the Liberal administration down the road to "accommodation," relief of Soviet "anxieties," and "general and complete disarmament."

U.S. News, in a 1963 summary of steps being taken toward disarmament, gave these further examples:

Military satellites. The Midas 'spy satellite' was killed after a decision that 15 extra minutes' warning of missile attack was not worth the millions still required to perfect it. Numerous other military space projects have been abandoned or delayed.

Navy carriers. Signs point to a cut of as much as one third in the Navy's fleet of 15 attack carriers. Construction is being delayed on an additional new carrier authorized by Congress last year.

Overseas bases. Flying bases in England, Morocco, Spain, France, Guam and elsewhere have or will be shut down . . .

Nuclear test-ban. The U.S. alone took the initiative in suspending atmospheric tests in June as evidence of good faith before formal test-ban talks with Russia. Military requests to continue testing were set aside.[22]

That these actions are aimed at "accommodating" the Soviets has been affirmed by both Kennedy and Johnson. The first step toward disarmament, Kennedy said in 1961, "is a treaty assuring the end of nuclear tests of all kinds, in every environment, under workable controls." An acceptable move in this direction was a "mutual ban on atmospheric testing, without inspection or controls"—after which still other items on the agenda of "general and complete disarmament" could be taken up for action.[23] The test-ban treaty was of course achieved in 1963. President Johnson, using language almost identical to Rock's, similarly cited the test-ban treaty, the cutback on atomic materials, the "hot line," and our concordat with Moscow on making fresh water from the oceans as efforts "to build the structure of agreement which can bring peace to the rest of the world."[24]

Also consonant with the unilateralist program is the fact that Secretary McNamara has been systematically slashing U.S. defenses across the board. In 1964, a confidential report of the Senate Armed Services Committee showed McNamara had cut more than $2 billion from "priority weapons systems requests" of the armed services. Included in the cutbacks were $240 million for nuclear-powered submarines, $311.4 million for the Minuteman missile, $40 million for the Titan missile, and $12.5 million for research on the effects of high megaton nuclear blasts on the reliability of missile guidance systems. Another $89.8 million projected for development of nuclear testing sites, overseas atomic facilities, and a nuclear detection system was also cut.[25]

One "reciprocal initiative" idea translated into official policy by our government was a so-called "bomber-burning" scheme which first came to light early in 1963. According to *The New York Times,* this proposal "calls for the United States to burn 30 B-47 bombers a month in return for the destruction by the Russians of an equal number of their TU-116 Badger bombers." The idea, in the official explanation, was to keep such aircraft from being sold off to other countries. U.S. officials explained that "the United States . . . is already phasing out its B-47 fleet, so the exchange would not involve a sacrifice."[26]

When Senator Barry Goldwater brought this matter up in March, 1963, his charges evoked official denials. Secretary of State Rusk, however, subsequently acknowledged the plan had "been discussed inside the disarmament agency and with the [other] departments as one possible step which might at some stage be seriously considered," in essence confirming Goldwater's allegations. The *Times* added that "the senator's attacks have baffled disarmament officials, who felt they had come up with a reasonable suggestion that was winning favor on Capitol Hill."[27]

A year later, the disarmament lobby was still working on the idea. Columnists Allen and Scott disclosed that "U.S. and Soviet diplomats have reached an agreement 'in principle' on a second-step disarmament treaty . . . Under this disarmament agreement U.S. B-47s and Soviet Badger bombers, similar to those sent to Cuba, would be destroyed in a large arms 'bonfire' under the supervision of the U.N."[28]

How this subliminal approach to disarmament works in practice, of course, is another matter. The United States has on occasion received verbal professions of compliance from the Soviet Union, but little else. Osgood and the Study FAIR authors tell us we can wait and see whether the Soviets respond to our initiatives, but neglect to explain how we can be sure the response is valid. If we cut back on our manned bombers, the Soviets can say they are doing the same; if we stop nuclear tests, the Soviets can say they are doing the same. But how do we know what they *say* corresponds to what they do?

That Soviet deception has not been suspended to suit the enthusiasms of Rock and Osgood has been previously suggested in our discussion of the 1963 test-ban treaty. It was confirmed in 1964, when the Johnson regime attempted to pursue the program of disarmament-without-treaty in the matter of nuclear materials. On April 20, 1964, President Johnson and Premier Khrushchev made simultaneous announcements that each side was cutting back the production of fissionable materials for nuclear weapons. These announcements were widely hailed as a great step toward peace. Johnson himself singles out the cutback as an important step toward building "the structure of agreement." Close analysis revealed, however, that while our cutback in fissionable materials was real, the Soviets' was purely verbal. Although the United States slashed its plutonium production by 20 per cent and its enriched uranium production by 40 per cent, the corresponding figures for the Kremilin, to the extent we can estimate in this always mysterious realm, were zero per cent and 15 percent. Thus, even assuming the Soviet pledges mean anything at all, the "structure of agreement" in this case wound up with the United States, in the words of Congressman Craig Hosmer, (R-Calif.) swapping one horse for one rabbit.*

* Congressman Hosmer, ranking Republican on the Joint Congressional Committee on Atomic Energy and an authority on nuclear subjects, gives this analysis on the transaction:

"On the subject of plutonium, Premier Khrushchev merely announced that the USSR is not going to finish off two production reactors. He did not indicate whether other unfinished reactors, if any, would be completed. He made no reference to reactors, in being and now supplying plutonium to nuclear weapons factories, the amount of their production, or how Soviet scientists might be planning to boost it to higher levels. Khrushchev not only promised no cutback whatever in plutonium production, he left entirely open the possibility that the Soviet Union might be increasing it considerably.

"In contrast, President Johnson confirmed . . . his order issued in January to shut down and mothball four plutonium producing reactors and slash the U.S. output by 20 per cent.

"On the subject of enriched uranium, Premier Khrushchev announced but he did not promise—what he termed a 'substantial' cutback in production 'over the next several years.' What did he mean by the 'next several years'? When does it start? When does it end? How big a slash in Soviet production of U235 does he believe warrants the adjective 'substantial'?

"A possible clue to the definition of this word is found in President Johnson's speech. He described the boost of his 25 per cent cutback announced in January to 40 per cent in April as 'substantial.' Thus, in the semantics of enriched uranium production, a 15 per cent variation appears to warrant the euphemistic adjective 'substantial.' "

★★ *Part IV:*

THE RETURN OF THE IPR

As it became more and more obvious that Chiang Kai-shek and the Kuomintang were doomed, the conduct of American policy became increasingly delicate. The problem was how to allow them to fall without making it look as if the United States had pushed them . . . The thing to do, therefore, is to let South Korea fall—but not to let it look as though we pushed it.

—Owen Lattimore

★★ 19. *Kennedy Was Right*

1. *Lattimores and Fairbanks*

ON JANUARY 30, 1949, a lanky young Congressman arose at a political gathering in Salem, Massachusetts, to discuss the subject of China. Then as now, it was not a happy topic. The Chinese Communists were at the time closing in for the kill against the discomfited armies of Chiang Kai-shek.

It was shocking to reflect, said the young man, that the Second World War had in large part stemmed from our desire to protect the territorial integrity of China—only to result in the sacrifice of that integrity to the Communists. The war had been fought, countless lives had been lost, so that America might stand by her ally, Chiang. Now the victory achieved on the battlefield had been thrown away.

"In 1944," the congressman charged, "Gen. 'Vinegar Joe' Stilwell presented a plan to arm 1,000,000 Chinese Communists, who had been carefully building their resources in preparation for a post-war seizure of power . . . This plan was supported by some State Department officials, including Ambassador Clarence Gauss. Chiang Kai-shek refused to co-operate with this plan, which would have presented the Chinese Communists with an easy coup. Chiang requested that Stilwell be recalled, which caused much bitter comment in this country; and Gauss resigned. From this date on our relations with the National Government declined."[1]

The young lawmaker pinpointed the Yalta conference as a major source of our difficulties, charging that "a sick Roosevelt, with the advice of General Marshall and other Chiefs of Staff, gave the control of the Kurile Islands as well as the control of various strategic Chinese ports, such as Port Arthur and Dairen, to the Soviet Union."[2]

Detailing further mistakes in American policy toward China, the congressman concluded that:

> Our policy in China has reaped the whirlwind. The continued insistence that aid would not be forthcoming unless a coalition government with the Communists was formed was a crippling blow to the national government. So concerned were our diplomats and their advisers, the Lattimores and the Fairbanks, with the imperfections of the diplomatic system in China after 20 years of war, and the tales of corruption in high places, that they lost sight of our tremendous stake in a non-Communist China.
>
> There were those who claimed, and still claim that Chinese communism was not really Communism at all but merely an advanced agrarian movement which did not take directions from Moscow. . . .
>
> This is the tragic story of China whose freedom we once fought to preserve. What our young men had saved, our diplomats and our President have frittered away.[3]

So spoke the youthful Democratic Congressman, John F. Kennedy of Massachusetts.

Two years later, Kennedy's indictment of American policy, and of the baleful influence upon that policy of "the Lattimores and the Fairbanks," was to be confirmed in full. The Senate Internal Security subcommittee, after a painstaking investigation, issued a heavily-documented report on an organization known as the "Institute of Pacific Relations." The IPR was the principal base of operations of "the Lattimores and the Fairbanks"—Owen Lattimore and John K. Fairbank both being prominent IPR associates—and it exerted a powerful influence on the course of American policy. As the paramount scholarly organization concerned with the Orient, it was a natural source of counsel and information for general public and government officials alike. Moreover, it could claim various members, such as Lattimore, who often were employed by the government in matters pertaining to China. With these excellent connections, it assiduously promoted the belief that the Chinese Communists were "agrarian reformers," and advertised the alleged corruption of Chiang Kai-shek.

The Senate subcommittee came to the following conclusions concerning this organization:

"The IPR has been considered by the American Communist Party and by Soviet officials as an instrument of Communist policy, propaganda and military intelligence.

"The IPR disseminated and sought to popularize false information including information originating from Soviet and Communist sources . . .

"Members of the small core of officials and staff members who controlled IPR were either Communist or pro-Communist . . .

"The IPR was a vehicle used by the Communists to orientate American Far Eastern policies toward Communist objectives . . .

"During the period 1945-49, persons associated with the Institute of Pacific Relations were instrumental in keeping

United States policy on a course favorable to Communist objectives in China . . .

"The net effect of IPR activities on United States public opinion has been such as to serve international Communist interests and to affect adversely the interests of the United States."[4]

A dozen years later, our young Congressman was to become President of the United States. The normal presumption was that a statesman who had shown such prescience in 1949, and who had been vindicated by a minute dissection of the record, would recall his own warnings and act on them. At a minimum, it would seem logical to expect he would not staff his State Department with alumni of the Institute of Pacific Relations; that he would not man his Pacific outposts with the "China hands" who had been associated with the ruinous policies of the 40s; that he would not employ defenders of the Yalta conference; and that he would not repeat the blunder of cutting off aid to anti-Communist governments to force them into coalitions with the Communists. Yet, after a year of his term had run, each and all of these presumptions would be proved wrong.

2. *The Man From Yalta*

With considerable accuracy, Congressman Kennedy had dated the beginning of the end for China from the 1945 Yalta conference, where the Communists were given vast and critical concessions in Asia and Europe. That Yalta had been a diplomatic disaster for the free world and a great uncalled-for triumph by the Communists is widely acknowledged by everyone who has assessed the record with any degree of objectivity. On this point, Kennedy was thoroughly sustained by the record.

It would therefore seem reasonable to have assumed that Kennedy, having been proved right about Yalta by the consensus of historical opinion, would *not* make it his business upon ascending to the White House to name the principal still-active alumnus of Yalta—and an inveterate defender of the agreements reached there—his trusted assistant in matters of foreign policy. Yet that is exactly what occurred when Kennedy selected Charles E. Bohlen as the new administration's "Russian expert."

"Chip" Bohlen entered the foreign service in 1929, and, according to *The New York Times,* "was chosen by the State Department as one of a half-dozen promising young men to specialize in Soviet affairs against the day when the United States recognized the Soviet Union."[5] He first went to Moscow in 1934, returning for two years in 1937. In 1953, he was named Ambassador to the Soviet Union, and remained there until 1957, when he was sent to the Philippines. In 1959, he became a special adviser to Secretary of State Christian Herter, and was appointed to a similar post in the Kennedy State Department.

Bohlen's "career" status makes him an important connecting link between the Kennedy-Johnson State Department and the heyday of the New Deal. According to Robert Sherwood, Bohlen got his real start as an "expert" under the sponsorship of Roosevelt's alter ego Harry Hopkins, who "asked him [Bohlen] all manner of questions about the Soviet Union and was surprised and impressed by the objectivity and lack of bias as well as by the considerable scholarship revealed in his answers."[6]

General John R. Deane suggested Hopkins' outlook during this period, writing that Hopkins had administered American aid to the Soviets "with a zeal which approached fanaticism." Hopkins' enthusiasm for helping Moscow, Deane says, "became so ingrained that it could not be tempered."[7] According to testimony of Col. Bogolopev, the Communists considered Hopkins their staunch and enthusiastic friend. Foreign Minister V. M. Molotov informed his

Communist colleagues, Bogolopev said, that Hopkins' desire "is to ask nothing and to give everything. What he wants is to keep us in the fight—and that is all. Mr. Hopkins is completely on our side and may be trusted absolutely."[8] *

Such was the man who took "Chip" Bohlen under his wing and was favorably impressed by his lack of bias in matters pertaining to the Soviets. "From then on," Sherwood records, "Bohlen's star was very much in the ascendant . . ."[9]

Bohlen subsequently turned up at the crucial conferences in Teheran and Yalta, where a "sick Roosevelt," as Kennedy had put it, made his concessions to Stalin. At Teheran, Stalin made his bid to hang on to the Polish territory east of the Curzon Line which his troops had captured in the sneak invasion of 1939. President Roosevelt was prepared to make the concession, but was worried about the political impact of it. The State Department documents on Teheran tell us:

"According to the American memo made of this conversation the President went on to explain that a national election in the United States was due in 1944; that while he would rather not run again he might have to if the war was still in progress. There were between six and seven million Americans of Polish extraction in the United States and he did not want to lose their votes . . ."[10]

Roosevelt got safely by the '44 elections, and in February 1945, the Polish deal was consummated at Yalta. Agreements were also arrived at which insured that the newly defined Polish nation would be controlled by a puppet government run from Moscow. In addition, Moscow was given, as Kennedy noted, control of Outer Mongolia, the arterial railroads of Manchuria, the ports of Dairen and Port Arthur, southern Sakhalin, and the Kurile Islands.

In the middle of all this sat Soviet expert Charles Bohlen, unbiased protege of Harry Hopkins. It was Bohlen who re-

* For his own part, Hopkins stated: "Since Russia is the decisive factor she must be given every assistance and every effort must be made to obtain her friendship."

corded Roosevelt's acknowledgment that he was ready to abandon the Poles, but not ready to abandon 7 million votes. He was, officially, an interpreter and stenographer, and his partisans try to picture his part in these conferences as relatively insignificant. Authorities who have reason to know, however, contradict this demure assessment. Edward Stettinius wrote that "Bohlen . . . was more than a professional interpreter. He was an expert, as well, on substantive matters."[11] Bohlen himself, trying to minimize his role, put it that: "At Yalta, I served primarily in the capacity of an interpreter for President Roosevelt, but was also an adviser to the delegation."[12]

Whatever his role, Bohlen has made it clear he does not disapprove of the Yalta concessions. When his appointment as Ambassador to Moscow came up in 1953, Senator Joseph R. McCarthy (R-Wis.), raised the Yalta issue. Bohlen, called to give his views on the matter, refused to acknowledge any default of U.S. policy. "I don't consider that the agreement at Yalta involved a surrender," he said. "It involved the opposite."[13]

The late Senator Styles Bridges (R-N.H.), opposing Bohlen's nomination as a State Department adviser, said: "The reason I'm opposed is that over a period of years Mr. Bohlen was associated with some of the basic failures in our dealings with Russia, and that apparently he still was defending those failures."[14] That was in 1959, at which late date Bohlen still had not repudiated Yalta. Nor, so far as the public record discloses, has he done so to this day.

During the 1953 debate, the subject of Bohlen's status in the government's loyalty-security files was also raised. Secretary of State John Foster Dulles, although at that time defending Bohlen, acknowledged the State Department's security chief had said "that, in view of the fact that this file contained some derogatory information, he did not wish to take the responsibility for clearance."[15]

Among Bohlen's early acts in the Kennedy administration

was his advice to the new president, reported by Thomas Ross and recorded in Chapter 17, to insert "Communist phraseology" in the March, 1961 message on defense, to insure that the Kremlin understood the intensity of our desire not to be "provocative."[16]

3. *Dean Rusk*

When Dean Rusk was appointed Secretary of State for the Kennedy administration, the most common response was: "Who is he?" The general public knew nothing about the soft-spoken Georgian, and experienced reporters recalled little except that he had always been a quiet sort of journeyman diplomatist. Nobody could state with any accuracy the nature of his opinions or predict the kind of policy a State Department under him would pursue.

Kennedy's Secretary of State, it developed, was an integral part of the IPR group Kennedy had himself disparaged. His name came up in this connection in the IPR hearings, during testimony of Dr. Edna Fluegel:

> Mr. Morris. Dr. Fluegel, who succeeded Alger Hiss as head of the postwar planning Division of the State Department?
>
> Miss Fluegel. Dr. Dean Rusk.
>
> Mr. Morris. Mr. Mandel [subcommittee research director], was Dr. Dean Rusk active in the Institute of Pacific Relations?
>
> Mr. Mandel. Dr. Dean Rusk was a member of the American Council of the IPR and actively supported an IPR request for a donation from the Rockefeller Foundation as late as 1950. He also suggested the use of IPR publications by the Chief of Military Intelligence, according to a letter in our files.[17]

Among the duties which Rusk took over from Hiss were those having to do with the United Nations. Under Hiss' administration of the Office of Political Affairs, "top-level" policy was that no steps should be taken to prohibit American

Communists from serving in the United Nations. The decision, according to testimony of State Department official Carlisle Humelsine, was to leave the matter up to the U. N. secretariat. When Rusk took over U. N. affairs, the policy was continued. During Senate hearings on this question, the following colloquy took place:

> Mr. Sourwine. It is the gist of our testimony that while Mr. Dean Rusk was in charge of United Nations Affairs, not only was no position of the Department in opposition to the employment of American Communists communicated to the United Nations but actually there was no such official position of the Department so far as you know?
>
> Mr. Humelsine. So far as I know.[18]

The omission was a damaging one. As the Senate Internal Security subcommittee's hearings showed, the U.N. harbored a large number of Americans, in important positions, with dubious security records.[19]

In 1950, Rusk moved up to become Assistant Secretary of State for Far Eastern Affairs, serving in this capacity through the hectic days of the Korean War. In this position, he was instrumental in shaping the policy General Douglas MacArthur described as a "catastrophic blow to the hopes of the free world"[20]—the policy giving the Communist Chinese a privileged sanctuary north and west of the Yalu River. On November 6, 1950, MacArthur was ready to send a bombing mission to knock out a bridge connecting Sinuiju, Korea, with Antung, Manchuria. Former President Truman tells of an emergency conference involving Secretary of State Acheson and Secretary of Defense Lovett. "Assistant Secretary of State Dean Rusk," Truman says, "pointed out that we had a commitment with the British not to take action which might involve attacks on the Manchurian side of the river without consultation."[21] Rusk, Truman goes on, added that the State Department was trying to get a "resolution" from the United Nations concerning the flood of Communist troops pouring across the river from China. "Mr. Rusk also mentioned the danger of involving the Soviets, especially in the light of the mutual-assistance treaty between Moscow and Peking."[22]

As a result, Truman says, Lovett called Air Force Secretary Thomas Finletter, "and instructed him to tell the Joint Chiefs what Mr. Rusk had set forth and to tell them that he (Lovett) and Acheson both felt that this action should be postponed until they were able to get a decision from me."[23]

The bombing mission was cancelled an hour and 20 minutes before the planes were scheduled to take off. MacArthur, after protesting, got permission to try to bomb the bridges—so long as he did not violate the air space to the west and north of them, or harm the staging points from which the Communists operated. The "privileged sanctuary" policy was established.

Nine days later, Rusk delivered an address supporting this policy. "We do not know," he said, "what the Chinese intentions are. It is of the greatest importance to find out whether the Chinese have limited objectives which are negotiable in character, or unlimited objectives which by their very nature are not negotiable . . . Put yourself in Peking, consider that you have been subjected to a barrage of Soviet propaganda about our alleged aggressive designs, and see whether you yourselves might not have some such misgivings."[24]

While Rusk was urging his listeners to look at it from the Chinese Reds' point of view, General MacArthur was having his own look in Korea: "Men and material in large force are pouring across all bridges over the Yalu from Manchuria. This movement not only jeopardizes but threatens the ultimate destruction of the forces under my command. . . . The only way to stop this reinforcement of the enemy is the destruction of these bridges and the subjection of all installations in the north area supporting the enemy advance to the maximum of our air destruction. Every hour that this is postponed will be paid for dearly in American and other United Nations blood . . ."[25]

Rusk had delivered yet another speech on the Chinese Communists earlier in 1950, describing them as revolutionaries comparable to the American patriots of 1776, suggesting their despotism was "not Russian in essence" and did not aim at dictatorship, but was "subject to perversion." He opined that there was a "conflict coming between Chinese nationalism and Russian imperialism masquerading as world Communism."[26]

Such sentiments coming from a high State Department official, commented the Washington *Post,* "made it clear that U.S. policy is based upon the hope that even Communist movements can be kept out of Soviet control, and indicated that so long as nationalist movements—Communist or otherwise—are not Soviet-controlled, the United States may deal with them."[27]

When Republican critics subsequently alluded to this speech, Rusk sought to deny everything. "There is not a shred of truth in the allegation that I ever compared the Communist revolution in China with the American revolt from the British in 1776," Rusk said, "or that I ever compared Mao Tse-Tung with George Washington and Patrick Henry. Nor did I ever say that the Communist Chinese revolution 'does not aim at dictatorship.' "[28]

The GOP immediately produced a story from the *Philadelphia Bulletin* for January 14, 1950, headlined: "Revolt in China Likened to '76: Rusk of State Dept. Gives Talk Here." The lead paragraph of the story reads: "The revolution now raging in China springs from the same basic causes as the American Revolution, the World Affairs Council of Philadelphia was told today. The statement came from Dean Rusk, deputy under secretary of the U.S. Department of State, at the start of the council's two-day session at the University of Pennsylvania."[29]

The GOP quoted several paragraphs of the news story on Rusk's remarks, including these:

"The upheaval in China is a revolution which, if we analyze it, we will see is prompted by the same things that prompted the British, French, and American revolutions," Rusk said.

The trend in China is not pro-Soviet, though it could become so, Rusk said.

"Americans would not want to freeze conditions in the Far East. What we are seeking is a direction for the revolution. The Chinese are not aiming toward dictatorship. Their revolution is not Russian in essence, but is subject to perversion . . ."[30]

4. *Arthur H. Dean*

In a previous essay, this writer discussed the return to eminence of two IPR luminaries under the ministrations of the Kennedy-Johnson regime. These were Owen Lattimore, who in 1961 popped up on a rather mysterious mission to Outer Mongolia, and John Stewart Service, who was given a high-ranking position in the Kennedy State Department. Both are relevant now as examples of the return to favor of IPR, but since they are discussed at some length elsewhere, they will be noted only briefly in this chapter.*

Service, more directly connected with this phase of our narrative than Lattimore, served as a U.S. diplomat in China during the 1940s, whence he filed reports disparaging Chiang Kai-shek. In 1945, he was arrested in connection with the *Amerasia* case, and charged with having passed secret governmental documents to an identified Soviet agent, Philip Jaffe. Charges against Service, under somewhat confused circumstances, were subsequently dropped.

After numerous "clearances" on loyalty-security charges by

* *Cf. The Liberal Establishment* (New York, 1965), pp. 218-232.

the State Department, Service was finally declared a "loyalty risk" by the Civil Service Loyalty Review Board, which looked with skepticism on the Jaffe transactions. In 1951, he was separated from the State Department. In 1957, however, the Supreme Court ordered his reinstatement; and in 1961, despite an adverse recommendation by State Department security official Otto Otepka, Service was given an important diplomatic assignment having to do with the travel of U.S. personnel abroad, and subsequently became U.S. consul general in Liverpool, England. He retired in 1962.

Lattimore, one of the most influential of all IPR functionaries, performed various governmental services in the early 1940s, then turned to extensive propagandizing in behalf of the Chinese Communists. The Senate Internal Security subcommittee, after questioning him at length, declared him to have been "a conscious, articulate instrument of the Soviet conspiracy,"[31] and asked that he be indicted for perjury. The perjury charges, on the technical grounds that "pro-Communism" did not admit of legal determination, were subsequently dropped. In 1961, Lattimore turned up with a passport issued by the Kennedy State Department in Outer Mongolia, a Soviet satellite in whose behalf he had previously expended considerable propagandistic energies. Fulton Lewis Jr. reported that the State Department intended to "consult" Lattimore about his findings in Mongolia when he returned. His account of conditions there was later published in *The Atlantic.* The visit occurred at a time when considerable agitation was afoot to have Mongolia admitted to the United Nations and to have the United States confer recognition on this Soviet satellite.

Lattimore is relevant to the Kennedy-Johnson years for reasons above and beyond his Mongolian connections. Intimately associated with the Institute of Pacific Relations, he rubbed shoulders with many diplomatic and literary figures who have continued to exercise Establishment prerogatives.

An examination of one of these figures will serve to cast some new light on the diplomatic record, as well as on Owen Lattimore himself.

The American government has, as we have earlier noted, engaged itself for countless months in a labor of Sisyphus which has for its *mise en scene* the attractive city of Geneva, Switzerland. In that celebrated spa, American missions have on and off convened with representatives of the Soviet Union to parley for the destiny of the United States. The immediate subject has been disarmament—ways and means of limiting and disposing of the nuclear arsenal which protects America from Communist aggression.

For some three years up until 1964, the head of this mission was one Arthur H. Dean, lawyer and diplomat. In this important assignment, Dean was called upon to weigh the motives and expose the artifice of the Communists. He was required to judge whether the Communists could be trusted to keep a disarmament agreement, whether they harbored secret intentions, whether anything might be settled with them on the basis of "good faith," *etc.* A mistake on his part could conceivably commit America to a course tipping the balance of world power to Communism. It would therefore have seemed essential that he be a man of proven discernment on the intricacies of Soviet deceit. But is Arthur H. Dean such a man?

Dean is an alumnus of the Insitute of Pacific Relations, an association which was neither incidental nor temporary. He was, in fact, vice chairman of the IPR, and actively engaged in an effort to silence internal protests against its policies.

In 1947, an IPR member named Alfred Kohlberg became concerned with the pro-Communist nature of much IPR activity and launched an effort to bring about an internal investigation. In a memorandum to the Internal Security subcommittee, Kohlberg told of submitting his request for an investigation, replete with documentation of pro-Communist influence, to the IPR board. He told the subcommittee the result:

"Mr. Arthur H. Dean, vice-chairman of the IPR, presided in the absence of the chairman, Robert G. Sproul. He answered my statement, saying that IPR was lily-white (not Red) and he could vouch for it. The vote cast by the nearly 100 persons present was unanimous against the resolution. A few days later, by letter, I resigned from the IPR. Since which time I have devoted little attention to it."[32]

Kohlberg's recollection is confirmed by a letter mailed March 17, 1947, by the officials of IPR. "The executive committee of the Board of Trustees," said the letter, "have investigated Mr. Kohlberg's charges and found them inaccurate and irresponsible. We, the undersigned, have been connected with the IPR over a period of years. We have observed its research and educational program closely and have no hesitation in stating that the charges are false. We believe that you will agree with us that the IPR has an enviable record for unbiased and scholarly research." Among the seven signers—Arthur H. Dean.[33]

Dean apparently did not vouch for IPR's impartiality out of ignorance of its workings. William L. Holland of the IPR told the Senate subcommittee the group had looked into Kohlberg's charges carefully before rebuking them; additionally, Holland said, "certain other inquiries were conducted, and some members of the executive committee, notably Mr. Arthur H. Dean (then a vice-chairman), did a considerable amount of research on their own."[34]

In the midst of the agitation for an inquiry into pro-Communist influence in IPR, a meeting of the trustees of the organization took place March 18, 1947. Among the topics discussed was whether Frederick Vanderbilt Field, a man frequently identified under oath as a Communist, should continue as a member of the IPR executive committee. As the Senate records show, Field bent every effort to make IPR policy favorable to the Soviet Union and to Communists everywhere. Correspondence between Field and Owen Lattimore, for example, shows that Lattimore rebuked his colleague for employing blatant Communist phraseology in preparing articles for the printer, and thus giving the game away. Field caught on, at one point writing Lattimore that: "while the analysis is a straight Marxist one, *and from that point of view should not be changed,*" the "over-used Communist words" would have to come out. (Italics added) [35]

Because of his obvious subservience to Moscow Field was one of Kohlberg's principal targets. A record of the proceedings of the March 18 trustees' meetings shows the reigning powers in IPR, however, found nothing amiss in Field's performance:

> During the course of the discussion, Mr. Dean and Mr. Gilchrist had pointed out that Mr. Field was one of the most valuable and objective members of the executive committee and that they had never known him to show any political bias whatever as far as the IPR had been concerned. They also argued that if Mr. Field were removed from the committee, it would be welcomed by Mr. Kohlberg, who would then concentrate his efforts on getting rid of other members who participated actively in IPR.[36]

Thus the contribution of Arthur Dean—who had allegedly looked into the matter with some care—toward an understanding of the pro-Communist activity of Frederick Vanderbilt Field. Needless to say, when Mr. Dean put the matter to a vote, the trustees decided overwhelmingly to keep Mr. Field in his position of honor.

A final footnote on Dean is instructive. In a letter written April 18, 1949, concerning an IPR approach to General George Marshall, Dean wrote:

". . . I think we might go back to the publications of the Institute and with the help of Larry Rosinger point out the difficulties our State Department is now facing in attempting to get up a constructive policy for China. I think we might make a very real contribution to the subject if we could state very objectively, but explicitly, problems which we now face in China. I am sure Owen Lattimore would be a great help in this."[37]

At that time, the policies favored by Owen Lattimore and Lawrence Rosinger were nothing more or less than total commitment to the cause of the Chinese Communists. Rosinger, moreover, has been identified under oath as a member of the Communist Party by three different witnesses. Lattimore, as noted, was characterized by the Internal Security subcommittee as a "conscious, articulate instrument of the Soviet conspiracy."

These were the men Arthur Dean recommended as a source of "constructive" thought on China. Wasn't Dean able to recognize pro-Communist chicanery when it was going on right under his nose? If not, was he more able when he represented us at Geneva?

★★ 20. *The Exiles Return*

1. *Philip C. Jessup*

AMONG THE KEY APPOINTMENTS decided upon by President Kennedy early in his administration was the elevation of Philip C. Jessup, former U.S. diplomat, to the International Court of Justice.

Jessup had been one of the leading IPR alumni in the U.S. State Department, and as such was highly influential in having IPR doctrine on China converted into official policy. From 1933 to 1946, he served on the IPR's Board of Trustees; in 1939 and 1940, he was chairman of the IPR's American Council; from 1939 to 1942, he was chairman of the IPR's Pacific Council. In 1944, he was chairman of the IPR's Research Advisory Committee.

During this period, IPR publications like *Far Eastern Survey* and *Pacific Affairs* were engaged in blatant propaganda in behalf of the Chinese Communists. Jessup, who held responsible positions affecting the content of these magazines, at no point in the record spoke out against that propaganda. On the contrary, William F. Buckley Jr. and L. Brent Bozell note, "but for the cooperation of Jessup, the *Far Eastern Survey* could not have developed into a militantly pro-Chinese-Communist magazine."[1]

Also of interest concerning Jessup is the fact that he, like Ambassador Dean, took it upon himself to speak highly of Frederick Vanderbilt Field. When Field considered dropping some of his IPR duties to take on a job with the Communist-front American Peace Mobilization, Jessup strongly protested his departure. In a memorandum to the IPR Board of Trustees, Jessup said of Field:

> I cannot acquiesce in his complete separation from the direction of the affairs of the American Council. I have therefore appointed him Staff Adviser with the understanding that he is to be on leave without salary for the next six months . . . We consider that it is in the best interest of the American Council that Mr. Field should remain as closely associated with it as possible. We should therefore like to see him continue as secretary of the Council, exercising the maximum amount of guidance in the determination of policy consistent with his desire to be relieved of the burden of administrative work and financial promotion.[2]

Like Dean, Jessup also opposed Alfred Kohlberg's efforts to have Communist and pro-Communist influence cleaned out of the IPR. With Dean and other IPR officials, Jessup was a co-signer of the March 17, 1947 letter to IPR members in refutation of Kohlberg's charges, stating "the charges are false. We believe that you will agree with us that the IPR has an enviable record for unbiased and scholarly research."[3]

In 1949, as the Chinese Nationalists slipped toward oblivion beneath the combined pressures of Communist assault and IPR-fanned hostility from the American government, Jessup was the State Department official in charge of editing the U.S. "white paper" explaining the necessity of abandoning Chiang Kai-shek, plumping for a "coalition" government, and acquiescing in Communist takeover. The release of this document was in itself a cruel blow to the anti-Communist forces, since it told them they had been written off by the American government.

The Senate Internal Security subcommittee says: "During this period Mr. Philip C. Jessup expressed to Admiral Cooke opposition to United States aid for the Nationalist government. General Chennault testified that he urged Jessup not to release the white paper as it would undermine the Nationalist government. The white paper was nevertheless released. Jessup acknowleged before the Foreign Relations committee that he edited the white paper . . . The mere issuance of the white paper jarred the morale of the Chinese Nationalists, and was, in fact, determined upon by the State Department in the face of warnings that such a publication would aid the Communist conquest of China."[4]

The content of the white paper, as one might surmise from what has gone before, was straight IPR doctrine: Chiang Kai-shek was corrupt and dictatorial, the Chinese Communists were popular, the fall of China was inevitable, the U.S. government could do nothing about it.

Short weeks after the white paper was issued, Jessup continued to purvey the IPR line and to press IPR doctrine and personnel into official service. In October, 1949, he presided over a U.S. State Department "round table" on China, attended by 25 "experts" on the subject—each of whom was a member or alumnus of the IPR. Chief guiding authorities at this conclave, according to the Internal Security subcommittee, were none other than Owen Lattimore and Lawrence K. Rosinger, those particular favorites of Ambassador Dean.

The conference unsurprisingly recommended recognition

of, U.N. membership for, and economic assistance to Red China, plus "recognition that Communist conquest in Asia was a natural and inevitable consequence of revolutionary ferment in Asia with its Communist nature being incidental."[5]

Information about this gathering was given the subcommittee by Harold Stassen (hardly a militant reactionary) and Prof. Kenneth Colegrove, both of whom were observers at the conference. The committee notes that "Governor Stassen conferred with Dr. Jessup off the record between sessions and according to Stassen's testimony Jessup asserted that greater logic lay with the findings of the majority present who expressed their views."[6]

During his years of IPR service, Jessup was greatly influential in setting up various IPR conclaves with State Department personnel. Discussing one such gathering, the subcommittee said: "According to the record, it was [Lauchlin] Currie, Alger Hiss, Joseph Barnes, and Philip Jessup, who, with [IPR executive secretary Edward] Carter, made the selection of conferees . . ."[7] (Currie, Hiss, and Barnes have all been identified under oath as participants in the Communist conspiracy). The committee also notes: "According to [witness Raymond] Dennett, and the correspondence in the record, recommendations for delegates from the American Council to the Hot Springs International Conference came from Philip Jessup and Lauchlin Currie . . ."[8] And again: "The other person making recommendations for delegates to the conference was Jessup . . . of the approximately 30 recommendations by Jessup, 10 were identified by witnesses as being associated with the Communist organization."[9]

The committee notes that the conference in question saw active propaganda work by Owen Lattimore: "Jessup presided at the caucus and Lattimore was the most vocal and dominant conferee. The conferees, who also included Frederick V. Field, Len De Caux, Frank Coe, and Miriam S. Farley,* agreed that their position should be one of pressing for changes in the internal situation of the Chinese government . . ."[10]

The committee concludes: "Thus did the IPR continue to establish pro-Communist influence at the Hot Springs International Conference. Thus were the various influential non-Communist delegates from the United States and foreign governments exposed to this influence."[11]

And thus the background and performance of Philip Jessup, who now sits as America's representative on the World Court, there presumptively to battle against the Communists and to protect the interests of the United States.

2. *Our Men In Tokyo*

America's recently-resigned ambassador to Japan, Edwin O. Reischauer, is a scholarly gentleman who has delved much into Japanese history. He also has a Japanese wife, which would seem to have qualified him well for his post in Tokyo. But he has, in addition, a rather faulty memory, which does not reflect quite so favorably on his talents.

President Kennedy's choice as Ambassador to Japan gave a somewhat curious performance when he appeared before the Senate Foreign Relations Committee March 23, 1961, to say his catechism. "I was never connected with the IPR in any way," he told the senators, but modified this in the same sentence to: "I think I never did join."[12] That Reischauer could state he was "never connected" with an organization in "any way" and then be in doubt as to whether he ever actually joined it suggests a peculiar kind of forgetfulness.

While the professor's memory may be somewhat hazy on IPR membership, the memory of William L. Holland, former Executive Vice Chairman of the IPR, was very clear.

* The first three identified under oath as members of the Communist Party, the fourth as a writer for Communist or pro-Communist journals by the Senate Internal Security subcommittee. IPR Report, pp. 152-53.

On September 28, 1951, Holland sent a letter identifying Reischauer to Robert Morris, then counsel to the Internal Security Subcommittee, which had been investigating Reischauer's part in the 1949 State Department conference. The letter from Holland read: "Edwin O. Reischauer: Member American IPR, 1944-48; contributor to *Far Eastern Survey* 1948; co-author of *Next Step in Asia*."[13] Reischauer, it also turns out, has had one book published by the IPR and has contributed to the IPR publication, *Pacific Affairs.*

Reischauer told the senators he was not very interested in the IPR because "my interests were not along those lines. At that time [presumably during the 1940s] I was primarily interested in ancient history." His preoccupation with history, however, does not explain "why the State Department appointed him Senior Divisional Assistant of the Division of Far Eastern Affairs in 1941 or why John Carter Vincent (an IPR stalwart), who during the late 40s was Director of the Office of Far Eastern Affairs, recommended Reischauer for a Far Eastern post," or why the State Department invited him to participate in its Round Table Discussion.[14]

Another curious statement by the professor before the Senate Foreign Relations Committee was that he had never advocated that the United States recognize Red China, merely that the U.S. should "consider" the recognition problem from time to time. Yet in the Round Table Discussion in 1949, as we shall presently observe, he certainly gave the impression he had made his mind up on the recognition issue for once and for all.

Chosen as Number-two man in the Tokyo embassy was John K. Emmerson, another "old China hand" from World War II days. Emmerson served in China during the final months of the war, as a co-worker of John Paton Davies, John Stewart Service, and Raymond Ludden—the group which worked overtime to convince the American government

Chiang Kai-shek was corrupt, and that America's support should go instead to the Chinese Communists.

Emmerson's field of specialization was Japan—as Stilwell's successor, General Wedemeyer, pointed out to the Senate Internal Security Subcommittee—and thus he did not involve himself much with the internal Chinese contest. Yet so far as the record discloses he did not dissent from the biased counsel being served up by his colleagues. As Wedemeyer put it: "The four political advisers on my staff—John Paton Davies, John Stewart Service, John K. Emmerson and Raymond P. Ludden—submitted oral and written reports. . . . The information embodied in the reports pertaining to the military situation uniformly was critical of the Chinese Nationalist Forces and invariably was complimentary to the Chinese Communist forces. Some of the reports included definite recommendations to the effect that I should provide U.S. equipment to and support the Chinese Communists on the grounds that they were fighting the Japanese realistically and would contribute more than the Chinese Nationalists to the overall war effort."[15]

Gen. Wedemeyer said Emmerson himself did not submit a written report to this specific effect but, his 1958 memoirs, made this further comment about Davies, Service, Ludden, and Emmerson: "Their sympathy for the Chinese Communists is obvious in their reports and in their recommendations that we back the Communists instead of the Nationalist Government."[16]

It is a matter of record that Emmerson did submit a written report congruent with this line concerning his own field of special interest. In a dispatch written November 7, 1944, he urged U.S. support for the "Japanese Peoples Emancipation League," a Chinese Communist effort to indoctrinate Japanese prisoners in Communism. The organization was headed by Susumu Okano, a Japanese Communist serving with the Chinese Reds in Yenan. The men trained by such an organization, obviously, would be sent back to Japan to stage a Communist take-over there. Emmerson, however, disclosed none of this in his dispatch urging support. In fact, his treatment of it gave entirely the opposite impression:

"The Japanese Peoples Emancipation League . . . has an estimated membership of 450 Japanese prisoners in North and Central China. *Its declared principles are democratic. It is not identified with the Communist Party.* Upon completion of a course of indoctrination the more able members voluntarily prepare propaganda leaflets and engage in propaganda activities on the front lines. There is no doubt that most of them are sincere converts to the anti-war principles of the league."[17] (Italics added.)

Having given this innocent-sounding description of the Communist effort, Emmerson urged: (1) organizing chapters of this group, "or a similar one," in numerous other countries—including the United States; (2) encouragement of "the organization of cells within Japan to spread defeatism and thereby reduce resistance at the time of invasion;" (3) setting up a radio transmitter to broadcast the group's propaganda into Japan; and (4) the training of "units of Japanese for activity with American pacification operations and with Military Government officials during occupation."[18]

Expanding on the fourth point, Emmerson said: "Such Japanese personnel, with invaluable knowledge of particular areas and of the language, could be extremely useful in assisting American Army officers in re-establishing order among the Japanese population."[19] They would also have been extremely useful to the Communists in establishing control of Japan—a fact which Emmerson, presenting the group as "not identified with the Communist Party," failed to point out. He also failed to point out that Okano, who was in charge of the effort, was a Communist and took his orders directly from the Chinese Reds.

In September 1951, the Senate Internal Security subcommittee took testimony from Eugene Dooman, World War II Chairman of the Far East Subcommittee of the State, War and Navy Coordinating Committee. Asked if he knew "what the attitude of the State Department, or any individuals in the State Department was with respect toward Japanese Communists," Dooman answered:

"Well some time in May I believe it was, May or June . . . 1945 . . . there returned from China a Foreign Service officer named John K. Emmerson, who, before the war, had been one of my subordinates at the American Embassy in Tokyo. I understand that he had been sent to Yenan. Yenan in China then was the capital of the Chinese Communists. There was present at that time in Yenan a Nosaka, the leading Japanese Communist, and other leading Communists.

"Mr. Morris. Is Nosaka the same as Susumu Okano, head of the Japanese Communist Party?

"Dooman. I believe the latter is a pseudonym. I believe that Emmerson had been sent to Yenan to study methods used by the Japanese Communists in Yenan in indoctrinating the Japanese prisoners of war taken by the Chinese. As I said, he returned to Washington in about May of 1945. . . .

". . . He brought back a report describing at considerable length the method used by the Japanese Communists with respect to Japanese prisoners of war, and as I recall, he recommended that Japanese prisoners in American stockades be then turned over to Japanese Communists in the United States for indoctrination along methods used by the Japanese Communists in Yenan."[20]

Emmerson seems to have been an enthusiastic promotor of the Communist indoctrination program outside office hours as well. In April, 1945, an IPR memo described a series of meetings in Washington, at one of which "Mr. John Emmerson of the Department of State . . . described plans of the Japanese Emancipation League in Yenan."[21]

In 1957, Emmerson was called before the Senate Internal

Security subcommittee and asked about his report from Yenan and the Communist connections of the Japanese Peoples Emancipation League. His answer:

". . . They were under complete control of the Chinese Communists, but the Chinese entrusted the actual operation to the direction of this Japanese Communist, Okano, who was then present in Yenan and directed the whole operation. He was a Japanese himself, but again he was subject to the orders."[22]

Pressed as to why he had not pointed these facts out in his report, Emmerson said "the Communists deliberately did not identify it as being a Communist organization because they expected that, by so doing, the effect would be greater among the Japanese . . ."[23] No doubt. Yet this would hardly seem to justify the language used in Emmerson's report. It is one thing to say an organization is controlled by the Communist Party, *but* the party does not publicly identify itself as the controlling element. That construction makes it clear the point being made has to do with surface appearances, useful in wartime propagandizing. But that is not the construction Emmerson used. He merely said the organization was "not identified with the Communist Party," period, which conveys the impression it was a non-Communist group.

The real effect of the program is described by Edward Hunter, authority on brainwashing and Asian Communism, as follows: "Red China for years has been providing a haven for Communist leaders in flight from Japan, and has engaged in a thorough brainwashing program for Japanese captured at the close of World War II. They return to their native land to engage in espionage and subversion."[24]

And Chinese Communist leader Chang Ting-ch'eng explained the program this way: "Education was given to the Japanese war criminals in detention to help them oppose war and support peace . . . The war criminals released in accordance with the policy of leniency expressed their desire and determination to oppose wars of aggression and fight for peace. After their return to Japan, many of them have been taking an active part in the peace movement. Former war criminals who have been released by China have taken part in the world conference to ban the atom and hydrogen bombs, and dispatched in the name of the 'War Criminals' Group' a telegram to the conference opposing the use of hydrogen and atomic weapons."[25]

3. *And Elsewhere*

The IPR operated, during the 1940s, through several channels at once. It had many sympathizers within the government, or closely associated with it. It had many others traveling throughout the world, working as foreign correspondents, some for important U.S. publications, some for high-brow magazines. It had still others working at important American universities.

The fabled Owen Lattimore is only one of the old IPR publicists who, with the advent of the Kennedy-Johnson administration, have been popping up in the public media. Just as the purveyors of the Mao-is-an-agrarian-reformer line have made their way back into the high echelons of our government, so have they found their way back into the communications media. Many of them have returned to the old standby of polishing up the image of Communist China. Others have attached themselves to current crisis spots—like Viet Nam—and are repeating, *mutatis mutandis,* their performance of the 1940s.

In 1965, for example, James Burnham noted the reappearance of three former IPR functionaries—Anna Louise Strong. Frank Coe, and Israel Epstein—all working blatantly for the Communists in Asia. Considering the background of these three, that intelligence was not particularly surprising: all had been identified, before the Senate Internal Security subcommittee, as Communists.

"Anna Louise Strong," Burnham commented, "is the veteran Communist who from Moscow, for many years, edited the English-language propaganda magazine, *Soviet Russia Today* . . . Many a respectable magazine—*Atlantic Monthly* prominent among them—printed her articles. She was an honored source for the Foreign Policy Association. Under Owen Lattimore's editorial direction, she was a featured writer for the Institute of Pacific Relations' quarterly, *Pacific Affairs*." Israel Epstein similarly wrote for IPR publications, and authored a book on China which IPR secretary Edward Carter beamed at influential members of the government. Frank Coe was an assistant in the Treasury Department to Harry Dexter White and, according to Whittaker Chambers, a member of a Communist espionage ring, as well as an active participant in IPR affairs. "I suppose it's some improvement," Burnham remarks, "that today Mao at least has to meet his own payroll for this particular set of hirelings."[26]

Here in the United States, the Vietnamese war also evoked activity from Lattimore himself, who fired off a letter to *The New York Times* comparing U.S. bombings with the Japanese aggressions of the 1940's, and a *cri de coeur* from the publishing firm of Marzani and Munsell, which offered two booklets by Edgar Snow, a pamphlet called "Bitter End in Southeast Asia" by two unnamed "experts," and "The Conscience of the Senate on the Viet Nam War," featuring the remarks of Wayne Morse and 15 other U.S. Senators who dissented from the Johnson policy in Viet Nam, with an introduction by Carl Marzani. The records of the House Committee on Un-American Activities have this to say about Carl Marzani, co-owner of the publishing firm in question:

"Marzani was convicted some years ago of concealing his Communist Party affiliation while employed in the U.S. government and served a prison term as a result therefore during the years 1949 to 1951. In his appearance before the Senate Internal Security subcommittee on June 18, 1953, and before this committee November 13, 1956, in response to questions relating to his Communist Party membership, he invoked the Fifth Amendment."[27]

These were not, however, the only purveyors of confusion to make their way back into action. Popping up in the public media in the United States have been such enthusiasts of the old IPR line as writers Mark Gayn, John K. Fairbank, and Theodore White. Since much of their activity falls outside the scope of this chapter, further examination of these publicists will be reserved until later. (pp. 486 *et seq.*)

Finally, IPR alumni and survivors of old loyalty-security battles in the U.S. government have also been turning up in diplomatic and official capacities outside the United States, where they play key roles in handling such matters as disposition of U.S. foreign aid dollars and direction of U.S.-financed activities of the United Nations.

One of these is Lauchlin Currie, "named in sworn testimony as having collaborated with agents of the Soviet intelligence apparatus."[28] Currie was a high-level assistant to President Roosevelt in the early 1940s, and worked closely, as the Senate subcommittee discovered, with Lattimore. When the subcommittee held its hearings, however, Currie was not around to testify: He had gone to the Latin American state of Colombia, where he had become a high-ranking adviser to the Bogota government.

The Chicago *Tribune* reported in 1961 that Currie, "who left the United States in the face of an investigation as an alleged Communist, is emerging in Colombia as a top planner there in the spending of money expected under the new Latin American Alliance for Progress program . . . Information received in the Commerce Department here from the Colombian-American Chamber of Commerce gives the details of Currie's plan, which he calls Operation Colombia. . . . The Currie plan presented to Colombian officials would combine land reform and industrialization. He recommended breaking up the land into small, highly mechanized farms operated by their owners. He suggested moving 1½ million people from rural areas into Colombia's four most populous cities to strengthen home building, public works, and factory output." Currie had originally gone to Colombia, the *Tribune* said, "to reorganize that government's administrative setup for a $150,000 fee."[29]

Yet another survivor of the hectic loyalty-security battles of the 1940s has achieved a measure of international celebrity—and a measure of influence over the way U.S. dollars are used abroad. Although not a member of IPR, he is a former official of the U.S. State Department whose case became famous at the same time the IPR battle blew to the surface. His name is Gustavo Duran.

Duran was one of the U.N. officials who served in the Congo during the crisis of 1960-63. He was U.N. political officer in the Congo from August 1960 to April 1961, and subsequently a special advisor to the U.N. on Civilian Operations in the Congo.

A former resident of Spain, Duran has enjoyed a varied career in the diplomatic world. A memorandum by James Shepley of *Time* magazine, as inserted in the Congressional Record by Senator Joseph R. McCarthy (R-Wis.), described this U.N. official as follows:

> The record picks up Duran in the early 1920's on arrival in Madrid from the Canaries with a friend known as Nestor . . .
>
> Sometime in this period he is reputed to have come to the attention of the GPU* which became interested enough in him to test him on a few practice missions. He turns up next crossing the Spanish frontier in the early thirties as the reputed representative of Paramount Pictures. Some sources indicate that by now he was a tested and 'live' agent of the GPU. DOS bio says he was employed by Paramount in Paris in 1933 and 1934, worked for a motion-picture company in Madrid in 1934 and 1936.
>
> The file shows him crossing into Spain, however, in 1931 as a

* GPU, Cheka, and MVD are all names used by the Communist secret police.

provocateur of the Spanish Republican Revolution, working on GPU orders.

All sources, including Duran, agree that he signed up with the Republican army after the Falangist uprising. The file reports his first act in behalf of the cause was to commandeer the convent of Siervas de Maria in the old Plazo Chamberi, and convert it to a Cheka for the detention of Falangist agitators. He is reported variously to have lived at Santa Engracia, 104 or 106, and at Hermosilla, Three. He is reported to have been a leading light in the pre-civil war days in the Juventudes Commistas y Socialistas.

In August 1936 he had a bout with typhoid, but eventually got back to his job of running the political prison. He became a fast friend of Serrano Poncela, chief of the Communist-dominated Republican political police. Prieto reports in a published document . . . that he appointed Duran chief of SIM for the Madrid zone.

There is little doubt that Gustavo was an able soldier. He grew close to the Red Brigade commanders Lister and Modesto, who are supposed to have fought World War II as general officers of the Red Army. He was a member of the general staff which executed the brilliant withdrawals from Talvera de la Reina, Maqueda, and Toledo.

The last days of Col. Gustavo Duran, according to the file, were spent in the Red Brigade headquarters at Taroncon. From here, following his escape, some sources say he went to Paris, then to Moscow. The DOS bio says he went to London . . .

Both Duran and * * * are considered flatly to be MVD secret agents. Remember that counterintelligence operations do not involve proof of assumptions. They are made on a working basis for the purposes of neutralizing foreign espionage and on occasion for disseminating false information. Please in no way associate any of the information in this research with any Federal agency.[30]

★★ 21. *The IPR Strategy*

1. *Recognizing Red China*

IMMEDIATELY after the fall of China to the Communists, elements in and around the American government moved to secure recognition for the new regime. In 1949, Philip Jessup presided over the State Department conference alluded to in the preceding chapter at which plans were laid for an immediate exchange of embassies. Prevailing sentiment at this conclave, says the Internal Security subcommittee, favored:

". . . (a) the recognition of Communist China; (b) normal trade relations between the United States and Communist China; (c) encouragement of trade between Japan and Communist China; (d) economic assistance to Communist China; (e) recognition that Communist conquest in Asia was a natural and inevitable consequence of revolutionary ferment in Asia with its Communist nature being incidental."[1]

Unfortunately for the conferees, the state of American public opinion would not then permit enactment of this bold new program. Many people, including a number of influential congressmen and senators, were unhappy about the loss of China. Calls were going up for an investigation. A few months later, Senator Joseph R. McCarthy (R-Wis.) launched his criticism of the State Department. In June, 1950, the Korean War began. These were not circumstances conducive to recognition.

The existence of a large articulate body of public feeling antagonistic to Red China imposed, quite obviously, certain difficulties.[2] Faced with such negativism, one had to go about the business of moving toward and advocating recognition while maintaining an appearance of *not* moving toward or advocating recognition. The result of this exercise—if the rapidly ascending Fog Index on those occasions when Red China gets discussed is any indication—has been a considerable amount of psychological strain on the recognitionists. At the surface, their attitude toward Peking is one of hostility. Beneath the surface thay have never ceased to edge as close to recognition as political caution would allow.

Liberal aspiration on this count is clear enough in the case of such relatively heedless verbalizers as Americans for Democratic Action and the authors of *The Liberal Papers.* Both of these groups have asserted the necessity and desirability of conferring recognition on Peking.

In 1951, ADA declared: "We believe that the principal objective of American policy in China must be the maintenance of communication and traditional friendly contact with the Chinese people. We believe that sooner or later we will be compelled to establish diplomatic relations with the Mao Tse-tung regime as the effective government of China, however much we detest its devotion to totalitarianism. Our continuing policy must be to counter any Kremlin policy of isolating China from the non-Communist world . . ."[3]

In 1964, in proposals to the Democratic platform committee, ADA retained the same kernels of thought, trimmed out in the tentative rhetoric of the hour: "It is . . . important that there be regularized channels for communication with the Red Chinese . . . We . . . urge the lifting of barriers to trade in nonstrategic goods with mainland China and the removal of all passport barriers preventing travel by Americans to China . . . Should the overall interests of the United States seem in the future to make a change of policy appropriate, we should be prepared to consider the initiation, together with our allies, of negotiations leading toward the diplomatic recognition of mainland China and its admission to the United Nations—not as indications of any moral approval of its repressive regime, but as a means of re-establishing normal channels of communication."[4]

In *The Liberal Papers,* James P. Warburg sets forth a similar view on Peking. It is about time, Warburg says, that we face up to the reality of "the most powerful nation in Asia," and start knuckling under to it. He urges us to recognize "Peking's unquestionably valid claim to the offshore islands" of Quemoy and Matsu, set in motion the machinery of diplomatic recognition, and accede in the entry of Red China to the United Nations.

Warburg says U.N. membership should be tied to certain provisions—specifically, "that the Peking regime will reaffirm the renunciation of force which it signed at the Bandung conference of 1955 and which it has since repudiated by its action with respect to the Indian-Chinese border; and provided further that the Peking regime will undertake the obligations imposed by the charter of the United Nations and agree to cooperate in working toward universal total disarmament under world law."[5]

Warburg's proposed U.N. membership for Communist

China thus comes attached to "conditions" which give it the appearance of a give-and-take proposition. The catch, of course, is that Red China's end of the bargain would consist of nothing but words—a "reaffirmation" of some previous words, already violated, and an "undertaking" to abide by the U.N. Charter. In return for this rigmarole, Peking would receive the very solid perquisites attendant upon its debut in the "family of nations." Once safely inside the U.N., it could and would violate any verbal pledges at its leisure.

The outlook of *The Liberal Papers* and the ADA—considering the intimate connection between these specimens of Liberal sentiment and the reigning opinions of the American State Department—would in itself seem to indicate high level willingness to recognize Red China. We have at our disposal, however, a good deal of other evidence which makes it unnecessary to rest content with that legitimate inference. Various of our officials have expressed themselves on the subject in terms which, once we decipher the cryptograms in which these affirmations are necessarily couched, demonstrate quite clearly that their objective is to get on with the recognizing as soon as possible.

There is, for example, the fact that Kennedy's ambassador to Tokyo—our most important emissary in the Far East—was Professor Reischauer, IPR alumnus, participant in the famous 1949 State Department round table, and an authority on record as believing the desirability of recognition to be manifest.

When Reischauer appeared before the Senate Foreign Relations Committee in 1961, he tried to suggest he had not favored recognizing Red China. The record, however, indicates otherwise. The official State Department transcript of the 1949 round table shows Reischauer saying: "*We seem to be in very general agreement about the desirability of recognizing the Communist government in China and recognizing it fairly soon.*"[6]

He thought, moreover, that we should recognize Red China even if that meant the Communists would earn the right to participate in the Japanese Peace Treaty. "I cannot see," said the professor in the transcribed discussion, "why the addition of Communist China to such a peace treaty would have a great influence. On the other hand, if you negotiated a peace treaty with the rump Kuomintang Government having membership at the table, I think it would only have an adverse influence on China. The Communists would be less likely to accept the results of that treaty."[7]

When Reischauer made his 1961 Senate appearance, his equivocal statements did not, on analysis, represent much of a departure. He was opposed to recognizing Red China, he told the senators, so long as it did not accept the independent status of Formosa. As we have seen in the case of James Warburg, this is in fact a convenient formula for achieving recognition. It means, I *am* in favor of recognizing Red China if it *does* accept the independent status of Formosa.

The same sort of mystic algebra has popped up at other places in our State Department, notably in the utterances of Policy Planning Chief Rostow. In a book entitled *An American Policy in Asia* (1955), Rostow rather circuitously works his way around to urging U.N. membership and U.S. recognition for Peking as follows:

"With Asia at peace, with a clear and positive Free World policy launched, there would be a reasonable case for United Nations membership for Peking: for United Nations membership does not imply approval, and it need not interfere with a constructive political role for Formosa . . .

"At least three conditions should attach to Communist China's entrance into the United Nations quite aside from the return of our prisoners and the pacification of Korea, Indo-China, and the Formosa Strait . . . [among them that] Formosa should retain a seat in the United Nations Assembly.

"Whether or not Peking would accept such terms for entrance into the United Nations, it may be well for the Free World to agree on such terms and make them known . . ."[8]

As for diplomatic recognition:

"There would be little reason to withhold recognition if the Chinese Communists were to accept Formosa's independent status in the Free World. Such action by Peking seems somewhat unlikely, however, even if a truce is established in the Formosa Strait."[9]

A related approach was used by Secretary of State Rusk when he was a member of the Truman State Department back in 1951. We have noted Rusk's 1950 address likening the Chinese Communists to the American revolutionaries, which Rusk later attempted to deny. Almost a year after this speech, Rusk delivered yet another pronouncement germane to the present discussion. To his credit, Rusk in the 1951 address spoke harshly of the Peking Chinese, and opined that the government on Formosa more nearly suited American notions of a legitimate regime. This is roughly the kind of rhetoric Rusk and other Liberals use toward Red China now, and certainly gives the appearance of a tough anti-Communist stance.

Rusk had comparatively little to say, however, about the shortcomings of the Chinese Communists as such, and a great deal to say about the domination of their leaders and consequently of China by the Kremlin. "The independence of China," Rusk said, "is gravely threatened. In the Communist world there is room for only one master—a jealous and implacable master, whose price of friendship is complete submission. How many Chinese, in one community after another, are now being destroyed because they love China more than the Soviet Union? How many Chinese will remember in time the fate of Rajk, Kostov, Petkov, Clementis, and all those in other satellites who discovered that *being Commu-*

nist is not enough for the conspirators in the Kremlin?" (Italics added.)[10]

Rusk went on in this vein, imputing tyranny in China to the fact that its "territorial integrity" has been breached by Russia; that China is losing "its great Northern areas to the European empire" of Moscow; that Soviet troops are on Chinese soil; *etc.* The problem, in short, is not the Communism of China, but Russian domination of China. Then, having said this in a half-dozen different ways, Rusk asserted that "as the Chinese move to assert their freedom to work out their destiny in accordance with their own historical purposes, they can count on tremendous support from free peoples in the other parts of the world."[11]

On comparison, this statement represents small improvement in understanding from Rusk's views of the preceding year. The difference between the two speeches arises solely from a changed estimate of the empirical balance of forces. In the first speech, the Chinese revolution was good, but "subject to perversion" if Russian imperialism got the better of it; in the second, the anticipated perversion had transpired, native aspirations (including, presumably, native Communist aspirations) had been squelched, and the regime was "not Chinese." Rusk's theoretical premises had not changed; what were conceived as new "facts" were simply fitted into the existing mould of ideology.

If the May 1951 speech does represent Rusk's present views, it appears to mean he would supply "tremendous support" to the Chinese Communists if there were a split between Moscow and Peking, and the Chinese began working things out "according to their own historical purposes." Interestingly enough, it is now the vogue among all foreign policy specialists with whom Rusk is known to consort to maintain that just such a split exists, and that it is of immense significance.

More recently, Rusk has said: "I see no present prospect

that normal relations could be considered or established with Peking, because the Red Chinese seem to feel that the abandonment of the government and people on Formosa would be a prerequisite."[12] This statement, in the usual manner, has been interpreted to mean Rusk opposes recognition; but what it obviously says, in a formula identical to that of Warburg, Rostow, *et al.*, is that "normal relations" *can* be considered at such time as the Red Chinese relent on the question of Formosa.

This approach was given its most significant formulation by Senator Fulbright in his March 25, 1964, address, previously referred to. Fulbright's phrasing is significant because it shows so unmistakably that all the verbal sinuosities about "the independence of Formosa" are in fact preliminaries to granting recognition.

Fulbright began his remarks on Red China by affirming that recognition is not desirable "under present circumstances," then worked his way forward to suggest the circumstances under which it would be desirable. *"I do not believe, however, that this state of affairs is necessarily permanent,"* Fulbright said:

"It would therefore be an extremely useful thing if we could introduce an element of flexibility, or more precisely, of the capacity to be flexible, into our relations with Communist China. We would do well, as former Assistant Secretary Roger Hilsman has recommended, to maintain an 'open door' to the possibility of improved relations with Communist China in the future. For a start, we must jar open our minds to certain realities about China, of which the foremost is that there are not really 'two Chinas' but only one, mainland China, and that it is ruled by Communists and likely to be so for the indefinite future.

"Once we accept this fact, it becomes possible to reflect on the conditions under which it might be possible for us to enter into relatively normal relations with mainland China.

One condition, of course, must be the abandonment by the Chinese Communists, *tacitly if not explicitly,* of their intention to conquer and incorporate Taiwan. This seems unlikely now, but far more surprising changes have occurred in politics . . ."[13] (All italics added.)

Fulbright thus makes it apparent that the "independence of Formosa" or "two China" approach opens the door for U.S. recognition of and U.N. membership for Peking, since it leaves attainment of both objectives up to the Communists themselves. Peking could assent to the "independent" status of Formosa and agree to let Chiang Kai-shek remain in control there; it might sign a dozen documents proclaiming it no longer harbored aggressive intentions in the Formosa Straits. In the Fulbright version, even this would not be necessary—the commitment would be merely "tacit." In which case, the logic of the Rusk, Rostow and Fulbright statements would clearly be that we *should* recognize Red China, our preconditions having been fulfilled. But when that has been done, and Red China is duly recognized and inducted into the United Nations, what is to prevent it from violating every piece of paper it has signed?*

These speculations about the drift of U.S. policy are rendered the more sobering by other evidence. In his study, *What China Policy?*, Vladimir Petrov writes: "As early as 1955, Arthur H. Dean suggested recognition of Communist China and its admission as a new member of the United Nations, while maintaining relations with the Republic of

* As for the possibility that we could prevent Red China from violating its pledges by the threat of withdrawing recognition or kicking it out of the U.N., nothing in the history of either Communism or U.S. foreign policy makes this even remotely possible. If we should recognize Red China after it has already violated so many commitments, why should it believe we will withdraw recognition of it if it should violate one more? More to the point, why would the United States withdraw recognition from Communist China for violating one pledge when it has not withdrawn recognition from Moscow for violating 50? Finally, the urge to conciliation which dominates Messrs. Rusk and Rostow would unquestionably prevent any move to impose sanctions on Peking once it had achieved the desired threshold of recognition.

China (on Taiwan) and supporting its position as a permanent member of the Security Council. The same year, Quincy Wright offered [the suggestion] . . . that: 'The United States is free to recognize Formosa and the Pescadores as an independent state under the Nationalist government . . . provided free and fair elections indicate that an independent state of Formosa under the Nationalist government conforms to the wishes of the inhabitants.' Two years later Wright repeated this proposal, adding that a 'two Chinas' solution would strengthen the United Nations provided that the Communists were given China's permanent seat in the Security Council."[14]

The "two Chinas" idea, obviously, has long been in the works. And, significantly, of these two early proponents of the idea, one—Arthur Dean—has been an official of the Kennedy-Johnson administration; the other—Quincy Wright—is a contributor to Ambassador Roosevelt's *Liberal Papers.*

High-level partiality toward recognition of Peking is also disclosed by Arthur Schlesinger, who records that Adlai Stevenson, Kennedy's U.N. ambassador, "had long argued as a private citizen that we must deal with realities and perhaps move toward a solution which would seat both Chinese governments" in the United Nations. As for Kennedy himself, Schlesinger notes that he "considered the state of our relations with Communist China as irrational," and "did not exclude the possibility of doing something to change them in the course of his administration." Kennedy realized, however, that admission of Red China to the U.N. would cause an "uproar," and therefore told Stevenson: "If we can buy twelve months, it will be more than worth it. We may be preparing the way for the admission of Peking in another year; but in another year things will be different."[15]

Even more direct evidence of official sentiment on this point was unearthed in mid-1964 by reporters Robert S. Allen and Paul Scott. A "policy paper circulating in top administration circles," they reported, disclosed that while we would resist Peking's acts of aggression in Southeast Asia, we would simultaneously seek conciliation. We should, the paper said:

". . . leave ajar possibilities for opening commercial, cultural and other contacts with Communist China. We should make clear that there is no final bar to the entrance of Communist China into more normal relations with the U.S., if it is prepared to modify its present policies . . ."[16]

Virtually the same programme was made public under sponsorship of the Johnson administration in late 1965, when the special advisory panel headed by Dr. Wiesner offered, among its varied suggestions for greater East-West collaboration, the idea that we should "initiate direct 'bilateral' talks with Red China to seek an agreement on arms control. The President is also urged to explore means of getting the Chinese Communists into the United Nations."[17]

In 1966, this campaign began to build up a noticeable head of steam. The Senate Foreign Relations Committee under Senator Fulbright staged a series of "China hearings," parading various "experts" before the public to urge augmented contacts with the Peking government. Prominent among these was none other than John K. Fairbank, singled out so long ago by Congressman Kennedy, who is a leader in a new group called "Americans For Re-Appraisal of Far Eastern Policy." Fairbank wanted, to no one's surprise, steps toward *rapprochement.* The cry was subsequently taken up by Vice President Hubert Humphrey, who urged "closer contacts," and Defense Secretary McNamara, who urged U.S. effort to "breach the isolation of great nations like Red China." A May, 1966, survey by Samuel Lubell appeared to show this line of advocacy was getting results: American attitudes toward recognition of, and U.N. membership for, Red China, Lubell reported, were softening perceptibly.[18]

So the advocates of recognition, despite public hostility,

continue to press forward, penetrating the upper councils of our government. No doubt the assembled experts who advanced this line at Philip Jessup's 1949 "round table" can take satisfaction from that outcome. Whether any one else can take satisfaction from it the reader may determine for himself.

2. *'Coalition'—Formula For Defeat*

The work of the Institute of Pacific Relations in assisting the communization of China was manifestly important in and of itself. But it was also important because it set the peculiar style of Cold War strategy in years to come. U.S. policy toward China in 1946-49 has been the prototype of Liberal policy in world crisis spots, with remarkably few exceptions, ever since.

The substance of IPR policy toward China was to disparage the anti-Communist leadership as "corrupt," dictatorial, and out of step with the times; the technique of IPR policy was to advocate the conjunction of Communists and anti-Communists in a "coalition" government. The pivotal event in turning U.S. policy into this IPR-indicated groove was the China mission of General George C. Marshall.

American policy during World War II had been one of support for Chiang Kai-shek. When the war came to an end, however, and the fighting between the Nationalists and Chinese Communists broke out again in earnest, a campaign was launched in the communications media and within the American government to portray Chiang as unrepresentative of China. By degrees this attitude permeated the U.S. State Department, and when General Marshall departed for China in late 1945, it represented the official American position.

The Internal Security subcommittee tells us that "until late in 1945, United States policy with respect to China was one of support to the Chinese Nationalist government. We sought to keep the Chinese army in the field to fight the Japanese. Officially, we took no hand in China's internal strife . . . In 1945, our policy changed to intervention; and our intervention thereafter was in aid of the Chinese Communists and in opposition to Chiang Kai-shek."[19]

This alteration in policy, the subcommittee notes, was vehemently urged by the IPR element, with Owen Lattimore personally exhorting President Truman to adopt it. The solution to China's ills, according to various officials, professors and journalists enamored of the IPR line, was a "broadly based" "reform" government uniting "all factions" in Chinese politics—which meant, quite simply, "include the Communists in."

A typical communique to this effect was John Stewart Service's famous memorandum No. 40, which declared that "we cannot hope to solve China's problems (which are now our problems) without consideration of the opposition forces—Communist, provincial, and Liberal."[20] A similar utterance was the journalistic assertion of Theodore White and Annalee Jacoby that "We must make clear to the Russians that what we want is a China in which the friends of Russia will have as large and free a voice as the friends of America, that a union of the two parties is as much our object as theirs."[21]

The desirability of such a coalition subsequently became the policy line of our government. The State Department's famous "white paper," edited by Jessup, reflects the official attitude:

> It seemed apparent to General Marshall that the government military leaders were in the saddle and were thoroughly convinced that the Communists would not carry out any agreement reached. The strong political clique in the Kuomintang was firmly convinced that the Communists would merely disrupt any government in which they participated . . . General Marshall was

very emphatic in stating . . . that it was useless to expect the United States to pour money into the vacuum being created by the government military leaders in their determination to settle matters by force and that it was also useless to expect the United States to pour money into a government dominated by a completely reactionary clique bent on exclusive control of governmental power.[22]

The complete victory of the IPR position was further illustrated by President Truman's 1946 statements on the coalitionist intentions of the Marshall Mission, by a joint communique to similar effect by the American, British and Soviet governments, and by the statements of Marshall himself as set forward in the white paper: ". . . he believed . . . that it was imperative that efforts be made to bring [the Communists] into the government."*[23]

The views of our State Department were made even plainer by two June 1946 statements from then Under Secretary of State Dean Acheson. "Too much stress cannot be laid," Acheson said, "on the hope that our economic assistance be carried out in China through the medium of a government fully and fairly representative of all important Chinese political elements, including the Chinese Communists." And: "The Communist leaders have asked, and General Marshall has agreed, that integration with the other forces be

* Also instructive is the passage in the IPR report concerning the role of IPR stalwart John Carter Vincent, identified by Louis Budenz as a Communist (which Vincent denies) and by the Senate committee as "the principal fulcrum of IPR pressures and influence in the State Department," and, after a long and confused loyalty-security battle in which he was first "cleared" by the State Department then "uncleared" by the Civil Service Loyalty Review Board, at last "requested" to resign from the State Department by Secretary of State John Foster Dulles on the grounds of "bad judgment." The Senate Internal Security subcommittee offered this sample of Vincent's bad judgment: "John Carter Vincent acknowledged having drafted . . . a memorandum that became a presidential message to Chiang Kai-shek transmitted on August 10, 1946, wherein Chiang was charged with using force against Chinese 'liberals' and with failing to understand the 'liberal trend of the times.' The letter threatened that unless the Chinese came to terms with the Communists it would become necessary 'to redefine and explain the position of the United States to the people of America.' "

preceded by a brief period of United States training and by the supply of minimum quantities of equipment."[24] American policy was not only committed to "coalition," but to training and supplying the Communists to get them ready for it.

General Marshall believed the Chinese Communists could, in some way never quite clearly determined, be "trusted." Freda Utley, then a correspondent in China, says:

> . . . it became apparent to those of us who were in Chungking at the time and were frequently invited to General Marshall's residence, that Chou En-lai had succeeded in captivating him. Any doubts General Marshall may originally have had as to the truth of the State Department thesis about the "progressive" Communists and the "reactionary" Nationalist government had obviously been dispelled. The fascinating Chou En-lai had evidently finally convinced General Marshall that the Chinese Communists were not "real" Communists, or that they could be "detached" from their Russian affiliations provided only they were helped by America to bring "democracy" to China. Marshall had long since come under the influence of his old friend, General Stilwell, who believed in the liberal professions of the Chinese Communists. Chou En-lai merely completed his conversion.[25]

Chiang Kai-shek was less enthusiastic. His long battle with the Communists, and his observation of their bland violation of truces insisted upon by Marshall, convinced him a "coalition" would be suicidal. And his contention that the Communists "would merely disrupt any government in which they participated," referred to in derogatory accents by the American State Department, was of course vindicated by the results.

Marshall nevertheless persisted in his demands and, when they were not acceded to, ordered an embargo of U.S. aid to Chiang. The result was to reverse the strategic situation in favor of the Communists:

At the end of 1945 when General Marshall left for China, the balance of power was with the Chinese Nationalists. Chiang's divisions were chasing the Communists northward and the prospect of victory by Nationalist China was at its highest. However, when General Marshall arrived in China, he undertook to bring about the coalition government which his directive demanded. And he commenced to bring pressure on Chiang in order to force his compliance. . . . Admiral Cooke testified that while he was in China in 1946, in charge of United States naval forces, General Marshall said to him during a conversation that the United States had armed the Chinese but then was disarming them.[26]

The behavior of the Communists in China was itself sufficiently recalcitrant, as even the white paper makes clear, to prove Marshall's dogged insistence on coalition wrong. But had the Communists obligingly concealed their hostile tendencies, his performance and that of the IPR claque generally would have been inexcusable. For the historical evidence on "coalitions" with the Communists, even prior to Marshall's China sojourn, was already substantial—as a brief review will indicate.

In 1944, the United States and Great Britain forced the establishment of a "coalition" government in Yugoslavia, involving the anti-Communist Prime Minister Subasic and the Communist Tito. In a matter of months, all anti-Communist ministers were driven from office and Yugoslavia went Communist.

In late 1945, a similar coalition was imposed on Rumania. The non-Communist leaders wanted no part of such an arrangement, but were chivvied into it by Averell Harriman, who performed there the role assigned to Marshall in China. At Harriman's urging, the Rumanian anti-Communists reluctantly entered the coalition, and not too long after that entered prison as well. Rumania went Communist.

Another effort at coalescence took place in Czechoslovakia,

where the Communists succeeded in getting control of the police—one of the offices they insist on whenever they enter a coalition. When Communist insurrection broke out in February, 1948, the police sided with the mob instead of with the Benes government. Czechoslovakia went Communist.

The dreary story was again repeated in Poland, when the Allies withdrew their support from the Free Polish government of Stanislaw Micolajczyk, and forced a "coalition" with the Soviet puppet regime in Lublin. Micolajczyk was harried into accepting a "government of national unity" in which the Communists held all the strategic posts. Within two years, the anti-Communists were driven out of the government and Micolajczyk fled to England.

In each of these cases, the "coalition" had already started to disintegrate, or had collapsed completely, when Marshall wrapped up his mission in China. Moreover, the record also included some very plain statements by the Communists about their settled intention of perverting coalitions to their own uses. "Coalitions including Communists," Gerhart Niemeyer notes, "have invariably ended either in Communist dictatorship or in a complete rupture between the non-Communist and Communist members of the coalition . . . There is no case of Communist cooperation in a coalition within the limits of the traditional parliamentary pattern in which parties accept and expect alternations between participation in power and opposition."[27]

If any of the examples we have cited in our brief survey deserves mention alongside China as a model of "coalition" diplomacy, it is Czechoslovakia. In essence, Czechoslovakia fell to Communism because its Socialist leadership, headed by President Benes, refused to grapple with the aggressive reality of Bolshevism. Until the very end Benes, in all particulars a blood brother of American Liberals in his wistful desire to accommodate the Communists, clung to the notion that his implacable enemies would listen to reason. And while

Benes was exhorting, the Communists were moving with stealth and purpose toward revolution.

On February 24, 1948, even as the Communists struck from the positions of power afforded them by the "coalition" to stir riot and rebellion, Benes sat down to write a pathetic, pleading letter which sums up, all too clearly, the impotence of rationalist cliche in the path of Bolshevik force. Expressing his belief that "the necessary cooperation of all can be achieved," and urging everyone "to find a peaceful solution and new successful cooperation through parliamentary means," Benes begged the Communists to reconsider their intransigence. "Let us all together begin negotiations again," he said, "for further durable cooperation . . ."[28]

That statement was made in the very hour of *coup d' état.* The cold-blooded revolutionists whom Benes was inviting to further negotiations had, for all practical purposes, already sealed Czechoslovakia's doom—and the president of the country could think of no recourse but new negotiations for "further durable cooperation." In that phrase, uttered in that hour, Eduard Benes intoned the epitaph of the Western Liberal intelligence.

The historical record when Marshall sought to impose a coalition government on Chiang Kai-shek was already impressive. With the Communization of China itself and the dismal history of Czechoslovakia super-added, the evidence that such arrangements are unworkable is more imposing still. Yet the same IPR-style program for "cooperating" with the Communists is with us today, 20 years later. In the 1960s, as in the 1940s, the urge to coalesce with the Communists remains a dominant force in American foreign policy.

★★ 22. *Encore In Laos*

1. *Special Obligations*

We come now to the closely-related cases of Laos and South Viet Nam, two nations created from the partition of French Indochina in 1954. Since the fall of China, and in particular since the French evacuation of the Indochinese peninsula, the Communists have sought to gain control of these nations. For various reasons having to do both with geography (Laos has a long common border with Communist North Viet Nam and with Communist China) and leadership (the anti-Communist leaders of Laos were neither so resolute nor so experienced as were those in South Viet Nam), Laos was the first to fall into serious danger.

The political history of Laos, from its founding in 1950 as a state within the French Union, has been extraordinarily confused. The nation, comprising the principalities of Luang

Prabang, Vientiane, and Champassac, had traditionally been ruled by a monarchy premised in a peace-loving and other-worldly Buddhism. At the end of World War II, two princes distantly related to the king—Souvanna Phouma and Souphanouvong—pitched in with the Viet Minh-led effort to oust the French. When this campaign met with indifferent success, Souvanna Phouma returned to Vientiane to work within the existing government; Souphanouvong continued to cooperate with the Viet Minh and launched the Laotian Communist group, the Pathet Lao. The King and Prince Boun Oum of Champassac remained loyal to the French.

Throughout the fifties, both before and after Dienbienphu, the Pathet Lao warred against the Royal Laotian government, setting up their own "resistance" government in the country's northern provinces, assisted by Ho Chi Minh, the Chinese Communists, and the Soviet Union. The government pursued a vacillating and contradictory course toward Souphanouvong, alternately inviting him into its ranks and arresting him. In May 1960, Royal Laotian army captain Kong Le staged a *coup d' état* in Vientiane, throwing in with the Pathet Lao. His action and subsequent confusion in government ranks provoked a counter-coup headed by strongly anti-Communist General Phoumi Nosavan, an ally of Boun Oum.

The Eisenhower administration, viewing this sad history of disorder, saw Boun Oum and Phoumi as the best hope of a highly uncertain situation. Although they were like most Laotians sometimes "unrealistic" by Western standards, they were anti-Communist, aware of their country's peril, and prepared to work with the United States to do something about it. If there were any chance of saving Laos from Communism, they obviously were it.

Senator Peter Dominick (R-Colo.) sketched the Laotian balance of forces when the Kennedy regime ascended to power. ". . . as we come up to 1961," Dominick said, we have aggression by the Communists in two groups in Laos, a pro-Western government in control, and a reaffirmation of support by our own government in this pro-Western government.

In 1961 the anti-Communist government, headed by Prince Boun Oum, chosen premier by 'strong man' Gen. Phoumi Nosavan, was endorsed as the legal government of Laos by a unanimous vote of the National Assembly on January 4. It was immediately recognized by the United States during the last weeks of the Eisenhower administration.

Thus, up until the time that President Kennedy took office there was no misunderstanding of this nation's attitude toward the pro-Communist Pathet Lao, the formation of a broad-based government in Laos, or the foreign aid to such a government. Our policy had been consistent and our actions had matched our statements. We had not vacillated from our determination to prevent a Communist takeover.[1]

At first, there were signs that the New Frontier was going to continue this policy and stand firm against the Pathet Lao. On March 23, 1961, President Kennedy took to the nation's television screens to explain the importance of Laos, its pivotal role in the defense of all Southeast Asia. ". . . all SEATO members," Kennedy said dramatically, "have undertaken special treaty obligations toward an aggression in Laos. No one should doubt our resolution on this point."[2]

Kennedy's presentation that day, his emphatic pledge to keep Laos out of Communist hands, and his apparent appreciation of the kingdom's strategic importance were all at the opposite pole from the policy which had brought about the fall of China. Yet in a few months the presentation and the pledge were seemingly forgotten, and the IPR strategy was once more fully in the saddle.

Returning from the Vienna conference with Khrushchev in June, Kennedy expressed the state of mind which had suddenly come to prevail among our diplomats. "The one area which afforded some immediate prospect of accord,"

Kennedy said, "was Laos . . . Both sides recognized the need to reduce the dangers in that situation. . . . Both sides endorsed the concept of a neutral and independent Laos."[3]

A ceasefire was arranged, and America lent its prestige to an International Conference on Laos which had as its objective the creation of a coalition government embracing pro-Communists and anti-Communists. The negotiations were conducted, throughout, on the premise that Moscow truly wanted a peaceful settlement. As Australian journalist Denis Warner comments: "Western policy, as it was presented at Geneva, was based on the assumption that the Communists had made an exception of Laos, that they wanted nothing more there than a truly neutral state. This assumption sprang from the Russian pledges made privately in Moscow and Geneva, coupled with the confidential note of urgency that we had to hurry up with the job to keep the Chinese out."[4]

Like Chiang, Prince Boun Oum and Gen. Phoumi resisted these assumptions, and the coalition that went with them; therefore, also like Chiang, they became "rightists" standing in the way of bliss and harmony. A campaign was mounted in the American press to portray them as villains preventing the United States and the Soviet Union from getting together.

In May, 1962, *The New York Times* reported the New Frontier's conviction "that Moscow shared its desire for a peaceful and political settlement." This belief was founded, *The Times* went on, in the idea that Moscow was showing "restraint," traceable to "a general Soviet desire to contain Chinese influence in Southeast Asia." The story additionally asserted the New Frontiersmen's belief that Moscow therefore was actually pleased with American "military motions" in the area. The story then went on to say:

"The administration, in turn, *is not entirely displeased* with some diplomatic by-products of last week's Communist offensive in Laos. The fighting proved the weakness of the right-wing Laotian army and thus destroyed many of the political pretensions of its leaders, Prince Boun Oum, the Premier, and his strong-man Deputy Premier, Maj. Gen. Phoumi Nosavan [Italics added.]

"Several times this week, President Kennedy has acknowledged his resentment of the rightists' refusal to join the proposed neutral coalition government in Laos. General Phoumi Nosavan has been told that he will be disowned entirely if he does not heed Washington's advice."[5]

In other words, the Kennedy regime was *pleased* with *Communist* successes against the anti-Communist government it was supposedly supporting. It felt it could trust Mocow's peaceful intentions, but could *not* trust the "rightists" and "strong men" of the anti-Communist government. Here is the IPR line in earnest, with a dose of Rostow-*Liberal Papers* credulity thrown in for seasoning.

In February, 1962, the New Frontier cut off its $3 million aid stipend to Laos, to force Boun Oum to coalesce. Boun Oum and Phoumi began seeking assistance from other anti-Communist governments in Asia, notably Thailand and Nationalist China. This made the New Frontier even angrier, and provided yet another pretext for attacking the anti-Communist leaders. In late May when the two Laotians were in the Philippines seeking support, the New Frontier criticized them for not "staying on the job" and battling the Communists.

"No one has been tending the store for our side," wrote R. H. Shackford of the Scripps-Howard newpapers, "during the recent flareup in Laos.

"The Communist Pathet Lao has remained on the job, but 'our' Laotian leaders have been junketeering.

"Premier Boun Oum and his so-called strong man, Vice Premier and Defense Minister General Phoumi Nosavan, have been gallivanting all over the Far East for most of the last three weeks. They were in Formosa seeking what they called the 'moral support' of Chiang Kai-shek.

"The U.S. government is not just disenchanted with these two men. It is fed up with them as unreliables who seek primarily, for their own personal prestige, to get U.S. forces entrapped in the jungles of a country whose people are unwilling to resist the Communists."[6]

Two weeks later, *The New York Times* reported mounting pressures against Phoumi. "Officials denied today," said *The Times,* "that the Assistant Secretary of State for Far Eastern Affairs, W. Averell Harriman, told the Laotian Ambassador, Tiao Kampan, last week that General Phoumi Nosavan should be removed.

"But it was understood that Mr. Harriman had expressed the wish that the general try to concentrate on military matters instead of confusing the political picture in Laos.

"There was growing suspicion here that General Phoumi Nosavan was hoping to provoke the United States and Thailand into intervening directly in the Laotian civil war.

"Concerning yesterday's pro-Communist attack, the State Department press officer said that, if the incident proved to be serious, *the United States would immediately call it to the attention of the Soviet Union.*

"Other officials recalled Moscow's recent reaffirmation of its desire to see the Laotian crisis settled diplomatically."[7] (Italics added.)

Thus the reversal was complete; the anti-Communist leaders were the villains; the Moscow Communists, striving faithfully to get things worked out, were our brothers in pacifism. President Kennedy believed, or (what amounts to the same thing) acted as though he believed, that Khrushchev's word could be trusted, and that his bona fides on Laos were good. The parallel with the "IPR strategy" in China was so blatant that even *The New York Times* took editorial note of it.

"The American policy," *The Times* commented, "is based on Washington's belief that the Lao are uninterested in political or ideological conflicts and, in contrast to the Vietnamese, will not fight. But to back up that policy and force the pro-Western leaders into the coalition with the Communists, even to surrender the army and the police, which they refuse, American authorities have tended to undercut the pro-Western government, even to accuse it of provocation, until the policy begins to resemble that which lost China."[8]

That the U.S. had "undercut" the Boun Oum government was putting it mildly. Joseph Alsop compared Harriman's effort to force Boun Oum into the coalition to the Mad Hatter stuffing the dormouse into the teapot. Alsop described an episode in which Harriman berated the anti-Red leaders:

> Governor Harriman looked at the Lao leaders one by one; pointed a stern forefinger at each of them in turn; and told them that he wished them to know they would be "responsible for the destruction of their country" if they refused to do his bidding. There was a brief silence, and General Phoumi then replied: "You know, Governor Harriman, we in Laos have many years' experience of colonial rule. But we were never spoken to in quite that fashion in colonial times."[9]

Alsop went on to add that Boun Oum and General Phoumi would have reluctantly entered a coalition government "if the price of the coalition had not been surrendering control of the police and the army. Such a surrender, they understandably considered, was tantamount to cutting their own throats with a blunt knife . . . if the Lao anti-Communists are now driven, by main force, into the coalition that has been so eagerly promoted, it will be equivalent to handing Laos to the North Vietnamese with a red ribbon prettily tied around it. No doubt this can be done, by withdrawing U.S. military aid, for instance, which Governor Harriman apparently told the British Ambassador here that he intended to recommend."[10] As it turned out, of course, the anti-Communists were driven into the coalition.

2. *Why We Backed Down*

Why was the New Frontier so intent upon enacting another China debacle in Laos? Why did it insist upon "coalition" and back its insistence with bitter attacks on the anti-Communist regime and a cut-off of aid? The official answer was that the Laotian anti-Communists were incapable of defending themselves, and that the only alternative to "neutralization" was massive commitment of American arms and personnel. Moreover, it was asserted, the important thing was the defense of South Viet Nam. We would make the best of a bad thing, cut our losses, and concentrate on the job of defending a position that was defensible.

The most obvious flaw in this explanation is that it is completely at variance with the Kennedy pledge of March 1961. But, equally to the point, it was at variance with the available facts about Laos:

1. Far from being unable or unwilling to defend themselves, the Laotian anti-Communists showed marked improvement in their ability to combat the Pathet Lao. So much so, in fact, that the Communists felt increasingly obliged to call on the assistance of troops from North Viet Nam and Red China.

2. Even if the situation could not be retrieved without outside help, this did not mean American troops would have to be sent into the battle. Thailand, the Philippines, and Nationalist China all wanted to pitch in with arms and men; the Kennedy regime, however, refused to give the go-ahead for this.

3. If the New Frontier's concern was to defend South Viet Nam, the best possible way of accomplishing that would have been to press the fight in Laos. With Laos in Communist hands, a common border with South Viet Nam lay open to the Viet Cong as a supply route through Laos into Diem's country. Subsequent New Frontier actions in Viet Nam also

punctured the "all or nothing" argument about that nation.

On the first of these points, Senator Dodd contested the assertion that the Laotians were not interested in defending themselves. "I do not accept the thesis that the Lao people are indifferent to Communism and that the Royalist forces are incapable of fighting," he said. "I remind the senators that it was a year ago last December that the Royalist Army, under General Phoumi, drove the highly touted Kong Le rebels out of Vientiane. I remind the senators, too, that certain units of the Lao army, in particular the 10,000 Meo tribesmen who are serving with it, have put up a truly heroic resistance in situation after situation." Fighting the Pathet Lao, he said, the anti-Communist regime held its own, but was having difficulties with "the hardened professionals of the North Vietnamese Communist army . . ."[11]

A similar view was offered in a *U.S. News and World Report* dispatch from Vientiane. The magazine's correspondent gave this summary of the struggle:

> Judging from the information available in Laos, Thailand, and South Viet Nam, the United States has not reassessed the situation in Laos since the spring of 1961, when the Kennedy administration apparently decided the best way out was to neutralize the Red-menaced country. . . .
>
> For example, it was assumed that the Communists and neutrals would overrun Laos in a matter of days unless a coalition government that included them was set up. In fact, the reverse has happened. In order to maintain Red power, Communist North Viet Nam has had to send in new battalions of its most experienced troops.[12]

Although the "cease fire" stipulated that no further action be taken by combatants on either side, the Communists blithely used it to strengthen their position, and the Soviet Union, to whose attention the Kennedy regime wistfully called violations of the agreement, was up to its ears in helping the operation along. "Communist North Viet Nam has put 10 identified battalions into the fighting area," said *U.S. News*. "The Communists now have a stranglehold on the supply corridor through Laos that connects North and South Viet Nam. The Russians airlift supplies to Tchepone, close to the South Viet Nam border, and have one other major airdrop zone . . . Right now, the entire Communist-neutralist force is dependent on a Soviet airlift and several weekly truck convoys from North Viet Nam."[13]

Such was the force with which the "non-fighting" Boun Oum government had to contend. Confronted by that situation, the administration assailed the anti-Communists for making it difficult to reach an agreement with the Communists.

As for possible U.S. involvement, Dodd related his findings on a swing through Southeast Asia during a crucial SEATO meeting on Laos. ". . . at the time this SEATO meeting took place," he said, "our Asian allies were prepared to provide all or most of the necessary ground troops. They took the stand that it was much better for Asians to fight in Asia and that, if SEATO did intervene, American participation should consist primarily of air and logistical support." By defaulting in Laos, moreover, we made augmented American involvement in neighboring Viet Nam inevitable.

The strategic significance of Laos was pinpointed by Gen. Rothwell H. Brown, who served as chief of program evaluation for the U.S. Operations Mission in Laos for three years. "A glance at any relief map in any good atlas," Gen. Brown observed, "will show clearly that below the mountains of Laos and west of the mountains along the coast of Viet Nam, there lies a great alluvial plain . . . lacking in major military defensive positions. Therefore, it is quite clear that once the mountain barrier is breached, the problem of defending the heartland of Southeast Asia becomes exceedingly difficult. . . . The only barrier protecting the great heartland of Southeast Asia, Thailand, Cambodia, and South Viet Nam lies in the mountains of Laos."[14]

3. *Umbrella and All*

On June 11, 1962, the three rival leaders of Laos announced the formation of a coalition government. On July 21, fourteen nations at Geneva, including Red China, the Soviet Union and the United States, ratified the plan, signing a declaration and protocol "guaranteeing" the neutrality of Laos.

East and West hailed the coalition and the associated "neutrality" agreements. President Kennedy, in a White House press release, remarked that "the kingdom of Laos, which has been torn for so long by fratricidal strife, now stands on the threshold of a new era. It now has the opportunity to become united and independent, free to pursue its own chosen course of neutrality."[15]

The happy future suggested by Kennedy was affirmed neither by the majority of America's military officials nor by the leaders of Southeast Asia. They saw little hope in a settlement which replaced pro-Western Boun Oum with "neutralist" Souvanna Phouma. Souvanna's armed forces were trained and supplied by Russian and Chinese Communists; his 19-member cabinet included a majority of Communists and neutralists; and he lived with and took advice from his Communist half-brother, the leader of the Pathet Lao, Prince Souphanouvong.

Suggesting the course that such "coalitions" have followed to date, the new regime tilted noticeably toward the Communists. Shortly after its formation, Souvanna Phouma departed the country, leaving the government in control of his Communist half-brother. Souphanouvong immediately demanded the withdrawal of U.S. troops from neighboring Thailand, and unleashed an attack on the embattled anti-

Red regime in South Viet Nam. Augmented aggressions occurred in 1963.

When it came to negotiating with the Communists, Harriman had not been quite so demanding as with Boun Oum. The backbone of the Pathet Lao army in Laos was composed of some 10,000 battle-hardened North Vietnamese; if there were to be even the pretense of "neutrality" in Laos, this army should have been disbanded and the Vietnamese expelled from the country. Yet the agreement provided no effective means of achieving this. Similarly, Harriman did not attempt to get Souvanna Phouma to rescind his agreement with the Red Chinese allowing them to build a military road from Meng La in China to Phongsaly, the Pathet Lao stronghold in Laos.

Moreover, the inspection commission, allegedly to insure that the agreement was adhered to, was given only "investigatory" powers and was in effect powerless. It could operate only if it were "acting with the concurrence of the Royal Government of Laos,"[16] an eventuality which the Communist prince could simply veto. The agreement would thus prove workable only if the Soviets and the Pathet Lao cooperated, which they did not.

As Sir Wilfrid Kent Hughes of the Australian Parliamentary Foreign Affairs Committee observed: "Averell Harriman . . . has the chance to go down in history as the Churchill or the Chamberlain of Southeast Asia. When I was in Bangkok, he seemed to have decided on the latter, umbrella and all."[17]

The Senate Internal Security subcommittee, examining the results of the Laos settlement, summed up the matter as follows: "On November 10, 1962, the International Control Commission for Laos reported that only 40 North Vietnamese soldiers withdrew from Laos at any of the designated checkpoints. The British government estimated that at the time of the cease-fire there were about 10,000 North Vietnamese troops in Laos . . . In April 1963 the Communist Pathet Lao forces renewed civil war in Laos . . . At the SEATO Ministerial Council meeting in Paris on April 8 to 10, 1963, Secretary Rusk declared that Communist forces from Viet Nam were still operating in Laos in violation of the 1962 Geneva agreements . . .

"Throughout April . . . serious fighting continued in the Plaine des Jarres. Communist Pathet Lao forces, now controlling two-thirds of Laos, pressed their attack against the neutralist forces . . . The Soviets charged the United States with sabotaging the Geneva agreements and placed blame for the new outbreaks of distorder on American subversive activities. *The New York Times* reported that this commentary . . . was the first public indication that the Soviets would remain adamant in refusing to join British diplomatic moves to restore the political balance in Laos . . . The British held that the Geneva accords were in jeopardy owing to Soviet failure to act responsibly."[18]

Thus we get this sequence:

1. President Kennedy proclaims American commitment to the cause of defending Laos against Communism;
2. The Kennedy regime squelches a move by SEATO nations to assist the pro-Western Laotian government;
3. The Kennedy regime reaches a "ceasefire agreement" through the good offices of Moscow;
4. Under cover of the ceasefire Soviet, Red Chinese, Vietnamese and Laotian Communists combine to strengthen the Red position against the pro-Western government;
5. The Kennedy regime calls violations of the ceasefire "to the attention" of Moscow, which is participating in them;
6. Assured by their new strength, the Communists demand a "coalition" government in which they control the key portfolios of defense and police;
7. The Kennedy regime, to force the anti-Communist government into this coalition, cuts off American aid;

8. When the pro-Western leaders travel to other nations to seek help, they are attacked for "junketeering" when they should be "on the job" against the Communists;

9. The pro-Western government capitulates and the "coalition" is formed in keeping with Communist desires;

10. The assault on South Viet Nam, now unencumbered by effective resistance in Laos, begins with renewed vigor.

At this writing, the political future of Laos remains in doubt. The various factions continue to ride off in all directions, and no one seems certain who is siding with whom. One fact, however, is already clear: The principal strategic value of Laos, owing to our default, is already in the hands of the Communists. The "Ho Chi Minh" trail connecting North with South Viet Nam is a broad highway along which reinforcements to the Viet Cong killing U.S. and Vietnamese soldiers pass in daily procession. And with every footfall they press a little deeper in the jungle mire America's brave words of 1961.

★★ 23. *Viet Nam: The Turn of the Screw*

1. *The Betrayal of Diem*

IN ITS APPROACH to Laos—both in making its commitment and in withdrawing it—the Kennedy regime had put a great deal of emphasis on South Viet Nam. In his original pledge to keep Laos out of Communist hands, Kennedy had stressed the strategic importance of Laos to the defense of its anti-Communist neighbor. In the series of actions which nullified that pledge, the New Frontier stressed that it would concentrate on Viet Nam *instead* of Laos. While the two positions contradicted each other, they at least had the common merit of recognizing the strategic significance of Viet Nam.

A glance at the map will confirm Viet Nam's importance. Directly to the South lies the vast archipelago of Indonesia, which has teetered close to overt communization. Eastward are the Philippines. Southward still from Indonesia is the subcontinent of Australia. Should Viet Nam fall, Thailand, the last remaining stronghold of anti-Communist sentiment on the Asian continent, would be hopelessly isolated. And the Pacific sea lanes from the Aleutians to the Spice Islands would be in the hands of the Communists. The New Frontier's insistence that it would stand or fall in Viet Nam, even as it consigned Laos to the limbo of "coalition," was in recognition of this fact.

That the significance of Viet Nam had thus been explicitly confirmed makes it all the more appalling that, once Laos had been disposed of, the IPR strategy was put into action in Viet Nam as well. The ink on the Laos agreements was hardly dry before the machinery was geared up to discredit the anti-Communist leader of South Viet Nam, Ngo Dinh Diem. This attack, both in the public media and in the councils of the American government, took two main channels: The first, that U.S. aid to Diem must be conditioned on "reforms". The second, that Diem, his brother Ngo Dinh Nhu, and his sister-in-law, Madame Nhu, were guilty of "religious persecution" of Vietnamese Buddhists.

The "reform" theme was first advanced, interestingly enough, by Walt W. Rostow, whose singular views on the Cold War we have already examined. In his book, *An American Policy In Asia,* Rostow had urged that "the United States should sharply reduce its exhortation and pressure for anti-Communist action in Southeast Asia," and that "we should not link economic assistance to military aid."[1] Such things, he believed, were offensive to Asian neutralists, and would not get the job done for freedom.

These views were to a large extent translated into American policy in 1961 when Rostow accompanied General Maxwell Taylor on an inspection trip to Viet Nam. Taylor's subsequent recommendations were heavily larded with the idea that U.S. military aid to Diem should be contingent on the enactment of "democratic reforms," demands which stretched U.S.-Vietnamese relations to the breaking point. Although sensitive to the problems of "offending" the various neutralists of Asia, Rostow and other Liberal theorists think nothing of laying down the law to anti-Communists like Diem.

The agitation for "reform," although a staple in the IPR strategy, was somewhat curious when applied to Viet Nam. For one thing, Diem himself had virtually created the Vietnamese nation by main strength out of the chaos bequeathed him by the French and the Communists. When Rostow raised the "reform" question in 1961, Diem had recently been elected over two opponents by more than 60% of the popular vote. He was engaged in all-out war for survival against the Viet Cong, threaded in among the domestic population, and in resettling refugees from the North, who then numbered better than one million human beings. In the midst of all this, he was to enact "reforms" if he wanted to continue getting American aid.

In early 1962, Edward Neilan, chief of the Asian Bureau of the Copley News Service, relayed an informed and plain-spoken commentary on this clamor for "reform." Neilan interviewed a Tokyo-based American businessman who had travelled frequently to Saigon and who contributes articles to Far Eastern newspapers. The resulting analysis of U.S. policy in Viet Nam:

"I have nothing against attempting to reform South Viet Nam. It probably can stand reform as much as any other place, and I am sure will not absorb enough of it to matter. The danger is that in going about reforming this and that, we will get diverted from the fact that the Communist Viet Cong guerrillas are using live ammunition and real bullets and are murdering school children and priests and businessmen too. Closing dancing halls and emphasizing a purer form of democracy is not much of a defense against that sort of thing.

"The villagers in the provinces are being turned into nervous terrorized wrecks not because of a lack of democracy in Saigon, but because they are being shot up in the night. It is silly to say that they would resist the Viet Cong harder if they believed in the government more. They will resist the Viet Cong whenever they come to believe that the government side has more guns and more ability to use them. So far the government does not have them and the Viet Cong are running rampant."[2]

Even more insistent than the "reform" theme was the rising clamor over "religious persecution" of the Buddhists. This boiled to a climax in May, 1963, when several Buddhist monks burned themselves alive in protest against the Diem regime. The press corps in Saigon was in full cry against Diem and Madame Nhu. Pressures began radiating from the American government. Rumors were rife that a coup would be attempted soon. *The Times of Viet Nam* claimed the CIA had been engineering a move against Diem, originally scheduled for August 28. Up to $24 million, the paper asserted, had been spent in this effort—going for propaganda, bribery of public officials, subornation of military personnel.[3] The story was denied.

Similar rumors had been circulating in Saigon for months. A dispatch from that capital in the fall of 1963 said: "The month of August, 1963, appeared to be the most auspicious time for the downfall of the government . . . The city of Saigon was buzzing with rumors of the coup. Virtually every general in the Vietnamese army had been named at one time or another as prospective head of the new government."[4]

Madame Nhu journeyed to the United States, where she was pointedly snubbed by the Kennedy administration and the State Department put pressure on newsmen to keep her out of the public spotlight. "An official of the Columbia Broadcasting System," reported the Richmond, Virginia, *News-Leader,* "appeared on a State Department platform at a

Washington press briefing to tell the editors that Madame Nhu's appearance on Face The Nation was being cancelled. To take her place, CBS chose Tran Van Chuong, Madame Nhu's father and her vocal opponent. The implication was, go and do likewise."[5]

Back in Viet Nam, American pressures against Diem had been mounting relentlessly. A USIA official in Saigon says the embassy's *chargé d'affaires* there had been ordered by Washington to apply "direct, relentless table-hammering pressure on Diem such as the United States had seldom before attempted with a sovereign friendly government . . . [and] resorted to a formal warning to Diem that if he continued repressive measures the United States would be forced to disassociate itself publicly from such actions, as indeed we did two months later. The warning was a momentous step. It amounted to a direct official command from the United States. Public disassociation could have disastrous results, encouraging the Viet Cong, strengthening the regime's foreign critics, perhaps even stimulating the Vietnamese army to try another coup."

The turning-point against Diem was the August arrival of Henry Cabot Lodge as America's new ambassador. Replacing Frederick Nolting, considered "friendly" to Diem, Lodge soon made it apparent no such accusation could be levelled against him. He provided exactly the "public disassociation" needed to trigger action against the anti-Communist leader.

Lodge placed American prestige squarely on the side of the Buddhists by calling on their leaders and having his picture taken with them, apparently before presenting his credentials to President Diem. Although it was later claimed Lodge merely happened to "drop in" at the American Aid Compound where he met the Buddhists, the place is many miles from the U.S. embassy in Saigon and a highly inconvenient spot for a newly-arrived ambassador to drop into. Moreover, inquiries concerning his whereabouts elicited the answer that "the ambassador went to call on the Buddhists."[6]

Reporter Jay G. Hayden of the North American Newspaper Alliance says: "From the day Lodge arrived as ambassador, events began building [toward the overthrow of Diem] . . ." Lodge's first official statement, Hayden notes, was in condemnation of Diem's action against the Buddhists and "the ambassador particularly antagonized the regime by granting refuge in his embassy to the leading Buddhist priest . . ."[7]

On September 2, President Kennedy appeared in a television interview and said the Diem government could not hope to win the war against the Viet Cong unless it made "a greater effort . . . to win popular support." The regime, said Kennedy, had "gotten out of touch with the people."[8] Twenty-two United States senators followed up with a declaration that, unless the Diem government reformed, American aid should be cut off. Then, precisely in the IPR pattern, U.S. assistance to Diem's "special forces" was halted, on the grounds that these troops were being used for purposes of religious persecution. As one commentator put it: "Washington is still hoping to 'get' Diem. That's why it cut the $250,000 monthly subsidy for Diem's 'special forces.' In essence, this is notice to all opponents of the Diem regime that the U.S. won't be unhappy if somebody manages to overthrow him."[9]

It became evident that the United States government was giving the go-ahead for the toppling of Diem. Secretary of Defense McNamara and CIA Director John McCone, Marguerite Higgins reported, opposed the coup. "But they were overruled by the pro-*coup d'état* faction led by Ambassador Henry Cabot Lodge, Under Secretary of State Averell Harriman, and Assistant Secretary of State for Far Eastern Affairs Roger Hilsman . . . On August 24, the State Department sent out word—without the knowledge of Secretary McNamara or of CIA Director McCone—instructing Ambassador Lodge to 'unleash' the Vietnamese generals with a view to toppling the Diem government if they could . . . On Sunday, August 25, Washington gave the generals a green light in a Voice of America broadcast that virtually called on the Vietnamese military to take over."[10]

The broadcast said: "High American officials blame police, headed by President Diem's brother, Ngo Dinh Nhu, for anti-Buddhist actions in the Viet Nam republic. The officials say Viet Nam military leaders are not, repeat, not responsible for last week's attacks against pagodas and the mass arrest of monks and students."[11]

This broadcast, according to the researches of Miss Higgins, had been the handiwork of Assistant Secretary of State Hilsman, who called in a UPI reporter, gave him the requisite background on the "official" view, then called VOA personnel and told them the resulting story "would be an accurate reflection of American policy." A State Department officer comments: "On that weekend Hilsman was a man in a hurry—and perhaps out of the most idealistic reasons. He thought that if he could publicize the threat to cut aid the generals would be bound to act quickly against Diem."[12]

Miss Higgins further tells us that "key Americans at the embassy were assigned to take soundings of the most openly revolt-minded generals . . . It took most of Monday and Tuesday (August 26 and 27) to complete this 'poll' . . . A total of seven generals were asked whether or not they were ready to revolt."[13]

The generals, as it developed, were ready, having been made so by President Kennedy's call for a change in policy and "maybe in personnel," the announcement that 1,000 U.S. soldiers would be withdrawn by the end of 1963 ("that convinced us that unless we got rid of Diem, you would abandon us"), and the cut-off of economic aid ("in cutting economic aid the United States was forcing us to choose between your country's help in the war and Diem").

One member of the junta summed up matters by saying: "We would never have dared to act if we had not been sure that the United States was giving us its moral support."[14]

Denis Warner, who can be accused of no partiality toward Diem, sums up this incredible performance as follows: "By every means short of direct involvement, and including Voice of America broadcasts, the suspension of aid, and a quite open campaign in Saigon to dissociate itself and the South Vietnamese people from the government, the United States floodlit the way for the enemies of the regime. Coldly, calmly Lodge set the scene."[15]

In November, while Madame Nhu was still in America, the blow fell. The Army overthrew the Diem government, murdering Diem and Ngo Dinh Nhu. Signs of United States approval were immediately in evidence. American authorities refused to give asylum to Diem's brother, and extended recognition to the new military junta. By way of contrast, the U.S. *had* given asylum to Diem's opponents, and had withheld recognition from a similar military coup in the Dominican Republic against the fellow-traveling government of Juan Bosch. *The New York Times* commented that recognition for Diem's slayers "symbolized what appeared to be a new climate of confidence between Washington and Saigon . . ."[16]

2. *The Buddhist Hoax*

What could have been the reason for so astounding a performance—in the very land where the New Frontier had pledged to give its all in the struggle against Communism? The answer was the "religious persecution" of Buddhists by the Catholic Diem. The self-immolation of several Buddhist priests, and the closing of Buddhist pagodas in August, vastly played up by the press corps in Saigon, had turned a great wave of global indignation against Diem. The Kennedy regime decided, against the advice of the Pentagon and the CIA, that because of his "persecutions" and the reaction against them, Diem would have to go.

Yet the fact of the matter is that the cries of "persecution" were propaganda, and the United States knew as much. In September 1963, 16 member governments filed a statement with the United Nations charging the Diem government was engaged in "serious violation of human rights."[17] On October 11, in response to this charge and at the request of Diem, the U.N. sent a fact-finding commission to Viet Nam. The commission learned what was already known to U.S. officials: The Buddhist agitation was the work of a small, politically fanatic element, and the "repressions" carried out by Diem were exactly the same things the regime would have been compelled to do had the demonstrators been Catholics or Doukhobors.

Ambassador Fernando Volio Jimenez of Costa Rica, whose motion led to the U.N. inquiry, told an interviewer: "It is my personal feeling that there was no policy of discrimination, oppression, or persecution against the Buddhists on the basis of religion. Testimony to this effect was usually hearsay, and was expressed in vague or general terms. When a witness tried to give some concrete proof to the mission, the incident he cited came down to individual or personal actions. On the basis of the evidence, there was not a governmental policy against the Buddhists on religious grounds."[18]

In a series of articles for the New York *Herald-Tribune,* Marguerite Higgins established the same point. The Buddhist protest, Miss Higgins noted, was political, not religious, centering in such items as the right of the Buddhists to fly their flag (a prohibition affecting all religions), and involving such other things as the desire of certain of the Buddhists to achieve a reconciliation with the Communist regime to the North. The mastermind of the Buddhist campaign was Thich Tri Quang, a former member of the Communist Viet Minh, who, according to French records, had been arrested twice for dealings with Red leader Ho Chi Minh. Thich Tri Quang's 1963 solution for Viet Nam was "neutralization." In an interview with Miss Higgins, he said: "We cannot get an arrangement with the North until we get rid of Diem and Nhu."[19]

The U.N. inquiry discovered that, under the direction of Thich Tri Quang, the "Buddhist" protest that aroused world indignation had been artfully manufactured. Senator Thomas Dodd says:

> The report reproduced at length the testimony of a 19-year-old monk who told the mission how he had been recruited by a "suicide promotion squad." The monk said that he had been informed that the venerable head of the Buddhist Association had been killed, that hundreds of Buddhists had been disemboweled, and that the Xa Loi pagoda had been burned. He was asked to volunteer to commit suicide for the sake of the Buddhist religion, was assured that he would be given drugs that would make him feel no pain, and was given prepared letters to sign. He was apprehended by the police in time to discover that the atrocity stories were complete fabrications.[20]

This incident, taken from the report of a U.N. body which had no bias toward Diem, offers a revealing insight into the Buddhist immolations. It is not difficult to extrapolate from the case of the 19-year-old monk who did not burn himself to the case of others who did. Such findings convinced the U.N. members who previously thought Diem was engaged in a religious pogrom to adopt the opposite conclusion. Costa Rica's Volio told Senator Dodd "the charges made in the General Assembly against the Diem regime had not been sustained." Before journeying to Viet Nam, Volio had been prepared to vote for condemnation of Diem.

In short, the "religious persecution" stories played up by so much of the press were false. Yet the numerous reporters who had given currency to them never bothered to retract what they had said, nor did they give comparable publicity to the important findings of the U.N. mission. Nor, finally, did they give publicity to the ironic fact that, in the weeks following the overthrow of Diem and the ascension of the junta, there were more suicides by fire on the part of the Buddhists than there had been under Diem, or to the parallel fact, reported by Pulitzer-prize correspondent Sanche de Gramont of the *New York Herald-Tribune,* that there were more than 500 arbitrary arrests carried out in the aftermath of the coup.

Subsequent agitation against the government of General Nguyen Cao Ky demonstrated the political motives and ruthless methods of the Buddhists even more conclusively. Correspondent Richard Critchfield of the Washington *Star* reported that Buddhists attempted to use newsmen as foils in a battle with Ky's troops, cynically endangering the lives of innocent by-standers to spread their propaganda. One newsman, Critchfield said, declared that "the Buddhists trapped us in the pagoda and then opened fire when we tried to get out." Critchfield added that "in a kind of shock treatment that stripped bare the almost incredible cynicism toward human life of Buddhist monks and rebel political commissars, newsmen were enticed inside for a fictional urgent announcement, then were told it was too dangerous to leave for the remainder of the night after Buddhist forces provoked a heavy firefight with surrounding paratroops and tanks." He concluded that the episode marked "the collapse of the myth that the Buddhists represented a just but repressed popular cause . . ."[21]

The basic reason behind Diem's "unpopularity," the alleged religious persecution, was a propaganda hoax. Yet our government premised the overthrow of a loyal anti-Communist ally on these grounds—knowing all the while that the charges were false. Miss Higgins quotes Roger Hilsman as saying: "After the closing of the pagodas on August 21, the facts became irrelevant."[22]

Small wonder Thich Tri Quang should have commented

to a reporter from the Saigon *Post:* "With the Americans it is not so interesting any more. They are too easy to outwit . . . some of them persist in thinking they can 'reform' me into agreeing with them . . . It is useful to smile sometimes and let them think so . . . We will use the Americans to help us get rid of Americans."[23]

The one extenuation for this dreadful business was that, in order to prosecute the war successfully against the Communists, Diem had to go. Yet it was apparent that by encouraging a coup the United States was also encouraging instability, leading to other possible coups in the future. Such instability could hardly strengthen the anti-Communist cause. As for "democratic reforms," a military junta is certainly less democratic, not more, than was the popularly-elected Diem regime. Finally, it is apparent that the effort expended in such internecine struggles is effort which cannot be directed at the danger of Communism. In every way, the administration's action diminished rather than increased the Free World's chances of winning the struggle in Viet Nam.

"If there was any slowdown in the war in September and October of 1963," Miss Higgins commented, "it was because the Vietnamese generals—under American prodding—were concentrating on thoughts of a *coup d'état,* while Diem and Nhu, out of fear of America, were concentrating on how to prevent a coup.

"It was not until after the *coup d'état* that the Vietnamese war took a decidedly downward turn. The military junta with its uncertain leadership, after purges of key (and scarce) officials, finally plunged much of the countryside into the confusion from which it was purportedly trying to save Viet Nam.

"No wonder the Viet Cong took advantage of the situation to seize the military initiative for the first time in many months. No wonder that, in the two months after the *coup d'état,* the military junta lost more real estate, lives and weapons to the Viet Cong than at any previous time in the war."[24]

Such was Liberal policy in Viet Nam for whose sake we had abandoned Laos. An ally besmirched by false propaganda, public criticism by the American government, withdrawal of aid in a time of crisis, and connivance in a military coup by force.

3. *Against the Grain*

The overthrow of Diem was perhaps the worst single blow struck by our government against the anti-Communist Vietnamese we were supposed to be supporting. But it was not the only one. The fall of Laos, as indicated, gave the Communists in Viet Nam the first prerequisite of successful guerrilla warfare—sanctuary and an easy source of supply. The advantage of sanctuary was redoubled by a United States policy of purely defensive action against the Viet Cong. As in Korea, initiatives against North Viet Nam itself were strictly verboten until 1965. In addition, initiatives by U.S. "advisers" against Communists *within South Viet Nam* had also been ruled out.

Captain Edwin G. Shank Jr., an American pilot killed in the Vietnamese action, called attention to this fact in some widely publicized letters written shortly before his death. On December 14, 1963, Captain Shank wrote to his wife in Winamac, Indiana: "The war is quiet because the Viet Cong are quiet. The funny thing is, I know, everyone knows, where some Viet Cong concentrations are, but they won't let us hit until the Viet Cong start something."[25]

U.S. soldiers in Viet Nam were instructed not to fire at a Communist guerrilla unless he fired at them first—a rule at last altered when servicemen protested this was more of a sporting chance for the Communists than they deemed necessary. Also inhibiting was a decree that no air attack could occur against the Viet Cong unless a South Vietnamese observer had pinpointed the target beforehand. This resulted in Viet Cong troop movements spotted by American reconnaissance going unmolested because a South Vietnamese wasn't on hand to join in the observing. *The Wall Street Journal* gave this report from Saigon:

> One night Viet Cong guerrillas began shelling Soc Trang airfield where the U.S. 1st Air Commando Squadron was on bomber alert duty. As the shells slammed down on the field two young American pilots raced for their planes and took off. They strafed the Reds with rockets and machine guns and drove them off.
>
> But instead of being decorated for their heroism the two men were reprimanded. They were judged to have violated the rules against attacking the enemy without a Vietnamese observer aboard to point out the target.[26]

"I'll bet you anyone you talk to," wrote Captain Shank in 1963, "does not know American pilots fight this war. The Vietnamese 'students' we have on board are airmen basics. They do not even know their own serial numbers. The only reason they are on board is, in case we crash there is one American adviser and one Vietnamese student. They are sacrificial lambs and a menace to have on board."[27]

Further complicating matters was the fact that the equipment supplied to U.S. personnel in Viet Nam was, according to numerous reports, obsolete. The airplane flown by Shank was a World War II vintage B-26. Stories were rife of these planes literally coming apart in mid-air. Secretary of Defense Robert McNamara testified in May 1964 that American soldiers in Viet Nam were receiving the best equipment available, yet when it came time to introduce new planes into the conflict, the Pentagon chose a craft called the Skyraider, a propellor-driven single engine plane left over from Korea.

Many Air Force men wanted America to use jet planes in Viet Nam, but this idea was for a long period vetoed by the administration on the grounds that it violated the Geneva agreement governing introduction of new equipment. The agreement says worn-out equipment can be replaced only by weapons "piece for piece of the same type and with similar characteristics."[28] America, however, was not a signatory to this agreement, and the Communists had blithely been violating it for years.

Viet Nam is one policy area in which the Johnson administration has, in several particulars of strategy, represented an improvement over the performance of the Kennedy regime. Certain nagging questions about Viet Nam, however, persist. For one thing, many elements in the government did not favor a "hard" policy in Viet Nam, and continued to work for a softening of the U.S. stance. Their efforts apparently began to bear fruit in the Christmas 1965 drive by the administration—with none other than Averell Harriman in a leading role—for a ceasefire.

From the beginning, it had not been entirely clear just how "hard" the Johnson policy in Viet Nam was intended to be. In his July, 1965 speech, the President said the aim of U.S. resistance in Viet Nam was to set the stage for negotiations. Precisely what these negotiations would consist of had never been made plain. A "negotiated settlement" in Laos had already been attempted, with particularly unfortunate results; there was little reason to believe a similar settlement in Viet Nam would be much better, or would justify the sacrifice of American blood and treasure which Viet Nam had evoked.

Problems in our Viet Nam strategy reflect the basic uncertainty of a war which aims at "negotiated settlement" with the Communists. When the President ordered a 1964 aerial retaliation to a Communist attack in the Gulf of Tonkin, he also announced the attack some 90 minutes before it took place, thus giving the Communists time to prepare for it. Johnson went on American television at 11:36 p.m., August

4, 1964, and announced that "air action is now in execution" against Red bases.[29] Yet our planes were not over those bases until 1:15 a.m. the following day, Eastern time. The attack on the northern most Communist base, Hon Gay, did not occur until 3:45 a.m., Eastern time—more than four hours after Johnson's announcement.

Two American planes were lost in the attack on Hon Gay. Whether this fact was in any way traceable to the advance warning the Communists were given, or whether it would have happened in any case is something we do not know. But the obvious fact is that, with such warning, an enemy is better prepared; without it, he is less prepared. Attempted extenuations of the advance warning by Secretary of Defense McNamara could not explain away the fact that, in counterattacking against the Communists, we had simultaneously handed them a long lead-time in which to get ready for us.

This strange policy ambivalence was continued in 1965. While U.S. air attacks were stepped up to 600 raids a week in early autumn, they were directed at targets which limited the resulting damage. Former Air Force Chief of Staff Curtis LeMay commented that "we have been sending more than 1,000 sorties a month since last spring over North Viet Nam. If this destructive power had been used against essential targets, there wouldn't be much left in North Viet Nam. However, it has been applied mostly to interdiction targets, roads, bridges, ammunition dumps, radar sites, etc. It is my position that this has not done the job. We have not done much damage to North Viet Nam and they think they can withstand this kind of attack. In effect, they have not gotten the message we are trying to send."[30]*

Reports of equipment inadequacy—denied by administration spokesmen—persisted. The Senate Preparedness Sub-

* The 1966 escalation of our bombing program to include oil depots near Hanoi and Haiphong was an apparent recognition of the fact that the LeMay analysis was correct and evidently represented a new ascendancy for "hard-line" advocates within the administration.

committee discovered "defective ammunition and shortage of essential supplies are plaguing U.S. fighting forces in Viet Nam."[31] Robert S. Allen and Paul Scott reported the investigators had found, "in several instances, faulty bombs and shells have caused casualties to U.S. and South Vietnamese troops," and "lack of communication equipment and repeated delays in obtaining parts for helicopters have hampered combat and other operations."[32]

The defective equipment was alleged to be 10-year-old ordnance which had not been "re-worked," and which had to be pressed into service because Secretary McNamara had curtailed Army and Navy funds needed for "re-working" and had ordered the selling off of $75 million worth of military equipment annually to foreign buyers: "To supply U.S. forces in Viet Nam the Army is being required to dip into stockpiles in Europe and to take equipment from divisions in the strategic reserve in the United States."[33]

Finally, even as American men were being sent into Viet Nam in increasing numbers, U.S. allies were doing a flourishing trade with Hanoi. In effect, other free world nations were supplying the Communists with the materials they needed to kill Americans. Although Republican spokesmen called for administration action to have this trade halted, the Johnson regime was either doing nothing about it or else doing it so quietly that no observable results were achieved in the behavior of our allies.

These reported misplays in the conduct of the Vietnamese war suggest the difficulty of conducting a single relatively "hard" campaign against the Communists within the context of an "accommodationist" program. When we add to these several confusions the fact that we have ourselves supplied the Soviet Union with wheat, while the Soviet Union is supplying the North Vietnamese with MIGs and missiles, it becomes obvious that maintaining a sensible and purposeful strategy in Viet Nam is a difficult proposition.

★★ *Part V:*

NEW WORLDS TO LOSE

[Khrushchev] thought that we're too Liberal to fight. He thinks that we'll sit on one hand and then on the other.

—Robert Frost

★★ 24. *Cuba: The Bay of Pigs*

AS A CASE STUDY of Liberal foreign policy, it would be difficult to improve on Cuba. From the first glad delirium over Fidel Castro to the last lingering illusion over the Soviet missile build-up, Cuba has been a prototype of Liberal diplomacy. The result has been an unrelieved disaster with few parallels in the annals of the Cold War.

In service to Liberal theorems, the American State Department has in rapid succession presided over: (1) The overthrow of anti-Communist Cuban President Fulgencio Batista and the installation of the Communist Castro in his place; (2) the abortive Bay of Pigs invasion in which Cuban freedom fighters were denied crucial air support; (3) an ill-disguised effort to accede to Castro's blackmail demands for tractors, bulldozers, and drugs; (4) an all-out build-up of Soviet missile power in Cuba threatening American cities; and (5) heavy traffic in strategic goods with Castro by nations fattened on American tax dollars.

1. *The Rise of Castro*

The communization of Cuba was, in all essential respects, a re-enactment of China. From Castro's arrival in the Sierra Maestra in December 1956 until his final triumph two years later, he was the obvious favorite of crucial elements in the American press and State Department, acclaimed as the George Washington of Cuba, vehemently defended against charges of Communism. He was the "agrarian reformer" par excellence. And, at a crucial stage in his battle with Batista, the United States government withdrew its aid to the Havana government, spiking the guns of the anti-Communists.

The story has been told in detail by a group of American ambassadors familiar with Cuba and the policies of the U.S. government during this critical era. The testimony of ambassador Earl E.T. Smith, who represented the U.S. in Havana during Castro's rise to power, who went to Cuba as an envoy considered friendly to Castro and unfriendly to Batista, and who was a personal friend of President Kennedy, is particularly significant.

In his book, *The Fourth Floor,* Smith lists in tabular form the actions of our government beneficial to Castro:

1. Suspending the sale of arms and ammunition to the government of Cuba . . .
2. Refusal to honor outstanding and prepaid orders for arms.
3. Suspending shipments of all replacement parts for combat equipment.
4. Advising the Department of Defense not to ship controversial military equipment . . .
5. Not fulfilling our commitment to deliver . . . 20 armored cars.
6. Not living up to our promise to deliver 15 training planes.
7. Issuing public statements that hurt the government of Cuba . . .

8. Intervention by innuendo—persuading other governments not to sell arms to the government of Cuba.[1]

Smith lists a dozen other actions taken by our diplomatists to weaken Batista and strengthen Castro. These included "playing down all activities" by our military advisers in Cuba "which could be deemed offensive to the revolutionaries"; harassment of Batista for using arms we had supplied in his effort to suppress Castro; non-enforcement of our Neutrality Law, allowing Castro's supporters in the United States to supply him with arms and ammunition; "asking the Immigration Department to be lenient on certain Cuban revolutionary exiles and permitting them to prolong their visits in this country"; "maintaining friendly contacts with representatives of the revolutionaries"; *etc.*[2]

Smith put much of this information into the official records when he testified before the Senate Internal Security subcommittee:

Primarily I would say that when we refused to sell arms to the Cuban Government and also by what I termed intervening by innuendo (which was persuading other friendly governments not to sell arms to Cuba) that these actions had a moral, psychological effect upon the Cuban armed forces which was demoralizing to the nth degree.

The reverse, it built up the morale of the revolutionary forces. Obviously when we refused to sell arms to a friendly government, the existing government, the people of Cuba and the armed forces knew that the United States no longer would support Batista's government.

. . . upon instructions, I spent 2 hours and 35 minutes on December 17, 1958, with Batista, and I told him that the United States or rather certain influential people in the United States believed that he could no longer maintain effective control in Cuba, and that they believed it would avoid a great deal of further bloodshed if he were to retire.

SENATOR EASTLAND. That was on instructions of the State Department?

SMITH. An ambassador never would have a conversation like that, sir, unless it was on instructions of the State Department.[3]

And:

We even did not fulfill our promise to deliver 15 training planes, which had been bought and paid for by the Batista government. In accordance with instructions from the State Department I informed Batista that delivery would be suspended, because we feared some harm might come to the 47 kidnaped Americans. The kidnaping by Raul Castro of 30 U.S. marines and sailors, 17 American citizens, and 3 Canadians occurred at this time.

After the kidnapped Americans were returned we still refused to deliver these training planes because we feared that bombs could be put on the planes even though they were strictly for training purposes.

I reiterate that decisions such as these may determine whether a government can remain in power.

Although they could buy arms and ammunition from other sources, the psychological impact on the morale of the government was crippling. On the other hand, it gave a great uplift to the morale of the rebels.[4]

And:

EASTLAND. Let me ask you this question. As a matter of fact, isn't it your judgment that the State Department of the United States is primarily responsible for bringing Castro to power in Cuba?

SMITH. No, sir, I can't say that the State Department in itself is primarily responsible. The State Department played a large part in bringing Castro to power. The press, other Government agencies, Members of Congress are responsible.

EASTLAND. Would you say that the American Government

then, including all of its agencies, was largely responsible for bringing Castro to power?

SMITH. The American Government, yes, sir, and the people in the American Government.

EASTLAND. Yes.

SMITH. We refused to sell arms to a friendly government, and we persuaded other friendly governments not to sell arms to Cuba. Yet on the other hand revolutionary sympathizers were delivering arms, bodies and ammunition daily from the United States. We were lax in enforcing our neutrality laws.[5]

Smith concludes that "our actions in the United States were responsible for the rise to power of Castro." And: "Without the United States, Castro would not be in power today."[6]

Similar opinions were expressed by Ambassador Arthur Gardner, Smith's predecessor in Havana, who said Batista's troops "got so discouraged by the position we had taken about not giving them arms and so on that they just didn't want to fight."[7] U.S. Ambassador to Mexico Robert C. Hill, who followed the Cuban situation closely, confirmed these judgments.

Castro's victory was, on this evidence, made possible by the denial of U.S. support to Batista. The Liberal elements whose counsel had helped that victory come about, however, refused to acknowledge error. The Kennedy regime's 1961 "White Paper" on Cuba, prepared by presidential adviser Arthur Schlesinger Jr., blandly opined that the problem in Cuba did not result "from the fact that the Castro government was established by revolution." On the contrary, it stated, "the hemisphere rejoiced at the overthrow of the Batista tyranny, looked with sympathy on the new regime, and welcomed its promises of political freedom and social justice for the Cuban people."[8] The problem, the White Paper asserted, was that the leaders of the revolution had "betrayed" its principles.

Thus, even in retrospect, American Liberals clung to the notion that the Castro movement had been praiseworthy and should have triumphed. This despite the fact that our ambassadors repeatedly warned of Castro's Communist connections, and despite the fact that our intelligence services knew Castro had been involved in Communist activities as far back as the Bogota, Colombia, uprising of 1948.

With Castro in power, recognizable as a Communist to all but the most ossified intelligence, many Americans began to get concerned. By the time the 1960 presidential campaign rolled around, Democratic candidate John Kennedy was calling loud attention to the danger at our doorstep. Kennedy cited Cuba as evidence that "our security and leadership are both slipping away". He wanted America to "let the Cuban people know our determination that they will someday again be free," and to "let Mr. Khrushchev know that we are permitting no expansion of his foothold in our hemisphere."[9] Kennedy declared that "if Communism should obtain a permanent foothold in Latin America . . . then the balance of power would move against us and peace would be even more insecure."[10] As an indication of how this threat should be countered, Kennedy made the following 1960 campaign statements:

"We must end the harassment, which this government has carried on, of liberty-loving anti-Castro forces in Cuba and in other lands. While we cannot violate international law, we must recognize that these exiles and rebels represent the real voice of Cuba, and should not be constantly handicapped by our immigration and Justice Department authorities."

"The forces fighting for freedom in exile and in the mountains of Cuba should be sustained and assisted, and Communism in other countries of Latin America must be confined and not permitted to expand."

"We must attempt to strengthen the non-Batista democratic anti-Castro forces in exile, and in Cuba itself, who offer eventual hope of overthrowing Castro. Thus far these fighters for freedom have had virtually no support from our government."

". . . We must firmly resist further Communist encroachment in this hemisphere—working through a strengthened Organization of American States—and encouraging those liberty-loving Cubans who are leading the resistance to Castro."[11]

These words led many people to believe that Kennedy, if elected, would follow a firm course toward Cuba. Those expectations were to be rudely disappointed.

2. *The Bay of Pigs*

During the latter months of 1960, the Eisenhower administration formulated a plan for the liberation of Cuba, envisioning the use of exile forces to invade and reconquer their homeland. Former Vice-President Nixon says Kennedy knew about this plan, and thus knowingly urged the government to do what the Eisenhower regime was already planning to do. Kennedy and various Liberal spokesmen vigorously denied this. Whatever the case in that controversy, the fact remains that Kennedy found waiting for him when he assumed office precisely the sort of program he had called for during his campaign.

The plan, submitted to Kennedy in February, 1961, was ready for action by mid-April. It called for an exile force of 1500 men to go ashore at Trinidad on the southern shore of Cuba, there to establish a beachhead and rally the surrounding population to their standard. In the event of a misfire, the exiles could disperse into the Escambray mountains and function as guerrillas.

Necessary to the success of the plan was the immobilization of Castro's air force. If this were achieved, the invaders could conduct the battle on substantially equal or even advantageous grounds. If it could not be achieved, they would be hopelessly exposed to attack. Three air strikes were therefore planned to knock out Castro's planes. The pilots were to be Cuban exiles trained by the U.S. but "covered" by the fiction that they were defectors from Castro's air force.

That was the general outline in mid-April as Cuban exiles trained diligently for action in Florida, Louisiana, and Nicaragua. Both the Central Intelligence Agency and U.S. military leaders, as things stood, believed chances for success were excellent. In rapid order, however, President Kennedy began subtracting from the plan various elements necessary to victory.

First, the invasion site was switched from Trinidad to the Bay of Pigs, about 100 miles further West. The given reason was that Trinidad was too large a city for such an undertaking to evade widespread notice and avert the censure of "world opinion." There would be many witnesses to the invasion, and to signs of U.S. involvement; civilians might be involved in the shooting. Wise and Ross, as we have noted, comment that "President Kennedy personally approved the change. The CIA believed that this was a political and foreign policy decision by the President, prompted by concern over potential world reaction."[12] Military planners believed the invasion would have smaller chance of success at the Bay of Pigs, because there was no alternative saving course available should something go wrong. The low swampy area offered little protection and was poor terrain for guerrilla operations.

Nevertheless, the CIA and the military assented, reasoning that the plan could still succeed. If Castro's air force were effectively neutralized, the invaders could hold their own. Kennedy, however, was not through changing the plan. As matters entered the final stages, the dominant urge at the White House became, not to insure success of the invasion, but to insure that America was not tagged with "involvement" in it. For this reason, the crucial air support was canceled.

The official version of this tragic episode was first set forward by Robert Kennedy, then attorney general in his brother's administration, as follows: "I can say unequivocally that President Kennedy never withdrew U.S. air cover . . . In fact, there never were any plans made for U.S. air cover, so there was nothing to withdraw."[13] The attorney general's statement on this point was backed up by his brother at a subsequent press conference.

Even a slight acquaintance with the known facts of the Bay of Pigs fiasco reveals these assertions to be inaccurate and misleading. What was at issue was a plan for U.S.-*supported* and U.S. *authorized air strikes,* prior to the invasion, against Castro's air force. These were cancelled by the express personal decision of President Kennedy himself. In effect, Robert Kennedy was playing verbal games with the phrase "U.S. air cover" to divert discussion into a false channel.

Under pressures from Liberal advisers, President Kennedy made three drastic changes in the planned air strikes. The first strike, on Saturday, April 15, was to be executed by 16 exile-flown B-26 bombers. The State Department argued this was too many planes to fit the "cover" story of defecting Cuban pilots. The number was therefore cut from 16 to 8.

Following this decision, the second air strike, scheduled for the morning of April 16, was cancelled altogether. "The reason given," says Dr. Mario Lazo, prominent Cuban expatriate and renowned international lawyer, "was the insistence of the State Department (and some of the President's other advisers) upon preserving the 'non-involvement image' of the United States."[14] This decision meant everything now depended on the success of the third air strike, planned for the morning of the invasion.

On Saturday, Cuba's U.N. representative loudly protested the first air strike, roiling the waters of "world opinion."

Adlai Stevenson, who had apparently accepted the "defecting Cubans" story at face value and premised the U.S. defense upon it, was deeply concerned. So were Secretary of State Dean Rusk and presidential aide McGeorge Bundy. Fear of world opinion became the first consideration of the President and his counsellors. Wise and Ross say: "Could the President permit another B-26 strike on Monday and still convince the world that somehow a new covey of Castro pilots had defected from the Cuban air force? The President decided he could not."[15]

Kennedy therefore called off the third air strike on which all hopes for the invasion depended. The exiles were left to die in the Bay of Pigs, scanning the skies in vain for air support which never came.

While all this was going on, Kennedy and Rusk repeatedly proclaimed that America would not, under any circumstances, become directly involved in the action against Cuba. The effect of these pronouncements was to seal the doom of the invasion even more certainly. Such public statements increased the psychological pressure against America's taking any action, emboldened Castro, and demoralized the Cuban population, supposedly being counted on to rise up against their Communist masters.

Kennedy biographers Schlesinger and Sorensen attempt to argue that the failure of the invasion was somehow traceable to the military, to the CIA, or to the preceding administration, who assertedly gave the president bad advice and sold him an unworkable plan. Kennedy himself, according to Sorensen, put the blame on his military counselors.

None of these extenuations jibe with the known facts of the matter. The crucial decisions which caused the failure of the invasion were taken by Kennedy himself, on the basis of exhortations by Stevenson, Rusk, and other non-military advisers. The CIA and the military, far from causing these decisions and therefore causing the failure, were almost uniformly *against* the steps Kennedy finally decided upon. Haynes Johnson, whose outlook is extremely favorable to Kennedy, says: "The realities of the Cold War, the life-and-death stakes involved, the gamble Cuba represented, the apparent success of the Brigade air attack on Saturday, the President's pledge against direct American intervention in Cuba, and the assurance of his advisers that the invasion had a chance of success without such American support, led him eventually to a decision: *the second air strike, scheduled for dawn Monday to coincide with the invasion, was canceled.*"[16]

CIA officials in charge of the operation pleaded with Kennedy to allow the Monday air strike, and were turned down. If any "advisers" thought things were working out under the revised arrangements they transparently were not military advisers. *U.S. News and World Report* reviewed the pros and cons of the air support issue, and came up with the following conclusions:

> . . . it was President Kennedy himself who made the decision that determined the fate of the Bay of Pigs invasion . . . It was President Kennedy who forbade the use of American military forces . . . The President forbade the Cuban fliers to make an aerial strike against Castro's air force that had been scheduled to coincide with the invasion . . . *President Kennedy's decision to forbid the second air strike by the invaders' own planes was made without consulting high U.S. military officials.*[17]

Cuban freedom fighters involved in the expedition also protested the Kennedy decision. Manuel Antonio de Varona, former Cuban Prime Minister and one of the top exile planners, says he was told by a representative of the U.S. government: "Don't worry. We will have complete control of the air, and Castro won't be able to move a single car or truck any place in Cuba." Varona commented that "to send such a force on such an invasion without air cover is a crime. It could mean death to all."[18] Other exiles tell the identical story.

One source who claimed to have confirmation of all this from Kennedy himself was editor Jack Gore of the Fort Lauderdale, Fla., *News*. Gore wrote that on May 10, 1961 Kennedy informed a group of Florida editors that air cover had been planned, and that he had personally canceled it. "On that day," Gore said, "less than a month after the invasion had failed miserably, the President told us air cover was available to protect the invaders, but that he had made the decision not to use air power."[19]

Gore's statement was backed up by other Florida newspapermen present at the meeting. Martin Anderson, publisher of the Orlando *Sentinel-Star,* said he remembered the conversation and added: "I have thought about it a thousand times. The air cover was cancelled about 3 a.m. the day of the invasion." John H. Perry, Jr., publisher of the Palm Beach *Post-Times,* seconded Gore's article, saying: "To the best of my recollection, that's substantially correct."[20]

Even Robert Kennedy, by indirection, confirmed the essential facts of the matter. In denying that his brother had "withdrawn air cover," the Attorney General went on to say what his brother *did* do—namely, "postpone" an "air strike." Here is the quotation in full:

"What happened was this: one air attack had been made on Saturday on Cuban airports. There was a flurry in the United Nations and elsewhere, and as a result, U.S. participation in the matter was coming to the surface. This surfacing was contrary to the pre-invasion plan. There was supposed to be another attack on the airports on Monday morning.

"The President was called about whether another attack which had been planned should take place. As there was this stir about the matter, he gave instructions that it should not take place at that time unless those having the responsibility felt that it was so important it had to take place, in which case they should call him and discuss it further.

"And that's what was postponed. It wasn't air cover of the beaches or landings. And, in fact, the attack on the airports took place later that day."[21]

Close reading of these paragraphs confirms, in its essentials, what critics of the fiasco have alleged. The original plan called for bombing raids to knock out Castro's air force on the ground; President Kennedy's "postponement" of this action proved to be decisive. Because of it, Castro's planes were able to cut the rebels to pieces. Whether they were able to do so because an air strike had failed to destroy them on the ground or because "air cover" failed to combat them over the beaches is a distinction which may be significant to Robert Kennedy, but was no doubt lost on the men abandoned to their fate in Cuba.

As these facts and more became generally known, official spokesmen made a final effort to exculpate the Kennedy regime. Both Robert Kennedy and his brother, along with their journalistic supporters, began stressing the fact that the invasion plans had been laid under the Eisenhower administration, thereby suggesting Eisenhower and Kennedy were somehow mutually to blame for what had happened. Haynes Johnson, for example, off-handedly asserts that the prisoners were a responsibility of "both a Republican and a Democratic administration."[22] This argument ignores the fact that while certain of the plans were laid under Eisenhower, the critical decisions *which caused the invasion to fail* were made exclusively by Kennedy. The first of these was the decision to attack at the Bay of Pigs, rather than at Trinidad, militarily a more favorable spot for a landing. The second was the decision to cancel the crucial air strike Monday, April 17. The two critical misjudgments which doomed the invasion had nothing to do with the Eisenhower administration. Both were the exclusive property of the New Frontier.

Dr. Lazo, moreover, contests Robert Kennedy's assertions as a disingenuous effort at cover-up. Lazo writes:

What was the "attack on the airports" that Robert Kennedy said "took place later that day" [Monday]?

On Monday, two Free Cuban bombers were authorized to hit the San Antonio airfield where Castro planes were based. The pilots were warned, however, to avoid any risk of lives or property. The planes took off from Nicaragua at 7:30 p.m. They arrived over the target four hours later, on a moonless night, with both the base and the nearby town blacked out and hidden by a low cloud ceiling. Unable to distinguish the target, the pilots obeyed their orders and *returned to Nicaragua without firing a shot or dropping a bomb.*

To call this Monday-night flight an "attack on the airports" and to equate it with the original air strike planned for Monday dawn (and then cancelled) . . . is not exactly an exercise in candor.[23]

All of this, as noted, was premised in the Kennedy regime's urgent desire to conceal U.S. involvement and thereby to placate "world opinion." As often happens in such cases, Kennedy's indecision managed to make the worst of both worlds: The invading force was destroyed; and the world knew almost instantly that America was involved—a fact which Kennedy himself subsequently confessed in a TV speech. We reaped no benefits whatever from the halting, abortive invasion, yet inherited all the hostility that would have accrued to us had we gone in up to the hilt.

3. *The Ransom Deal*

Having abandoned the exile invaders to their fate, the New Frontier decided to make an effort at gaining the release of those who had survived and been taken prisoner. Following a lead set by Castro himself—who had called on the United States to "indemnify" Cuba for the invasion by sending over tractors and bulldozers—the administration launched a tortuous effort to ransom the prisoners.

There were two separate ransom attempts—the first involving the bulldozers and tractors, the second involving drugs. In both cases, the administration tried to convince the public the ransom attempt was a private matter, which had the sympathy of the government but nothing else. On Wednesday, May 24, 1961, after an assertedly private "Tractors for Freedom" committee had been announced, with Eleanor Roosevelt, Walter Reuther, and Milton Eisenhower as its leading members, President Kennedy said: "The government of the United States is not and cannot be a party to these negotiations."[24] When the tractor exchange fell through, yet another "private" effort was launched, involving attorney James B. Donovan. Donovan succeeded in negotiating an arrangement whereby the prisoners were released in exchange for some $53 million worth of drugs contributed by American pharmaceutical companies. The agency publicly identified as superintending this transaction was the Red Cross.

The truth was that both of these "private" ransom efforts were thoroughly engineered by the administration itself and were run from start to finish by government officials. Having "invaded" Cuba without really invading it, the administration now tried to ransom the prisoners without really ransoming them.

Dr. Milton Eisenhower recounts that when Kennedy told him of the "Tractors for Freedom" committee and asked him to serve, the President said he would "explain the matter to the American people the next day." Eisenhower agreed, but was astounded when Kennedy subsequently disclaimed responsibility for the committee. "Now I had the awful truth," Eisenhower says. "I now realized in chilling clarity that the President intended to maintain the fiction that all aspects of the case, from negotiation to critical decision, from raising funds to actually freeing the prisoners, were private."[25] Meanwhile, congressional spokesmen were ripping the

"Tractors" committee as a concession to Communist blackmail. Dr. Eisenhower found himself in a position not unlike that of the prisoners he was trying to rescue: He had been promised support if he undertook a New Frontier-sponsored operation—but when the shooting started, the support wasn't there.

The nature and extent of governmental involvement in the tractors deal was apparent from the beginning. As the Associated Press put it, Kennedy's approval of the deal "was seen in a variety of direct or indirect aids from several Federal agencies which indicated White House approval."[26] These included use of a Coast Guard plane to ferry representatives of the prisoners from Cuba to Florida; State Department readiness to approve the transaction even though the tractors were on the embargo list; Treasury willingness to grant tax deductions for contributions going to the purchase of the tractors; and a White House statement that the Committee was not in violation of the Logan Act, which forbids negotiations with foreign powers by private citizens.

This same pattern was evident in the negotiations conducted by Donovan. Representatives of the exiles were sent to Donovan by Robert Kennedy, who assured Donovan the deal was "in the national interest" and that his role would not violate the Logan Act. Kennedy also addressed drug manufacturers and urged them to participate in the deal, while Justice Department officials assured them they would not be open to antitrust prosecution for working in concert and Treasury officials told them their contributions would be tax-deductible.

Attorney General Kennedy also ordered one of his aides, Lou Oberdorfer, to devote full time to the project. Oberdorfer's office, staffed with private attorneys, became headquarters for the operation. The Internal Revenue department, for its part, maintained a staff of 12 people on continuous call to answer questions and issue rulings about the transaction.

As a cover for all this activity, Oberdorfer and Assistant Attorney General Nicholas de B. Katzenbach enlisted the American Red Cross. Haynes Johnson says:

> The Justice Department officials pointed out that contributors would feel more comfortable if the name of the Red Cross were involved in the transaction. The Red Cross agreed; the operation, therefore, was conducted officially in its name. In actual fact, however, the operation at all times remained centered in the Justice Department, where the major plans and decisions were made. But the participation of the Red Cross helped to overcome public opposition to dealing with Castro.[27]

★★ 25. *Cuba: The Missile Crisis*

1. *Eyeball to Eyeball*

WITH CASTRO'S TOTAL VICTORY in the Bay of Pigs, the strategic situation in the Caribbean was dramatically transformed. Cuba was no longer an embattled outpost vulnerable to exile initiative. It became, so far as American policy was concerned, an impregnable fortress capable of threatening the safety of the hemisphere. The point of the lance was reversed: We were no longer the attackers, but the attacked.

Sometime in late 1961 the Soviet Union began moving increased quantities of men and materials into Cuba. By the spring of 1962, this influx became heavy enough to attract public comment in America, and by summer Cuban exile reports had it that the island was becoming an armor-plated garrison capable of striking the United States. In particular, the reports said, Soviet missile components were being shipped to Cuba, and work was under way to construct launching sites for them.

Republican spokesmen, led by Senator Kenneth Keating of New York, began looking into the matter. Through late summer and early fall, Keating and other GOP legislators marshaled and presented to the nation evidence that missiles were being installed in Cuba. Between August 31 and October 12, Keating alone made ten Senate speeches and 14 other statements documenting the build-up and calling for government action.

Throughout, the Kennedy administration consistently denied these allegations of danger. At first it denied that anything at all untoward was taking place in Cuba. When the flood of exile reports continued to indicate otherwise, the official view held that, although there was a build-up, it was not "offensive" in character, and that there was nothing to worry about. As late as October 14, presidential aide McGeorge Bundy appeared on national television and declared: "I know there is no present evidence, and I think there is no present likelihood, that the Cubans and the Cuban government and the Soviet government would in combination attempt to install a major offensive capability."[1]

On the night of October 22, however, President Kennedy himself affirmed that what Keating and Sen. Homer Capehart had been warning of was indeed the case: Precisely as they had charged, Cuba was bristling with Soviet rockets capable of hitting almost every major city in the United States.

How had it happened? How could our government have stood by and allowed the weapons of destruction to be installed 90 miles from American soil? And why, up until the last possible minute, had our officials so emphatically told us nothing was amiss? These are questions to which we still do not have satisfactory answers, although the succeeding months and years have been fertile of official and semi-official utterances on the subject.

According to the orthodox version, no real evidence of the missile build-up came to hand before mid-October, 1962. Such spokesmen as Schlesinger, Sorensen, Roger Hilsman, Stewart Alsop and Charles Bartlett maintain the White House received its first credible information about Soviet "offensive" weapons on October 14, when U-2 reconnaissance photographs revealed missile installations in an advanced state of construction. Having received this proof of Soviet treachery, the Kennedy administration then went to work to have the missiles removed, successfully marshalling our forces and "facing down" Khrushchev in "eyeball to eyeball" confrontation. The missiles were removed, the crisis resolved, American security restored. So runs the official version.

This presentation is, however, open to serious question in almost every particular. In the first place, highly-detailed refugee reports indicating a Soviet military build-up in Cuba had been flooding into Washington at least since mid-August. What were these reports if not "evidence"? In the absence of photographic proof, would we simply have dismissed all other traditional forms of intelligence?

The truth was that our government had every reason to believe a military build-up was going on in Cuba but allowed its ideological *assumptions* about the nature of Soviet strategy to block out the facts. Only the absolute and belated proof of the U-2 flights could overcome this ingrained tendency to think the Communists somehow would not try to destroy us. Reporters James Daniel and John Hubbell tell us in their important book, *Strike In the West:*

> In early August [1962], it is now known, the Central Intelligence Agency's John McCone began warning responsible officials that the temptation to Khrushchev to plant attack missiles in Cuba would be almost irresistible. At that time, Soviet ships had

been landing massive quantities of war material and troops in Cuba. But Washington's Kremlinologists could not bring themselves to believe that Russia would do what it did until they saw the U-2 pictures. If the test of "hard intelligence" had always been this "hard," no precautions against aggression would have been taken at any place and at any time prior to the development of photo-reconnaissance techniques in World War II.[2]

Obviously, the information available to McCone was available to the major decision-makers in Washington; and just as obviously, the decision-makers had as much information as did Keating. The difference was that McCone and Keating understood the intentions of the Communists; they did not allow implausible theories about Communist "mellowing" to obscure their observation of the facts. Such as McGeorge Bundy, if we may believe their statements, were so steeped in Liberal ideology that they refused to believe what any common-sense assessment of the record would have told them was occurring.

Even assuming it was legitimate to rely only on photographic evidence, however, still other questions remain: Foremost among these is why it took so long for the U-2 flights to come up with photographic evidence. The official answer is that weather conditions conspired to delay the flights for several days, that for some reason early photographs had not been taken in western Cuba, and that on balance, it "is something of a miracle that the missiles were discovered as early as they were." Roger Hilsman, a participant in the crisis, gives this reading: "A flight over western Cuba was proposed on October 4, approved at a special meeting on October 9, and readied on the 10th. The aircraft stood by, waiting for good weather, on the 11th, the 12th, and the 13th. On Sunday the 14th, the flight was made as planned and without incident."[3]

This is a rather extraordinary effort to explain away a lapse of 10 days at best, and possibly much longer. If we assume the administration had no reason to look for missile sites before October 4—stretching things in view of what had been going on for at least a month—why wasn't the flight approved until a special meeting on October 9? Every day counted. What was the administration doing over that five day span other than attacking Republican spokesmen who warned about the Cuban build-up?

For the days between the 9th and 13th of October, Hilsman uses the adverse weather explanation. Daniel and Hubbell, however, tell us:

> Why nothing effective was done for . . . eleven perilous days . . . is a question that only a congressional investigation is ever likely to disclose. Meanwhile, one reason given to newsmen by White House sources is demonstrably false. The explanation . . . was: "The weather intervened. Hurricane Ella delayed flights for a week and then a cloud cover blocked high-level surveillance." . . .
>
> Official U.S. Weather Bureau maps show clear weather over western Cuba for October 5th through October 9th, with some afternoon shower activity. A detailed report prepared for Congress, and at hand as this is written, indicated picture-taking weather prevailed on the mornings from October 10th through October 14th, with the afternoons of October 10th and 11th questionable.[4]

In short, there *is* no very good explanation of the fact that 10 or 11 days intervened between the decision to photograph western Cuba and the actual job of photographing it. And there is even less explanation for the fact that our government should have been waiting around for these photographs when every other intelligence source indicated a lethal threat to American security.

After the photographs were obtained, still another delay took place. It was not until October 22 that President Kennedy made his famous address to the nation. This span was taken up, according to the semi-official Alsop-Bartlett story in *The Saturday Evening Post,* by a long round of arguments within the administration as to what ought to be done. In the intervening period Democratic spokesmen continued to deny everything and to flay Republicans warning against the build-up. The Pentagon, in response to a question about Soviet missiles, stated that "no information indicating the presence of such weapons in Cuba" had come to hand.[5] As late as October 22, the very day of Kennedy's address, Senator Mike Monroney of Oklahoma denounced a Republican urging action on Cuba by saying: "Does he want to go to war now? A blockade is an act of war; one overt act would lead to the use of force, I am certain."[6] Across the land during that same week, Democratic spokesmen were similarly decrying calls for action on Cuba, and condemning the idea of a blockade. All this while the Democratic administration in Washington knew the Republican charges were correct, and was preparing to impose a blockade.

Thus things came to a head the last week in October, 1962, with America acting—not before the threat occurred, or while it was abuilding—but with the missiles already in place and trained on our cities.

2. *The Deal*

At this point in the narrative, the court historians depart from defensive obscurantism and portray our government's performance as heroic. Khrushchev, confronted by an ultimatum and a "quarantine" (*i.e.* the blockade denounced as an "act of war" by Lyndon Johnson and others), was "faced down." He removed the missiles from Cuba, the threat was gone, and the Kennedy regime had won a famous victory.[7]

To the extent that President Kennedy did stand firm, and to the extent that firmness won an abatement in the immediate threat to our security, all Americans can be thankful. But certain problems remain. We are instructed to believe, for example, that Khrushchev backed down in the missile crisis because he knew he was beaten. No "deal" of any sort, supposedly, was reached. Yet the evidence is clear that, in general terms, a "deal" *was* reached, and grounds for suspicion exist that a specific deal within that larger framework was also consummated.

The large deal was a pledge by the United States that, if the missiles were removed, we would not try to invade Cuba again. When Rep. William Miller alluded to such an arrangement in the 1964 presidential campaign, he was denounced by official spokesmen. State Department press officer Robert J. McCloskey said: "Any suggestion that there has been a secret agreement is untrue. There is no such agreement, secret or otherwise."[8]

The cold record, however, tells a different story. On October 27, 1962, President Kennedy replied to a message from Khrushchev as follows:

> As I read your letter, the key elements of your proposals—*which seem generally acceptable as I understand them*—are, as follows: (1) You would agree to remove these weapons systems from Cuba under appropriate United Nations observation and supervision; and undertake, with suitable safeguards, to halt the further introduction of such weapons systems into Cuba. (2) We, on our part, would agree—upon the establishment of adequate arrangements through the United Nations to ensure the carrying out and continuation of these commitments—(a) to remove promptly the quarantine measures now in effect and (b) *to give assurances against an invasion of Cuba.* (Italics added.)[9]

Such were the outlines of the larger "deal." In denying Miller's charge, official spokesmen say that the proposed transaction did not go through because Khrushchev did not agree to on-site inspection and therefore did not render satisfactory performance. This may be—but if so it means Kennedy did *not* in fact face Khrushchev down, did not require the presumptively minimal performance outlined in Kennedy's letter as necessary to protect American security. On the other hand, if we are to believe the Establishment story that Cuba was a victory, and that we did receive satisfactory compliance, there would seem to be no reason for Kennedy not to have followed through on the assurance contained in his letter.

That such a pledge was in fact understood to have been obtained from the Communists' point of view was made plain in an interview Castro granted Barnard Collier of *The New York Herald-Tribune.* Asked if agreements existed covering possible attacks, Castro answered: "Yes. Yes. Formal agreements. Between the U.S. and USSR and Cuba and the USSR. Essentially, I think, what is in the compromises is known to the world. *There is to be no invasion of Cuba by the U. S. That is formal. It is binding on the U. S. government under any president, any government. . . . When Khrushchev proposed that there be no invasion of Cuba Kennedy said yes. We knew about the compromise.*" (Italics added.)[10]

Supporting this assertion is the fact that, since the 1962 crisis, our government has kept a tight rein on Cuban exile activities. In early 1963, for example, it was reported that the exiles were being kept under strict watch, their arms confiscated, and their attempted raids against Cuba thwarted by the U.S. Coast Guard. Former U.S. diplomat Paul Bethel, an authority on Cuba, said: "These people are not even permitted out of Dade County [Miami]. Over 600 officials have been sent in to keep track of them, and Coast Guard strength has been built up more than 20 per cent to make sure they do not undertake raids against Castro."[11]

A more specific kind of deal was alleged in the case of U.S. missiles in Italy and Turkey. Subsequent to the Cuban crisis, it was announced that 45 1,500-mile missile bases in these countries would be dismantled—a move which had been talked of as a possible "trade" with Khrushchev. Senator Milward Simpson, Republican of Wyoming, charged "we are in fact witnessing our end of the reciprocity agreement under which chairman Khrushchev threw his puppet Castro to the propaganda winds and withdrew a portion of his missiles from Cuba."[12]

The official response was that the pullback of missiles in Italy and Turkey had been settled upon *before* the Cuban crisis, and so could not have been part of a deal. If this was so, however, certain loose ends demand explanation. Why, for example, had the Defense Department issued a statement as late as October 29 defending the necessity of IRBM bases around the globe, including Turkey? And if a decision had already been arrived at to withdraw these bases, how could the idea of withdrawing them have been brought up as a new idea—and professedly a distasteful one—in the meetings at the White House?

In their article for the *Post,* obviously based on data supplied them by the administration, Alsop and Bartlett allude to the subject as follows: "Only Adlai Stevenson, who flew down from New York on Saturday, dissented from the . . . consensus. There is disagreement in retrospect about what Stevenson really wanted. ('Adlai wanted a Munich,' says a nonadmiring official who learned of his proposal. 'He wanted to trade the Turkish, Italian and British missile bases for the Cuban bases.')

"The Stevenson camp maintains that Stevenson was only willing to discuss Guantanamo and the European bases with the Communists after a neutralization of the Cuban missiles."[13]

Now, whatever the particulars about Stevenson's proposal, one thing becomes clear from this passage: Withdrawal of our missiles from Turkey and Italy must *not* have been decided prior to these conversations. Had it been decided,

Stevenson could not have *suggested* withdrawing them. That the issue was controverted at all means a decision had not been arrived at previously. Which means, since the withdrawal subsequently took place, there are grounds to suppose the "Munich" alluded to in the Alsop-Bartlett piece actually transpired.

3. *Are The Missiles Gone?*

Despite assurances given to or received from Khrushchev, the clearing smoke of the "crisis" left a major issue unresolved. Do we in fact know the missiles were removed from Cuba? The demand for on-site inspection, after all, did not succeed. Khrushchev *said* he would withdraw the missiles, and ships were seen departing Cuba with something that looked like missiles on board. But did Khrushchev really do what he said? Did the departing ships really contain missiles? And if they did, did they contain *all* the missiles?

By early 1963, these questions had gained enough currency for the administration to feel an answer was called for. Secretary of Defense McNamara therefore staged what afterwards became known as his "magic lantern show," February 6, 1963. In an elaborate presentation to the press, a McNamara aide showed and explained before-and-after picture slides, taken by U-2 reconnaissance planes, demonstrating certain missile sites in Cuba had indeed been dismantled. Information obtained in this way, McNamara said, enabled the government to estimate accurately the number of missiles implanted in Cuba, and how many of them had been removed. On the basis of this reasoning McNamara stated: "I believe beyond any reasonable doubt that all weapons systems have been removed from the island and none have been reintroduced."[14] And he categorically affirmed: "There are today no offensive weapons systems in Cuba."[15]

This presentation did not satisfy Republican critics. Senator Keating and Representative Donald C. Bruce of Indiana, in particular, continued to raise embarrassing questions. Bruce had stated that "there are 40 or more Soviet missiles still in Cuba today and the highest officials in the United States government know it."[16] The number of missiles originally introduced into Cuba, he said, had in fact been between 82 and 88 and accounting for the removal of only 42 meant upwards of 40 still remained.

Senator Keating said: "There is incontrovertible evidence that they [the Soviets] are building a base there. They are building barracks, making it a permanent installation. They are continuing to maintain medium-range missile sites. And they've been working at these activities in some parts of Cuba around the clock. This gives rise to the very real possibility that the Russians hope to return heavy missiles to Cuba or—even more ominous—that they may have missiles left on the island and need only to wheel them out of caves."[17]

The possibility that the Soviets had simply taken missiles off the launching pads and put them into caves was, and is, a very real one. Cuba is honeycombed with caves—and the Cuban exiles who proved themselves knowledgeable about such things in 1962 contend those caves are full of military hardware. As early as November, 1962, the Cuban Student Directorate published a detailed rundown on caves in Cuba containing missiles and other lethal weaponry, based on the observation of agents on the ground. According to the student committee, "secret military underground or camouflaged installations (caves, tunnels, and covered ditches)" in Cuba consisted of "airfields with underground hangars; missile platforms in covered ditches; intercontinental and short-range ballistic missiles; and storage for rockets, missiles, and all sorts of military equipment."[18]

That missiles could in fact be concealed in Cuba, in caves or elsewhere, has been conceded by the highest governmental spokesmen. "Absolute assurance on these matters," said CIA chief John McCone, "could only come from continuing, penetrating on-site inspection."[19] And the Senate Preparedness Subcommittee said:

"Strategic weapons may or may not be now in Cuba. We can reach no conclusion on this because of the lack of conclusive evidence. . . . The current intelligence estimate that they are not present is based largely on the negative evidence that there is no affirmative proof to the contrary. This, of course, was precisely the status of the matter prior to last October 14."[20]

And: "There is no doubt that there are literally thousands of caves and caverns in Cuba and that it is feasible to use many of these for the storage and concealment of strategic missiles and other offensive weapons. It is also true that military activity has been observed in connection with these caves. Our intelligence people are of the opinion that some of the caves are in fact utilized for the storage of military items and equipment other than strategic missiles, such as ammunition, explosives, etc."[21]

Without the on-site inspection which the Kennedy administration failed to secure in its "victory" over Khrushchev, we have no real way of knowing whether those caves also contain long-range missiles—except for exile reports, proved accurate in the past, that the missiles in fact are there. Not, after going "eyeball to eyeball," a very comforting outcome.

During 1964, reports mounted that there were indeed missiles back in Cuba. In his interview with Barnard Collier, Castro himself hedged the question "are there still long range missiles in Cuba?" by saying: "I have always refused to answer that. I think the government of the U.S. is well informed on that situation."[22] He gave a similarly evasive answer on the subject to C. L. Sulzberger of *The New York Times*. On August 18, Castro's sister, Juanita, told a Brazilian interviewer that ". . . in Cuba there are long-range ballistic missiles which are well camouflaged."[23] Exile sources, moreover, began to relay back information much like that conveyed by them in the summer and fall of 1962.

Among these reports were stories of a vast explosion in Pinar del Rio province in March, 1964, in which missile components were blown over an area of more than 10 square miles. Cuban peasants were warned to say nothing of the incident, says Paul Bethel, on pain of death. "We checked this out five or six different ways," Bethel said in September, 1964. "The reports all coincided. There can be no doubt that it occurred."[24] Bethel also cited an eye-witness who spotted a 26-wheel truck trailer being used to haul long-range missile components in Matanzas province in August 1964.

"We have solid reports that missiles were introduced into Matanzas in August," Bethel said.[25] Similar reports persisted, from exile sources and elsewhere, through 1965 and 1966.

4. *Outpost of Subversion*

Nor is the presence of missiles in Cuba the only threat Castro offers to the security of the Western hemisphere. His very existence, of course, is a flagrant and standing violation of the Monroe Doctrine, not only permitted by us but, on the evidence reviewed, guaranteed and protected by us. With this privileged status, Castro is relatively unhampered in his effort to spread subversion throughout the hemisphere. His agents have been at work in Chile, Mexico, Panama, Bolivia, and Venezuela. As a U.S.-certified sanctuary for hemispheric subversion, Cuba is in some ways more dangerous than as a base for Soviet missiles.

On this score, too, however, the administration has professed to see no evil. Concerning the Monroe Doctrine, of course, it is silent as the tomb. No more is heard of Kennedy's '60 campaign rhetoric. As for subversion, certain of our officials have simply argued it isn't there. In his lantern-show briefing McNamara stated: "I have no evidence that Cuba is being used as a base for subversion directed against other Latin American countries. It is a matter that is of constant interest to us and one we are monitoring continuously."[26]

The Senate Preparedness Subcommittee rejoined with its own equally flat statement that "the evidence is overwhelming that Castro is supporting, spurring, aiding, and abetting Communist revolutionary and subversive movements throughout the Western hemisphere and that such activities present a grave threat to the peace and security of the Americas."[27]

At almost exactly the same time McNamara was offering his assurances, moreover, a special committee of the Organization of American States declared: "It is clear that Cuba is being used as a base for training in Communism and its spread in America . . . the military strengthening of Cuba by the Soviet Union, by greatly increasing the capacity of the Cuban government to send arms into neighboring countries and to intensify other subversive activities, renders the threat to hemispheric security much more serious, a threat that assumes an urgent character with respect to the security of the countries of the Caribbean region. This has become evident, sometimes in a dramatic manner, in the recent wave of terrorism, sabotage, and other subversive activities that Castro has unleashed in some of the Latin American countries."[28]

Finally, less than two weeks after McNamara's assertions, a representative of the State Department, assistant secretary of state Edwin M. Martin, gave a House Foreign Affairs subcommittee a review of Communist terror and subversion emanating from Cuba. Martin noted bombings, burnings, blowing up of U.S. oil installations and smelting plants, and guerrilla raids "in an increasing rhythm of disorder, terrorism, and revolutionary activity"—all stemming from Cuba.[29]

Under Lyndon Johnson, our policy toward Cuba has not changed appreciably. One of Johnson's earliest acts was a much-publicized aid cut-off to countries trading with Cuba, as mandated by Congress. It developed, however, that this step was merely window-dressing, compliance with the letter of the congressional resolve which violated its spirit. Aid was withdrawn from Britain and France, each of whom was receiving only a few thousand dollars in U.S. assistance—an act greeted with derision in both countries.

The *Chicago Daily News* reported: "The U.S. government has come close to making itself ridiculous by 'stopping aid' to Britain as punishment for Britain's continued trade with Cuba. British newspapers tried hard not to laugh at this tap on the wrist . . . when they pointed out that the sum involved was $7,400 . . . The American gesture made a particularly silly impression here because it was obviously made only in order to conform with the aid bill and not with any idea on the part of President Johnson that it was going to dissuade Britain from trading with Cuba. The British had even been asked in what form the announcement should be made."[30]

As for France, the *Daily News* said, the move was met with "stony silence and apparent indifference": "The American move was generally described in Paris as one that could improve President Johnson's chance of being re-elected more than it could harm the already poor relations between France and the United States."[31]

Untouched by Johnson's action—thanks to a loophole allowing him to continue aid if he finds it "in the national interest"—were a dozen or so nations receiving healthy amounts of aid from America and doing a booming business with Cuba. The Johnson action was designed to show the American people something was "being done" about Cuba; in fact nothing was being done at all.

★★ 26. *The Dominican Republic*

1. *Another Cuba?*

THERE IS AN AXIOM which holds that the worst possible practice in any contest with a dangerous adversary is to "shake your fist, then shake your finger." That is, in all too many instances, the practice of American diplomacy.

The Kennedy administration was profligate of "hard" declarations about the U.S. intentions, and of vaunts about "resolution," the limits of our patience, our willingness to risk our cities. President Kennedy was rhetorically quite militant. But fighting words were seconded, in Laos, in Viet Nam, in Cuba, by gelatinous follow-through. We talked tough, but we backed down.

President Johnson has, if anything, been even more militant in his foreign policy pronouncements than was Kennedy. Johnson's early statements on Viet Nam were generally marked by stern anti-Communist sentiment, and his July 1965 address on the subject was, in part, a ringing manifesto on the follies of appeasement. In one foreign policy crisis, however, the Kennedy pattern of reversal has to some extent been repeated.

In May, 1965, when the Dominican Republic was threatened by leftist revolution, Johnson moved swiftly to send in American troops, making a deliberate statement of his reasons. "I want you to know," he said, "that it is not a light or an easy matter to send our American boys to another country, but I do not think that the American people expect their president to hesitate or vacillate in the face of danger just because the decision is hard when life is in peril. The revolutionary movement took a tragic turn. Communist leaders, many of them trained in Cuba, seeing a chance to increase disorder, to gain a foothold, joined the revolution. They took increasing control. And what began as a popular democratic revolution, committed to democracy and social justice, *very shortly moved and was taken over and really seized and placed into the hands of a band of Communist conspirators.*" (Emphasis added.)[1]

Johnson's action was roundly applauded, supported by spokesmen for both political parties, and favored by the American public. Moreover, his statement about "Communist conspirators" was seconded by information gathered by U.S. intelligence and various authorities on Latin politics. Yet within a month the thrust of our intervention was blunted, and within four months totally reversed. Our forces, sent to Santo Domingo to restrain the pro-Communist rebels of Colonel Francisco Deno Caamano, wound up restraining the anti-Communist government of Gen. Antonio Imbert Barreras.

Just why this reversal occurred has not been officially explained, although certain clues have sifted their way to the public. While some Liberal spokesmen like Senator Fulbright objected to the intervention and downgraded the presence of Communists in the rebel movement, the evidence in favor of Johnson's original estimate was considerable. Associated Press correspondent William Ryan reported, two months after the policy reversal, that U.S. intelligence stuck by its assessment of the Communist following attracted by rebel leader Caamano. "The U.S. says Communist leaders played a leading part," Ryan wrote, "in distributing arms, sometimes controlling the distribution. Other Communists—identified by name—incited mobs to destroy and burn, kill police, and loot stores and homes . . . U.S. sources in Santo Domingo estimate that more than half the rebel civilian army came from the [Castro-dominated] 14th of June movement . . . Communists now hold big quantities of arms, U.S. sources say . . ."[2]

Similar testimony came from the investigatory team dispatched to look into the matter by the Organization of American States. One of the ambassadors on this mission, Alfredo Vazquez Carrizosa of Colombia, said there were "numerous persons" on the rebel side who, "if they are not members of the Communist Party, are actively in favor of Fidel Castro's system of government for political purposes." Many Latin diplomats, Carrizosa said, "are firmly convinced that on that side there are many persons, I do not say members registered in an officially organized Communist Party, but persons who have leanings toward a well-known political trend which is prevalent in Cuba"[3]

Ambassador Marinho of Brazil similarly declared: "The whole committee agreed that the Caamano movement could be rapidly converted to a Communist insurrection that was susceptible of gaining the support of the Marxist-Leninist powers."[4]

Senator Thomas Dodd (D-Conn.) noted the findings of the OAS ambassadors were representative of much concerned opinion in Latin America. Dodd pointed out that advices from the Dominican labor federation CONATROL, from the Inter-American Regional Organization of Workers, and from numerous Latin newspapers all gave warning about "Communist control of the rebel movement," and approved U.S. intervention. Dodd gave this summary of the available evidence:

> The administration has published details about 77 identifiable Communists, many of them with training in Castro Cuba, who occupied command positions in the rebel movement . . . Apart from the Bosch party [Juan Bosch, ousted former president] whose leaders abandoned the revolt and sought refuge after the first few days, the political support for the rebellion came from the three Communist parties . . . which, between them, had a membership of several thousands . . .
>
> The Dominican revolt was characterized . . . by the highest degree of precision and professionalism . . . It was, if anything, a textbook operation in the seizure of political power which could only have been conducted by trained professional revolutionaries.
>
> . . . I believe that anyone who takes the trouble to analyze the propaganda output of the Dominican rebel movement in the early days of the revolt and afterward would have to agree that the radio and TV broadcasts and the printed literature all bore the heavy and unmistakable imprint of trained Communist propagandists . . .[5]

U.S. News and World Report said in a May dispatch from Santo Domingo: "Two weeks ago 52 trained Communist agents slipped into the country—32 of them from Castro's Cuba where they had been trained in guerrilla warfare schools. The rest were from similar training schools in Russia, China, and other Communist countries . . . those in the rebellion ranged all the way from known Castro agents—carbon copies of Castro's revolutionaries—to bands of criminals intent on looting . . . The violence that spread through

Santo Domingo gave the appearance of utter chaos. Actually, it was cut to the standard Communist pattern. Bands of young toughs . . . roamed the streets, carrying burp guns and other weapons. Others sat on rooftops sniping."[6] The mobs dragged victims from their homes and shouted "To the wall!"—the standard cry of the mass executions conducted in Castro's Cuba.[7]

Concerning the excesses charged to the rebels, and subsequently denied by several Liberal spokesmen, further confirmation of Johnson's original indictment was supplied by the Citizens Committee for a Free Cuba. Executive Secretary Paul Bethel managed to get hold of a ship's log from a Panamanian vessel anchored off rebel territory during the fighting. The log says: "The mobs now are in control, and the sacking, the rapes, the robbing and killing are uncontrollable . . . A policeman was killed, his head put on a long stick, and it is being paraded around the neighborhood to incite the mobs . . ."[8]

That sampling yields a picture of Communist revolution in the all too familiar pattern—a revolution our government supposedly set out to scotch. But despite the fact that the evidence vindicated President Johnson's action, and that his stand was strongly backed by the American people, the public direction of our policy was suddenly reversed. Without substantial alteration in either of the contesting parties, the United States appeared to switch sides. At a crucial point in the proceedings, as the anti-Communist junta was on the verge of finishing up the revolutionaries, we withdrew our support of the government and began pressing for "reconciliation." The rebels, at the time, controlled one city block of Santo Domingo, were running low on food and ammunition, and were obviously in no position to withstand a final assault. As Latin American authority Jules Dubois reported:

"The United States concurred in, and contributed to influence the obtaining of a precarious cease-fire through the

Organization of American States at a time when the anti-Communist military junta was ready to crush the Communist-dominated rebels in a final and decisive cleanup.

". . . the United States tried to dump Brig. Gen. Elias Wessin y Wessin, the anti-Communist leader in the army. Had he been dropped, the entire Dominican Army would have been demoralized beyond repair.

"The United States has blocked the immediate defeat of the Communists by preventing the employment of two-thirds of the fire-power of the Dominican armed forces—the air force and the navy."[9]

Thanks to our pressures, the junta stepped down and a provisional regime headed by Hector Garcia-Godoy, former lieutenant of Bosch, came to power. A symbolic representation of the change occurred almost immediately: Anti-Communist leader Wessin y Wessin, surrounded by American troops, was deported; pro-Castro leader Bosch was repatriated, and made his arrival in Santo Domingo the occasion of a bitter diatribe against the United States.

Shortly after landing in Miami, September 10, General Wessin expressed his shocked disbelief at what had happened: "When the North American troops arrived in the Dominican Republic—after the men under my command had received the brunt of the attack from a Communist mob drunk with vengeance and death—I never imagined that the same troops, making common cause with the enemies of democracy, would kick me out of my country. I have arrived in Miami without passport, without money . . . In these moments I have to dismantle my home, to sell my furniture and my house, and to separate myself from my family . . ." Viewing that example, he asked, "what military man will be disposed to assume responsibilities when Communism launches its final attack against our fatherland?"[10]

General Wessin's ordeal was not yet ended. On September 24, columnists Allen and Scott reported "the State Department is seeking to exile General Wessin y Wessin again—this time from the U.S. On direct orders from the White House, Secretary Rusk is sounding out diplomats here to find a Latin-American government willing to accept the dedicated anti-Communist general when he is again deported." The administration had decided, the reporters said, "that Wessin had to be silenced."[11]

The Senate Internal Security subcommittee, however, decided the ranking general in the Dominican army, a leader in the coup against Rafael Trujillo, and a direct participant in these bizarre events, should more logically be heard than silenced. The committee travelled to Miami and took testimony from Wessin about the drift of events under the former Bosch regime and the provisional government of Garcia-Godoy. Wessin discussed Dominican politics in considerable detail, supplying documents to back his charge of alarming deterioration in Santo Domingo.

In essence, Wessin's testimony added up to the fact that the Dominican Republic was in danger of becoming precisely what President Johnson said he wanted to prevent—a second Cuba. Under the Bosch regime, it had been making rapid progress in this direction; and under Garcia-Godoy, that development had been resumed and intensified. Wessin's testimony indicated the Garcia-Godoy regime, despite its public presentation as a "reconcilation" government containing elements from both the rebel faction and the anti-Communist junta, was canting noticeably toward the Communists. Wessin singled out nine individuals in the new government known to him as active in the Communist-dominated rebel movement or, in some instances, as Communists. These included the personal counsel to Garcia-Godoy, the attorney general, the secretary of labor, the secretary of agriculture, the head of the radio station, the press secretary, the director of the passport office, and others. By way of contrast, Wessin said so far as he knew no member of the anti-Communist

Imbert government had been included in the "reconciliation" regime.[12]

Similar evidence was marshalled by the *Tribune's* Dubois, who reported from Santo Domingo in mid-November, 1965, that "Communist influence, . . . terror, and . . . fear reign here only two months after provisional president Hector Garcia-Godoy assumed his precarious seat in the national palace." Although the "Act of Reconciliation" was supposed to favor neither rebels nor junta, Garcia had made it plain his sympathies lay with the Caamano forces:

> Caamano is regularly received in the palace and only he is consulted by Garcia about certain conditions . . . All key appointments have gone to "constitutionalists," and, chiefly, to well-known Communists. . . . The announcers and staff from the rebel radio still function from [the government radio-TV station] and broadcast propaganda in favor of the leftist-Communist rebels and their party lines. . . . The judiciary is now virtually in the hands of the Communists. The chief justice and most of the associate justices are avowed partisans of the rebels . . . Most of the judges appointed throughout the country are either Communists or fellow-travellers . . . The attorney general appointed by Garcia is one of the most recalcitrant members of the pro-Castro 14th of June revolutionary movement. Most of the provincial governors and mayors have been chosen from avowed Marxists.[13]

One non-Latin diplomat in Santo Domingo confirmed this estimate. "The Communists are stronger now than they ever have been in this country," he is quoted. "They have come out in the open, publish their own newspaper, hold conventions, even call themselves Communist, openly. All the concessions are being made to the Communists—none to the other side. . . . In one edition of *Patria* [the rebel newspaper] the Communists bragged in one statement that they were the power in the revolution. In these months of revolution, the Communists have built up their political and military apparatus far beyond anything they ever had here before."[14]

Another high-ranking Dominican military officer seconded the lugubrious analysis of General Wessin. America, he said, "seems to be protecting the Communists . . . The Communists publish their newspapers—but the anti-Communists are ordered off the air . . . We cannot understand your government. You send thousands to fight Communism in Viet Nam —but give in to the Communists here."[15]

What accounts for so strange a turn of events? In Cuba, at least, the issue was in doubt. Our vacillation there turned an uncertain situation into defeat. But in Santo Domingo, the doubt had been largely eliminated—the pro-Communist rebels were virtually beaten. Our policy there overturned a certain victory. The given reason was that, by seeking compromise, our diplomats could work within the Garcia government, separating non-Communist rebels from Communist ones. The Imbert-Wessin axis, supposedly, was too militarist and not good for the country. What was needed was a government of "the democratic left," with the Communists cleaned out of it, and return to the 1963 constitution of Juan Bosch. As one U.S. official reportedly put it, "the first job was to clean house on the right."[16]

This pat theory, all too familiar from previous foreign policy debacles, was properly skewered by Representative William Bray (R-Ind.). The "divide and conquer" strategy, Bray noted, was a technique in which the Communists themselves were particularly adept. "For reasons that are obscure to me," he added, "we chose to turn our attention to the Dominican right wing first, when it seems the most logical course would have been to move against and destroy what Communist power and influence existed there . . . We may well have allowed the Dominican Communists time to gain a foothold in this strategic Caribbean republic and, in so doing, once again seized defeat from the jaws of victory."[17]

2. *"The Democratic Left"*

On the face of it, our performance in the Dominican Republic did not make sense. If the Imbert-Wessin regime was so obnoxious its leaders had to be ousted, and if the rebels were worthy of our protection, then the reasons given by Johnson for the original intervention were wrong. If Johnson's statement was right, as the evidence indicates it was, then our actions from mid-May to September, 1965, could not possibly have been correct.

To reconcile these things, it is necessary to get beneath the surface, and to note that the dominant influences in our Latin American policy are people to whom anti-Communist military regimes of the Imbert-Wessin class are intolerable. The hope of Latin America, according to these people, rests with something called "the democratic left"—a group of Latin leaders who may be described, in their most favorable aspect, as revolutionary socialists. They and they alone, according to prevailing Liberal theory, can "save" the Western hemisphere from Communism.

It is impossible to analyze the Dominican situation accurately without understanding this romance with the "democratic left." In fact, very little of United States policy South of the border or the general drift of events there is comprehensible without some understanding of the Socialist leaders who make up this group, among whom Juan Bosch is preeminent. They include Romulo Betancourt of Venezuela, Victor Paz Estenssoro of Bolivia, Victor Raul Haya de la Torre of Peru, and former Governor Luis Munoz Marin of Puerto Rico, among others. The general stance of these leaders may be gathered by pausing for a moment to inspect a few of the principals:

I. VICTOR PAZ ESTENSSORO

Paz Estenssoro of Bolivia, ousted by military coup in 1964, gained power in Bolivia through the combined strength of the proto-Nazi "National Revolutionary Movement," a Bolivian variant of Peronism, and the Communists. During World War II, Paz and his colleagues threw their support to the Axis. In December, 1943, they engineered a military coup, supported by the Nazis and by Argentina, after which Paz travelled to Buenos Aires to seek financial support. When the fortunes of war began to change, he and the MNR moved back into the allied camp. After a post-war decline, the MNR reasserted its influence in 1952 when, with overt Communist support, Paz succeeded in getting control of the government. His faction controlled Bolivia, with occasional lapses, up until 1964.

Paz Estenssoro transformed Bolivia into a thoroughly Marxist and thoroughly totalitarian state. Recipient of more aid per capita than any other Latin American nation, Bolivia remains that continent's No. 1 candidate for bankruptcy, thanks to its Marxist policies. As Latin American expert William Stokes says:

"Paz and his advisers evidenced from the very beginning a passionate intolerance of the opposition. They arrested a former foreign minister, former minister of economic affairs, former chief justice of the supreme court, leaders of the major political parties, and many other prominent, even distinguished, figures.

"Secret police, organized under a bureau known as political control, ferreted out the opposition, using unconstitutional methods that rivaled in ferocity those employed by the Nazi and Communist tyrannies.

"The jails were literally filled with thousands of political prisoners, and President Paz Estenssoro created concentration or 'work' camps to accommodate the overflow . . ."[18]

While continuing to give the Communists free rein in Bolivia, in accordance with the understanding which had secured their support, Paz found nationalization of the Bolivian tin mines had brought the nation close to economic ruin and required assistance from the United States. So, for Washington's consumption, he uttered the right sentiments in international circles while continuing his close alliance with the Communists at home.

Former Bolivian official Alberto Ostria Gutierrez recounts the Communist style terror, the murders, imprisonments, tortures, and routine acts of demagogy and economic folly that marked Paz Estenssoro's career and renders the somber verdict we have quoted in chapter 8.[19]

II. ROMULO BETANCOURT

Venezuela's Betancourt, on his own testimony, is not only a Marxist but a former Communist Party member whose differences with Moscow stem from the Titoist issue of "national" Marxism for Venezuela. In the 'thirties, when he was in exile in Costa Rica, Betancourt wrote: "You know that I have acted here as director of the Communist Party," and kept up a running barrage of correspondence and journalistic exhortation on ways and means of bringing Communism to Venezuela. Among the recipients of these missives was Raul Leoni, Betancourt's long-time coadjutor and his "hand-picked successor" as president of the country.[20]

Betancourt's theory on the best way of achieving Latin Communism was spelled out in a famous pamphlet written in 1931. "We can introduce Lenin and Stalin to these people by using vaseline," he wrote. "We can build a passionate hatred of private property and a vital and active determination to get rid of the capitalist system. We can do all this without using that word which reeks of sulphur and brimstone, Communism." Despite assertions of Betancourt's subsequent break with Communism, he played a key role in the 1948 Bogota uprisings sparked by the Communists. Betancourt's own newspaper in Venezuela, *El Popular,* proudly proclaimed Betancourt was in the forefront of the demonstrations. Also, according to the researches of Nathaniel Weyl, Betancourt helped introduce Fidel Castro into Colombia. Bogota security chief Alberto Nino commented that "nearly all incoming foreign Communists went first to Venezuela."[21]

Betancourt is now pictured as a defector from Communism and a leader in the anti-Communist cause. This argument is belied by his own statements. Betancourt's notion of "fighting Communism" is indicated in his 1956 book, *Venezuela: Politica y Petroleo,* in which he describes the formation and purposes of his Democratic Action Party—which he calls "a belligerent and disciplined party, which daily waged a struggle against the anti-historical forces opposed to national progress."

The objective of his party, Betancourt says, "was to form a vast resistance front against the deforming imperialist penetration and against the undigested remnants of feudalism, which on the political and economic fronts blocked collective progress. We did not deny but admitted the doctrine of the [Communist] Party and its daily conduct, the characteristics of the workers and peasants as the most revolutionary and coherent sections of the nation; and we strove successfully to incorporate them in our ranks and helped them to organize in their labor unions for economic struggle."[22]

Betancourt's preference, in short, is for a kind of national Communism for Venezuela, severed from the Communist international.

Betancourt's management of the Venezuelan economy was reminiscent of Paz Estenssoro's performance in Bolivia. Increased governmental control of vital resources—in this case oil—meant declining prosperity. As veteran Latin American specialist Edward Tomlinson notes, the rise of Betancourt was the occasion for "leftists and Communists" to gain increased influence in the oil workers' unions. "Although Betancourt described himself as a liberal and permitted the Communists quite a free rein, he was in fact a dictator and kept a firm hand on the oil industry."[23] The resemblance to Paz Estenssoro's arrangement is obvious.

Latin authority Hal Hendrix reported in 1962 that "Communists have infiltrated deeply into labor unions, the nation's press, student organizations, almost every sector of commercial and industrial activity and the government body itself. Betancourt cracks down only occasionally."

And Congressmen William Cramer recalled in 1963 that as recently as four years previously Betancourt "was asked to leave this country as an undesirable alien and is now being given a 21-gun salute and welcomed with open arms." In another speech, Cramer charged that "lawlessness, Communist terrorism, and daylight thefts and assaults are rampant throughout Venezuela today, particularly in the major cities. The situation is described as 'chaos' by many American newspapermen visiting that country."[24]

There seems to be little question these days that the Betancourt faction in Venezuela is on the outs with Fidel Castro, which is certainly a point in Betancourt's favor. But there is equally little question that, as a supposed barrier against the advance of Communism, Betancourt leaves a thing or two to be desired.

III. JUAN BOSCH

If Betancourt is a dubious adviser for American policy in the Caribbean, Juan Bosch is, if only for his specific vested interests in Santo Domingo, even worse. We have noted General Wessin's testimony about the waxing of Communist influence under the Bosch regime. When Bosch was president,

Wessin stated, 40 Communist indoctrination centers were established and operated openly, one of them in a government building "turned over to the Communist Dato Pagan Perdomo to install a school of political science."[25] These schools taught, among other things, hatred of the United States and the techniques of guerrilla warfare.

Bosch himself established a "peasant militia" outside the armed forces, patterned after Castro's performance in Cuba. This is a classic Bolshevik maneuver—used also by Paz Estenssoro in Bolivia—to break down a potential source of resistance to revolution. Bosch in addition surrounded himself with members of the Communist-dominated 14th of June movement. "The way they allowed the Communists to gain belligerence in the Dominican Republic . . ." Wessin said, "there is no doubt that Juan Bosch wanted to turn over the country to the Communists."[26]

The Citizens Committee for a Free Cuba notes that Bosch had himself worked closely with the 14th of June revolutionaries. "In early March [1965]," the committee reports, "Bosch met . . . Felix and Rafael Tavares of the Communist pro-Castro June 14 movement and agreed to cooperate with the Communists in the overthrow of Donald Reid Cabral [civilian president]. The June 14 representatives went back to Santo Domingo and made common cause with Jose Brea Pena, Finance Secretary of Bosch's PRD.

"On March 16, the Central Committee of the PSP-D (Communist Party) issued a manifesto saying that 'the entire population must fight in the streets, in the plazas, in the factories, in the fields, for the return of Juan Bosch at the head of the constitutional government.'

"With Communist organizational ability and vigor bolstering Bosch's traditionless and weak party apparatus, the collaboration was complete."[27]

U.S. News confirmed this report, noting that "leaders of the plot had been working with Juan Bosch, former President who had been overthrown in September, 1963, and had taken refuge in San Juan, Puerto Rico. Bosch was not known as a Communist, but he knew that Communists were in on the plot to restore him to power, and he worked with them. . . . [By the third day of the revolt] some followers of Juan Bosch were seeking asylum in foreign embassies. The open take-over of the rebel movement by Castro-type Communists was more than they were willing to accept."[28]

Finally, in December 1965, Juan Isidro Tapia Adames, a defector from the Dominican rebels, and Alfonso L. Tarabochia, a staff member of the Internal Security subcommittee with experience in Dominican affairs, gave testimony to the committee confirming Bosch's ties to the Dominican Communists. "These new hearings," commented Senator Dodd, "present important new evidence that Bosch and his lieutenants maintained indirect contact with Communists even after the uprising. Mr. Bosch evidently thought he could use the aid of the Dominican Communists and other leftist agents, while secretly distrusting them. It also seems that the Communists held Mr. Bosch in deep contempt as a bourgeois element disposed to cooperate with 'Communism.' But the hard fact emerges that, despite mutual suspicions, the Bosch people and the Red activists did maintain liaison for the purpose of cooperation."[29]

Upon his return to Santo Domingo after the elevation of the Garcia government, Bosch bitterly denounced the United States and demanded $1 billion in reparations for the U.S. intervention.

Bosch's 1963 constitution, which our State Department said it wanted to see restored in the Dominican Republic, provides further evidence of Bosch's leanings. "The 1963 constitution," says the Citizens Committee, "is a Bosch constitution, rammed through a largely illiterate and incompetent Bosch congress. It is deliberately vague. It is a blank check."[30] Among the provisions of this document are sections saying expropriation of property may take place in the "general interest," that foreign nationals are divested of all land rights except what the government chooses to grant, that "excessive" land-holding is outlawed (without definition of what is excessive), that oil and mineral rights, as in Cuba, are declared to be the property of the state, *etc.*

In his Kennedy memoir, Arthur Schlesinger stresses the connections of the New Frontier with all of these Latin leftists. "My talks with Betancourt, Haya de la Torre, Paz Estenssoro and others," Schlesinger says, "had given me the strong impression that the democratic left in Latin America had turned decisively against Castro . . ."[31] And so forth at some length. This partiality for the "democratic left", *i.e.,* revolutionary Socialists, has marked all of the present administration's dealings in Latin America. In 1963, Paz Estenssoro was a welcome guest at the White House, accorded a 21-gun salute. Betancourt has been consulted repeatedly as an oracle on Latin affairs. Bosch was a particular favorite of the Kennedy regime.

The devotion of Washington Liberals to these "democratic left" leaders is suggested by the tribute paid Betancourt by Kennedy-Johnson Latin American specialist Richard Goodwin. "He is a leader and a guiding spirit of the democratic liberalism which offers the only hope for a Latin America in which steadily increasing human welfare can be combined with human freedom and dignity," Goodwin says.[32] Vice President Hubert Humphrey similarly opined that Betancourt "is one of the great leaders of our hemisphere," and a stalwart foe of Communism.[33]

In like manner, Schlesinger remarks of Bosch: "An old friend of Munoz, Figueres, and Betancourt, Bosch was strongly in the progressive democratic tradition." Schlesinger approvingly quotes Bosch on the Alliance for Progress, and records that Kennedy "instructed our government to give

Bosch full support." Bosch's failure Schlesinger attributes to the fact that he was "essentially a literary figure, better as a short story writer than as a statesman."[34]

The Marxist-Socialist bent of the "Alliance for Progress," remarked in Chapter 8, was a direct result of consultation between Kennedy advisers Schlesinger, Goodwin, *et al.,* with leaders of the "democratic left." Schlesinger's discussion of the "Alliance" and all its appurtenances is a hymn of praise to these Socialist leaders and their "democratic revolution," and a denunciation of U.S. efforts to promote "free enterprise" and "private initiative" in the Latin countries.[35]

Considering this long-standing romance between domestic ADAers and Latin Socialists, the blunting of a U.S. policy in support of a "right wing" military junta in the Dominican Republic is hardly surprising. In particular, that durable regard for Juan Bosch—a charter member of the leftist camarilla—would obviously predispose Liberal foreign policy specialists to seeking a solution favorable to his aspirations. And so, in fact, it turned out.

If we go back to Johnson's speech of May 3, we find him announcing, even as he declared U.S. willingness to combat Communist encroachment, that we were seeking the opinion and counsel of precisely these leaders. "We are in contact," Johnson said, "with such distinguished Latin American statesmen as Romulo Betancourt and Jose Figueres. We are seeking their wisdom and their counsel and their advice. We have also maintained communication with President Bosch who has chosen to remain in Puerto Rico."[36]

Thus, even as the intervention was launched, the seeds of confusion were sown. The President declared "the American nations cannot, must not, and will not permit the establishment of another Communist government in the Western hemisphere."[37] Yet the administration was simultaneously seeking out "wisdom, counsel, and advice" from Marxists Betancourt and Bosch, the latter having helped launch the revolution in open collaboration with the Communists, whose background and previous performance hardly equipped them to fulfil that noble resolve.

It is apparent, Jules Dubois observed when the first signs of our policy turnabout appeared,

> that the Dominican Republic policy of the White House is geared to the revived influence of the so-called democratic left of Latin America, and the Americans for Democratic Action . . . The Latin American democratic left is known as the Caribbean club . . . Its leaders are: Luis Munoz Marin, ex-governor of Puerto Rico, former President Romulo Betancourt of Venezuela, Jose Figueres of Costa Rica, Juan Bosch of the Dominican Republic, Ramon Villedes Morales of Honduras, and Victor Raul Haya de la Torre, head of the American Popular Revolutionary Alliance in Peru.[38]

Dubois added that "Munoz, Betancourt, and Figueres were summoned to Washington after the revolt erupted here to confer with Vice President Humphrey, who sought their recommendations to resolve the crisis here. Those recommendations, of course, were heavily weighted in favor of a solution desired by Bosch. History is thus fateful in itself. During the fateful days of April 17-19, 1961, Munoz and Figueres made similar appearances in Washington. Both strongly urged the late President Kennedy not to use the might of the United States to support the Bay of Pigs brigade."[39]

Carrying the ball for the "Caribbean club" within administration ranks was then-presidential assistant McGeorge Bundy, reported in June as "insisting that a 'compromise' junta be set up to replace the Imbert Barrera junta."[40] Bundy again popped up as a chief advocate of exiling General Wessin from the United States. Allen and Scott put it that "the 'second exile of General Wessin' was decided by Secretary Rusk and presidential assistant McGeorge Bundy. They were told by President Johnson at an announced meeting of administration policy-makers that Wessin had to be silenced." The columnists report Johnson as saying Wessin "shouldn't have been brought to this country in the first place. Action must be taken immediately to silence him. His appearance at the Capitol could touch off a bitter foreign policy inquiry that could embarrass us both in this country and abroad."*[41]

A parallel account of how our policy got turned around—written from a different point of view—is given by Tad Szulc of the *New York Times*. Szulc says the "new approach" was launched by presidential adviser Abe Fortas, who contacted Bosch and asked him "to seek a compromise formula." Bundy and Defense Department official Cyrus Vance followed up. As a "compromise" was sought, Szulc says, "the rebels were confined to a small section of downtown Santo Domingo," with U. S. troops, "in a sense, protecting them." Finally, "the Johnson administration struck down its erstwhile protegé by depriving General Imbert of financial support."[42]

What happened in the Dominican Republic, then, was a "reversal" in one sense only. In the public presentation, and in reports concerning the "hard" analyses of officials like Assistant Secretary of State Thomas Mann and U.S. Ambassador Tapley Bennett, the purpose of the intervention was to defeat the pro-Communist rebels and to lend support to the Imbert-Wessin regime. But in the view of those enamored of "the democratic left," that could hardly have been the objec-

* A previous conjunction of Betancourt advice and exile of an anti-Communist leader occurred in 1963 when the Kennedy administration denied asylum to anti-Communist former President Perez Jimenez of Venezuela. The action against Jimenez was pushed in the Federal courts by Dean Acheson's law firm Covington & Burling, the registered U.S. agent for the Betancourt government. "To send the former President Perez Jimenez in chains into [Betancourt's Venezuela]," said Rep. Henry Schadeberg at the time, "would be the greatest contribution which the United States could make to Venezuelan communism. It would be a public sign that the United States was not following a sincere anti-Communist policy in Venezuela. It would be a weak admission of American neutrality in the struggle between the Communists and the anti-Communists in Venezuela." Jimenez was extradited.

tive. Considering the relative strength of the two forces, it is altogether probable that had the United States not intervened the anti-Communist junta would have won. Because the United States intervened, the junta lost. For those who find the counsels of Romulo Betancourt and Juan Bosch edifying, the dispatch of American troops and that grim result would not be inconsistent at all, but a simple matter of ends and means.

In 1966, the Dominican people had their chance to show, in a free and open election, what they thought of "the democratic left." They overwhelmingly rejected the candidacy of Bosch and the gaggle of leftists supporting him in favor of Joaquin Balaguer. They obviously wanted no more of Bosch, the revolutionaries who backed him, or the violence which had been touched off in his name. Incoming president Balaguer, however, had his work cut out for him. The consensus was that the Communists—who geared up during the election for continual efforts at subversion and, if need be, guerrilla warfare—would do everything in their power to stir new trouble and new violence. Additionally, Balaguer inherited the leftists who had been threaded into the government during the caretaker regime of Garcia-Godoy. The forces of "the democratic left" had been proved devoid of popular support, but thanks to the nine-month tenure of Garcia-Godoy still held important positions of strength.

★★ 27. *War In Katanga*

FROM WORLD WAR II forward the United States, in obedience to Liberal doctrine, has pressured its European allies to abandon their colonial possessions. Among the powers which have felt these pressures have been England, France, the Netherlands, Portugal, and Belgium. The principal holding of the last-named was the Belgian Congo, a vast and fabulous region in the center of Africa. After long hectoring Belgium agreed to grant independence to the Congo, which was in consequence to take its place among the free nations of the world, June 30, 1960.

The new government wound up, by virtue of a rigged election, in the hands of Patrice Lumumba, former convict and a collaborator with the Communists. Congolese terrorists then went to work staging a saturnalia of mayhem and violence, in which no European and few non-Lumumbist Africans were safe. An alarmed Belgian government sent its troops back to Leopoldville to protect its nationals, Lumumba called upon the U.N. to protect him from resurgent "colonialism," and the U.N., to no one's surprise, responded with alacrity.

After some months of disorder, Congolese President Joseph Kasavubu parted with Lumumba. The ousted premier took refuge with the ever-helpful United Nations, and sought to make his way to the pro-Soviet outpost of Antoine Gizenga in Stanleyville, in the midst of which sojourn he was arrested by central government forces under Col. Joseph Mobutu. Throughout this period, the United Nations lent its support to Lumumba, protecting him and hindering the efforts of his various opponents. The United States in turn gave its support to the U.N.

Meanwhile, a crucial region of the Congo, comprising some 2 million people, remained relatively stable. Under the leadership of anti-Communist, pro-Western President Moise Tshombe, mineral-rich Katanga province was peaceful and orderly. Wanting things to remain that way, and viewing the Lumumbist anarchy with understandable alarm, Tshombe withdrew from the Congo. Katanga declared itself independent.

As four Methodist medical missionaries who served in Katanga put it: "Tshombe urged secession of Katanga because he feared the marked Communist leanings of powerful men in the central government, such as Lumumba and Antoine Gizenga. Tshombe himself is fiercely democratic and severely anti-Communist. He determined that secession was the only route to follow if any semblance of democracy was to be preserved in Katanga. Knowledge of the facts substantiates this as the course of wisdom . . . He is in fact the only Congolese leader who has been elected to office . . . [and he] had a peaceful country . . ."[1]

In 1961, at the urging of the central Congolese government, the United Nations sent its troops into Katanga. This action was directly in conflict with the Security Council's resolution of August 9, 1960, which said: "The U.N. forces in the Congo will not be a party to, or in any way intervene in, or be used to influence the outcome of internal conflict, constitutional or otherwise."[2] On September 13, 1961, U.N. forces nonetheless staged an all-out assault against Elisabethville, Katanga's capital city.

The United States lent its full support to this action, provided airplanes to fly supplies to the United Nations troops beleaguering Katanga, and paid the lion's share of the bill. In 1962, as previously noted, President Kennedy threw himself into the effort to achieve an appropriation of $100 million to meet the U.N.'s financial obligations. The purpose of all this was to force anti-Communists, "neutralists" and Communists into a coalition government, and to bring Katanga under its dominion. Meanwhile, the pro-Communist element in the Congo, headed by Lumumbist Antoine Gizenga, had set up its own shop in Stanleyville. No U.N. action was taken, however, to bring that faction into line. All the violence was directed at anti-Communist Katanga.

1. *Fighting Communism*

The stated purpose of U.S. support for the U.N. in Katanga was to prevent dismemberment of the Congo and the eruption of conditions in which "the Communists would pick up the pieces."[3] According to Under Secretary of State George Ball, Tshombe's secession was "playing into the hands of the Communists."[4] The State Department further alleged that "while [Premier Cyrille] Adoula's government has been following a policy friendly to the West, Mr. Tshombe has done nothing to aid the cause of anti-Communism."[5] It was also suggested that the U.N. action *must* have been anti-Communist, because the Soviets opposed it. These arguments, it developed, were incorrect in almost every particular.

To begin with the last assertion first, the Soviet Union did *not* oppose U.N. action against Katanga, but enthusiastically supported it, voting for and acclaiming the November 24, 1961, Security Council resolution authorizing the use of force against Katanga.

As for the inclinations of the central government, the Moscow *New Times* remarked: "The members of political parties of the national bloc which was headed by Patrice Lumumba have 23 seats in this government, or an absolute majority. The composition of the new cabinet proves that the adventurous effort to liquidate the government of Lumumba completely failed."[6] Adoula himself, at a September 1961 conclave of neutralists in Belgrade, Yugoslavia, bitterly attacked the United States, denounced "the capitalist nations," and said recently deceased U.N. chieftain Dag Hammarskjold "was the victim of certain financial circles for whom a human life is not equal to a gram of copper or uranium."[7] In August, 1962, Adoula made available to the rebel-terrorist forces of Holden Roberto military sanctuary for guerrilla raids against the neighboring state of Angola.

If these signs were not enough to suggest the true nature of the "pro-Western" government to which our State Department lent its support, Senator Dodd offered a detailed analysis of certain people in the Adoula regime which made the matter crystal clear. In a speech to the Senate September 8, 1961, Dodd declared:

> Under the guise of assisting the central government and reestablishing parliamentary rule, the United Nations, although it may not recognize this fact, has been preparing the way, step by step, for a Communist take-over in the Congo.
>
> The United Nations first gave its unconditional support to the regime of Patrice Lumumba. When Lumumba was dismissed by President Kasavubu in September 1960, his chief aid, Antoine Gizenga, a Prague-trained Communist, set up an independent regime in Stanleyville, the capital of Oriental Province.

The U.N. did nothing to interfere with Gizenga's action in setting up this independent, Moscow-oriented regime. It did nothing to curb the reign of terror which Gizenga instituted against the white residents of Oriental and Kiwu Provinces and against anti-Communist political opponents. It did nothing to prevent the massive influx of Communist arms to Gizenga, via Cairo.

To round out the picture, it did everything in its power to prevent and restrain President Kasavubu from re-asserting the authority of the Central government over Oriental Province.

Within recent weeks, the U.N. has fostered the creation of a so-called coalition government, so heavily weighted in favor of the Communists that, unless we do something to reverse the course of U.N. policy, the outcome is virtually a mathematical certainty.

The Prime Minister, Adoula, is, by reputation, not a Communist, but simply a neutralist. The Vice-Premier, however, is Antoine Gizenga, a cadre Communist, while the key position of the Ministry of the Interior has been awarded to Gizenga's most notorious henchman, Christophe Gbenye . . . (who) incidentally, as Minister of the Interior in the pro-Communist regime in Oriental Province, was directly responsible for instigating the murder and rape and terror against the white residents of the province.[8]

On September 22, Dodd spoke on the question of who would run mineral-laden Katanga once it was subjugated to the central government. "It is clear," he said, "that there must have been some conflict within the coalition government between pro-Western elements and pro-Communist elements over the selection of a man who would fill the post of administrator for Katanga. Who was appointed? Egide Bochely-Davidson, an ardent Lumumbist, a former member of the Gizenga government, and a man who, according to the Western press, is considered strongly pro-Communist by Western diplomats."[9]

Dodd added that "my own information from a reliable American source is that Bochely-Davidson is not only a

Communist, but an agent of the Soviet secret police. The State Department has said it has no proof Bochely-Davidson is a Communist, but it admits that he is a Gizenga follower and that he would probably take his orders from Gizenga."[10]

Early in 1962, Gizenga was overthrown in an internal coup. His place was taken by still another Lumumbist, Christophe Gbenye. Concerning this transition, Dodd said:

> There have been other claimants to the mantle of Lumumba. Most notable of these is Christophe Gbenye, Minister of the Interior under Gizenga in Stanleyville, and again Minister of the Interior in the Leopoldville government today.
>
> Gbenye, who is even more responsible than Lumumba for the reign of terror in Leopoldville in the summer of 1960, told me proudly that he considers himself the legitimate heir to Lumumba as leader of the National Congolese Movement. Gbenye is a force to be reckoned with since he controls the largest single group of deputies in the Parliament, and the largest single group inside the Congo's gargantuan cabinet of 44 members.
>
> When I was in Leopoldville, I was told that sharp personal differences had developed between Gbenye and Gizenga. Apparently, Gbenye was determined to assert his undisputed claim to No. 1 position in the radical nationalist movement.
>
> The vote . . . against Gizenga in the Congolese Parliament does not signify a total victory for the forces of moderation. On the contrary, what it signifies is that the Lumumbist bloc, under Gbenye's leadership, voted solidly to take action against Gizenga.[11]

2. *U.N. Aggression*

That the U.N. was guilty of aggression against Katanga can no longer be open to serious dispute. We have it on the authority of the man who was in charge of the U.N. operation that the 1961 action was unprovoked and that the U.N. tried to cover up that fact by trading in falsehood. These charges are made by Dr. Conor Cruise O'Brien, the Irish diplomat who superintended the offensive.* A partisan of the U.N. and bitter opponent of Katangan independence, O'Brien says he is aware his revelations will "play into the hands" of U.N. critics but that nevertheless the truth must be told.

When open fighting between Katangese and United Nations forces first broke out in September, 1961, the world body said its action was a "defensive" one. The day after hostilities began, the U.N. issued a statement saying "arson" had been discovered at the United Nations garage in Elisabethville. U.N. troops heading for the scene, according to this communique, were treacherously fired upon. This supposedly started the fighting.

All of which came as distinct news to Dr. O'Brien. "If this is an accurate account of what took place in Elisabethville on the morning of September 13," he writes, "my name is Titus Oates."[12] The Katanga action began, not as a result of the U.N.'s defending itself, but as a result of premeditated United Nations attack. The purpose of the aggression, O'Brien says bluntly, was simply to subjugate Katanga by force. The code name of the operation was "Morthor," a term whose significance O'Brien explains as follows: *"Morthor is a Hindi word. It does not mean 'sound the alarm; there is arson in the garage' or 'Now let us assist the provincial authorities to maintain order.' It means 'Smash.'* "[13]

Why did the U.N. put out a false version of the fighting? Secretary General Hammarskjold, O'Brien says, "was subjected to the most intense pressures, both psychological and

* *Cf.* also the four medical missionaries we have quoted, who say: "From Americans in Elisabethville during the United Nations conflicts of September, 1961 and December, 1961, we have learned that upon both occasions the fighting was started by the United Nations. This is contrary to the pose of self-defense which the United Nations has assumed. In fact, in December, the hour of the offensive was made known to the Americans so they could be at home and out of the line of fire."

diplomatic, to draw back from what the U.N. had undertaken—which was in fact the ending of the secession of Katanga by the use of force."[14] (O'Brien concedes such use of force was "plainly contrary" to certain clauses in the U.N. resolutions concerning the Congo.) Responding to these pressures, Hammarskjold "allowed the world to be given an official version which was so phrased as to conceal the reality of what had happened, making what had been an active intervention by the United Nations look like a defensive action."[15]

Thus the man actually in charge of the U.N. forces on the scene says the official U.N. version—not to put too fine a point on it—was a lie. He acknowledges that the fighting, which launched a long bloody war, began with an act of aggression by the organization which is alleged to be the hope of world peace. Throughout this discussion, moreover, O'Brien makes it clear that, had it not been for the support of the Kennedy administration, the U.N. action in the Congo would have gone nowhere.

In the 1962 offensive against Katanga, also advertised as "defensive," there was equally convincing proof of U.N. aggression. This came in the form of an *aide-memoire* circulated at the U.N. in the fall of 1962, which was smuggled into the hands of *National Review* magazine. The document spelled out the moves which would be taken to launch a new aggression against Katanga, including preliminary steps to "affirm Tshombe's intransigence," "repeat UN determination to achieve Congolese unity," and "affirm the continued presence of mercenaries in the Katangese gendarmerie." These steps to prepare "world opinion" would be followed by an order to "the UN occupation force to take control of the mining centers and the frontier exit points."[16] The *aide-memoire* even became so explicit as to discuss alternative plans of aggression—an attack against the key mining center of Kolwezi, occupation of frontier stations only, or simple bombardment of Katanga's lines of communication.

The authenticity of this document was attested by a number of subsequent disclosures. In November, 1962, U.N. correspondent William R. Frye gave a rundown of U.N. plans which matched the *aide-memoire* almost point for point. U Thant, said Frye, was "fed up with interminable bickering and delays," and wanted to get the Katanga situation mopped up in a hurry. He planned "to swoop down on nests of Katanga mercenaries believed to be hiding out in Jadotville, Kipushi, and Kolwezi—three centers now barred to U.N. troops by Katanga president Moise Tshombe."[17]

In December, further confirmation came from *Chicago Daily News* correspondent Milt Freudenheim, who reported "the U.N. force is slated to begin moving into Kolwezi, Jadotville and Kipushi in southern Katanga around the third week in January."[18] The article reported various steps being taken by U.N. and American military commanders to get their forces ready for the aggression.

Early in January, the action spelled out in these advance reports occurred, triggering a final confirmation from U.N. Under Secretary Ralph Bunche. As with the previous aggression, U.N. headquarters in New York tried to float a false story of what had occurred. The Jadotville attack, said the U.N., had been launched because "its communications with the Congo broke down"—an announcement which led the Associated Press to state that the troops "evidently entered the city without orders to do so from higher echelons."[19] On the day following the Jadotville attack, however, Bunche *"declared the capture of Jadotville had been part of a plan approved by Thant last October."*[20]

These acts of aggression took place, as usual, with the assent and active encouragement of the United States. The AP disclosed: "As the U.N. troops paused, U.S. Air Force Globemasters flew armored cars and amphibious tanks into

Elisabethville to bolster [the U.N.] forces. . . . In Washington, the United States was understood to be advising the United Nations and the governments of Belgium and Britain that it would make little sense to stop the U.N. advance when the Tshombe forces were on the run."[21]

3. *U.N. Atrocities*

The official version of what the U.N. and the U.S. were doing in the Congo, as set forth by Ambassador Edmund Gullion, our emissary to Leopoldville, was that the U.N. had "prevented what might have been a Korean-type power struggle between the super-powers in the heart of Africa" and had "spared the Congolese people the ravages of a step-up from cold war to hot war."[22]

The U.N.'s method of sparing ravages became apparent on the morning of January 3, 1963, when it was learned that U.N. troops had brutally murdered two women near Jadotville. Newspapers around the world displayed a photograph of the wounded husband of one woman, falling to his knees before the marauding Indian troops of the U.N. "peace force." TV stations showed a remarkable newsreel of the same episode. All three of the individuals under attack by the U.N. heroes were civilians, unarmed and travelling in a distinctly non-military looking Volkswagen.

To blunt the horror of this event, the U.N. advertised it as a "mistake" which "should never have happened."[23] Yet the killing of civilians, far from being an exception to the usual orderly performance of the U.N. troops, was standard performance.

The Jadotville murders were committed by Indian Gurkhas. One of the officers who commanded these units, Col. E. S. Mitra, had expressed his philosophy of warfare to the Paris daily, *Figaro,* in 1961. "As for me," Mitra said, "I do not take any white prisoners. I ordered my men to kill all mercenaries and to finish off the wounded." Asked whether "any European may be considered a mercenary by your troops even if he isn't armed," Mitra replied: "Certainly there is a risk."[24]

The "mistake" alibi for the Jadotville slayings is also contradicted by the fact that the entire U.N. performance in the Congo was marked by atrocities, including numerous attacks on civilians. The U.N. obviously was forced to concede what had happened at Jadotville simply because photographers had been on hand to get a picture of it.

Consider the following account of U.N. behavior from a Baltimore, Md., missionary in Elisabethville:

> Eyewitnesses have seen the Indian United Nations troops shoot down Katanga soldiers with their hands raised in surrender. They have thrown Katanga troops off the top of the Post Office Building. They have fired on civilians. They have carried ammunition in trucks carrying Red Cross flags. Their every tactic has been Gestapo-like and contrary to the usual conventions of war . . . We are all so ashamed of the United Nations behavior.[25]

The Baltimore Sun, which published this account, concluded by quoting the missionary as saying "it was the Congo army which, 'by pre-arrangement, destroyed public order' . . . The army was infiltrated by Communists who triggered the revolt."

In January, 1963, the Brooklyn *Tablet* of New York carried an article headlined "U.N. Troops Violate Churches, Hospitals," which contained the following quotation from the Catholic Vicar General of Elisabethville:

> According to reports I personally received, the Ethiopians [of the UN command] completely looted St. Benedict's church and broke into the tabernacle of another church in the Kaspa suburb of Elisabethville.
>
> St. Boniface's church was hit by two mortar salvos. Sisters

took shelter in the cellar all night while their convent was being severely bombed.

The reports also confirm the cruelty of the killing of Katangese civilians. Seventy corpses were brought to Prince Leopold hospital. . . . I feel helpless and sad at hearing that my people are being maltreated and that any intervention is interpreted as political interference.[26]

Another eye-witness account, from a high European official stationed in Elisabethville, says:

I could fill pages with the simply horrible things the United Nations has done here . . . Did you hear that the U.N. Ghurkas attacked the Elisabethville radio station at 4 a.m. and killed 25 Katanga soldiers and police who had received orders not to fire first? Many of them were asleep inside the building and a Red Cross ambulance which came up to help the wounded was also put out of action. The Red Cross people later gave a description of the state of the building when they were eventually admitted to take out the dead, and it made appalling reading. The reason for the attack on the radio station was that the news commentaries were anti-U.N.[27]

A similar report came from Harold Soref, a businessman visiting the Congo, in a letter to the London *Times:*

I witnessed two passing jeeps attacked by U.N. machine guns. The Katangese occupants, who had not fired a shot, were slaughtered without warning. Shortly afterwards an unarmed police jeep was machine-gunned from the almost adjacent U.N. Red Cross hospital. The wounded Katangese were left to die. When a Red Cross Katangese ambulance arrived it was attacked by a U.N. armored car. Any attempt to render aid was repulsed by trigger-happy U.N. troops. On several occasions I saw press photographers similarly threatened, and one was wounded whilst taking a shot which might well have been embarrassing to the United Nations' apologists. Such incidents were not isolated. On the following morning I witnessed another unarmed Katangese ambulance, carrying an enormous Red Cross flag, attacked and the driver seriously wounded.[28]

U.N.-commanded troops also engaged in systematic plunder of conquered territory. David F. Renwick, himself a former U.N. official, declared there was a "massive amount of black marketeering, pilfering, and outright stealing by certain U.N. military personnel" in Katanga. He added that "the U.N. will do nothing about this owing to political pressures from New York and more especially by the governments of the troops concerned."[29]

These varied assertions were confirmed by no less an authority than *The New York Times,* which reported in 1961 that "at least 15 white women were raped by Congolese soldiers" under United Nations command in the Congo's Kasai Province:

Belgian refugees . . . put the number of women raped at 15. Other sources said the count was accurate. Three of the women were said to be in serious condition. One jumped from a window to escape assailants. She suffered a broken arm and an injured back . . . the troops [according to one report] began a search for a radio transmitter believed to have been used as a link between Belgians sympathetic to Katanga. The Congolese troops were said to have moved from house to house arresting Belgians as spies and herding all the men together at a hotel. Then, with the men under armed guard, some of the soldiers went back after the women.[30]

A week later, *The Times* added that "in the village of Mweka, about 50 Europeans were arrested and beaten by the police. Four Nigerian soldiers were immediately sent to the village to free the whites. They, too, were arrested. Other Nigerians had to be sent to free these men."[31]

The Times reported that the U.N. command was unhappy

with the performance of the Congolese troops (under whose absolute control the U.N. was trying to place Katanga). But other reports indicated that, at best, U.N. chieftains were indifferent to the atrocities committed by forces under their command. Smith Hempstone, African correspondent of the *Chicago Daily News,* reported: "The Congolese troops . . . put villages to the torch, slaughtered women and children, and sent an estimated 10,000 families fleeing to the south . . . at Luluabourg, Congolese soldiers had arrested 400 whites, raped 15 women including some nuns, and beaten up some missionaries . . ." Even Italian airmen serving the U.N. itself were set upon by the U.N.'s Congolese troops: "Drunken Congolese soldiers accused them of being Belgian mercenaries, beat them, shot them all, and then dismembered their bodies."[32]

Hempstone charged that chief of U.N. operations Sture Linner, who had replaced O'Brien, would not discipline his troops. Result: "One month later, 22 Belgian priests were murdered by the same troops whom Linner had found it 'inopportune' to disarm after the Kindu massacre."[33]

Other details provided by Hempstone: ". . . firing was indiscriminate enough for Georges Olivet, Swiss international Red Cross representative in Elisabethville, to cable an appeal to his Geneva office to call on the U.N. to stop firing on Red Cross vehicles . . . Fifty U.N. mortar shells rained down on the Prince Leopold Hospital one night as African patients crawled screaming into the corridors . . . Indian Canberra jets . . . roared in over Shinkolobwe and shot up the former Uranium mine's hospital, leaving two children and two men dead. Four pregnant women were wounded, as were 44 other Africans. The hospital was clearly marked with a huge Red Cross on its roof and was more than 1,500 yards from the nearest building"[34]

Prof. Ernest Van Den Haag, after an on-the-scene 1962 study in Elisabethville, came to these conclusions: "The city is still terrorized by ignorant and suspicious soldiers hired by the U.N. They arbitrarily arrest people suspect to them, regardless of documents and permissions signed by their own superiors. No provision has been made to discipline these U.N. troops; or to offer a protection to the civilian population against abuses by these troops; or to investigate and adjudicate claimed abuses; or to prevent them; or to punish the soldiers guilty of abuses or unauthorized actions."[35]

On December 19, 1961, Van Den Haag relates, a civilian named Alazraki was on an automobile trip in Elisabethville when "Ethiopian machine gunners shot at the car and wounded Alazraki. He left the car and dragged himself for a small distance His attackers continued to shoot. He was killed."[36]

Among the eye-witness accounts quoted by Van Den Haag: "Maurice Mwanza, five years old, has been at the hospital Prince Leopold since December 17. On that date, Ethiopian soldiers killed his father with bayonets. The child took refuge in bed. An Ethiopian soldier slashed him there with his bayonet." And: "I saw Mr. Dedeken with a book in his hand, standing in the garden. An Ethiopian soldier, hidden behind a tree, shot him down at a distance of about 30 metres."[37]

When Tshombe was ousted in January, 1963, there should have been no further occasion for violence. But the same pattern of atrocities continued. Early in April, *Time* magazine reported that " an elderly shopkeeper" had been shot to death in Elisabethville by a soldier of the central Congolese government. "As the man lay groaning on the pavement," *Time* added, "Congolese troops shoved away a doctor who tried to save his life." This "cold-blooded killing," the magazine said, "pointed up the grim fact that nearly three months after United Nations troops crushed secessionist Moise Tshombe's regime and placed the province under Premier Cyrille Adoula's central government, peace is far from restored in Katanga . . . In recent weeks, trigger-happy Congolese soldiers in Elisabethville have killed at least one civilian per day."[38]

As the acts of terrorism continued, the crisis precipitated, irony of ironies, the return to power of Tshombe—deemed to be the one man who could put the Congo's troubled affairs back in order. Tshombe set to work, over the loud protests of Afro-Asian "neutralists," to clean the pro-Communists, led by Christophe Gbenye, out of the Congo. Since accomplishing that job, he has again been ousted, and the country is, at this writing, under the military rule of Gen. Joseph Mobutu. The ultimate fate of the Congo is yet to be determined. But the record suggests that, if it is at last saved from Communism and chaos, that outcome will be in spite of, and not because of, United Nations intervention.

★★ 28. *How the Other Half Dies*

THE COMMUNIST DYNAMISM which has conquered China, Yugoslavia, Czechoslovakia and other once-free nations during the course of the Cold War; the so-called "liberation movements" manipulated by the Communists in Laos, Viet Nam, and the Dominican Republic; the endemic confusion which has marked American policy. These are the components which have produced the communization of half the globe. If our story ended there, we would have reason enough to be dismayed. But the fact is that all these elements are today at work in still other places, places which have not received the attention accorded Cuba or Viet Nam or the Congo.

In the preceding chapters, we have touched on some of the major episodes in which half the world has been lost to Bolshevik aggression; in this one we shall note, in a brief review of a number of subsidiary trouble spots, how the other half dies.

1. *Panama*

American vacillation and confusion have recently been most manifest in Panama, where pressures mobilized by "neutralists" and pro-Communists have provoked the Johnson administration to an epic venture in conciliation. In 1963, following popular agitation and pressures from Panamanian authorities, the U.S. government agreed to compromise on the long-standing issue of where and how the American flag should be flown inside the Canal Zone. Although the Zone was by the treaty of 1903 fully subject to American sovereignty, Panamanians felt their flag should fly alongside of or, preferably, in place of our own. Attempting to quiet this agitation, our government yielded almost everything.

On January 10, 1963, a joint U.S.-Panamanian communique announced that "the flag of the Republic of Panama will be flown together with the flag of the United States of America on land in the Canal Zone where the flag of the United States is flown by civilian authorities . . ."[1] American citizens in the Canal Zone vehemently protested, to no avail. An order was handed down in late 1963 by Canal Zone governor Robert J. Fleming, Jr., directing that the dual flag policy be put into effect.

Among the places where the U.S. flag was no longer supposed to fly alone was Balboa High School at the Pacific end of the Canal Zone. U.S. students there, however, raised an American flag and stood watch during the night to prevent its removal. Panamanian demonstrators thereupon launched a series of riots which were, according to Latin American authority Hal Hendrix, "fanned by pro-Communist elements on the Panamanian side of the border."[2]

The Spillway, authoritative Canal Zone publication, gave this on-the-scene report of what happened: "The mob upset and burned an unoccupied automobile at the intersection of Roosevelt Avenue and Frangipani Street . . . About 2 or 3 minutes later, part of the mob started to burn and sack the Ancon freight house . . . a crowd estimated between 5,000 and 6,000 was gathering along Fourth of July Avenue. Molotov cocktails were being thrown against buildings in the Canal Zone and a number of cars had been set on fire . . . A Molotov cocktail was thrown through the windshield of an automobile that came out of Panama into the Canal Zone at Frangipani Street, etc."[3]

Although America had already gone the extra mile, President Johnson met these outbursts with still other offers of conciliation. In April, Johnson agreed to "review" the treaty with Panama whereby the United States has sovereignty over the Zone. In November Hendrix reported: "It is felt here the U.S. is willing to drop from the treaty the clause granting the U.S. perpetual sovereignty in the 10-mile-wide zone."[4] Hendrix added that both governments had agreed to put the matter off until after the 1964 elections.

Negotiations on the subject continued through 1965. In September, 1965, Johnson announced the U.S. and Panama had agreed to revise the 1903 treaty and to draft a new one which would "effectively recognize Panama's sovereignty over the area of the present Canal Zone."[5]

Rep. Daniel Flood (D-Penna.) summarized what had happened:

> When the Panamanians sat down they demanded that the Treaty of 1903 be abrogated, so the Americans agreed. The second point made by the Panamanians was that sovereignty be established in the Republic of Panama over the Canal Zone territory and the Americans agreed. Third, the Panamanians insisted that the tolls be raised and a greater profit come to them with increased payments from the Canal, and the Americans agreed.

The net effect of these agreements, Flood said, was "a complete and abject surrender to Panama of our indispensable sovereignty and authority with respect to the Panama Canal." A mixture of authorities over the Zone could "only lead to unending conflicts and recriminations that always accompany extra-territorial jurisdictions where two masters are concerned." Flood added that

> the grant of complete jurisdiction of Panama over the Canal Zone means that all laws made by the U.S. Congress for the Government of the Zone and the operation and maintenance of the Canal may be scrapped at any time by Panama, and superseded by Panamanian law. Also, all civil activities in the zone—courts, police, and fire departments, schools, roads and public utilities—will be taken over by Panama. All this means, sooner or later, the elimination of United States citizen employees in the Canal enterprise with substitutions of Panamanians.[6]

The result, in short, was that a vital link in America's security system would fall under the control of a regime heavily influenced by anti-U.S. agitation and subject to the violent oscillations of an unstable political system. Flood drily concluded that "for our officials to proclaim Panama, which since 1955 has not been able to collect its own garbage from the streets of Panama City and Colon, as a partner of this great interoceanic public utility is, to say the least, unrealistic . . ."[7]

Walter Trohan commented in the Chicago *Tribune:*

> In Panama we are preparing to haul down the American flag. President Johnson has abrogated the 1903 Panama Canal Zone treaty to surrender sovereignty to Panama, a nation which owes its existence to the United States. The United States performed all its responsibilities under the treaty, building and guarding the canal, and developing and maintaining the Canal Zone, which was bought with American tax dollars.
>
> The Communists have long wanted the United States out of the canal. When Fidel Castro took over in Cuba, almost his first

act was to launch an expedition against the canal, which proved abortive.

Now the United States is giving up on its own . . .[8]

The United States, which had created Panama out of whole cloth, sustained it financially, and obtained an unbreakable lease, thus drifted from one act of "conciliation" to another. Having first compromised on the question of the flags, we indicated our vulnerability to calculated pressure. When that pressure was accordingly applied, we agreed to cashier the treaty and give Panama sovereignty over the Canal.

Even this, however, has not proved enough for certain Liberal spokesmen. Sen. J. William Fulbright, for one, suggests we go even further. With characteristic lucidity, Fulbright says that "surely, in a confrontation so unequal, it is not unreasonable to expect the United States to go a little further than half-way in the search for a fair settlement."[9] The 1903 treaty, Fulbright says, is not "sacred," and ought to be revised; we are unjust to the Panamanians, not paying them enough, treating them as a colony. Then, Fulbright offers this statement:

"The Soviet Union is of course one of the users of the Panama Canal, albeit a minor one, and this fact suggests an 'unthinkable thought': the possibility of Soviet participation in a consortium constituted to build and operate a new Central American canal. I am not advocating Soviet participation, but neither do I think it must be ruled out as 'unthinkable.' "[10]

Stating his reasons for this proposal, Fulbright asks: "Is there not something to be gained for world peace from bringing a difficult and dangerous nation into one more enterprise in which co-operation in the performance of practical tasks would be permitted to do its eroding work on the ideological passions that divide us?"[11] Is there not something to be gained for world peace, that is, by dealing America's chief enemy in on the management of a defense and transportation link essential to our survival?

2. *British Guiana**

Among various Latin American statesmen who have been looked upon with favor by the U.S. government is Cheddi Jagan of British Guiana. In 1961, Jagan received a sizeable and crucial injection of "aid" money approved by U.S. authorities and journeyed to the United States, where he was politely received by President Kennedy as a guest at the White House. In 1962 and 1963, he was welcomed to our shores again.

Precisely at the time of Jagan's 1963 visit, the government of British Guiana was seizing and jailing leaders of a small opposition party whose leaders claimed to have evidence that Jagan's political faction, the People's Progressive Party, "had received more than 127,000 West Indies dollars from the Soviet government . . . " Such a charge, in Jagan's British Guiana, was a matter of "sedition." Jagan's wife Janet, the Home Affairs Minister of the government, said documents assertedly backing up the charge were "forged."[12]

Mrs. Jagan's own credentials are not, however, of the best. She is the former Janet Rosenberg of Chicago, a former Communist functionary. A British Commission looking into the history of the Jagans reported that she "was a member of the Young Communist League in the United States before 1943."[13] Senator Dodd said she had been described as "the director of the Communist terror apparatus in British Guiana."[14]

As for Jagan himself, the House Committee on Un-American Activities reported:

* Now Guyana

. . . an official British Commission of Inquiry into the February [1962] disturbances in British Guiana found that some of the opposition to Dr. Jagan and his local government was motivated by the belief that his local government policies were "leading the country toward Communism." The Royal Commission observed that Dr. Jagan had evaded answering its questions as to whether he was a Communist. The Commission concluded: "There is very little doubt that many of his speeches and some of his deeds gave rise to the apprehension that despite his evasions and profession to the contrary, he was acting as a Communist." The Royal Commission quoted statements made by Dr. Jagan . . . showing that the British Guiana Premier was an admitted Marxist who had publicly declared that "Communism is winning throughout the world—it will win everywhere."[15]

The questions asked of Jagan, and his answers, were most revealing:

Dr. Jagan: "I believe the tenets of Communism to mean: From each according to his ability, and to each according to his need. And I believe that represents the Communist belief, and I accept it."

Question: "Dr. Jagan, you have a clear idea of the tenets of Communism. Do you accept these tenets of Communism?" Dr. Jagan: "I do."

Question: "Then Dr. Jagan, according to your own acceptance of these tenets, you are a Communist?" Dr. Jagan: "I am a Communist, in accordance with my own views of Communism."

Question: "Are you an admirer of Fidel Castro?" Dr. Jagan: "Yes."

Question: "Did you declare him to be the greatest liberator of the 20th Century?" Dr. Jagan: "Yes."

Question: "Are you also an admirer of Nikita Khrushchev?" Dr. Jagan: "Yes."

Jagan also declared : "I have always said that I am a Marxist . . . Now, sir, by saying that I am a Marxist, I could be at one and the same time anti-colonialist, an anti-imperialist, a democrat, a Socialist, a humanist, and a Communist."[16]

The British concluded that "on the evidence as a whole we have no doubt that there was a very powerful Communist influence within the PPP. At the time of the [1963] elections at least six of the party's most prominent leaders, specifically Dr. Jagan . . . [and] Mrs. Jagan . . . accepted unreservedly the 'classical' Communist doctrines of Marx and Lenin; were enthusiastic supporters of the policies and practices of modern Communist movements; and were contemptuous of European social democratic parties, including the British Labor Party."[17]

After Jagan's election in 1961, *The New York Times* chided those who had called him a Communist by saying that "If British Guiana is handled by the United States with some understanding, sophistication, and sympathy, there is every reason to hope it will become a desirable member of the inter-American system."[18]

That commentary prompted Senator Dodd to remark that "Cheddi Jagan talks like a Communist. He behaves like a Communist. He has played a leading role in Communist front organizations. He has consorted with international Communist leaders. He has distributed official Communist literature. He has sided with the Kremlin in every conflict of policy with the free world. He has hailed Communist victories in Cuba and in China and has himself been hailed and supported by the Communist propaganda apparatus."[19]

Despite the mass of evidence on Jagan, the Kennedy regime helped make a sizeable foreign aid grant available to him immediately before the crucial 1961 elections ". . . we fortified Jagan's position," Dodd noted, "by providing him with technical assistance and by approving [a] World Bank loan of $1¼ million, which was personally signed for by Jagan himself. I have been told by Americans who were in British Guiana at the time that, had we wanted to help Jagan win, we could have taken no more effective measure than the granting of this loan in the weeks immediately preceding the election. Indeed, when we consider that Jagan won by only a few seats, I do not think it is too much to suggest that this loan made the difference between victory and defeat for the forces of Communism in British Guiana."[20] And, if the aid stipend served to strengthen Jagan's hand, we can only imagine the impact of his 1961 role as honored guest of the American President.*

Arthur Schlesinger Jr. describes the 1961 meeting between Jagan and Kennedy, in which the historian was a participant, at an uneasy but basically friendly gathering. Kennedy, Schlesinger says, was somewhat troubled by Jagan's refusal to say anything critical of the Soviet Union, but stressed to Jagan that America did not object to his pursuing a Marxist course, trading with Moscow, or nationalizing our property in British Guiana so long as he did not become an overt member of the Soviet bloc. When Jagan expressed his admiration for flaming left-wing Socialist Aneurin Bevan of England, Schlesinger says, "we all responded agreeably to this, citing Bevan's faith in personal freedom and recalling his belief that the struggle of the future would be between democratic socialism and capitalism." Schlesinger records that he himself entered a demurrer to some Jagan enthusiams for American pro-Communists, and concludes that Jagan "had that kind of deep pro-Communist emotion which only sustained experience with Communism could cure."[21]

In late 1964 Jagan's party suffered a defeat at the hands of an anti-Communist coalition and the premiership passed

* Jagan's stay at the White House also proved useful to Leo Huberman, self-styled "independent Marxist-Socialist" who headed the "Friends of British Guiana" in the United States. In a session with the House Committee on Un-American Activities in which he repeatedly invoked the Fifth Amendment, Huberman was able to counter the assertion that Jagan had "himself conceded that he is a Communist" with the retort that "he was a guest at the White House."

from his hands. That result owed little, however, to the public prestige conferred on him by our government, and it leaves him as a factor still to be reckoned with in Latin politics.

3. *Indonesia*

Yet another professed "neutralist" and *de facto* pro-Communist who has been gifted with large sums by our government is Achmed Sukarno of Indonesia.

In his effort to drive the Dutch from the East Indies, Sukarno was the beneficiary of U.S. pressures against Netherlands "colonialism"—much as Lumumba was the beneficiary of U.S. pressures against Belgian "colonialism." Since the mid-1950s, Sukarno has collaborated with the Communists, and the Partai Komunis Indonesia (PKI) has often been cited as the largest Communist Party outside the Iron Curtain. In his internal affairs, Sukarno was a thoroughgoing despot, presiding over a hand-picked parliament and congress in the name of "guided democracy." He has sought to crush anti-Communist, Christian elements of resistance in the Spice Islands and elsewhere in his ocean kingdom.

William R. Kintner and Joseph Kornfeder comment:

> President Sukarno's program of "guided democracy" has been an encouragement to leftist groups who saw in it a reflection of Soviet thinking. In his appointed cabinet of June, 1960, the PKI had the largest representation of any group, and PKI leaders Aidit and Njoto (both Politburo members) were appointed members of the Supreme Advisory Council. Sakirman (also a Politburo member) was appointed a member of the National Planning Council, as was Wikana (a Central Committee member). The program of the PKI has evidently been to make the Indonesian economy so dependent on Soviet-bloc aid that it cannot afford to alienate the Communists.[22]

While pursuing this course, the Sukarno-PKI axis was able to rely on United States aid, with no notable deterrent effect on Indonesia's pro-Communist tendencies. The "aid," it might be added, has been moral and military as well as economic. Consider the Indonesian aggression against Netherlands New Guinea, spurred on by the world Communist movement and agitated in particular by the PKI. Should New Guinea fall into Communist hands, the Bolshevization of the Pacific would become virtually complete: the process begun in China, and extended in Laos and Viet Nam, would conclude with the final Communist onslaught against Australia. Senator Dodd, in a 1962 memorandum on this subject, recalled the words of an Australian official: "We see the tide of Asian Communism creeping down toward us, and we know that if it succeeds in conquering Southeast Asia and Indonesia, we are doomed":

> In a future that may lie only several decades ahead . . . Indonesia and New Guinea might be used as springboards for an Asian-Communist invasion of Australia. But long before this comes about, . . . the entire strategic position of the Free World would be gravely compromised if the forces of world Communism held control of the whole Pacific littoral, from the Bering Straits to Singapore, and of the southern island chain from Sumatra to New Guinea. For if this ever came to pass, the Communists would, in effect, have cut the world in half.[23]

Indonesian control of West New Guinea—to which Sukarno had no claim in law, religion, or ethnic association—would thus be gravely damaging to the hopes of the Free World. Instead of backing our Dutch allies against the pro-Communist Sukarno, however, our government focused its pressures on the Netherlands. The Dutch were advised to yield to Sukarno, and when they sought to prepare themselves against a threatened invasion, were denied use of American bases. Senator Dodd commented:

Many people have been disturbed by the fact that we have taken no action and made no protests when the Indonesian government has flouted the United Nations charter by its repeated public announcements that it planned to take West New Guinea by force, if it were not ceded peacefully.

They have been even more disturbed by the fact that when our Dutch NATO allies sought to transport troops to New Guinea in order to defend a non-self-governing territory of which they are recognized as the legal administrators by the U. N., against a threatened invasion in violation of the U. N. charter, we reacted to this situation by denying our NATO allies the right to land and refuel their transport planes at American Pacific bases.

But they have been most disturbed by the persistent reports that we are endeavoring to persuade, or perhaps I should say, to pressure our Dutch NATO allies to cede West New Guinea to Indonesia without a fight. . . . The Washington *Star* carried an AP story which spoke of a reported United Nations proposal that the administration of West New Guinea be switched from Dutch to Indonesian control over a two-year period. According to this story, the reported proposal met with stiff opposition from The Hague, which still insists that self-determination under U. N. auspices is the only proper way to dispose of the fate of the Papuan people.[24]

Arthur Krock of *The New York Times* summed up the New Frontier's performance: ". . . in the role of intermediary between Indonesia, the military aggressor in West New Guinea, and the Netherlands, administrator of the territory, the Kennedy administration has endorsed a 'solution' which guarantees the triumph of the aggressor. . . . The State Department has . . . voiced gratification for Sukarno's agreement to wait a little longer to gobble up West New Guinea, and for the agreement of the Dutch to negotiate the issue on the principle of Washington's proposed solution. But neither the so-called 'concession' nor the guarantees to the Papuans will do more than delay the eventual triumph of the aggressor, Indonesia, assisted by the foreign policy of the United States."[25]

In 1965 the Communists moved to seize total power in Indonesia. Sukarno, beneficiary of our long solicitude, refused to condemn the Communist effort at take-over, and according to numerous reports sided with the pro-Peking faction in its aspirations for *coup d'etat.*

Earlier in the year, Sukarno had taken a number of steps strengthening the Peking Communists' hand, including an indoctrination program for civil servants under the supervision of a PKI supporter, suppression of an important anti-Communist political party, and banning of a Moscow-oriented rather than Peking-oriented group of Communists. On the night of September 30, the pro-Peking Reds made their bid for power, provoking a strong counterattack from army elements under General Nasution. In the aftermath, Sukarno urged leniency toward the Communists, refused to disown the leaders who had attempted the coup, and moved to diminish the influence of General Nasution. "The conviction is gaining ground," wrote Richard D. Benson in *National Review,* "that . . . Sukarno himself was in on the Communist plot."[26]

4. *Algeria*

While still a member of the United States Senate, John F. Kennedy made his principal bid as an authority on world affairs with a speech on Algeria which demanded, in effect, that the French clear out.

That speech was a true index to the policy followed by the New Frontier when Kennedy assumed the presidency. With the French ousted, the OAS quashed, and Ben Bella in power, the new regime came high up on the Kennedy administration's list of most-favored nations.

In 1962, when Charles de Gaulle turned Algeria over to

Ben Bella, the reaction in the Communist world was electric: "History does not stop with the defeat of just a part of the imperalist system," said radio Havana; "the victory of the Algerian people is also a direct defeat for U.S. imperalism." Similar words of exultation proceeded from Moscow, Peking, Prague, Pyongyang, and East Berlin.

These cries of Bolshevik felicity were soon justified by events. In 1963, Ben Bella journeyed to Cuba, where he proclaimed his ties of friendship with Fidel Castro. In 1964, it was reported the Algerians had installed a Soviet-built missile complex near the Tunisian frontier, had given the Soviets a submarine base, and were flying Soviet MIGs. Ben Bella demanded that the United States pull out of its Guantanamo base in Cuba, get out of South Viet Nam, recognize Red China, etc. Algerian terrorists were sent to Cuba to train young Cubans in guerrilla warfare.

Former State Department officer Ray Colby commented in *U.S. News and World Report* that "Algeria is now beyond question the newest Soviet satellite and will spearhead the Red drive into Africa." The Communist take-over there, Colby said, "was a *fait accompli,* quietly and skillfully executed by the Communists, although it is not certain that we realize what has happened."[27]

Yet Ben Bella, too, received large quantities of American aid, totalling, as of June 30, 1964, some $149 million. In 1963, after Ben Bella visited America and was received (like Jagan and Paz) at the White House, he journeyed directly to Cuba where he was praised by Fidel Castro and extended his own praises in return. Following this episode, Foreign Aid administrator David Bell was questioned on Capitol Hill by Rep. H. R. Gross:

Gross: "Do I understand that we are going to give more aid to Ben Bella?"

Bell: "Yes. We are preparing a substantial aid program for Algeria."

Gross: "How in the world can you justify giving aid to that kind of government? Ben Bella is another Castro. He came to this country and then went directly to Cuba and pledges his support for that Communist regime. Now Castro is going to Algeria, and both are training guerrillas for the invasion of Portuguese Angola and Latin America. Why are we giving a single thin dime to Algeria under the circumstances?"

Bell: "As far as the basic political relationship between the U.S. and Algeria is concerned, I must say I am not too fully informed. Ben Bella is seeking progress for the people of his country and we are helping him to achieve that with our aid."[28]

In 1965, Ben Bella was apparently consumed, Jacobin fashion, by the revolutionary forces he had himself unleashed. Algeria, the recipient of generous quantities of U.S. tax money, continued to hew to the pro-Soviet line.

5. *Egypt*

American policy toward the government of Gamal Abdel Nasser in Egypt provides one of the few instances in which there has been a concerted effort in Congress to get our odd diplomacy turned around. Faced with that opposition, the executive establishment has flexed its muscles, fought for aid to Nasser, and won.

Up through June 30, 1964, the United States had extended to Nasser's United Arab Republic some $952 million in aid—supposedly to bring him closer to the Western orbit. While thus accepting plentiful quantities of American tax money, Nasser steered a course obviously plotted in Moscow.

In 1963, a Senate Government Operations subcommittee came to these conclusions:

> More than any other single individual, Nasser has been responsible for keeping the political cauldron boiling furiously in the strife-torn Middle East. For more than eleven years he has

poured oil on whatever brushfire breaks out there, seeking his own and Egypt's aggrandizement, in that order.

And he is doing that with the assistance of the U.S., which still continues to prop him up, and whenever he gets over his head, to bail him out.

The U.S. is pouring hundreds of millions in aid dollars into Egypt, while Egypt is pouring them out in foreign war, and in preaching subversion and violence in other Middle Eastern countries. It can rightly be said that U.S. dollars are enabling Egypt to wage war in Yemen, to foment trouble in Jordan and Saudi Arabia, and to attack Israel just as surely as though they were being spent directly for that purpose.

In addition, U.S. aid dollars are being used to build a police state with the government owning and operating everything through nationalization of industries and business. U.S. aid dollars are being used to prove that such totally socialist type police states can work economically.[29]

As examples of American aid money winding its way through Nasser into the camp of America's enemies, reporters Robert S. Allen and Paul Scott cite our government's moves to replenish the UAR treasury when it was emptied through the purchase of Soviet arms. An estimated two-thirds of Egypt's cotton crop, the reporters note in a June, 1964 dispatch, "went to the Soviet bloc in payment for tanks, planes, rockets, naval vessels and other armaments Nasser is furiously piling up. . . . As a direct consequence of the Egyptian dictator's sinister weapons build-up and costly military intervention in Yemen, his hard currency reserves have sunk from $277 million in 1957 to a low of $15 million this year. To help him bolster these crucial reserves, the State Department early this month again went to bat for Nasser . . . the International Monetary Fund, under State Department insistence, ladled out a $40 million loan to Nasser at one per cent interest. The Treasury and other Monetary Fund members sharply objected, but the State Department had its way."[30]

Nasser meanwhile was holding the neighboring state of

Yemen by force, airlifting Soviet-supplied arms to the pro-Communist rebels in the Congo, and openly attacking the United States. This continued show of hostility aroused a number of congressmen in both parties to take punitive action, and on January 26, 1965, the U.S. House of Representatives voted, 204-177, to end all "food for peace" aid to Nasser. The Johnson administration thereupon dug in and, working through Vice-President Humphrey and Senator Fulbright, managed to reverse the situation in the Senate. Result: In June, 1965, the Johnson regime authorized yet another $37 million in aid for Nasser.

Nasser has used our money to facilitate his trade with the Communist bloc and to shore up his Mideast aggressions. "The figures are clear," charged Sen. Ernest Gruening (D-Alaska) "that wheat sold to Egypt, for its own currency which remains there, has been utilized in violation of public law 480 . . . The result is that Nasser has greatly improved his foreign exchange position at the expense of that of the U.S., and to finance his incessant aggressions . . . Wheat sold to Egypt has not been used to increase the food supply of the people of that country, but rather to free rice, which otherwise would be consumed within Egypt, for sale and barter to Cuba, Russia, Red China, East Germany, Bulgaria, and Indonesia. Egypt's violation of its written agreement with the U.S. under public law 480 enabled Nasser to ship more than 60,000 metric tons of rice to Cuba in 1964."[31]

Rep. Otto Passman (D-La.) questioned Foreign Aid administrator David Bell about the use of our aid in support of Egypt's occupation of Yemen, where some 60,000 Egyptian troops had overturned the legally-constituted government:

Bell: "In the case of Egypt it is not our intention by economic or military aid to support a military force for aggressive purposes."

Passman: "Have they ever used their military forces for aggression?"

Bell: "It depends on how you describe their action in Yemen."

Passman: "How do you describe it?"

Bell: "The way I believe the Secretary of State would describe it, as a situation where the Egyptians sent forces in support of one side of an internal dispute."[32]

★★ 29. *The Double Standard*

1. *Ghana*

THE AFRICAN STATE of Ghana came forcibly to American attention in 1964 when two professors from the United States were fired from the state-run university of the Gold Coast and a mob laid siege to the U.S. embassy.

The outlook over in Ghana was suggested by the editor of the government-controlled newspaper in Accra during the demonstration at the embassy. "We are fed up with your imperialist American dollars," he intoned. "We will massacre you. You killed President Kennedy. American imperialism is a filthy civilization."[1]

That outburst occurred despite the fact that Ghana had been a favored recipient of American largesse. Upwards of $400 million had been funneled to the regime of Kwame Nkrumah, although the exact figures as recited by our aid officials are somewhat confused. The largest single part of this outlay has been for the Volta River project, a power-producing dam to be used in the manufacture of aluminum (in competition with American producers already hampered by a world surplus). An estimated $133 million was obligated for this enterprise.

"In granting this assistance to Ghana," Senator Dodd noted, "Congress and the American people have been led to believe that Nkrumah, although he frequently sides with Moscow, is not a Moscow Communist and that Ghana is not a Communist state."[2] Dodd charged that, on the contrary, "Kwame Nkrumah's Ghana had become the first Soviet satellite in Africa, just as Cuba is the first Soviet satellite in the Americas."[3]

Dodd's evidence included the testimony of a scholarly exile from Ghana, Professor Kofi Abrefa Busia, former faculty member at the University of the Gold Coast; innumerable articles from the Ghanaian press (strictly controlled by the Nkrumah government) praising Moscow and Peking; similar articles from the Communist press praising Nkrumah; and a report by former Ghanaian trade unionist Alex Hammah citing chapter and verse to establish that "Ghana is going Communist."[4] Hammah named a dozen Communists high up in the Nkrumah administration, and pinpointed the presence of Russians in the country (150 Russians, he said, were on the staff of the Ghana airways).

Senator Dodd, summarizing this and other evidence about developments in Ghana, made the following points:

1. Nkrumah himself, in his own autobiography published on the eve of Ghana's independence in 1957, boasts of the fact that he associated with American Communists when he was a student in this country 25 years ago.

2. He boasts of the fact that he decided even then that the philosophy of Karl Marx and Lenin was 'capable of solving' his 'problems.'

3. He boasts of the fact that he had the same kind of Communist associations in Great Britain. It was in Great Britain where he founded a secret organization known as 'The Circle,' composed of 'persons who are trained and engaged in political revolution as a profession,' to serve as the 'vanguard' for the 'creation and maintenance of the Union of African Socialist Republics.'

4. When Nkrumah became Ghana's Prime Minister, he invited American and British Communists to celebrate his inauguration and others to serve under him thereafter. These included a member of Elizabeth Bentley's Red underground group of document thieves in the United States. They also included the Britisher, Alan Nunn May, who pleaded guilty to selling his country's atomic secrets to the Soviet Union for $700 and a few bottles of whiskey.

5. Nkrumah has pushed Ghana closer and closer and more and more brazenly into the Communist orbit ever since he achieved power. In 1962 the Kremlin awarded him the Lenin 'Peace' Prize, which has caused his own newspaper to acclaim him as the 'Lenin of Africa.'

6. Nkrumah has steadily been reducing the number of moderates in his entourage and replacing them with known pro-Communists and extremists.[5]

America's "obstinate refusal to accept the facts about Nkrumah's Ghana," Dodd concluded, "is just as difficult to understand as our failure to face up to the facts about Castro."

In early 1966, Nkrumah was deposed by a military coup—an event which brought the people of Ghana into the streets cheering. At the time of his overthrow Nkrumah was paying a series of cordial visits to Communist capitals in the East. How much sooner he might have fallen had he not been sustained by massive injections of American aid is to a topic for melancholy speculation.

The successor regime revealed, in June, 1966, that it had uncovered some 30,000 documents showing that Nkrumah had organized a vast spy network and school for assassins, set up and run by European Communists, and a guerrilla training camp superintended by agents from Communist China. Purpose of this enterprise, the new government said, "was to undermine and, if necessary, overthrow any African leader unsympathetic to Nkrumah's vision of Africa's future."[6]

2. *Zanzibar*

In January, 1964, a Castro-style revolution occurred in the small island state of Zanzibar, off the East Coast of Africa. In charge of the insurrection was one John Okello, a military type of uncertain nationality who called himself "Field Marshal" and who came to Zanzibar fresh from a Castroite "freedom fighter's" camp. Okello declared Zanzibar a "people's republic," said he agreed with Khrushchev that "capitalism, colonialism, and imperialism should be buried," and set about creating a dictatorship.[7]

The temper of the new government was described by African authority Elspeth Huxley as follows: "A rigid censorship was clamped down, newspaper correspondents turned out and the European residents, all unharmed, turned their eyes to the wall. A lot of Arabs were murdered and a good many people disappeared."[8]

As for the political complexion of the regime, a "Moscow man," Kassim Hanga, was the new prime minister—"his wife is an American Negro who has worked with Professor Potehkin in Moscow"—while "Peking's champion, Abdul Rahman Mohamud Babu, is Minister for External Affairs." The Zanzibar government, Miss Huxley said, "*vis à vis* the Cold War, has clearly changed sides."[9]

Among other symptoms of side-changing, reminiscent of contemporary outbursts in Ghana, was a bitter assault on the U.S. consulate in Zanzibar, the rounding up of American diplomats at gunpoint, and the ouster of American personnel. Under the headline, "Zanzibar Regime Seizes U.S. Consul at Gunpoint," *The New York Times* reported that "Frederick P. Picard 3d, U.S. Consul, was marched out of a Zanzibar hotel to an undetermined place tonight with a gun at his back."[10]

Zanzibar had been ruled for centuries by an Arab minority under British auspices, and the withdrawal of British power led, as Miss Huxley notes, to violent attacks on the Arabs. Yet these acts of terrorism inspired, strangely enough, no protest from the self-anointed leader of the Arab world, Nasser. "At least," notes Victor Lasky, "he said nothing publicly. What he did do, however, was quickly recognize the new Zanzibar regime."

Zanzibar's subsequent federation with Tanganyika, allegedly muting the Communist overtones of the revolt, looks somewhat different in view of the techniques by which this association was achieved. Former Communist and new Zanzibar Foreign Secretary Abdul Rahman Mohamed ("Babu") turned up in Dar-es-Salaam, the Tanganyikan capital, with Okello, a week after the revolution. "It might have been just a coincidence," Lasky writes, "but at midnight that night 1,600 enlisted men of the Tanganyika rifles—most of the standing Army—arrested their British officers."[11] Subsequent to this uprising, quelled by the British, came the federation, and a new leftward drift for Tanganyikan policy. In Zanzibar itself, the Castroites remained firmly in control. In January 1965, Tanganyika evicted two American diplomats on charges of subversive activities.

Zanzibar, Lasky concludes, "had become a convenient base for the Communist infiltration of Tanganyika. Soviet and Chinese arms poured into the mainland. Soviet and Chinese instructors trained the raw Tanzanian army. And Soviet and Chinese specialists trained guerrillas along Tanzania's borders to attack the neighboring Portuguese province of Mozambique."[12]

In view of all this, imagine the surprise of editorial writer Richard Wheeler of the *Oakland Tribune* when he discovered, in the summer of 1964, that U.S. aid was being funneled to this blatantly pro-Communist regime, which had begun by avowing its hostility to America and inflicting humiliation on U.S. diplomats.

"Buried deep in a press release from the Agency for International Development," Wheeler wrote, "was an obscure, brief item about four grants, totalling $925,000 to the United Republic of Tanganyika and Zanzibar . . . According to the release, 'film, photographic, audio-visual aids, projection and graphic equipment and supplies costing up to $40,000 will be purchased in the U.S. to promote community development activity.' The release does not explain what 'community development activity' means, but the type of equipment would indicate that it will be used for propaganda. In short, it appears that the U.S. government may be supplying the educational tools with which Zanzibar Communists will 'educate' their peoples."[13]

3. *South Africa*

While the United States thus lends aid and comfort to African regimes which are pro-Communist and harshly authoritarian, there are *some* governments in Africa which excite official hostility in Washington. These are not Communist governments like the Soviet Union or Cuba, pro-Communist regimes like Algeria or British Guiana, or one-party dictatorships like Ghana or Indonesia. They are instead the Western-oriented, anti-Communist regimes of South Africa, Rhodesia, and Portuguese Angola.

America's hostility toward these governments has been evident chiefly in the United Nations. Although the U.N. will not rebuke Communist aggression in Viet Nam or Cuba or Hungary, it *will* attack the "colonialist" policies of these anti-Communist governments. And America has, all too quiescently, gone along.

The three states under discussion stand charged with

"colonialism." But since the shape of this crime is in each case quite particular and distinctive, we shall consider them separately, beginning with South Africa.

South Africa is the wealthiest, most advanced, and militarily the strongest nation in Africa. It is ruled by the "Afrikaners," descendants of the Europeans of Dutch extraction who have lived in South Africa for more than 300 years.

The white inhabitants of South Africa are depicted as interlopers who have subjugated the native Bantu population. The fact is that the Afrikaners have quite as much claim to the land as do the Bantus, since both of them entered the territory at about the same time. As to the relative claims of the two groups to the civilization that has been constructed on the land, no one would deny that it has been the Afrikaners who have built the cities, developed the wealth, and brought about its industrialization and prosperity.

The *tu quoque* of South African official F. W. Waring, therefore, seems to the point. "The record of the Europeans in South Africa," he notes, "compares more than favorably with that of Europeans who in the 18th and 19th centuries advanced into other countries then occupied by non-whites. No one speaks of 'tolerating' the presence in the United States of white Americans, in Canada of white Canadians, in Australia of white Australians or in New Zealand of white New Zealanders."[14]

In point of fact, the Afrikaners' claim to rule in South Africa is quite as valid as the white American's claim to rule in the United States, or as the claim of various other ascendant groups that have taken charge in other countries, including those in Africa.

As former British Prime Minister Harold Macmillan has said, "the nationalism of the whites of South Africa is the first in point of time of the African nationalisms." Paul Giniewski observes that "the white South Africans have as legitimate a claim to the territory they occupy as the Ghanaians or Congolese to theirs."[15]

The Afro-Asian bloc in the United Nations, however, believes otherwise. It insists that the white Afrikaner regime in Pretoria is intolerable and must be ousted. Point of departure for this insistence is South Africa's policy of "apartheid" and "separate development" for the races, which holds present political power in the hands of the Afrikaners while envisioning creation of a separate state for the Bantu population in the Transkei. Important elements in America, including several with key influence in our government, agree with the Afro-Asians.

When the Afro-Asian bloc in the U.N. pressed for an international arms embargo against South Africa in August, 1963, American Ambassador Adlai Stevenson took a leading role, declaring that "Just as my country is determined to wipe out discrimination in our society, it will support efforts to bring about a change in South Africa." And: "We continue to believe that this matter is of proper and legitimate concern to the United Nations. We have often stated our belief that the Assembly can properly consider questions of racial discrimination and other violations of human rights where they are a member's official policy."[16]

That the South African government's policy is authoritarian may be granted—although such close students of the matter as Giniewski believe the "separate development" policy offers the best possible hope for both black and white in South Africa. Yet it is certainly *not* as despotic as was, say, Nkrumah's one-party monolith in Ghana, where no opposition to the government was allowed at all, or the politics of Algeria or Indonesia. Yet the United States and the United Nations, for some reason, have nothing to say about these dictatorships while they excoriate South Africa.

Even more to the point, the Soviet Union, Cuba and the other Communist regimes which sit in the United Nations (casting votes against South Africa) are among the most brutal, grinding tyrannies known to history, having among them routinely murdered, tortured and imprisoned many millions of people. Yet the Afro-Asian bloc, and Liberals in the American government, are able to look quite complacently on these regimes. It is for anti-Communist South Africa that their spleen is reserved.

One interesting measure of conditions in South Africa is immigration. If South Africa were the world's worst despotism, and the nativist regimes were enlightened, one would imagine the African populace would flee Henrik Verwoerd's nation into the embrace of such as Nkrumah. The actual population movement, however, is just the other way around. This fact was brought out in 1966 hearings on South Africa by the House Foreign Affairs Committee—hearings aimed, as it happened, at discrediting South Africa and stirring stronger U.S. action against the Verwoerd regime.

The relevant testimony was given by one Kenneth Robinson of the United Automobile Workers, like most witnesses profoundly hostile to South Africa. Robinson testified that "despite the disparity . . . between white, colored and black workers in South African industry . . . there is little question but what the economic standards compared to the rest of Africa are high . . . It is not surprising, when you consider the poverty level that exists in most of the new nations of Africa, those bordering nations. . . . that there are workers who are moving into South Africa for jobs, because they find that there is a greater economic return to them there than perhaps in their own country."[17]

There are many different ways of voting in this world, and it is unfortunate that, throughout Africa, the free ballot as we know it in America does not prevail. But there still remains the privilege of "voting with your feet," and it appears that that privilege is being exerted in favor of, rather than against, South Africa.

Finally, the U.N. Charter says, Article II, Chapter I: "Nothing contained in the present charter shall authorize the United Nations to intervene in matters which are essentially within the domestic jurisdiction of any state or shall require the members to submit such matters to settlement under the present charter . . ."[18] The U.N.'s actions against South Africa, and Ambassador Stevenson's remarks in support of them, are in direct violation of that provision.

4. *Angola*

There is a momentum to defeat as there is to so many other human experiences. Each Communist and pro-Communist victory makes the next that much easier. The fall of China leads to the assault on Laos, the "neutralization" of Laos to increased pressure on Viet Nam, etc. The same sort of baleful chain reaction has been under way in Africa. Our attempted extirpation of Tshombe and support for pro-Communists in places like Algeria, Egypt, Ghana and Zanzibar has made Marxist efforts in Africa that much simpler. The 1962 "neutralization" of the Congo, in fact, contributed directly to efforts to subvert the neighboring state of Portuguese Angola.

Despite the fact that the Adoula regime in Leopoldville was advertised as "friendly to the West," it showed notable partiality for a native terrorist named Holden Roberto, who has made it his task to wreak murder and destruction in Angola until the Portuguese are forced to clear out. In 1962, Roberto maintained headquarters in Leopoldville, the Congo, and when he wanted to launch a guerrilla raid into Angola, did so at his pleasure and then retired to his U.S.-supported base of operations.

Lloyd Garrison of *The New York Times* reported that "the National Front for the Liberation of Angola announced today that it had established a military training camp for Angolan rebels in Congolese territory. The announcement said it had been 'generously donated' by the Central Government of Premier Cyrille Adoula. . . .

"The training camp in the Congo will be supervised by 24

Angolans who recently returned from Tunisia after more than six months of training by the Algerian nationalist army . . .

"The establishment of the base also has important political consequences. It is viewed as adding to the prestige of Holden Roberto's exile government. . . ."[19]

In other words, a notorious band of terrorists trained by the Marxists in Algeria, and commanded by the Marxist Roberto, achieved privileged sanctuary on soil made safe for them by American treasure, and were thus enabled to wage aggression with relative impunity against an American ally.

The United States government—which turned aside Tshombe and Madame Nhu—has welcomed Roberto to our shores, just as it welcomed Jagan, and Ben Bella, and Paz Estenssoro. We have joined with the Soviet Union in the United Nations to vote against Portugual in Angola, backing a proposed investigation of Portuguese internal practices and an imposition of trade barriers against Angola. We have thus clearly taken sides against the Portuguese authorities, and in favor of Roberto. Jacqueline Hallowell, writing for the New Bedford Mass., *Standard-Times,* discusses the activities and affiliations of our new ally this way:

It is a war for black supremacy. Holden Roberto, the self-appointed leader of the terrorist movement, who maintains his headquarters in Leopoldville in the Congo Republic to the north, rejects any thought of compromise. In press conferences he repeatedly said that it is "too late" for reforms and declared for nothing less than complete and immediate "independence."

The terrorists launched their race war in surprise attacks against the settlers in northern Angola March 15, 1961. Shouting "mata branco" (kill the whites), they butchered and maimed in one day more than 1,000 white and mulatto men, women and children—and any friendly blacks who got in the way. Severe reprisals by the whites followed.

The war is openly supported by Ghana, Guinea, and other

new African states to the north, accompanied by the applause of the Communist nations and the Afro-Asian bloc in the United Nations.[20]

That the uprising was not the result of spontaneous "nationalism," but of Roberto's agitation, is supported by none other than Robert H. Estabrook of the Liberal *Washington Post.* "There is much evidence," Estabrook wrote after a 1961 trip to Angola, "that the terrorism starting March 15 had been organized outside Angola, by the Union of the People of Angola, headed by Holden Roberto, an expatriate now living in Leopoldville." Previous uprisings, Estabrook added, had been "attributed to the Popular Movement for the Liberation of Angola (MPLA), headed by Mario de Andrade, another expatriate who at that time had his headquarters in Conakry, Guinea. Andrade is thought—and by foreign observers as well as Portuguese officials—to have Communist connections and support."[21]

After a similar trip to Angola, Brig. Gen. Frank Howley, Vice President of New York University, commented: "The current uprising against Portugal in Angola is a part of a Communist conspiracy to gain control of the rich African province."[22] And Sir Alec Douglas-Home, then Foreign Secretary of Britain, charged that "the responsibility for the breakdown of law and order must be laid at the door of international Communism."[23]

Small wonder that, reviewing the administration's record of support for Roberto, Prime Minister Salazar of Portugal should observe: "The United States seems to be less favorable to an ally than to a neutral or an enemy and to follow political conveniences of the moment rather than an ideal."[24]

In that gloomy reflection, Senor Salazar joins the sadder but wiser ranks of Chiang Kai-shek, Boun Oum, Madame Nhu, Moise Tshombe, and the exile leaders of Cuba, who have learned the hard way that, in the IPR strategy of the

American State Department, there is small comfort for anti-Communists.

5. *Rhodesia*

The double standard of morality that pervades the mind of American Liberalism surfaced once more in the 1965 dispute over Rhodesia.

By a vote of 108 to 2, the U.N. called on Great Britain to deny Rhodesia its independence because the government there was controlled by the white population and not by the African majority. When Rhodesian prime minister Ian Smith broke with England, the U.N. gathered to vote economic and other sanctions against the alleged autocrats holding forth in Salisbury.

The U.N. moves against Rhodesia were reportedly launched on the initiative of Ghana. Ghana thus could take credit for no less than three such actions by the U.N., since it also played a leading role in U.N. condemnations of Portugal and South Africa back in 1962.

These actions were enthusiastically endorsed by American Liberals, who denounced Rhodesia as a dictatorship, acclaimed the Ghana-led U.N. offensive as a blow for liberty, and underlined the whole with repeated press and TV commentary lamenting the plight of Rhodesian Negroes, denied the right to majority rule.

The apparent nobility of the U.N. action dissolves, however, when we consider the prominent role of Ghana, and reflect that five years previously, when Ghana made final its own break with Britain and became an autonomous "republic," no sanctions were voted by the U.N., and no such ringing affirmations of majority rule were offered by the fuglemen of American Liberalism. Yet there was not then, and there was not at the time of the Rhodesian crisis, majority rule in Ghana.

Indeed, Ghana under Kwame Nkrumah was a complete and perfect dictatorship in every respect. The nation obsessed with majority rule in Rhodesia was as perfect a despotism as any found behind the Iron Curtain. It had no free press. It had only one political party, that of Nkrumah. As early as 1957, Nkrumah's party had begun persecuting its political opponents, locking up and deporting those who dared to disagree with the official line. Even before independence, an effort was launched to secure "deification" of Nkrumah. In 1959, the opposition leader, K.A. Busia, was forced to retire, and fled the country. The International Commission of Jurists, reviewing the evidence, concluded that in Ghana "the liberty of the subject is disappearing."[25]

In early 1964, when Ghana was officially declared a one-party state, the *Manchester Guardian* called the election so ordaining a "mixture of ballot rigging which ranged from the brutal to the farcical." The Chicago *Sun-Times* commented: "There was no secret vote, no privilege of casting a vote in solitude. Ghana newspapers specifically warned their readers that the use of a 'secret vote to fool us' was gone. There was a climate of fear that was real and encouraged . . . Ballot boxes to receive votes in opposition to Nkrumah were sealed before the election started."[26]

This was the regime which led the way in demanding sanctions against Rhodesia for violating the canons of majority rule—the regime whose initiatives our own government endorsed. It would be difficult to conjure up a more flagrant instance of hypocrisy in a long and distinguished chronicle of international four-flushing.

Early in 1966, a fact-finding committee from the American-African Affairs Association journeyed to Rhodesia to get a first-hand look at things there. Members of this committee were Rep. John Ashbrook (R-Ohio) Dr. Max Yergan, and journalist Ralph de Toledano. Their conclusions about the situation of the Rhodesian people, black and white alike, contrast notably with conditions in Ghana. Among the findings of this committee were the following:

"It remains a fact that the 14 African members of the Rhodesian parliament . . . do not favor the surrender of the country to the African nationalists . . . For many of the Africans, the fear is not of more white government but of return to that brief period when nationalist terrorists, financed by Peking, Cairo, et al, were allowed to employ the 'persuasion' of bomb and knife. . . ."

Africans in Rhodesia vote for their own representatives on what is called the "B" roll, and, if they pass certain literacy and citizenship qualifications, can vote on the "A" roll for the majority of the parliament. The committee said that "the qualifications for the A roll are higher than those for the B roll. But there are Africans in the A category and white men in the B category."

Additionally, the committee observed: "African education is the single largest expenditure of the Rhodesian government, and it has trebled in the last seven years. . . . African pupil enrollment has tripled in the past 10 years, with approximately 700,000 students now attending school."

Finally, the committee noted that the African tribes are also represented in the government by the Council of Chiefs, who stand in the official structure for the persistent fact of tribal organization. The committee concluded that Rhodesia had "a stable government, geared to the needs of a counry in south central Africa," which "commands the virtually unanimous support of the white population and the respect of a preponderance of Africans."[27]

This is the government that we, in company with the British, set out to destroy, even as we had blinked away the totalitarianism of Ghana and co-operated in Nkrumah's various agitations for "Uhuru."

Part of the discrepancy between the two cases might be traceable to the fact that the government in Rhodesia is white, and the government in Ghana is Negro. Yet the U.N.

has in the past shown itself quite ready to stamp out Negro governments (as in Katanga) when those did not meet its lofty requirements. So the answer must be sought elsewhere.

The distinction seemingly arose from the fact that Ghana was a pro-Soviet "neutralist" while Rhodesia was pro-Western and anti-Communist. And the United Nations, for reasons we have noted, has proved itself greatly concerned about the possible authoritarianism of anti-Communist governments and yawningly indifferent to the iron despotism of Communist and pro-Communist governments.

Equally illustrative of the two-way stretch that characterizes our Cold War policy was the alert response of our government when Britain sought to embargo oil imports to Rhodesia. We have noted the inability of the Johnson administration to halt British trade with Cuba and with Viet Nam; to attempt to stop such things, in the words of Senator Fulbright, is to exhibit delusions of "omnipotence." But when our allies seek to have us stop collaborating with *anti*-Communists, that is an entirely different matter. No sooner had the British made their desires known than we hastened to assure them we would take all feasible steps to comply with their embargo and lent them our planes to help negotiate some attendant difficulties. Where our effort to cut off trade with Communists waging war against us is concerned, we get zero compliance from the British; but where their effort to cut off trade with anti-Communists *not* waging war against us is concerned, the British get maximum compliance from us. The British action was also backed by the Security Council, which voted 10 to 0 to urge Britain "to prevent, by the use of force if necessary," the arrival of oil imports to Rhodesia.

U.S. News and World Report commented: "Britain . . . insists on trading with warmaking North Viet Nam, whose troops are killing Americans. The British also continue to trade with Communist China and Cuba. American urgings to halt such trade are rejected. The whole question of this trade has been ignored by the U.N."[28]

★★ *Part VI:*

TELLING IT THE WAY IT ISN'T

The IPR had . . . a near monopoly on the presentation to the public of material dealing with the Far East . . . the IPR stalwarts constituted for the American reading public during those years a virtual screening and censorship board with respect to books on the Far East and the Pacific.

—Report of the Senate Judiciary Committee

★★ 30. *"I Got My Job Through The New York Times"**

IN A PREVIOUS ESSAY the present writer tried to show, through a survey of American political journalism, how the operations of Liberalism in government and in the public media complemented and reinforced one another.

This pattern of mutual support and interaction is, if anything, even more notable in matters of foreign policy. Themes of discourse and action programs favored by Liberals in government are routinely but powerfully supported by certain newspapers, TV networks, mass magazines, and—perhaps even more decisive in some specialized areas—motion pictures and popular fiction.

* This is the tag line of *The Times'* classified advertising section, first used by *National Review* cartoonist John Kreuttner as a caption for a cartoon about the Cuban reportage of *The Times'* Herbert Matthews and subsequently adapted by William F. Buckley Jr. as the subtitle for an article on the same subject.

Generalizations about the over-all performance of the media in this respect are both difficult and undesirable. Important newspapermen, TV commentators, and magazine journalists have accepted and advanced official illusions on many critical occasions. Others have fought against prevailing misconceptions. Human nature being what it is, some journalists have on certain occasions done one thing and then the other. Since the matter is therefore too complex for inclusive statement, it is best to let the record speak for itself.

1. *The Soviet Union*

Specific instances in which Liberals in the media have seconded the effort of Liberals in government to advance the themes referred to in this volume are legion. One of the earliest examples on which we have solid evidence is the performance of the American press corps in Moscow during the great Russian famine of 1932-33. Moscow's much-heralded collectivization of agriculture had turned out to be a stupendous failure, resulting in the loss of some four million or more lives through starvation. Reports of forced starvation in Russia would have comported, of course, neither with the contemporaneous drive for U.S. recognition nor with the general desire of "progressives" in America and elsewhere to portray the Soviet Union as a splendid experiment in social justice.

The famine wound up not getting itself reported. Eugene Lyons, then a correspondent in Moscow, notes that widespread starvation was everywhere apparent; in certain parts of the USSR, according to eye-witness accounts, the roads "were lined with stiff corpses like so many logs." Most of the Western correspondents had seen pictures of the famine conditions, and "around every railroad station in the capital hundreds of bedraggled refugees were encamped. . . . The famine was accepted as a matter of course in our casual conversation at the hotels and in our homes."[1]

None of this was reported to the West. And—when the facts began to filter out—the Moscow press corps attempted to rationalize or explain them away. "The circumstance that the government barred us from the afflicted regions," Lyons says, "may serve as our formal excuse," but since the same reporters were relaying home daily accounts of asserted Soviet industrial triumphs which they had never seen, they had small reason not to report a famine which was common knowledge. The prohibition against entering the famine areas itself, Lyons observes, should have confirmed any possible doubts about the immensity of the disaster.[2]

The first reliable report of the famine was offered by a British journalist named Gareth Jones, who gathered up the observations of other correspondents together with his own and returned to the West telling of the horror which raged in Russia. Correspondents in Moscow thereupon received inquiries from their papers asking for details; but since the episode coincided with preparations for the hoked-up "spy trial" of some British engineers in Moscow, Lyons says, "the need to remain on friendly terms with the censors at least for the duration of the trial" was deemed a professional necessity:

> Throwing down Jones was as unpleasant a chore as fell to any of us in years of juggling facts to please dictatorial regimes—but throw him down we did, unanimously and in almost identical formulas of equivocation. Poor Gareth Jones must have been the most surprised human being alive when the facts he so painstakingly garnered from our mouths were snowed under by our denials. . . . We admitted enough to soothe our consciences, but in roundabout phrases that damned Jones as a liar.[3]

As word of the famine continued to leak out, some correspondents, notably Walter Duranty of *The New York Times,* undertook to explain it away. "There is no actual starvation or deaths from starvation," Duranty wrote, "but there is widespread mortality from diseases due to malnutrition."[4]

Of similar kidney was a later *Times* story which stated: "Any report of famine in Russia is today an exaggeration or malignant propaganda. The food shortage which has affected almost the whole population in the last year and particularly in the grain-producing provinces—the Ukraine, North Caucasus, the lower Volga region—has, however, caused heavy loss of life."[5]

Such "philological sophistries," Lyons concludes, "served Moscow's purpose of smearing the facts out of recognition and beclouding a situation which, had we reported it simply and clearly, might have worked up enough public opinion abroad to force remedial measures."[6]

This exaggerated tenderness toward Soviet atrocities continued throughout the 1930s—some of it, particularly in Liberal journals like *The Nation* and *The New Republic,* persisting right through the notorious purge trials of 1935-38.[7] With the advent of World War II, of course, the Western press, along with just about everyone else in the allied camp, entered the most notorious phase of its honeymoon with the Soviets, routinely describing them as "our noble allies" and coating their most scarlet sins with a double layer of whitewash. Since this episode has been publicly rehearsed on other occasions, however, and since the exigencies of warfare and of sustaining public support for an ally introduce special mitigating factors, we shall not enter into it here.* Instead, let us inspect another episode in which these mitigating factors did not, for the most part, obtain.

2. *China*

While Western correspondents in Moscow studiously ignored the grosser by-products of the Soviet experiment, various of their colleagues were conceiving an even more fervent

* See William Henry Chamberlin, *America's Second Crusade,* pp 232-257, Eugene Lyons, *The Red Decade,* passim, and pp. 92-127 in particular.

enthusiasm for yet another group of Communists—the Chinese revolutionaries captained by Mao Tse-tung. Beginning in the late 1930s, Western journalists in China filed countless stories portraying Mao and his followers as energetic advocates of reform, a kind of peasants' party, largely independent of the Soviet Union, and—after the war-time amenities toward Chiang Kai-shek were disposed of—depicting the anti-Red Kuomintang as a corrupt force which should give way to the Communists.

This was, as noted, the principal "IPR line" on China and eventually the policy adopted by the U.S. State Department. Through the IPR and its excellent connections in book publishing, book-reviewing, and journalistic enterprise in general, the "agrarian reform" view of Chinese Communism was diligently sold to the American public. A sample may be glimpsed in Mark Gayn's contributions to *Collier's* in 1944 and 1945. Gayn declared, for example, that the situation in China demanded "immediate political reforms, including the democratization of the government, a clear and unequivocal understanding with the Communists, and the end of the North China blockade." Another Gayn piece advocated, "if not a coalition, at least a truce between Chungking and the Communists."[8] During this same period, *Collier's* carried numerous other articles of similar tendency, praising not only the Chinese Communists but the Soviet Union.*

The *Saturday Evening Post,* not to be outdone, countered Gayn with Edgar Snow, author of several best-selling books on the subject of China and the Soviet Union. Snow contributed no less than 45 separate *Post* articles on China, most of them touting the cause of Mao's forces. In a May, 1945 piece Snow told *Post* subscribers that

* In a June, 1945, editorial summary of one of these articles, *Collier's* opined that Russian ideas on various subjects were "not very far from those in Cincinnati." evidently demonstrating that a Red with a knout is no more dangerous than one with a first baseman's mitt.

> For the foreign reader it is somewhat confusing that the Chinese agrarian reform movement is called 'Communism'. . . . Communism in China is a watered down thing today . . . Having built up their armed power long after Moscow had more or less forsaken their struggle as hopeless, the Chinese Red leaders have a strong feeling of independence.[9]

In other dispatches, Snow opined that "there has never been any Communism in China, even in Communist areas," and that the Chinese Reds had "renounced years ago now any intention of establishing Communism in China in the near future."*[10]

Virtually the same line was offered up in *Thunder Out Of China* by Theodore H. White and Annalee Jacoby, who, as their book publisher noted, "constituted the Chungking bureau for *Time* during the war years."[11] White and Jacoby preached the doctrine of Chiang Kai-shek's corruption, the great popularity of the Communists, and the necessity for some kind of coalition government between the two factions. The book everywhere conjured up the "inevitability" of Communist-style revolution, and said the only question was whether the U.S.A. would contest it, stand by and do nothing, or step in and cooperate with it. The authors preferred the last-named version.**

* Similar ideas were expressed by Snow in his books, *People On Our Side,* and *Red Star Over China.* Freda Utley offers this comment: "In the original edition of his best-selling book, *Red Star Over China,* Ed Snow had painted a most favorable picture of the Chinese Communist regime in the Northwest. But he also included some passages critical of the Comintern and showing the subservience of the Chinese Communists to Moscow. My . . . impression of Snow as an honest journalist was altered when he eliminated, in the second edition of his book, a number of passages distasteful to Moscow."

** *Eg.* "Both parties lied, cheated, and broke agreements; but the Communists had the people with them, and with the people they made their own new justice. . . . Chiang's . . . lust for power, his calculating ruthlessness, his monumental stubbornness . . . [are] a force in national politics . . . His one passion now became and remained an overriding lust for power. . . . The leaders of the Communist Party were a highly interesting group . . . These simple, earthy men did not look like any terrible threat to Chungking and world stability. But when you examined their thinking, and listened to

Thus the views conveyed to the American people by correspondents of three major mass-circulation magazines. They were, of course, precisely the views advanced by such authorities as Owen Lattimore and John K. Fairbank, and urged on the American State Department by such foreign service officers as John Stewart Service, John Carter Vincent, and John Paton Davies.

Both Gayn and Snow, interestingly enough, came to the attention of the Senate investigators looking into the IPR. The *Collier's* correspondent was one of those arrested in the 1945 *Amerasia* scandal, and later released when the charges were dropped. An FBI agent testified that among the 1,700 stolen government documents found in the offices of *Amerasia,* "one document contained six latent fingerprints of Mark Gayn," and that several typed documents "were typed on a machine belonging to Mark Gayn."[12] Ralph de Toledano records that during the FBI's surveillance of Gayn, "he was seen to enter the *Amerasia* offices and emerge with a full briefcase," and that when he took some papers from the briefcase to read them on a bus, "an FBI agent, peering over his shoulder, could see enough to identify them. They were classified documents."[13]

Snow was also of interest to investigators of the tangled affairs of the IPR. The Internal Security subcommittee

---

their conversation, you found a stubborn, irreducible realism . . . There was no formal hierarchy among the Communists, but Mao was set on a pinnacle of adoration . . . By 1944 the Chinese Communist Party was rooted in its own soil, Sinified, nationalistic . . . eventually agents of change must creep into the peasant's village and tell him there is another system, a system by which the masters are wiped out and the land divided, a system in which the village elders no longer rule, but the peasants decide their own fate. Liberty is a glistening word of many faces, and the peasant will believe that that system is best and offers the most liberty which gives him the quickest solution to the troubles of his daily life . . . If we move to halt this tide, we are lost . . . We must make clear to the Russians that what we want is a China in which the friends of Russia will have as large and free a voice as the friends of America, that a union of the two parties is as much our object as theirs."

found Snow to be a member of the "active inner core" of the Institute and, although not an IPR official, one of those who "were frequent contributors to IPR publications, in close touch with IPR staff members, or active on the executive, nominating or other committees. . . ."[14] IPR lavishly praised Snow's *Red Star,* and the IPR publication *Pacific Affairs* observed that "it is curious how much of their good reputation abroad the Chinese Communists owe to one man—Edgar Snow."[15] In his testimony before the subcommittee, former Communist official Louis Budenz asserted that Snow "amended one edition" of *Red Star,* "as I recall, at the request of the Communist Party." In colloquy with committee counsel Robert Morris, Budenz gave this further information: *Q.* "Did you know Nym Wales, who was the wife of Edgar Snow? . . . Did you know that she was a Communist?" *A.* "Most decidedly. She was, so far as official reports went, a Communist before Snow was." *Q.* "Before Edgar Snow was?" *A.* "That is right."[16]

The IPR-oriented view on China purveyed to readers of *Colliers* and the *Saturday Evening Post* by Gayn and Snow was also made to prevail in the book-publishing and book-reviewing industry. Lattimore, Snow, Fairbank, White, and others conscientiously reviewed each others' books in *The New York Times, The New York Herald-Tribune,* and the *Saturday Review of Literature.* Snow reviewed Lattimore's *Solution in Asia* for the *Times,* Gayn reviewed Snow's *People on Our Side* for the *Saturday Review,* Snow reviewed White's *Thunder Out of China* in the *Saturday Review,* Fairbank reviewed *Thunder Out of China* in the *Times,* Snow's wife Nym Wales reviewed one of Lattimore's books for the *Saturday Review,* and so forth. The same group was handed all of the occasional anti-Communist books on Asia to review, and uniformly panned them.

With such blanket coverage in the opinion-moulding fields, the pro-Mao journalists made the task of their soulmates in government a good deal easier. With public opinion constantly subjected to the theory that the Chinese Communists were "agrarian reformers" and Chiang Kai-shek a corrupt despot, it became much simpler to persuade the American government to wash its hands of Chiang, as the Acheson-Marshall group in the State Department finally succeeded in doing.

Also instructive is the fact that many of these people are now back in circulation, most of them impenitently preaching variations on the old themes, and are receiving notable cooperation from the higher echelons of the Establishment.

Mark Gayn, for example, popped up in the 1960s as a correspondent for the Toronto *Star,* returned to China, and wrote dispatches syndicated by the *New York Times* news service. His outlook has not changed appreciably. In the *Amerasia* affair, an FBI agent noted that Gayn in his writings "compliments the Russian educational system, the freedom of speech, and the puritanical attitude of the people."[17] In his dispatches from Communist China 20 years later, Gayn compared what he saw there to the former condition of the country, as follows:

"Because China was hungry its people were servile. Now the servility is gone. Instead, those I met displayed inordinate pride in their country and its achievements.

"In old Shanghai thieves were like locusts. Today, honesty is commonplace.

"All these—the new pride in China, the puritanism, the confidence, the dedication, the honesty—form the texture of the spiritual revolution . . .

". . . China has become conscious of the rudiments of public sanitation and cleanliness.

"Public education has become a national obsession . . ."[18]

Edgar Snow, also, is back at the same old stand. In 1962, Snow brought out yet another book on China, entitled *The Other Side of The River.* This production, which praised the record of the Communist Chinese and blackguarded Chiang Kai-shek, was lavishly greeted by *Newsweek* magazine. It was, *Newsweek,* said, "a massive, thickly documented assault on the whole arsenal of U.S. illusions, attitudes and misconceptions about Red China . . . written with open admiration for the Chinese people and a barely controlled fury at American folly . . . The Chinese revolution, Snow maintains, is a success in nearly every way, it has made enormous economic progress over anything that China has ever known, and it enjoys the support of China's 650-750 million people."[19]

Just about the only thing wrong with Snow's homage to Peking, *Newsweek* concludes, is that it had "the extraordinary bad luck" to be released just as Red China was committing aggression against India, and so "stands to get buried in a new barrage of irrelevant slogans."[20] Bad luck, indeed!

Not content with lauding Snow's propaganda, *Newsweek* also set about to rewrite his previous record. It described *Red Star* as "the first extensive information about the leaders of the Red revolution and their struggle against Chiang Kai-shek's corrupt and plutocratic Kuomintang. Later, when parlor Liberals took over the Chinese cause, Snow tried in vain to demolish the notion that the Reds were 'agrarian reformers' or anything else but doctrinaire Communists."[21]*

The Atlantic, for its part, referred Snow's 1962 opus to reviewer John K. Fairbank—another old IPR wheelhorse—who dutifully found Snow's work, with a nice touch of auld lang syne, to be a masterpiece of good sense and compassion.

Thus two of the old IPR-line correspondents who helped sell America a false bill of goods about China have been restored to public esteem, and are hard at work vending the new IPR-style line about China and Viet Nam. Also back in

* Readers who have difficulty reconciling these assertions with Snow's 1945 statement that "there has never been any Communism in China, even in the Communist areas" are referred to the publishers of *Newsweek* for their explanations.

public esteem, of course, is Theodore White, who is cranking out best-selling books about the merits of Liberal candidates for President and the demerits of Conservative ones, and who became a kind of television fixture as an expert commentator for the CBS network during the 1964 election campaign.

3. *Cuba*

The performance of the IPR coterie in merchandising Mao Tse-tung as an "agrarian reformer" was duplicated in almost every particular by Liberal journalists in the late 1950s covering the activities of Cuban revolutionary Fidel Castro. Foremost among these, but by no means alone, was Herbert L. Matthews of *The New York Times.*

Matthews had journeyed to Oriente Province in 1957 and interviewed Castro in his mountain fastness there, emerging with a scoop picturing Fidel as the salvation of Cuba. "He has strong ideas of liberty, democracy, social justice, the need to restore the constitution, to hold elections," Matthews said.[22] Castro's movement, he added, is "democratic, therefore, anti-Communist."[23] And: "There is no Communism to speak of in Fidel Castro's 26th of July movement."[24] The echoes of White, Snow, *et al.,* from China in the 40s were clearly audible.

As for Castro himself, Matthews wrote: "The personality of the man is overpowering. It was easy to see that his men adored him and also to see why he has caught the imagination of the youth of Cuba all over the island. Here was an educated, dedicated fanatic, a man of ideals, of courage and of remarkable qualities of leadership."[25]

Numerous other correspondents followed Matthews' example, among them the late Edward R. Murrow of CBS, who subsequently went to work as head of the USIA for President Kennedy. Despite copious documentation on the fact that Castro had been a Communist functionary since 1948, he was uniformly portrayed to the American people as a brave reformer devoid of Bolshevik connection.

With that kind of press treatment, it is small wonder the American public did not become aware of Castro's Bolshevism until it was too late. Moreover, the favorable journalistic picture of Castro also affected two special areas of opinion of critical importance—literate Cubans and the American government. One Cuban exile leader, Luis Manrara of the Truth About Cuba Committee, says he and his friends in Havana first formed a good opinion of Castro by reading Matthews' articles in *The Times.* They were later to learn by personal experience how wrong Matthews had been.[26]

Also important was Matthews' direct influence on U.S. policy, which turned against Batista and toward Castro at a crucial point in the battle for Cuba. Figures in the American State Department, particularly Caribbean desk man William Wieland, seemed impressed by Matthews' good opinion of Castro. Former Ambassador Earl E. T. Smith testified that when he was briefed on his Havana assignment by Wieland, he was told to consult Matthews. Smith said: "In February 1957 Herbert L. Matthews wrote three articles on Fidel Castro which appeared on the front page of *The New York Times,* in which he eulogized Fidel Castro and portrayed him as a political Robin Hood, and I would say that he repeated those views to me in our conversation."[27]

Smith added that "when I was ambassador . . . I . . . sometimes made the remark in my own embassy that Mr. Matthews was more familiar with the State Department thinking regarding Cuba than I was." Smith concluded that "until certain portions of the American press began to write derogatory articles against the Batista government, the Castro revolution never got off first base."[28] Former Ambassador to Mexico Robert Hill affirmed this conclusion, remarking that "individuals in the State Department and individuals in *The New York Times* put Castro in power."[29]

Something more than two years later, when Castro refused to supply any of the boons he had said he would provide—including the elections—Matthews interviewed him again, and found everything as rosy as ever. Regarding the unheld elections, Matthews blandly asserted: "Premier Castro is avoiding elections in Cuba for two reasons. He feels that his social revolution now has dynamism and vast popular consent, and he does not want to interrupt the process. Moreover, most observers would agree that Cubans today do not want elections."[30]

On other points, while conceding things were not proceeding in precise democratic order, Matthews was also optimistic. The revolution might appear to be Communist "in form," Matthews said, but "in substance" it was something else again. "Cuba has been transformed . . . the revolution has caught on . . . for Cubans a world is dying; a world is coming to life . . . Fidel Castro and his associates need a good five or ten years more to carry through the process of institutionalization . . . and to put the country on its feet and going strong . . .

"[Castro's revolution] has done many right things as well as many things wrong . . . [the country has] a purposefulness to life that is rare in Latin America and new in Cuba . . . the young are gay; the women are as feminine as ever . . . Cubans have at last grasped what is required of them, what they may or may not hope for . . ."[31] Thus did Matthews describe the slave system which has destroyed Cuba's economy, killed and imprisoned thousands, and made the nation an outpost of Communist aggression against the West.

Matthews' extenuations for Castro were supported elsewhere in the *Times* by correspondent Tad Szulc, who said "Dr. Castro," in refusing to hold elections, was "searching for a complete definition of democracy." Cuba's theorists, Szulc wrote, "already seem convinced that what Dr. Castro called . . . 'our so pure, so clean democracy' can function better without the cumbersome process of holding elections."[32] Only the subdued irony of the last phrase implied criticism of Castro's cynical alibi for despotism—a fine point submerged in *The Times'* headline for the story—"Cuba Formulates A New Democracy." Had the individual in question been a right-wing dictator, would *The Times* have treated the matter in jargon about "new democracy," or would it have called tyranny by its proper name?

4. *The Congo*

The Szulc example suggests one of the peculiarities of much Liberal press treatment of world crises: The different kinds of language used to describe Communists on the one hand and anti-Communists on the other. In this story and many others Fidel Castro is referred to as "Dr." Castro. Fulgencio Batista, on the other hand, is generally referred to as "dictator Batista"—just as Castro's other arch-enemy, Rafael Trujillo of the Dominican Republic, was referred to as "dictator Trujillo." This judicious deployment of emotive phrases is a common characteristic of Establishment journalism.

In press coverage of the fighting in Katanga, for example, the white troops employed by Premier Tshombe—many of them Europeans who had lived in the area for years—were invariably referred to as "mercenaries," as though this highly-pejorative and emotion-laden term were a common everyday factual description. The native Katangan troops, for their part, were always referred to as Tshombe's "gendarmerie," a term apparently deemed suitable for the armed forces of an illegitimate state. United Nations troops flown into Katanga from all over the world to wage aggression against a state they had never seen were of course never referred to as "mercenaries" or "gendarmerie." They were the "peace force."

As an example of this raw journalistic bias, consider a 1961 dispatch in *Life* magazine describing the U.N.'s attack on Katanga.

> In the Congo, [says the *Life* piece] . . . tough proud United Nations troops are acting resolutely in the cause of peace. One recent morning they struck boldly and, in a commando operation, began arresting and expelling the white mercenary officers who led Moise Tshombe's private army in the secessionist state of Katanga.[33]

The bold resolute action of the tough proud U.N. forces thus described was, as we have seen, in fact a wanton act of aggression which resulted in bountiful atrocity—facts which do not get themselves mentioned in the *Life* story. Instead, the magazine portrayed the U.N. sojourn in Katanga as "a story of unheralded individual courage, initiative, wisdom and idealism . . . of U.N. heroes facing up to their unusual tasks." (What could be more unusual for a hero than gunning down unarmed civilians?) The aggression was described as a "brilliant thorough coup" which was a "huge step forward for the Congo" while the U.N. troops from Ghana, India, and other outposts of liberty were depicted as demigods manfully routing and shaming Tshombe's "mercenaries" and "gendarmerie":

"From the Congo, a front-line report on soldiers of peace waging a war against war . . . Calm and confident after rounding up Katanga mercenaries in Elisabethville, members of the U.N. Irish contingent await their next assignment . . . The U.N. heroes are not all soldiers [some being administrators] . . . [Most U.N. people in the Congo] are worth more than money can pay . . . These disciplined Ghanaian soldiers . . . performed deeds brave enough to win medals in any war . . . I will never forget [their] sheer guts . . . this show of courage [by Indian Gurkha troops] . . . The remarkable esprit and coolness applies at the command level as well as among the troops in the field . . . It became clear to me that the U.N. on the whole has been highly successful in the Congo, particularly in its operations against the hired guns of Katanga . . ."[34]

The *Life* rhapsody—which makes Herbert Matthews look serenely objective by comparison—avoided mention of such of the U.N. demigods as were (a) killing civilians, (b) raping, (c) shooting at Red Cross lorries, or (d) lying to the world about what had actually happened in the Congo.

5. *Viet Nam*

Press bias toward the official line was equally apparent in Laos and Viet Nam. We have already noted the hearty denunciations of the assertedly "junketeering" anti-Red leaders of Laos by Scripps-Howard journalist R.H. Shackford. In Viet Nam, the treatment of Diem was, if anything, even worse.

In September, 1962, to take but a single example from the upper-brow press, *Harper's* suddenly blossomed with a lengthy lead article by a professor returned from Saigon, blasting the Diem regime as "inefficient," "corrupt," and "hated." The Vietnamese people in the cities were not at all apathetic about the war, said the author. "Nor, according to the battle reports that filtered through to us, were the peasants apathetic. The young ones [i.e., the Viet Cong] seemed to be fighting against the Diem regime with courage and initiative, as guerrilla fighters must if they are to survive. And the peasants on the whole seemed to support them with food, shelter, and intelligence. The Viet Cong—the Communist-led guerrilla force—had, by these means, taken and held the better part of the countryside from an army equipped and trained by the United States."[35] (The bulk of the article is given over to describing the author's "ordeal" at the hands of the Diem regime, which consisted of actually being detained and questioned by the government because he had been friendly with some Vietnamese who had flown low over the Diem palace and dropped bombs on it.) Similar attacks on Diem were to increase as the months went by.

The theme sounded in *Harper's* was taken up in earnest by certain members of the daily press in 1963, when the Buddhist furor evoked by Thich Tri Quang pushed Diem toward disaster. Marguerite Higgins records that many members of the Western press corps in Saigon took Thich Tri Quang's assertions at face value, without checking into his background and often without checking the incident in question to see whether his account was accurate. Although the Buddhist fracas by every authoritative report was confined to political circles in Saigon and did not have any observable effect on the war effort, it was widely discussed as if it were ruining Diem's chances of beating the Communists. Similarly, the documentation is overwhelming that the Buddhist uprising was a political rather than a religious matter, but press accounts referred to it as a "religious conflict" and as the outcome of Diem's "crushing the Buddhist religious movement."[36]

Miss Higgins recounted one notable incident in which a Buddhist spokesman told correspondents some 365 Buddhists had been arrested by Diem's men in one Saigon suburb, a "fact" duly relayed to the waiting world by a number of correspondents without checking it. Miss Higgins, who did check it, found it to be completely without foundation.[37]

The picture of persecution and seething discontent was etched most effectively by correspondent David Halberstam of *The Times*. Quoting anonymous observers and officials, Halberstam asserted that ". . . some United States civilian officials fear that the present government can no longer wage a successful war against the Communist guerrillas of the Viet Cong . . . Most observers say the key question centers on the regime's ability to unite the population at a time when it is engaged in a shooting war with a real enemy . . .

"As recently as last March a high State Department official on a visit said, 'The thing that bothers me about this government is that the only people who are for it are Americans . . .'

". . . the Ngo Dinh Diem of today is considered an isolated man, removed further and further from the population, hearing finely sifted reports about his people . . . He sees himself representing God to the people and believes that it is the duty of the population to honor him . . . "[38]

Halberstam gave this summary of the situation:

> As a climax to the crisis drew near, the protest was a complicated force. It was in small part Buddhist against Catholic; it was in much larger part the protest of a large segment of the people who happened to be Buddhist against an authoritarian government that happened to be Catholic-dominated: It was also, in small part, have nots protesting against the haves; it was in much larger part twentieth century Asians protesting against older Asians molded from a mandarin past.[39]

As disclosed by Miss Higgins and the inquiries of the U.N., however, the Buddhist uprising turned out to be none of these things so much as it was a calculated endeavor by a small politically fanatic element to undermine Diem. Halberstam, for his part, quotes Buddhist leader Thich Tri Quang with solemn respect—but makes no mention of his ties to the North.

That Miss Higgins' version of what was going on in Viet Nam was correct and that Halberstam's was not is evidenced by the fact that, following Diem's overthrow and murder, the domestic affairs of that troubled country became more turbulent, not less. In the two years following the coup, successive governments took office in Saigon in dizzy rotation, none of them any more "democratic" than Diem, and all less effective in combatting the Communists.

Despite this discrepancy, and despite the fact that the U.N. fact-finding commission found against Halberstam's version of events and in favor of Miss Higgins', Halberstam was awarded a Pulitzer Prize for his efforts. Even in their heydays, Edgar Snow and Herbert Matthews had not been able to accomplish the feat of plying the American people with misinformation and then receiving journalism's highest honor as a reward for having done so.

★★ 31. *To Russia, With Love*

1. *Nuclear Terror Is Better Than Ever*

IF SEGMENTS OF THE MEDIA have been successful in merchandising Establishment doctrine in specific instances, they have been even more dilligent in spreading the general themes which form the policy background for particular misplays. These are, as we have seen, the idea that the Soviet Union, when all is said and done, is *not* dangerous, and that our own military leaders in the possession of atomic weapons *are* dangerous.

Widespread misinformation about various aspects of nuclear weapons has been a key element in this campaign—particularly in advancing the psychology of disarmament. Some of this has been set forward in flat exposition—as in the "missile gap," fallout, and tactical nuclear weapons questions. This approach has, however, been only partly successful. Discussion of such matters in technical terms does not always penetrate to the public. Also, a purportedly factual discussion lends itself to refutation, which makes the business of promoting it rather tedious.

It is interesting to note, therefore, that most of the really choice misinformation about nuclear weapons has been propagated, not explicitly through political journalism, but in fictional form, through novels and motion pictures. The advantages of such propagandizing are apparent. "Entertainment" goes down far more easily than some dry book of controversy, and the ideology it contains can be well coated with a love story, glamorous names, and drama contrived to the taste of the author or director. Equally important, the fictional form affords a license to be as free with the truth as one's needs or predispositions require.

A major breakthrough for the disarmament lobby in the field of popular fiction was the success of Nevil Shute's 1957 novel, *On The Beach.* This story, which appeared during the first sustained agitation over radioactive fallout, purports to describe the total destruction of the human race as the result of an "accidental" nuclear war. Egypt attacks the United States with nuclear weapons delivered in Soviet aircraft, destroying Washington and everyone in it, and "someone" (the author does not specify who) in the military hierarchy decides the Soviets are the guilty parties. America therefore bombs Moscow. Although Shute is vague about how this cataclysm occurs (his characters, questioning each other about it, characteristically respond, "I don't think anybody knows"),[1] the general outline of the "accidental" war he suggests is sufficiently tangible to be judged against the known facts about our nuclear defenses and to be found inaccurate.

This is, however, a minor theme—a kind of offhanded and underdeveloped pretext for getting at the main business—which is the total destruction of every human being on earth through the workings of radioactive fallout. Fallout was Shute's principal villain, and it was hysteria over fallout which the novel, and the motion picture based on it, succeeded in spreading among hundreds of thousands of people.

Writing in the *Saturday Evening Post,* Stewart Alsop—himself a Liberal and hardly an advocate of nuclear holocaust—nailed Shute's ghastly melodrama for what it was worth. "A great many people," Alsop wrote, ". . . have assured us that *On The Beach* is a technically accurate presentation of the radioactive side-effects of a nuclear warfare. And that it certainly is not. The plot of *On The Beach* is based on two assumptions about the nature of radioactive fallout. Both assumptions are false. And they lead directly to the false assumption . . . that anything, including surrender to Communism, is better than nuclear war."[2]

The two assumptions, Alsop notes, are that "there is no protection against radioactivity," and that "radioactive fallout remains lethal indefinitely"—premises which between them assure, in Shute's scenario, that the human race is extinguished. "This is technically a lot of nonsense," Alsop says, since shelters obviously provide protection against fallout, and since, even more important, "radioactivity from fallout dies away very quickly—a vital fact which is virtually disregarded in *On The Beach,* but which could save millions of lives in case of nuclear warfare."[3]

As *On The Beach* employed technical falsehood to sell fear over fallout, so have other works of fiction and motion pictures employed other points of technical misinformation to spread terror about other aspects of nuclear weaponry. Perhaps the most famous of these was a 1962 novel called *Fail-Safe,* authored by two college professors in California for the avowed purpose of alerting the nation to the dangers of "accidental" nuclear war.

Fail-Safe tells the story of a group of American pilots in a time of international crisis, awaiting instructions to proceed toward Moscow or to return to base. Because of a mechanical failure, the signal does not go through and the pilots make their run at Moscow. To demonstrate that the whole thing is an accident, the President of the United States has our own Air Force bomb and destroy New York City, killing his wife in the process. Thus are the dangers of accidental warfare among nations owning nuclear weapons made apparent to hundreds of thousands of readers and, in cinematic form, to millions of moviegoers.

It would be difficult to imagine a more blood-curdling effort to provoke fear of our own nuclear arsenal. And that this was precisely their intention the authors make clear. "The people in this novel," they wrote, "are our contemporaries and they deal with a problem that is already upon us. It is being discussed daily in Washington, Moscow, London, and elsewhere by heads of state, diplomatic and military experts. Men of good will and ill have been agonizing over the problem for years. They have found no solution."[4]

The authors conclude that "the element in our story which seems most fictional—the story's central problem and its solution—is in fact the most real part. Men, machines, and mathematics being what they are, *this is, unfortunately, a true story*. The accident may not occur in the way we describe but *the laws of probability assure us that ultimately it will occur*. The logic of politics tells us that when it does, the only way out will be a choice of disasters."[5] (Italics added.)

This discussion and the novel it is meant to justify are almost completely false. The accident the authors describe as happening could not in fact happen, either in the way they suggest or in any way approximating it, for the simple reason that the fail-safe mechanism is in fact *precisely the opposite* of what the authors say it is. That is, our bombers do not proceed in the absence of a command to turn back; they come back in the absence of a command to proceed. The blowing-out of a condenser, in the contingency envisioned by the authors, would *not* result in an unauthorized bombing raid on Moscow, with all the horrible consequences suggested; it would result instead in a return to base.

As pointed out in Chapter 15, the real danger incurred by our elaborate system of nuclear checks and counterchecks is that, should urgent need arise, we actually might *not* be able to use our weapons. That some set of fantastic circumstances might conspire against 1,000,000 to one odds to produce an "accidental" attack is not, of course, totally inconceivable; it is merely beyond the realm of all probability, and a good deal *less* likely to come about, given existing arrangements, than the opposite danger of total misfire. Yet the authors of *Fail-Safe* have blandly informed millions of Americans that an accidental war is not only possible, or probable, but inevitable.

The comment of Prof. Sidney Hook is apposite:

> . . . given the assumption that *Fail-Safe* tells the truth, then it is our system of defense and not the avowed design of a hostile totalitarian government that is the chief enemy to our survival. Thus the abandonment of our nuclear defense, our own disarmament (unilateral, if need be) becomes a plausible and perhaps the only viable alternative.
>
> The publication and reception of *Fail-Safe* is evidence of a widespread syndrome of political defeatism. It sees in the deterrent shield of defense, behind which the main centers of free culture have until now survived, an instrument not of safety but one that insures a world-wide calamity. Rather than accept this "certain" disaster, any other course would appear preferable: appeasement, unilateral nuclear disarmament, even outright surrender to the Soviet government.

Hook adds that:

> In discussing *Fail-Safe,* we are discussing not merely a best-selling book but a movement, not merely the views of two men

but of many, not merely a technical question in the weaponry of defense but an entire political strategy upon which the future of freedom depends.[6]

Exactly so. *Fail-Safe* is indeed the product of a "movement," the movement discussed at various places in this book. It is a movement which includes the trust-and-assist Moscow theorists, the Vincent P. Rocks, the Jerome Wiesners, the politicians who tell us we must fear our own defenses more than we fear the Communists. And it is in this representative capacity, in its conformity to the goals of the disarmament lobby, that *Fail-Safe* and its central vitiating falsehood are most relevant.

Appearing almost simultaneously with *Fail-Safe* was yet another best-selling novel entitled *Seven Days in May,* which also sought to focus public anxieties on our defense establishment; not, this time, on the danger of accidental warfare, but on the danger of a military coup by fascist-minded generals.

In this novel, an American President named Jordan Lyman is trying to achieve ratification of a nuclear disarmament treaty with the Soviet Union. A group of military officers led by General "Gentleman Jim" Scott, a militant anti-Communist who thinks the treaty is "appeasement," plot to overthrow the government. Thanks to a plucky marine major, the plot is foiled, the reactionary generals are banished, the President delivers some homilies on "civilian control" and embarks to Vienna to sign the disarmament treaty. Music up and out. Any similarity between this yarn and the Fulbright Memorandum, the views of the disarmament lobby, and the Establishment line generally is, obviously, the product of right-wing paranoia.*

* Interestingly enough, Liberal Sen. Eugene McCarthy of Minnesota is quoted on the cover of this volume as saying it is "more than a thriller" and "should be read seriously" (this is precisely the counsel which numerous enthusiasts for *Fail-Safe, On The Beach* and *Dr. Strangelove* have given us).

The combined wisdom of *Fail-Safe* and *Seven Days in May* was subsequently assembled in a motion picture and novella entitled *Dr. Strangelove—Or: How I Learned to Stop Worrying And Love The Bomb,* concerning, among other things, a mad scientist who feeds insane policy directives to the President of the United States, military usurpation of authority *and* a breakdown of fail-safe procedure. In the *Strangelove* version—by coincidence precisely topical during the 1964 election—a military commander who has been given stand-by authority to use nuclear weapons in the event of a communications breakdown goes berserk and orders an attack on Moscow. The planes proceed to destination, devoid of all contact with Washington.

The technical procedures depicted in *Strangelove* are as far removed from the truth as those of *Fail-Safe.* The military has no authority to initiate orders for strategic nuclear attack; any orders or purported orders received by them must be verified by elaborate procedures; and once a plane had passed the fail-safe point it would not be unreachable by Washington, as the plot of *Strangelove* insists it should be. In short, the movie and book are simply further examples of falsehood in the service of nuclear hysteria.

It will be objected, of course, that *Strangelove* is a farce, which of course it is. But what might be the imagined effect of this farce coming on top of (a) the *Fail-Safe* assertion that accidental nuclear war is not only possible but "inevitable," (b) the *Seven Days in May* assertion that a military coup is also a possibility, and (c) the general campaign of the disarmament lobby, preaching the undesirability of nuclear weapons generally and the immense dangers of possessing

---

Even more interesting, the fly-leaf of the book in its paperback form (published in September, 1963), does not give the name of the humane President as "Jordan Lyman" as it appears in the book, but as "Lyman Johnson." That slip of the copy-writer's pen no doubt gave 1964 readers of *Seven Days In May* an even clearer understanding of its burning relevance.

them? Since the theme of *Strangelove* is merely a fusion and extension of these things, its underlying themes will obviously be accepted as purveying truth, beneath its surface veneer of mad fun, by anyone who accepted its predecessors.

And what, we may well wonder, was the political impact of *Strangelove* in election year 1964 when the American people were called upon to vote, among other things, on the question of whether the NATO commander in Europe should have the power, under certain circumstances, to employ battlefield nuclear weapons? Is it conceivable that anyone who had absorbed the contents of *Fail-Safe, On The Beach, Seven Days in May,* and *Strangelove* would *not* have cast his ballot against Barry Goldwater?

These fictional exercises in the art of inducing nuclear terror are not, as it happens, totally new departures. They are a culmination of a long-developing effort to induce fear of our own nuclear defenses and the people manning them which dates at least as far back as Howard Fast's 1951 novel, *The Fallen Angel,* which preaches the evil of those who seek to develop new weapons for the defense of the United States.

This novel is particularly interesting because it was written when Fast was still preaching the overt Communist line and was a publicly identified Stalinist. Yet in 1965, atop the wave of hysteria fostered by *On The Beach, Fail-Safe, Seven Days in May,* and *Strangelove,* this 14-year-old dreadful portraying developers of new weapons for America as maniacs and people subverting that development as tormented noblemen was dredged up, refurbished, and made into a major motion picture called *Mirage,* starring Gregory Peck. Its contribution to the dialogue over American defenses may well be imagined.[7]

The matter we have reviewed suggests, quite clearly, a mood impatient of truth, in which fact is serviceable as it conforms or fails to conform to the ideology of disarmament. Whether falsehood is involved or not, the point is the readiness of the media to seize upon and advance the accommodationist specialties of the Establishment. *On The Beach* and *Fail-Safe* and *Strangelove* are in the final analysis important, not because of the specific falsehoods they embody, but because they illustrate so great a readiness to disseminate pacifist propaganda *irrespective* of truth or falsehood and to advance the Establishment line through assertedly non-ideological channels.

It is interesting to note that these confessedly inaccurate efforts have received the praises of people who know they are inaccurate. Dr. Ralph Lapp, a popularizer of nuclear disarmament views, makes this revealing comment:

> . . . I am inclined to believe that the scientist-layman gap was and remains so great that we must give nonscientists much credit for translating the scientists' fears into terms which the layman could understand, even though very often the scientist deplored the text of the translation. For example, Nevil Shute's *On The Beach* did not conform very neatly with scientific fact but it got the message across to the average person. So, too did *Fail-Safe* and *Dr. Strangelove*. The novel and the drama appealed to many millions of people who would otherwise have had their lives untouched by the scientists' obsession.[8]

That statement affirms the overtly propagandistic nature of the "entertainment" in question. It also demonstrates the willingness of "the scientists", *i.e.,* those members of the scientific community favoring disarmament, to have falsehood merchandised if it serves their ideological ends. And it raises the question of why, in all three cases, the "scientists' obsession" with nuclear holocaust had to be gotten over to the people by means of critical misrepresentation. Wasn't it possible to *tell the truth* and to make the point the "scientists" wanted made? Or could it be that the truth will not sustain the kind of program the "scientists" want to see enacted?

2. *The Hiroshima Hero*

The importance of falsehood in spreading pacifist propaganda is well-illustrated by the bizarre case of Major Claude Eatherly, the so-called "Hero of Hiroshima" ballyhooed as a martyr to nuclear madness. The Eatherly case demonstrates that, just as the movies have adopted nuclear fantasies to their uses, so have the proponents of atomic hysteria, quite literally, taken over from the movies falsehood which suits their purposes, and promoted it as if it were fact.

Major Eatherly, on the presentation of his fans in the nuclear disarmament claque, was the pilot who "led" the American bombing raid against Hiroshima in 1945. According to a story circulated nationally by *Newsweek,* a number of newspapers, and the NBC television network—and internationally by such nuclear pacifists as Lord Bertrand Russell—Eatherly was ridden by a "guilt complex" and took to a life of crime by way of atonement.

As *Newsweek* told the story, Eatherly was a "Hero in Handcuffs." He had scouted Hiroshima, accompanied the "Enola Gay" on its bombing run, circled over the city to take scientific measurements; he repeated this mission at Nagasaki, subsequently received the Distinguished Flying Cross, stayed in the Air Force "for a time" after the war, was mustered out after seven years' service, then returned to his home state of Texas.

> To his family, [*Newsweek* said], Eatherly somehow seemed changed. His wife said he used to wake up at night shouting: "Bail out! Bail out!" When he came to, he would say that he dreamed he was in a burning plane that had been shot down over Tokyo. In 1950 he voluntarily entered the Veterans Administration hospital of Waco for treatment of extreme nervousness.[9]

After a while things became even worse: Eatherly started committing crimes, broke up with his wife, served a term for forgery, was questioned about some armed robberies. Eatherly is quoted as saying "I don't know why we did it. We didn't need the money."[10] The story concludes on the lugubrious note that Eatherly had once again been arrested, this time for breaking into post offices in West Texas.

Anyone acquainted with the temper of nuclear pacifism can imagine the impact of this story on the world's militant disarmers. Before long Eatherly was the centerpiece of an elaborate morality play in which his crimes were merely the acting out of his unassuaged guilt for the crime of Hiroshima. As Lord Russell put it: "The world was prepared to honor him for his part in the massacre, but, when he repented, it turned against him, seeing in his act of repentance its own condemnation."[11]

Not a word of this—or of a number of other Eatherly memorabilia passed about in America and Europe—was true. Indeed, many of the alleged facts about Eatherly were derived, incredibly enough, from a movie script. Retracing Eatherly's career step by step, William Bradford Huie came to these well-documented conclusions:

Eatherly did not "lead" the raid on Hiroshima; he did conduct a weather reconnaissance mission before the attack, but was hundreds of miles away when the city was bombed; he did not accompany the "Enola Gay"; he did not circle over the city and take measurements; he did not go to Nagasaki; he did not receive the Distinguished Flying Cross; and he did not have nightmares in which he woke up screaming "Bail Out! Bail Out!"

Even more to the point, according to everyone who knew him, Eatherly did not have the slightest feelings of "guilt" about his part at Hiroshima, having on the contrary tried to stay in the Air Force after the war and asked his crew to stay in also. He was at last ousted from the service for cheating on an exam. In 1947, this sensitive pacifist attempted to take part in a gun-running expedition aimed at a *coup d'etat* in

Cuba, and bragged about this episode as late as 1961. And the purpose of his many criminal activities was, as Huie proves beyond warrantable doubt, to raise money for the gambling to which he was addicted.

Finally, asserted "facts" about Eatherly's "guilt," attempted suicide, "nightmares," and cries of "Bail Out! Bail Out!" were derived from a movie script prepared in Hollywood by scenario writers Paul I. Wellman and A. B. Guthrie Jr. Huie, who quotes the relevant passages of the script in detail, notes a bit of by-play in which the movie Eatherly refuses his Air Force pension as "blood money" (the real Eatherly accepted his pension). Huie notes that "this script indirectly became the *source* for factual stories . . . Whether through Claude Eatherly or not, the 'blood money' story was circulated. The French journalist Ferdinand Gigon heard it and wrote it as fact. The *Observer* in London in reviewing Gigon's book, extracted it as fact. John Wain read the review after which he wrote his poem 'A Song About Major Eatherly.' The poem was published as truth by a firm like Macmillan; and it was read dramatically as truth over BBC."[12]

A like paternity is established for the screams of "Bail Out! Bail Out!" and the two suicide attempts reported by *Newsweek;* neither of these items has anything to do with the real Eatherly; both are based on the movie-script Eatherly. Yet these "facts" and others equally as spurious have been broadcast throughout America and Europe as the tragic, true-to-life story of a man mutilated by the horrors of atomic weaponry.

"I believe the story of Claude Eatherly and his publicists curiously illuminates the time in which we live," says Huie.[13] That it most assuredly does.

3. *Spies for Peace*

In company with the notion that our own nuclear defenses are dangerous goes the idea that the Communists in Moscow are *not* dangerous. As preached by the Establishment ca. 1964, this argument took the form of asserting that the real foreign policy danger (to the extent that there was one) stemmed not from Moscow, but from Peking; that, in view of the "split" between these two world centers of Communism, we should be able to cooperate with the Communists in Moscow; *etc.*

Motion pictures have long been an avenue for the expression of such views. During the Second World War, moviegoers were treated to *Mission To Moscow, Song of Russia, North Star* and other epics which painted the Soviet Union in the rosiest of hues. As William Henry Chamberlin observes, these films, portraying happy peasants, earnest priests, burgeoning larders and the good life of Mother Russia could not have been shown to a Russian audience because "there would have been too much spontaneous laughter."[14]

Fail-Safe's portrayal of the Communists is in this same fantastic vein. Just as the authors describe our own defense system as dangerous, they show then-Soviet Premier Khrushchev as compassionate, understanding, patient and realistic. This contrasts strangely with the chief candidate for the title of villain in the book, an American defense strategist who, as the story develops, is seen as lusting for nuclear war.

As Professor Hook comments: "The authors present Khrushchev as a man of tragic dimension, more sinned against than sinning, reluctant to demand a cruel and gratuitous price for an accident which he agrees is no one's fault, a humanist and reflective critic of Bolshevik-Leninism . . . He leaves the stage a philosopher pledged to reasonable compromise, a man whom the free world would do well to trust to insure peace."[15]

Who would recognize in this portrait, Hook asks, the real flesh-and-blood Khrushchev who was the butcher of the Ukraine, the assassin of the Hungarian freedom fighters, the man who secreted rockets in Cuba to threaten the survival of the United States? Obviously, any one who accepted *Fail-Safe's* message on this point would have a totally erroneous notion of what Communism is, and what Communists in the Soviet Union are like.

The massiveness with which this notion of the Soviets as rather likeable and sympathetic chaps has been brought into play may be suggested by examining a *genre* of fictional entertainment which, by its nature, touches directly on the Cold War and purports to be founded in the Cold War world —the spy story. A survey of some of the principal novels and motion pictures in this field will show, with some precision, just how the Establishment line on accommodating the Kremlin has been propagated. The natural candidates for inspection in this category are, of course, the immensely popular James Bond novels of Ian Fleming and the motion pictures based on them.

As any good Fleming addict knows, the novelistic Bond is, among his other accomplishments, a dangerous enemy of the Kremlin. In the novel, *From Russia With Love,* Bond tangles with the Soviet Secret police organization, SMERSH, which commits horrible crimes and employs despicable agents, and over which Bond triumphs with his customary flourish.

The net impact of *From Russia With Love,* the novel, is exactly the opposite of what we have described as the general Establishment line on Moscow: If the Soviets are what Fleming makes them out to be in this book, then they obviously are *not* the kind of people with whom we can or should do business. So let us note what happened to this story when it became a motion picture.

In the filmed version of *From Russia With Love,* the villains are no longer the Soviets and SMERSH; they are instead an amorphous group of international bad men operating through an altogether extraneous Fleming invention, imported from other novels, called SPECTRE. The theme of the film is that *both* British intelligence and the Soviets are being victimized by SPECTRE, plotting to set these two forces at odds. Fortunately, Bond and a beautiful female Soviet agent are able to foil the plot. Moscow is no longer the villain, the Soviets are innocent victims of SPECTRE along with Bond, and Bond-plus-beautiful-Russian agent triumph over the "third force" villain.

Similar liberties were taken in the motion picture version of another Bond success, *Goldfinger.* The villain of this piece is a bizarre madman who wants to steal all the gold in Fort Knox and take it to Moscow. In the film, Goldfinger's Moscow attachments are effaced and his assistants in the assault on Fort Knox suddenly turn out to be—Chinese.

The violence done *From Russia With Love* and *Goldfinger* was likewise perpetrated on the first of the Bond novels to be made into a film, *Dr. No.* Fleming buff O. F. Snelling notes of this transposition:

> When this book was written the Cold War was very cold. By the time the film of the book was made things had warmed up considerably, and it would hardly have been polite, to say the least, to accuse a friendly power like Russia of financing such a project [Dr. No's missile-sabotage installation in the Caribbean]. On the screen, you will find that the Russian government had nothing to do with it. Here, Dr. No works for that sinister organization called SPECTRE—one purely devoted to private enterprise.[16]

In this same category, it is interesting to note that the most highly acclaimed spy novelist of recent years (and the best-selling after Fleming), is "John Le Carré," who takes a notably soft line on the Cold War. Le Carré's most famous work, *The Spy Who Came In From the Cold,* preaches that there is no essential difference between East and West, and that whatever difference there is consists in the fact that the West is apparently a little more inhuman and beastly, while the East is a little more put upon.* Le Carré's follow-up novel, *The Looking Glass War,* informs us, as the title implies, that the whole business of Western intelligence and counterintelligence against the Communists is a sort of make-believe and farce.

In an earlier novel, *Call For the Dead,* Le Carré makes his point of view even clearer, as he describes a death struggle between a Communist agent, Dieter Frey, and a British agent, George Smiley. Le Carré states of the conflict between these representatives of East and West: "Dieter, mercurial, absolute, *had fought to build a civilization.* Smiley, rationalistic, protective, had fought to prevent him."[17] (Italics added.) Dieter the communist agent, Smiley the British agent, are substantially equal—old friends placed at odds by an irrational fate.

" 'Rational, protective' types," comments Professor Hugh Kenner, are comfortable to have around; we accept that designation of our side; but does not the heart go out all the same to the 'mercurial,' the 'absolute,' the fiery civilization builder? How sickening is a Cold War, say these books, that sets in lethal combat men whose difference is chiefly an affair of endocrinal balance."**[18]

* *This* message was *not* changed in the ensuing motion picture.

** The most successful effort to translate the spy-story fad to television was an amusing program launched in 1964 called "The Man From U.N.C.L.E." As everyone knows, U.N.C.L.E. is a mythical worldwide organization devoted to maintaining law and order. Its opponents are various vaguely identified dictators, including Latin Americans, Europeans, and Asians. Some of the Asians are clearly Chinese Communists; the others are so generalized that they might be malefactors of either the left or the right. But the one thing they apparently *cannot* be is agents of the Russians in Moscow, since it is clear from the premise of the program that the Russians and the Americans are working through U.N.C.L.E. together, as a cooperative venture: The two chief agents being an American (Robert Vaughn-Napoleon Solo) and a Russian (David McCallum-Illya Kuryakin).

Conclusion

If you believe . . . the outcome of the struggle in China, in Korea, in Indochina; the Communist penetration of Asia, Africa, the Middle East, and Latin America; the absence of any effective countering force to the Communist Party; the relative decline in Western influence. . . . could not have been helped, then you already are a Marxist.

—Dr. Charles Malik

★★ 32. *The History Theory of Conspiracy*

DURING THE FIRST TWO DECADES of the Cold War the United States and the Free World have been losing, and losing badly. Certain of the reasons behind these staggering losses have been suggested in the course of our narrative—foremost among them the chronic inability of the Liberal to perceive the nature of the world we live in and to close with the thrust of Communist aggression. We have been losing a street fight because we insist on behaving as though we were attending a debate at the Oxford Union.

The chief Liberal extenuation for this unhappy record is that it has been dictated by the nature of things—by the inevitable course of 20th-century revolution. To suggest that human failure contributed importantly to the way things came out, or that purposeful action could have made them come out otherwise, is to adopt the "Conspiracy Theory of

History." Belief that the machinations of the Communist apparatus require forceful counter-measures is viewed by certain Liberal spokesmen as prima facie evidence of delusion. Our world has been wrought for us, not by human effort or human failure, but by the sovereign force of history.

This inevitabilist view of the Cold War, as Dr. Charles Malik of Lebanon has pointed out, is one of Communism's most powerful assets. It is of course the Communist argument *par excellence* that "history" makes men and institutions rather than the reverse, and that Marxist revolution is ordained by the mesh of impersonal circumstance. He who posits historical inevitability as the reason for Communist triumph has, Malik observes, become something of a Marxist himself: He has swallowed the Marxists' variant of the self-fulfilling prophecy and accepted their vision of man and society and the future.

The episodes we have inspected suggest there has in truth been nothing "inevitable" about free world failure and Communist victory. The communization of China, to take the obvious case, was the result of considerable effort by people devoted to that task, acting upon other people prepared to let Asia slip from the Free World in a dream of befuddlement. The communization of Poland, Yugoslavia, Czechoslovakia, and other East European nations resulted from the same dismal convergence of Western default and Bolshevik resolve—as did the fall of Cuba, the abortion in the Bay of Pigs, the fall of Laos, the overthrow of South Viet Nam's Diem. Greater effort on our part or a different kind of effort could have brought about a different outcome. There is nothing very mysterious about the Communists' having won so many battles when they have been trying to win and we have not.

That Communist advances are traceable not to necessity but to American waffling was most clearly demonstrated in the aftermath of World War II, when the Soviets were enfeebled by the long struggle and we were at the height of our powers. It is interesting to speculate what the "inevitable" course of history might have been had not the Roosevelt regime made its startling concessions at Yalta and had not the IPR succeeded in dominating our China policy. Once the concessions had been made, of course, global Communism assumed something like a position of real strength. It was able to menace Western Europe and the littoral states of the Asian mainland. But even then Communism was inferior to the Free World in material and military power, dependent upon Western vacillation for its successes. The chief utility of the gains it had wrested from America's surrealistic statecraft was to supply the West with new rationalizations for retreat. Throughout the 50s and 60s, the principal gains of Communism—Cuba being the most prominent example—continued to take place through the aquiescence and in some cases the support of the American government.

Interpreting this lugubrious record as something ordained by history, the Liberal shows himself afflicted by a clinical disorder which has yet to be fully analyzed, but which deserves the attention of our modern-day specialists in mental health. He is suffering from something which might be described as "reverse paranoia"—a congenital inability to grasp the notion of conspiracy, to observe the impact of human striving upon the course of events, to perceive that ideological maunderings are no match for purposeful effort. The Liberal tries to foist off on "history" the residue of his own omissions and vacuities. He is hiding behind the History Theory of Conspiracy.

If there are at work in the world any deep-going currents of social and political sentiment, their natural tendency seems to be against the success of the Communist program. Revolutionary Marxism, with its grinding tyranny and jerry-built economics, cuts against the grain of human nature; it denies the normal human desire for personal expression and, contrary to Liberal report, does not deliver the goods. Wherever Marxism goes, there also go misery and poverty. To the extent that any great shifts in popular feeling can be counted upon to supply Cold War leverage, those shifts operate—not in favor of Marxist tyranny—but against it.

How far from "inevitable" has been the Marxist advance came clearly to light in 1964 and 1965 when, despite the best efforts of the Kremlin and Foggy Bottom, one Marxist dictator after another was toppled from power. Included in this number were Ahmed Ben Bella of Algeria, Cheddi Jagan of British Guiana, Victor Paz Estenssoro of Bolivia, Kwame Nkrumah of Ghana, and Achmed Sukarno of Indonesia. Each of these men had been busy constructing a dictatorship at home and following the international Communist line abroad. That all of them should have been brought low by popular upheaval is sufficient answer to the notion that cosmic tides of Marxism are sweeping the globe. The point becomes even more emphatic when we note that in every case these men had been actively supported by international Communism *and* by the United States. Yet their own people cashiered them all. In 1966, as we have noted, a similar fate befell Juan Bosch of the Dominican Republic—also despite our previous history of solicitude in his behalf.

The downfall of these six Marxists supplies an interesting measure, not only of the "inevitabilist" argument, but of Liberal foreign policy in general. The American taxpayer is entitled to wonder why the United States government was supporting men who were obviously Marxists, working hand in glove with international Communism, and anathema to their own people. We can only imagine how much sooner the Sukarnos and Nkrumahs might have been dismissed had not America showered them with dollars and prestige, or, perish the thought, had actually used its strength to assist forces in their nations friendly to the Western cause. If they were overthrown despite the fact that we were aiding them, it is reasonable to suppose they would have been ousted long since without our assistance. And it is also reasonable to conclude other Marxist dictators now receiving American largesse might be equally vulnerable if we stopped supporting them with American dollars.

The recent events in Ghana, Indonesia, *etc.*, are victories for the West, although inadvertent and, so far as the record discloses, unsought. Yet the lesson they teach is precisely the same as the lesson of our many setbacks: The "inevitable" advance of revolutionary Marxism is not inevitable at all. It is the product of conscious effort by the Marxists and feckless complaisance on the part of the United States. By supporting a Nkrumah or a Sukarno, by conciliating "Uncle Joe," by giving tax-subsidized wheat to the Soviet Union on the theory that Marxist revolution is bound to happen, we are in fact helping to make it happen.

Certain guidelines toward a more successful policy therefore suggest themselves. If one does not want to be swarmed under by a determined enemy, one's most obvious step is not to do things which strengthen the enemy. If a hold-up man confronts you on the street, you do not offer to give him the jackknife you have in your pocket or supply him with a few vitamin pills because he seems a little peaked. If we seriously intend to resist Communist aggression, our first indicated move is to stop doing things which strengthen the adversary. We should stop giving aid, direct and indirect, to Moscow and other Iron Curtain countries; curtail the East-West trade which helps fuel the Bolsheviks' creaking industrial machinery; enforce the Battle Act and other legislative measures seeking to forestall trade by U.S. aid recipients with Communist nations; stop cultural exchanges which make for improved Soviet espionage; stop Soviet scientists from touring our restricted installations; stop foreign and diplomatic aid to people like Sukarno and Nkrumah; stop paying the bills for Communist U.N. members, *etc.*

If these few steps toward rationality can be achieved, our next move is also obvious. As we stop strengthening the Communists, we should stop weakening ourselves. In particular, we should use the diplomatic avenues available to us to resume those parts of our nuclear testing program necessary to insure the workability of our intercontinental ballistic missiles; break off our endless quest for disarmament agreements with a foe which honors such understandings only in the breach; proceed with all possible speed toward the development of a new and effective manned bomber force; re-install, if military authority finds it requisite, intermediate-range missiles; re-activate the Skybolt missile program to increase the life and range of our manned bombers; move swiftly to develop and deploy an effective anti-missile defense system; do, in short, all those things which a realistic assessment of our enemy indicates need doing, and which our lotus-dream of a "mellow" Kremlin has prevented us from doing.

Our third elementary step back toward reality is to stop hurting, and start helping, the world anti-Communist forces we are supposed to lead. We should stop waging our fanatical crusades against anti-Communist leaders like Mihailovich, Micolajczyk, Chiang, Batista, Wessin y Wessin, Tshombe, Rhee, Boun Oum, Diem. We must call off our ideological feud with nations like South Africa, Portugal, and Rhodesia. And we should, with a judicious understanding of what serves both the long-term as well as the short-term interests of the Free World, give such aid and technical assistance to anti-Communist governments as is necessary to help them resist the encroachments of Marxist revolutionaries. Above all, we must end the masochistic hypocrisy of helping stamp out a Katanga or a Rhodesia in the name of "democracy" while backing the play of brutal Marxist despots like Nkrumah.

On the record before us, the mere act of *stopping* a sizeable percentage of the things we are now doing could work a profound transformation in strategic relationships. Denial of our support for this or that United Nations vendetta against an anti-Communist state would, in most cases, be sufficient to jar that particular campaign to a halt. The withdrawal of our aid funds from such as Nkrumah and Sukarno would in many cases be sufficient to touch off internal forces of resistance which can bring about a change of regime. And, most evident of all, the mere act of withholding our unnumbered financial and other favors from the Bolsheviks themselves would remove from the Communist enterprise the material supplements it needs to keep its staggering economy in motion—while a concerted effort to close off Moscow's chief avenues of espionage would do a like service in the matter of vital technical information.

By the same token, rational build-up and deployment of our strategic arsenal could work an important restraining effect on Communist adventurism. Were we to confront the Soviets with the full range of offensive and defensive power our technology is capable of providing, while securing our own base with an effective anti-missile defense system, Soviet nuclear blackmail, whatever its true resources, would be effectively ended. What is now conceived as strategic stalemate would become, from the Communist point of view, checkmate. The penumbra of menace under which Moscow has pressed its proxy and guerrilla wars and drawn out the protracted conflict against the West would be removed. What has heretofore been a battle of attrition against the Free World could be turned back upon the Communists, and the problem of crumbling interior positions, of putting out now this brush fire and now that, could become the Soviets' concern rather than ours.

Most important of all, the combination of these various steps—the merest securing of our own resources to our own purposes—would reverse the *psychological* equation in our favor. It would notify the Communists that we shall no longer retreat before their initiatives, and therefore tend to discourage Soviet gambles like the Cuban missile crisis, the crushing of Hungary, and the Berlin blockade—gambles all made, in the main correctly, on the calculation that we had a tendency to fade in the stretch.* It would simultaneously inform the anti-Communist forces of the world they have a leader in fact as well as in name, who can be counted on not to abandon them in the rough going on the strength of bogus assurances from Moscow. Just as there is a momentum to defeat—which we have for too long experienced—so can there be a momentum to victory. A clear example is Viet Nam, where our 1965 policy of somewhat limited firmness obviously contributed to the renewed determination of the anti-Communist elements of neighboring Indonesia. Weakness is contagious; firmness can be contagious, too.

None of this is to say merely stopping the mistaken things we are now doing would in itself constitute an effective foreign policy; it would constitute only a more effective policy than we have now. The Communists have gone too far, and by now have at their disposal too many different avenues of approach to work our distress, for a "Fortress America" stance to get the job done. We would move several paces forward by a policy of Stopping, but we should have to do other things as well. We must give effective aid to our friends and allies overseas; but, beyond that, we should work to improve the defensive strategy we have heretofore employed. Even in those cases where we have momentarily broken through the web of confusion about Communist amiability we have been so constrained by other species of Liberal abstraction that we have

* Former Soviet agent Oleg Penkovskiy says of the Hungarian crisis: "We in Moscow felt as if we were sitting on a powderkeg. Everyone in the General Staff was against the 'Khrushchev adventure.' It was better to lose Hungary, as they said, than to lose everything. But what did the West do? Nothing. It was asleep. This gave Khrushchev confidence. . . . If the West had slapped Khrushchev down hard then . . . all of Eastern Europe could be free." *The Penkovskiy Papers* (New York, 1965), p. 206

failed to make our defense effective. Again Viet Nam is the most obvious recent example.

In that struggle, from 1961 to 1965, we attempted to help the anti-Communist regime in Saigon defend itself from aggression. But we simultaneously granted the Communists a perfect access route for aggression in Laos and guaranteed the chief proximate center of aggression, the North Vietnamese capital of Hanoi, immunity from counterattack. Despite our 1965 effort to hit some Communist leverage points, America's Vietnamese strategy remained essentially a business of searching out infiltrators rather than cutting them off at some major arterial point, in Laos, or at the source, in Hanoi. Our strategy was rather like that of an exterminator who tries to kill ants with a rolled-up newspaper as they come out from under the baseboard. Any experienced exterminator can tell you such an approach will never get the job done. A truly successful defense strategy can never be mounted on purely defensive *tactics.* We need an offense as well.

The possible shape of the Western offense has been suggested by a number of authorities whose credentials in the matter of Communism have been validated by the test of experience. Such people as James Burnham, Robert Strausz-Hupe, General Curtis LeMay and countless other respected analysts of the Cold War have observed that we can successfully defend ourselves against the Communists only by turning the tables; we must give them something to worry about in their own back yard so that they do not have quite so much leisure to make trouble in ours. How this should be done will of course vary according to circumstances. In the case of Viet Nam, as the Johnson regime has in part now acknowledged, it should consist in an effort to knock out at least some of the major strategic elements of Hanoi and to stop the flow of trade into the port of Haiphong. It should also consist of an effort to re-activate anti-Communist strength in Laos, where our 1962 default left the Ho Chi Minh trail wide open for Viet Cong use. If Laos could be drawn back toward the anti-Communist camp, the struggle in Viet Nam would be a great deal easier.

In Latin America, our foremost objective should be to topple the regime of Fidel Castro, an act which would immediately relieve nine-tenths of the Communist pressure on other nations in the Hemisphere, including the Dominican Republic, Panama, Venezuela, Nicaragua. To work Castro's downfall, we should first move to halt the vast flow of Free World trade (and U.N. aid subsidized by us) to Castro, which has helped strengthen his faltering grip on the Cuban people. We should then do what President Kennedy originally set out to do in 1961: Support Cuban exile forces in their legitimate hope of restoring their country to the ranks of civilization. As in Viet Nam, we need an offense in Cuba as well as a defense. At present we have neither.

The first rule of successful guerrilla warfare is sanctuary and the first rule of successful counter-guerrilla action is to eliminate sanctuary. In both of our sample cases—Viet Nam and Latin America—our primary objective should be to move against the sanctuary from which the Communists operate. In Viet Nam, the sanctuary consists of Laos and the northern part of Viet Nam; in Latin America, it is Castro's GHQ for hemispheric subversion in Havana. Even in our best moments, our reigning policy assumptions have required us in some wise to give the Communists this asset when they wanted it—in Korea, Laos, Viet Nam, Cuba. If we are to relieve the free world from the pressures of aggression, we must stop guaranteeing the Communist that their bases of operations will be immune to our attack.

If this were successfully attempted in Cuba and Viet Nam, we would achieve a victory of a wider sort as well. The example of a truly resolute defense of Viet Nam, rather than a graceful "negotiated" retreat, plus the liberation of Cuba, would carry reverberations to every corner of the globe. Two such emphatic reversals of the Communist advance would signify to the world that the Bolshevik dream of conquest is waning. The aura of invincibility which has in the past helped the Communist enterprise would be dissolved. The effect of that transformation upon anti-Communist forces, upon the "uncommitted," and upon the captive peoples behind the Iron Curtain would be incalculable.

Such, on the merest impressionistic rendering, are the opportunities which await the United States and the Free World if we would but seize the nettle and take the necessary measures of self-protection. But they are opportunities which will never be engaged so long as our policies are in thrall to Liberal abstraction. We cannot move forward to do intelligent battle with our external adversary until we have thrown off the confusions that cripple us from within. There can be no hope of successful performance in the Cold War until we have cashiered the so-called "experts" who have steered us upon the shoals of calamity.

Liberalism has given us a foreign policy whose major achievements have been the liquidation of Western hegemony in every quarter of the globe, the transfer of one billion people from the Western world to the armed camp of Communism, and the establishment of a Communist beachhead 90 miles from American shores. Now the people who have negotiated these disasters inform us they alone are qualified to tend to our diplomacy, and that he who faults them for their conduct is suffering from mental aberration. Common prudence suggests that they, and not their critics, are the more appropriate candidates for analysis. If a man sets up shop as a race track tout or a tree surgeon or some other sort of specialist, we expect him at some point along the way to do something right. And if he routinely picks long strings of losers and kills every tree he touches, we feel justified in calling in another authority. The standards of performance ought to be at least as high for men who presume to guide the destiny of nations.

Notes

INTRODUCTION

Chapter 1: The Danger Is Internal

1. Walt Whitman Rostow, *The United States In The World Arena* (New York, 1960), p. 549
2. Fred Warner Neal, *U.S. Foreign Policy And The Soviet Union* (Center for the Study of Democratic Institutions, 1961), p. 59
3. Harlan Cleveland, address to the Arlington, Va., branch of the American Association of University Women. Reproduced in *Washington World*, October 2, 1962
4. *See* "Rusk Hits U.S. Policy Critics," Associated Press dispatch for June 1, 1962, *Indianapolis Star;* "Rusk Assails Goldwater's 'No Win' Charges," by R.H. Shackford, Scripps-Howard dispatch for June 1, 1962, *Indianapolis Times;* "The Counterattack on Victory," *Washington Report* of the American Security Council, July 2, 1962, analyzing remarks of Harlan Cleveland; "Victory—Theory And Practice," *Washingon Report*, October 8, 1962, analyzing remarks of Dean Rusk.
5. Secretary of Defense McNamara has estimated that, between 1958 and

1966, "there have been no less than 164 internationally significant outbreaks of violence—each of them specifically designed as a serious challenge to the authority, or the very existence, of the government in question." *U.S. News and World Report,* May 30, 1966.

6. James Burnham, *Suicide of the West* (New York, 1964), p. 112

Chapter 2: The Face Of The Enemy

1. *Facts On Communism,* Report of the House Committee on Un-American Activities, December 1960, p. 84
2. *Ibid.*
3. *Ibid.*
4. *Contradictions Of Communism,* Report of the Senate Internal Security Subcommittee, p. 44
5. *Ibid.*
6. *The Communist "Peace" Offensive,* report of the House Committee on Un-American Activities, April 1951, p. 2
7. Stefan Possony, *A Century of Conflict* (Chicago, 1953), p. 133
8. *Ibid.,* p. 134
9. *Ibid.*
10. *Conquest Without War,* edited by N.H. Mager and Jacques Katel, (New York, 1961), p. 49
11. Anthony T. Bouscaren, *Soviet Foreign Policy: A Pattern of Persistence* (New York, 1962), pp. 28–29
12. *Ibid.,* p. 64
13. *Ibid.,* p. 12
14. *The Great Pretense,* report of the House Committee on Un-American Activities, May 1956, p. 1
15. Quoted in *Peace And Freedom* (American Security Council, 1964), p. 109
16. *Soviet Political Agreements and Results,* Report of the Senate Internal Security subcommittee, 1956, p. ix
17. "When F.D.R. Recognized The Soviet Union," by Louis P. Lochner, *The American Legion Magazine,* October 1965.
18. *Soviet Political Agreements And Results,* p. viii
19. Lochner, *loc. cit.*
20. *Ibid.*
21. *Soviet Political Agreements And Results,* p. viii
22. *Ibid.*
23. Study released by Congressman Hosmer, May 10, 1959
24. *Soviet Political Agreements and Results,* Report of the Senate Internal Security subcommittee, third revision to January 1, 1964, Vol. II, p. 1
25. *Ibid.*
26. *The Burden And The Glory,* speeches of President Kennedy, Allan Nevins, ed., (New York, 1964), p. 91
27. Hosmer, *loc. cit.*
28. *The Great Pretense,* p. 7
29. *Khrushchev's Strategy and Its Meaning For America,* Report of the Senate Internal Security subcommittee, 1960, p. 6
30. Richard V. Allen, *Peaceful Coexistence: A Communist Blueprint for Victory* (American Bar Association, 1964), p. xix
31. *Conquest Without War,* p. 75

32. Allen, *op. cit.*, p. 15
33. *Ibid.*, p. 17
34. *Ibid.*
35. *Ibid.*, p. 19
36. *Ibid.*, p. 45
37. *Ibid.*, p. 59
38. "Report of the Central Committee of the Communist Party of the Soviet Union to the Twentieth Party Congress," in *The Communist Conspiracy,* House Committee on Un-American Activities, Part 1 Section A; 1956, p. xxv

PART I

Chapter 3: The View From The Top

1. This statement is from an article by Daniel Schorr, "Bohlen Returns to the Russian Challenge," in *The New York Times Magazine,* October 18, 1959. Schorr says the statement, among others, "summed up" Bohlen's "basic approach to the Soviet Union."
2. Statement by George F. Kennan. See M. Stanton Evans, "The Liberal Against Himself," National Review, December 22, 1956.
3. Statement by George F. Kennan in *Pacem In Terris,* Edward Reed, ed. (New York, 1965) , p. 82
4. Statement by Walt W. Rostow, *U.S. News and World Report,* May 7, 1962
5. J. William Fulbright, *Old Myths and New Realities* (New York, 1964), p. 9
6. *The Liberal Papers* (New York, 1962), p. 213
7. Statement by Harlan Cleveland, quoted by Frank Kluckhohn in *Lyndon's Legacy* (New York, 1964), p. 216
8. Statement by John F. Kennedy, in *The Burden and The Glory,* p. 57
9. Statements by Lyndon Johnson, *The New York Times,* December 28, 1963; *U.S. News and World Report,* May 11, 1964
10. Statement by Lyndon Johnson, *U.S. News and World Report,* May 11 1964
11. *The Burden and the Glory,* pp. 56–57
12. Theodore Sorensen, *Kennedy* (New York, 1965), p. 515
13. *Ibid.*, p. 243
14. "Military Cold War Education and Speech Review Policies," supplement to hearings of the Senate Preparedness subcommittee, Part 7, June, 1962, pp. 3283–3307
15. Alan L. Otten, "Big Election Victory Would Alter Johnson's Approach To Presidency," *Wall Street Journal,* August 25, 1964
16. Lyndon B. Johnson, *My Hope For America* (New York, 1964), pp. 103–106
17. *Ibid.*, pp. 103–104
18. *East Minneapolis Argus,* January 12, 1945
19. *Ibid.*

20. *Ibid.*
21. Hubert H. Humphrey, *The Cause Is Mankind* (New York, 1964), pp. 136–137

Chapter 4: The Rostow Line

1. Freda Utley, *The China Story* (Chicago, 1951) , p. 136
2. Robert Murphy, *Diplomat Among Warriors* (New York, 1965), p. 483
3. Earl E.T. Smith, *The Fourth Floor* (New York, 1962), pp. 225, 231
4. "What's Wrong With The State Department?" series of eight articles published by The New Bedford (Mass.) *Standard-Times,* June 1962, p. 6
5. *Ibid.*
6. Dean Rusk, *The Winds of Freedom,* Ernest K. Lindley, ed. (Boston, 1963), p. 350
7. *Ibid.,* pp. 7–8
8. "Senators Told Why 'Victory' Is Censored: State Department Says Word Has 'Aggressive' Ring," *Washington Star,* May 27, 1962
9. "What's Wrong With The State Department?" p. 4
10. *U.S. News and World Report,* May 7, 1962
11. "Draft Foreign Policy Revision Bowing To Reds," by Willard Edwards, *Chicago Tribune,* June 17, 1962
12. "Rostow On Communism," Manion Forum radio broadcast, October 14, 1962
13. *Ibid.*
14. *Ibid.*
15. "Rostow Paper Scuttles Chiang," *Phoenix Gazette,* May 14, 1962
16. United Press International dispatch, *The Indianapolis News,* September 23, 1959
17. Schorr, *loc. cit.*
18. *Ibid.*
19. *Ibid.*
20. *Ibid.*
21. Speech delivered May 3, 1956. "The Liberal Against Himself," *loc. cit.*
22. *Ibid.*
23. *Ibid.*
24. *Ibid.*
25. *Ibid.*
26. *Realities Of American Foreign Policy* (Princeton, 1954), pp. 89–90
27. *Russia And The West* (Boston, 1961), pp. 394–397
28. *Ibid.,* p. 398
29. *On Dealing With The Communist World* (New York, 1964), p. 14
30. *Ibid.,* pp. 11, 13, 14
31. *Ibid.,* p. 16
32. *Pacem In Terris,* pp. 81, 82
33. *American Diplomacy* (New York, 1952), p. 109

Chapter 5: The Fulbright Doctrine

1. *Old Myths And New Realities,* p. 8
2. *Senator Fulbright: A Legislator's Thoughts On World Issues,* Karl E. Meyer, ed. (New York, 1964), p. 46

3. *Ibid.*
4. "Senator Fulbright: The Man And The Memo," by Irene Corbally Kuhn, *The American Legion Magazine,* January, 1962
5. Meyer, *op. cit.*
6. "Arkansas' Senator Fulbright," by Willard Edwards, *Human Events,* February 3, 1962
7. *Ibid.*
8. *Ibid.*
9. Kuhn, *loc. cit.*
10. *New York Times,* March 26, 1964
11. *Old Myths and New Realities,* p. 30
12. Edwards, *loc. cit.*
13. *Ibid.*
14. *Ibid.*
15. "Memorandum On Propaganda Activities of Military Personnel Directed At the Public" ("The Fulbright Memorandum"), *Congressional Record,* August 2, 1961, p. 13437
16. *The Elite And The Electorate* (Center for The Study of Democratic Institutions, 1963), pp. 3–7
17. *Congressional Record,* July 26, 1965, p. 17609
18. *Ibid.,* pp. 17612–17616
19. *Ibid.,* p. 17616
20. "The Fulbright Memorandum," *loc. cit.*
21. *Ibid.*
22. *Ibid.*
23. *Ibid.*
24. C. Wright Mills, *The Causes Of World War Three* (New York, 1958), p. 54
25. *The Liberal Papers,* pp. 97–98
26. Seymour Melman, *Our Depleted Society* (New York, 1965), pp. 231 *et. seq.*
27 *Ibid.,* p. 301
28. "Smearing The Military," *The Indianapolis News,* September 5, 1964
29. *The Worker,* July 16, 1961
30. *The New Frontier Of War* (Chicago, 1962), p. 136
31. "The U.N. At 20: Should It Live to be 21?" by J.W. Fulbright, *Pageant* magazine, November, 1965
32. *Russia and the West,* p. 398
33. Vincent P. Rock, *A Strategy of Interdependence* (New York, 1964), p. 87

Chapter 6: The Liberal Papers

1. *The Liberal Papers,* p. 6
2. *Ibid.,* p. 30
3. *Ibid.,* pp 20, 21, 35, 55
4. *Ibid.,* p. 35
5. *Ibid.,* p. 23
6. *Ibid.,* p. 28
7. *Ibid.,* p. 53
8. *Ibid.,* p. 35
9. *Ibid.*
10. *Ibid.,* p. 54

11. *Ibid.*, p. 75
12. *Ibid.*, p. 68
13. *Ibid.*, p. 307
14. *Ibid.*, p. 41
15. *Ibid.*, p. 58
16. *Ibid.*, p. 116
17. *Ibid.*, pp. 121 *et seq.*
18. *Ibid.*, pp. 155 *et seq.*
19. *Ibid.*, pp. 229 *et seq.*
20. *Ibid.*, pp. 261–262
21. *Ibid.*, p. 278
22. *Ibid.*, p. 296
23. *Ibid.*, pp. 303 *et seq.*
24. *Ibid.*, p. 328
25. Charles E. Osgood, *An Alternative to War Or Surrender* (Urbana, Illinois, 1962) , p. 86
26. *The Liberal Papers,* pp. 203–204
27. *Ibid.*, pp. 184–189
28. *Ibid.*, p. 188
29. *Ibid.*, p. 189
30. News release from Republican National Committee, March 20, 1962
31. *Time* magazine, April 6, 1962
32. Lou Hiner Jr., "Democrats Take Wallops for Appeasement Papers," *Phoenix Gazette,* March 28, 1962
33. *The Liberal Papers,* p. 17
34. *Ibid.*, p. 325
35. *Ibid.*, p. 308
36. *Ibid.*, p. 196
37. *Ibid.*, p. 34

Chapter 7: The Phoenix Papers

1. Quoted by Walter Trohan, *Chicago Tribune,* February 8, 1964, see also *Peace And Freedom,* p. 25
2. United States Arms Control and Disarmament Agency, "Statement on the Phoenix Paper I Contract Study Conducted By the Institute for Defense Analysis For the State Department," March 24, 1964
3. *U.S. News and World Report,* November 18, 1963
4. *Ibid.*
5. Rock, *op. cit.*, p. 48
6. *Ibid.*
7. *Ibid.*, p. 16
8. *Ibid.*, pp. 45–46
9. *Ibid.*, p. 39
10. *Ibid.*, p. 28
11. *Ibid.*, p. 37
12. *Ibid.*, p. 33
13. *Ibid.*, p. 78
14. *Ibid.*, p. 61
15. *Ibid.*, pp. 60, 61
16. *Ibid.*

17. *Human Events,* April 11, 1964; see also *Peace And Freedom,* pp. 25–26
18. USACDA statement, *supra*
19. *U.S. News and World Report,* Nov. 18, 1963
20. USACDA statement
21. *Ibid.*
22. *U.S. News and World Report,* Nov. 18, 1963
23. *Ibid.*
24. *Ibid.*
25. *Ibid.*
26. *Ibid.*
27. *The Cause Is Mankind,* pp. 135, 140–141
28. "Proposal for a Democratic Party Platform," a presentation by Americans for Democratic Action, to the platform committee of the Democratic National Convention, Atlantic City, N.J., 1964
29. *The Burden And The Glory,* pp. 55, 57
30. *U.S. News and World Report,* Nov. 18, 1963

PART II

Chapter 8: The War For Men's Minds

1. David Cushman Coyle, *The United Nations And How It Works* (New York, 1955), p. 157
2. Thomas B. Ross and David Wise, *The Invisible Government* (Random House, 1964), pp. 20, 47
3. C.L. Sulzberger, *The Unfinished Revolution* (New York, 1965), p. 37
4. Henry A. Kissinger, *The Necessity For Choice* (New York, 1961), pp. 6–7
5. *To Turn The Tide,* Speeches of John F. Kennedy, John W. Gardner, ed. (New York, 1962), p. 141
6. *U.S. News And World Report,* May 30, 1966
7. P.T. Bauer, *United States Aid And Indian Economic Development,* (American Enterprise Association, 1959), pp. 75, 100
8. "The Underdeveloped Nations," by Karl Brandt, in *The Conservative Papers* (New York, 1964), p. 99
9. Arthur M. Schlesinger, Jr., *A Thousand Days* (New York, 1965), p. 196
10. *Ibid.,* pp. 187, 189
11. *To Turn The Tide,* pp. 163, 164
12. *Ibid.,* p. 172
13. See Philip A. Ray, *South Wind Red* (Chicago, 1962), pp. 124–125; also Ross Hermann, "Aid Means $22 Million Loss," *The Indianapolis News,* December 14, 1965. Friedman comment quoted in "Statement of Indiana Citizens Foreign Aid Committee," February 15, 1963
14. Smith, *op. cit.,* p. 41
15. *Ibid.,* p. 42
16. "Agriculture And Food Situtation In Cuba," U.S. Department of Agriculture, 1962; quoted in "Cuba Disproves The Myth That Poverty Is The Cause of Communism," published by the Truth About Cuba Committee, (Miami, 1963)

17. *Cuba And The Rule Of Law* (Geneva, 1962), p. 11
18. *American Foreign Aid Doctrines* (American Enterprise Institute, 1963), pp. 14–15
19. *The Tragedy of Bolivia* (New York, 1958) , p. 223
20. Fulton Lewis Jr., *The Indianapolis News,* Nov. 23, 1965
21. *The Winds Of Freedom,* p. 109
22. *To Turn The Tide,* p. 146

Chapter 9: The United Nations

1. Quoted by Max Ascoli in *The United Nations Reconsidered,* Raymond Moore, ed. (Columbia, S.C., 1963), p. 86
2. *Ibid.*
3. *The Winds of Freedom,* p. 304
4. Lyndon B. Johnson, *A Time For Action* (New York, 1964), p. 163
5. Charter of the United Nations, reproduced in Coyle, *op. cit.,* p. 172
6. *The Liberal Papers,* pp. 320–321
7. *Pageant* magazine, November, 1965
8. *Ibid.*
9. See Douglas MacArthur, *Reminiscences* (New York, 1965), pp. 415 *et seq.*
10. *Baltimore Sun,* October 28, 1961
11. *The United Nations Reconsidered,* pp. 9–10
12. *Newsweek,* June 4, 1962
13. Quoted by James F. Byrnes in "The United States And The United Nations" (McGraw-Edison, 1962)
14. *The Progressive,* November, 1965
15. See Goldberg's statement in *New York Times,* August 17, 1965

Chapter 10: Aiding The Enemy

1. "U.S. Foreign Aid To Red China Urged Here," by Ross Hermann, *The Indianapolis News,* January 11, 1966
2. Statement by Senator Thomas Dodd, September 9, 1965
3. *U.S. News and World Report,* February 17, 1964
4. *Ibid.*
5. Statement by Congressman Glenard Lipscomb, *Congressional Record,* September 2, 1965
6. "Are We Financing Missile Trainees?" Republican Congressional Committee Newsletter, February 28, 1966
7. UPI dispatch, *The Indianapolis News,* February 12, 1963
8. *The Indianapolis News,* February 15, 1963
9. "United Nations Loan," Report of the House Committee on Foreign Affairs, 87th Congress, second session; Report No. 2176; minority views of E. Ross Adair, p. 18
10. Statement of Congressman Durward G. Hall, Manion Forum radio broadcast, April 14, 1963
11. *Ibid.*
12. United Nations Children's Fund, Financial Report And Accounts for the year ended 31 December 1958 and Report of the Board of Auditors (United Nations, 1959), p. 26
13. "UNICEF Funds Aid Red Agent," Fulton Lewis Jr., *The Indianapolis News,* January 19, 1966

14. "U.S. Aid Helped Build Chinese, Soviet Projects," Fulton Lewis Jr., *The Indianapolis News,* July 7, 1962
15. Clark Mollenhoff, *Despoilers of Democracy* (New York, 1965), p. 15
16. *Ibid.*
17. Statement by Congressman Richard Roudebush, June 9, 1962
18. Statement by Congressman Richard Roudebush, January 1, 1966
19. *Ibid.*
20. *Ibid.*
21. "U.S. Foolishly Tries To Woo Red Rumania," by Robert Morris, *The Indianapolis News,* January 8, 1966
22. "Freedom Winds Not Blowing In Red Satellites," by Fulton Lewis Jr., *The Indianapolis News,* January 4, 1966
23. Powal Monat, *Spy In The U.S.* (New York, 1963), p. 133
24. *Congressional Record, loc. cit.,* July 26, 1965
25. Lewis, *loc. cit.,* January 4, 1966
26. See my "Tito's 'Freedom of Maneuver,'" *National Review Bulletin,* July 10, 1962 also "'Neutrals' Appeal to U.S., Russia," *The Indianapolis News,* September 5, 1961

Chapter 11: East-West Trade

1. "President Is Told Tariff Barriers Threaten West," by Felix Belair, *New York Times,* January 8, 1962
2. Quoted by Allan H. Ryskind, *Human Events,* March 12, 1962
3. *Ibid.*
4. *East-West Trade,* Report of the Permanent Subcommittee on Investigations of the Committee on Government Operations, July 1956; p. 46
5. *Ibid.*
6. *Ibid.*
7. Quoted by Fulton Lewis Jr., in syndicated column for June 8, 1961, King Features Syndicate, New York
8. Statement by Congressman John Ashbrook, August 31, 1961
9. Ryskind, *loc. cit.*
10. "D.C. Favors Soviet Trade," *Baltimore Sun,* December 14, 1962
11. "Red Trade Pushed To Businessmen," Robert S. Allen and Paul Scott, *The Indianapolis News,* December 16, 1964
12. New York *Daily News,* June 3, 1964
13. "U.S. Reverses Stand, Will Seek East German Trade," *The Indianapolis News,* June 30, 1965
14. Congressman Howard Robison, *Congressional Record,* April 29, 1965
15. Congressman Edward Derwinski, *Congressional Record,* July 1, 1965
16. Lipscomb, *loc. cit.*
17. Statement by Senator Thomas Dodd, October 1, 1963
18. Samuel F. Clabaugh and Richard V. Allen, *East-West Trade: Its Strategic Implications,* (Washington, 1964), p. 97
19. Statement by Senator Thomas Dodd, September 9, 1965
20. Quoted in Lipscomb, *loc. cit.*
21. *Ibid.*
22. Testimony of Secretary of State Dean Rusk before the Senate Foreign Relations Committee, January 28, 1966; reproduced in *The Viet Nam Hearings* (New York, 1966), p. 31
23. Republican Congressional Committee Newsletter, May 9, 1966

Chapter 12: Cultural Exchanges

1. *The Technique of Soviet Propaganda,* a study presented by the Senate Internal Security subcommittee, 1960; p. 13
2. Report of the Senate Internal Security subcommittee for the year 1958, August 27, 1959; p. 19
3. "The United States Through the Eyes of Soviet Tourists, an analysis of their published reports" prepared by the staff of the Senate Internal Security Subcommittee, 1960; pp. 3–4
4. "Report of the Central Committee of the Communist Party of the Soviet Union to the Twentieth Party Congress," in *The Communist Conspiracy,* p. xxiii; *Conquest Without War,* p. 75
5. "The United States Through the Eyes of Soviet Tourists," p. 2
6. "Beware! Tourists Reporting on Russia," by Eugene Lyons, an analysis of tourist testimony on Soviet Russia prepared for the Senate Internal Security subcommittee, February 1960; p. 21
7. Testimony before Senate Internal Security subcommittee, in "Scope Of Soviet Activity in the United States," April 12, 1956; Part 14, p. 781
8. *Ibid.*
9. Testimony before the House Committee on Un-American Activities, March 17, 1959; p. 3
10. *Ibid.*
11. Statements by Congressman Roudebush, June 23, 1961, and June 15, 1961
12. "The United States Through The Eyes of Soviet Tourists," p. 2
13. Testimony before the House Subcommittee on Appropriations, March 4, 1965; reproduced as *FBI Appropriation,* p. 68
14. Pierre J. Huss and George Carpozi Jr., *Red Spies in the U.N.* (New York, 1965), p. 11
15. *Ibid.,* p. 43
16. Statement issued by Senator McCarran, January 28, 1953
17. Huss and Carpozi, *op. cit.,* p. 43
18. Letter from Senator Birch Bayh to Robert J. Miller, August 18, 1965
19. Hoover testimony, *loc. cit.,* p. 67
20. "Exposé of Soviet Espionage," prepared by the Federal Bureau of Investigation, for the use of the Senate Internal Security subcommittee, May, 1960; p. 7
21. *Ibid.*
22. Statement by Senator Jack Miller on radio program "Comment," December 13, 1965
23. Sanche de Gramont, *The Secret War* (New York, 1962), p. 411
24. *Ibid.,* p. 409

PART III

Chapter 13: Is There A Stalemate?

1. Melman, *op. cit.,* pp. 22, 26

2. "Study FAIR Volume 3: Unilateral Arms Control: A Survey," by Barry M. Casper and John Phelps (Institute for Defense Analysis, 1963), p. 2
3. Martin Caidin, *Countdown for Tomorrow* (New York, 1958), pp. 210, 212, 219
4. Testimony before the Preparedness Investigating Committee of the Senate Armed Services Committee, November 27, 1957, in "Inquiry Into Satellite and Missile Programs," pp. 193 *et seq.* This testimony and the whole question of our "intelligence" knowledge are developed in the author's monograph, "Memorandum On Intelligence" (Indianapolis, 1960).
5. Hanson Baldwin, *The New York Times,* March 25, 1959
6. See M.J. Ruggles and A. Kramish, *The Soviet Union and The Atom: The Early Years* (Rand Corporation, 1957)
7. For comment on this assessment, see *Cleveland Plain-Dealer,* February 9, 1959
8. Hanson Baldwin, *The Great Arms Race* (New York, 1958), p. 22
9. See Colin Clark, "The Real Productivity of Soviet Russia," a study published by the Senate Internal Security subcommittee, 1961; *Growthmanship* (London, 1961); and G. Warren Nutter, "Some Observations on Soviet Industrial Growth," *American Economic Review,* May, 1957; *The Growth of Industrial Productivity in the Soviet Union* (Princeton, 1962)
10. James M. Gavin, *War And Peace In the Space Age* (New York, 1958), p. 162
11. *The Speeches of Senator John F. Kennedy, Presidential Campaign of 1960,* report of the Senate Commerce Committee, September 1961; pp. 973, 427, 489–90, 895
12. Victor Lasky, *J.F.K.: The Man and The Myth* (New York, 1963), p. 513
13. Sorensen, *op. cit.,* pp. 611, 613
14. "Study FAIR Volume I: Studies On Information and Arms Control," by Rosemary Klineberg, Janice Lyon, and Bruce Russett (Institute for Defense Analysis, 1963), p. 10
15. *U.S. News and World Report,* August 3, 1959
16. Oskar Morgenstern, *The Question of National Defense* (New York, 1959), p. viii
17. *Washington Daily News,* October 8, 1957
18. *Pacem In Terris,* p. 82
19. Raymond Garthoff, *Soviet Strategy in the Nuclear Age* (New York, 1958), p. 187

Chapter 14: The Nuclear Terror

1. Winston Churchill, speech before the Mid-Century Convocation of the Massachusetts Institute of Technology, March 21, 1949; quoted in William F. Buckley Jr. and L. Brent Bozell, *McCarthy And His Enemies* (Chicago, 1954), p. 3
2. *Program of the Communist Party of the Soviet Union* (New York, 1961), p. 62
3. F.J.P. Veale, *Advance to Barbarism* (Appleton, Wis., 1953), p. 136
4. Stefan Possony, *Resistance Or Death? The Perils of Surrender Propaganda* (Philadelphia, 1963), pp. 14–15

5. Quoted by Earl H. Voss in *Nuclear Ambush* (Chicago, 1963), p. 6
6. *New York Times,* March 30, 1958
7. "Background Material for the Development of Radiation Protection Standards," Staff Report of the Federal Radiation Council, May 13, 1960; p. 26
8. "Summary-Analysis of Hearings on the Nature of Radioactive Fallout and Its Effects on Man," Joint Congressional Committee on Atomic Energy, August, 1957; p. 4; Edward Teller and Albert Latter, *Our Nuclear Future* (New York, 1958), p. 123, and Voss, *op. cit.*, p. 22
9. Voss, *op. cit.*, pp. 9–10
10. "Background Material for the Development of Radiation Protection Standards," *loc. cit.*, p. 11
11. C.L. Dunham, "Radioactive Fallout," in the *Journal of the American Medical Association,* January 5, 1963
12. *Ibid.*
13. "Radiation Level Reported Safe," Associated Press dispatch, *Indianapolis Star,* August 23, 1962
14. "Soviet Nerve Gas," *The Indianapolis News,* October 14, 1961
15. J.V. Neel and W.J. Schull, *The Effect of Exposure to the Atomic Bomb on Pregnancy Termination in Hiroshima and Nagasaki* (National Academy of Sciences, 1956), p. 117; see also pp. 150, 162, 183, and 191.
16. Springfield, Ohio, *Sun,* April 21, 1958
17. Marshall Brucer, "The Great Fallout Controversy," *Journal of the American Medical Association,* January 6, 1962
18. See the author's "Trends" column in *National Review Bulletin,* April 1, 1961
19. "The Nuclear Test Ban Negotiations and the Quest for Peace," speech by Senator Thomas Dodd, February 21, 1963
20. *Ibid.*
21. *Ibid.*
22. Quoted in Kissinger, *op. cit.*, p. 275
23. *Ibid.*, p. 269
24. Quoted in Republican Congressional Committee Newsletter, August 10, 1962

Chapter 15: The Great Reversal

1. *The Burden and the Glory,* p. 59
2. Erie, Pa, *Morning News,* September 26, 1963
3. Television address by President Kennedy, March 2, 1962, reprinted in *Indianapolis News,* August 9, 1963. For some reason this paragraph is omitted from the collected speeches of President Kennedy (*The Burden and the Glory,* pp. 44–52)
4. *Wall Street Journal,* September 27, 1963
5. Text of the test-ban treaty, reproduced in *The Indianapolis News,* July 31, 1963
6. *Time,* September 25, 1964
7. *Ibid.*
8. *Ibid.*
9. *Ibid.*
10. *Ibid.*
11. *Ibid.*

12. *Ibid.*
13. *U.S. News and World Report,* September 28, 1964
14. *Ibid.*
15. Statement by Richard M. Nixon, *The Indianapolis News,* October 15, 1964
16. *Ibid.*
17. *Ibid.*
18. Sidney Hook, *The Fail-Safe Fallacy* (New York, 1963), pp. 13–14

Chapter 16: The Disarmament Lobby

1. Norman Cousins, *In Place of Folly* (New York, 1961), pp. 149, 148
2. *Ibid.,* pp. 101, 102
3. *Ibid.,* p. 123
4. "Is U.S. Giving Up In The Arms Race?" *U.S. News and World Report,* August 5, 1963
5. Sorensen, *op. cit.,* pp. 730–731
6. Melman, *op. cit.,* p. 251
7. *Washington Post,* December 15, 1963
8. *New York Times,* January 5, 1964
9. Melman, *op cit.,* p. 36
10. John Finney, "Top Scientist On The New Frontier," *The New York Times Magazine,* September 3, 1961
11. John Lear, "Peace: Science's Next Great Exploration," *Saturday Review,* December 10, 1960
12. *The New York Times Magazine, loc. cit.*
13. Rock, *op. cit.,* p. 354
14. Speech before the Sixth Pugwash Disarmament Conference, Moscow, November 29, 1960 (copy in author's possession).
15. Jerome Wiesner, *Where Science and Politics Meet* (New York, 1965), p. 288
16. Quoted by W.A. Manahan in "Program For Betrayal," photographic reproduction of *Factors Operative in a Post-Arms Control Situation* (North American Aviation, Inc., 1965).
17. Quoted by Edith Kermit Roosevelt, "The Balanced Deterrent," syndicated newspaper column for March 10, 1963
18. Speech before Pugwash Conference, *loc. cit.*
19. Earl Ubell and Stuart H. Loory, "The Death of Nike-Zeus," *Saturday Evening Post,* June 1, 1963
20. National Citizens' Commission, Report of the Committee on Arms Control and Disarmament, Washington, D.C., November 28-December 1, 1965; pp. 16, 17
21. *The Liberal Papers,* p. 111
22. Quoted by Senator Thomas Dodd, *Congressional Record,* February 21, 1963
23. Stewart Alsop, "Our New Strategy: The Alternative To Total War," *Saturday Evening Post,* December 1, 1962
24. *The Atlantic,* December, 1965
25. *The Liberal Papers,* p. 60
26. Arthur I. Waskow, *The Limits of Defense* (New York, 1962), pp. 83, 84
27. Quoted in Burnham, *op. cit.,* p. 80
28. "Proposals for a Democratic Party Platform," *loc. cit.*

29. *Ibid.*
30. Rostow, *op. cit.,* p. 549
31. Quoted by Walter Trohan, *Chicago Tribune,* October 23, 1963
32. *To Turn The Tide,* p. 215
33. "Blueprint for the Peace Race, outline of basic provisions of a treaty on general and complete disarmament in a peaceful world," United States Arms Control and Disarmament Agency Publication 4, May, 1962; p. 33. Similar language appears in Department of State Publication 7277, "Freedom From War," September, 1961, pp. 18–19
34. *Los Angeles Times,* March 31, 1962
35. *Washington Daily News,* April 19, 1962
36. *Ibid.*

Chapter 17: Easing Soviet Anxieties

1. Mills, *op. cit.,* pp. 110, 116
2. Walter Millis and James Real, *The Abolition of War* (New York, 1963), pp. 100, 101
3. *Chicago Sun-Times,* March 31, 1961
4. *Ibid.*
5. *To Turn The Tide,* p. 56
6. Sorensen, *op. cit.,* pp. 609, 610
7. Schlesinger, *op. cit.,* pp. 500, 502
8. *To Turn The Tide,* p. 56
9. *The Burden and The Glory,* pp. 57–58
10. *U.S. News and World Report,* August 5, 1963
11. "Study FAIR Volume 3," *loc. cit.,* pp. 9, 14
12. *Ibid.,* p. 9
13. Rock, *op. cit.,* p. 154
14. *Ibid.,* p. 39
15. Sorensen, *op. cit.,* pp. 725–745
16. Schlesinger, *op. cit.,* p. 499
17. *Ibid.,* p. 504
18. *U.S. News and World Report,* August 5, 1963
19. *Ibid.*
20. Rock, *op. cit.,* p. 368
21. Quoted by Walter Trohan, Chicago *Tribune,* February 8, 1964
22. Rock, *op. cit.,* pp. 155–156
23. Schlesinger, *op. cit.,* p. 499
24. Thomas C. Schelling, "The State of The Arms Race," in *The Prospects for Arms Control,* James E. Dougherty and John F. Lehman, eds. (New York, 1965), p. 52
25. *Chicago Sun-Times,* March 31, 1961
26. "Study FAIR Volume 1," *loc. cit.,* p. 18
27. *Ibid.,* pp. 13, 15
28. *Ibid.,* p. 22
29. "Study FAIR Volume 2," Studies on Accidental War, by John Phelps, Bruce Russett, Matthew Sands and Charles Schwarz, p. 4–14
30. *Ibid.,* p. 4–15
31. Ibid., p. 4–13; "Study FAIR Volume 1," p. 29; "Study FAIR Volume 3," pp. 27 *et seq.*

32. "Study FAIR Volume 2," p. 4–11
33. *Factors Operative In a Post-Arms Control Situation, loc. cit.*
34. *Ibid.*

Chapter 18: A Realistic Plan

1. *To Turn The Tide,* pp. 212, 213
2. Sorensen, *op. cit.,* pp. 608–609
3. *Newsweek,* December 6, 1965
4. *U.S. News and World Report,* "Is U.S. Giving Up in Arms Race?" August 5, 1963, and "New Cutback in Big Bombers: Effect on U.S. Defense," December 20, 1965
5. Robert S. Allen and Paul Scott, "McNamara Refutes Own Testimony on Arms," *The Indianapolis News,* September 2, 1964
6. General Thomas S. Power, *Design For Survival* (New York, 1965), p. 62
7. Robert S. Allen and Paul Scott, "Behind Goldwater Missile Charge," *The Indianapolis News,* January 22, 1964
8. *U.S. News and World Report,* August 5, 1963
9. Fulton Lewis Jr., "Senators Agree With Goldwater on U.S. Missiles," *The Indianapolis News,* January 30, 1964
10. *Ibid.*
11. *Congressional Record,* February 20, 1964, p. 3072
12. James Atwater, "Last Stand of the Big Bomber," *Saturday Evening Post,* June 20, 1964
13. *Ibid.*
14. "New Bomber Called Poor Substitute for Plane Air Force Really Needs," AP dispatch, *Indianapolis Star,* December 12, 1965
15. "The Department of Defense Decision To Reduce the Number And Types of Manned Bombers in the Strategic Air Command," report of subcommittee Number Two of the House Armed Services Committee, April 4, 1966, p. 6579
16. *Chicago Sun-Times,* March 31, 1961
17. "Study FAIR Volume 3," *loc. cit.,* p. 26
18. *Ibid.,* p. 18
19. *Ibid.,* p. 4
20. Report of the Committee on Arms Control and Disarmament, *loc. cit.,* p. 15
21. *Chicago Sun-Times,* March 31, 1961
22. *U.S. News and World Report,* August 5, 1963
23. *To Turn The Tide,* pp. 212–215
24. *My Hope For America,* pp. 103–104
25. Robert S. Allen and Paul Scott, *The Indianapolis News,* September 30, 1964
26. "Arms Plan Draws Goldwater Scorn," *New York Times,* April 3, 1963
27. *Ibid.*
28. Robert S. Allen and Paul Scott, "U.S. And Soviets Talking Toward Bomber Bonfire," *The Indianapolis News,* February 15, 1964; "U.S. Offers Plan to Burn 480 B-47s," *New York Times,* March 20, 1964; "Goldwater Hits Bomber Burning," *New York Times,* March 21, 1964
29. "Interlocking Unilateral Arms Control," *Washington Report* of the American Security Council, May 11, 1964

PART IV

Chapter 19: Kennedy Was Right

1. Speech delivered January 30, 1949; inserted in *Congressional Record,* August 23, 1961, by Congressman Donald Bruce
2. *Ibid.*
3. *Ibid.*
4. *Institute of Pacific Relations,* Report of the Senate Judiciary Committee, 1952 (hereinafter referred to as "IPR Report"); pp. 223–225
5. Schorr, *loc. cit.*
6. Robert E. Sherwood, *Roosevelt and Hopkins* (New York, 1948), pp. 774–775
7. John R. Deane, *The Strange Alliance* (New York, 1947), p. 90
8. Quoted by Felix Wittmer, *The Yalta Betrayal* (Caldwell, Idaho, 1953), p. 19
9. Sherwood, *op. cit.,* p. 775
10. Cairo-Teheran Papers, pp. 594–596; see Anthony Kubek, *How The Far East Was Lost* (Chicago, 1963), pp. 84 *et seq.,* also Sherwood, *op. cit.,* p. 796
11. Edward Stettinius, *Roosevelt and The Russians* (New York, 1949), p. 103
12. *U.S. News and World Report,* July 7, 1959
13. Quoted by James Burnham, "Was Bohlen a Blunder?" *The Freeman,* May 4, 1953
14. *U.S. News and World Report,* July 27, 1959
15. Quoted in Burnham, *loc. cit.*
16. *Chicago Sun-Times.* March 31, 1961
17. "Institute of Pacific Relations," hearings of the Senate Internal Security Subcommittee (hereinafter referred to as "IPR hearings"), 1952; p. 2870
18. "United States Citizens Employed by the United Nations," hearings of the Senate Internal Security subcommittee, 1952; p. 331
19. Statement issued by Senator Pat McCarran, January 28, 1953
20. *Life,* February 13, 1956; also see MacArthur, *op. cit.,* pp. 419 *et seq.*
21. *Memoirs by Harry S. Truman, Volume II: Years of Trial and Hope,* (New York, 1956), p. 374
22. *Ibid.*
23. *Ibid.*
24. Quoted in Utley, *op. cit.,* p. 122
25. Truman, *op. cit.,* p. 375
26. *Washington Post,* January 14, 1950
27. *Ibid.*
28. Republican Congressional Committee Newsletter, September 20, 1965; Don Maclean, "Did Rusk Liken China's Reds To Our Revolution?" *Washington Daily News,* September 16, 1965
29. *Ibid.*
30. *Ibid.*
31. IPR Report, p. 224

32. IPR hearings, p. 4942
33. *Ibid.*, pp. 5359-5360
34. *Ibid.*, p. 5366
35. IPR Report, pp. 118-119
36. IPR hearings, p. 3920
37. *Ibid.*, p. 2519

Chapter 20: The Exiles Return

1. Buckley and Bozell, *op. cit.*, p. 109
2. IPR Report, p. 111
3. IPR hearings, p. 5359
4. IPR Report, p. 211
5. *Ibid.*, p. 212
6. *Ibid.*, p. 213
7. *Ibid.*, p. 183
8. *Ibid.*, p. 193
9. *Ibid.*, p. 194
10. *Ibid.*
11. *Ibid.*, p. 195
12. Quoted by Allan H. Ryskind, "The Forgetfulness of Professor Reischauer," *National Review*, April 22, 1961
13. *Ibid.*
14. *Ibid.*
15. IPR hearings, p. 2535; also, 777-778
16. General Albert C. Wedemeyer, *Wedemeyer Reports!* (New York, 1958), p. 312
17. Treasury Department, Division of Monetary Research communiqué, December 8, 1944, transmitting Emmerson memorandum, "Proposed Projects Against Japan," dated from Yenan, November 7, 1944
18. *Ibid.*
19. *Ibid.*
20. IPR hearings, pp. 746-747
21. *Ibid.*, p. 5062
22. Testimony before Senate Internal Security subcommittee, March 12, 1957
23. *Ibid.*
24. Edward Hunter, *The Black Book On Red China* (New York, 1958), p. 17
25. *Ibid.*, pp. 17-18
26. James Burnham, "Nobody But Us Agrarians," *National Review*, August 10, 1965
27. "Manipulation of Public Opinion By Organizations Under the Concealed Control of the Communist Party," report of the House Committee on Un-American Activities, 1961; p. 183
28. IPR Report, p. 148
29. *Chicago Tribune*, August 19, 1961
30. *Congressional Record*, November 14; 1951; see Nora de Toledano, "Time Marches On McCarthy," *The American Mercury*, February 1952; Buckley and Bozell, *op. cit.*, pp. 140-146

Chapter 21: The IPR Strategy

1. Buckley and Bozell, *op. cit.*, pp. 119-120
2. See, *e.g*, summary of popular, congressional and political opposition to

recognition in "Statement on American China Policy," Committee of One Million, New York, December 31, 1963
3. Clifton Brock, *Americans for Democratic Action* (Washington, 1962), p. 144
4. "Proposals for a Democratic Party Platform," *loc. cit.*
5. *The Liberal Papers*, pp. 77–79
6. Quoted in Ryskind, *loc. cit.;* see also Ralph de Toledano, *Spies, Dupes, and Diplomats* (New York, 1952), p. 207
7. *Ibid.*
8. Walt W. Rostow, with Richard W. Hatch, *An American Policy in Asia* (New York, 1955), p. 54
9. *Ibid.*, p. 55
10. "The United Nations and China," address before the China Institute in America in New York City, May 18, 1951; reprinted by the Committee of One Million (New York, 1961)
11. *Ibid.*
12. Quoted in *Newsweek*, February 6, 1961
13. Fulbright, *op. cit.*, pp. 39–40
14. Vladimir Petrov, *What China Policy?* (Hamden, Conn., 1961), p. 117
15. Schlesinger, *op. cit.*, pp. 479–480
16. Robert S. Allen and Paul Scott, syndicated column for June 26, 1964; the Hall Syndicate, New York
17. Report of the Committee on Arms Control and Disarmament, *loc. cit.*
18. Fulton Lewis Jr., "Campaign To Remake Image of Red China Gaining Steam," *The Indianapolis News*, June 7, 1966; McNamara speech in *U.S. News and World Report*, May 30, 1966; Lyle Wilson, "Is Administration Trying To Appease Red China?" *The Indianapolis News*, March 22, 1966; "China Confusion," *The Indianapolis News*, May 17, 1966
19. IPR Report, p. 198
20. IPR hearings, p. 787
21. Theodore H. White and Annalee Jacoby, *Thunder Out of China* (New York, 1964), p. 323
22. Utley, *op. cit.*, pp. 20–21
23. *Ibid.*, p. 22
24. *Ibid.*, pp. 14–15
25. *Ibid.*, p. 11
26. IPR Report, pp. 204, 205
27. Gerhart Niemeyer, *Communists In Coalition Governments* (American Enterprise Institute, 1963), p. 2
28. H.L. Trefousse, ed., *The Cold War* (New York, 1965), pp. 109–110

Chapter 22: Encore In Laos

1. *Congressional Record*, May 17, 1963, p. 8920
2. *To Turn The Tide*, p. 40
3. Quoted by Dominick, *Congressional Record, loc. cit.*
4. Denis Warner, *The Last Confucian* (Baltimore, 1964), p. 305
5. *New York Times*, May 16, 1962
6. R.H. Shackford, "U.S. Is Fed Up With 'Pro-Western' Leaders of Laos," *Indianapolis Times*, May 17, 1962
7. "U.S. Loses Faith In Laos General," *New York Times*, May 29, 1962

8. *New York Times,* May 12, 1962; reproduced in *Congressional Record,* May 21, 1962; p. 8120
9. Joseph Alsop, "Mad Hatter's Tea Party," *New York Herald-Tribune,* April 23, 1962
10. *Ibid.*
11. "Laos And the Southeast Asia Crisis," *Congressional Record,* May 21, 1962, p. 8116
12. "U.S. 'Giving Away' Laos To Communists?" *U.S. News and World Report,* May 14, 1962
13. Dodd, *loc. cit.*
14. "Laos: The Explosive Domino In Asia," *Washington World,* July 31, 1962
15. Quoted by Allan H. Ryskind, in monograph, "Laos And The Future of Free Asia" (Washington, 1962)
16. *Ibid.*
17. *Ibid.*
18. *Soviet Political Agreements And Results,* revised to January 1, 1964, *loc. cit.,* pp. 95–96

Chapter 23: Viet Nam: The Turn Of The Screw

1. Rostow and Hatch, *op. cit.,* p. 13
2. Copley News Service dispatch from Tokyo, January 9, 1962
3. See *Times of Viet Nam,* Saigon, September 2, 1963; also September 26, 1963
4. Private letter from Saigon, autumn, 1963
5. "Managing The Nhus," Richmond (Va.) *News-Leader,* September 30, 1963
6. Marguerite Higgins, *Our Viet Nam Nightmare* (New York, 1965), pp. 100, 185–186
7. Jay G. Hayden, "How New Frontier Spurred Coup Against Diem," *The Indianapolis News,* November 7, 1963
8. Higgins, *op. cit.,* p. 202; see also Schlesinger, *op. cit.,* p. 992 and Sorensen, *op cit.,* pp. 658–659
9. Research Institute Recommendations, Research Institute of America; quoted in *The Indianapolis News,* November 7, 1963
10. "Saigon Summary," speech and insertions by Senator Thomas Dodd, *Congressional Record,* January 14, 1964
11. Higgins, *op. cit.,* pp. 198–199
12. *Ibid.,* p. 199
13. *Ibid.,* pp. 199–200
14. "Saigon Summary," *loc. cit.*
15. Warner, *op. cit.,* p. 237
16. Quoted in *The Indianapolis News,* November 15, 1963
17. "Report of the United Nations Fact-Finding Mission To South Viet Nam," published by the Senate Internal Security subcommittee, February, 1964; p, 23
18. *Ibid.,* p. v
19. "Saigon Summary," *loc. cit.*
20. "Report of the United Nations Fact-Finding Mission," *loc. cit.,* p. vi
21. Richard Critchfield, "Real Story Behind Viet Unrest," *The Indianapolis News,* May 31, 1966

22. Higgins, *op. cit.,* p. 186
23. *Ibid.,* p. 33
24. "Saigon Summary," *loc. cit.*
25. "Letters of Slain Flyer Describe War In Viet Nam," *Chicago Tribune,* April 5, 1964; also, "Air Captain's Letters Say Vietnamese War Is Unfair," *The Indianapolis News,* March 28, 1964
26. Norman Sklarewitz, "Special Ground Rules For Viet Nam War Irk U.S. Military Advisers," *Wall Street Journal,* October 1, 1964
27. "Letters of Slain Flyer Describe War In Viet Nam," *loc. cit.*
28. Geneva Agreements, July 20, 1954, Article 17b, in Marvin Gettleman, ed. *Viet Nam* (New York, 1965), p. 143
29. Congressman Ed Foreman, *Congressional Record,* August 13, 1964
30. *Baltimore Sun,* November 22, 1965
31. Robert S. Allen and Paul Scott, "Faulty Equipment Plagues U.S. Soldiers In Viet Nam," *The Indianapolis News,* November 24, 1965
32. *Ibid.*
33. *Ibid.*

PART V

Chapter 24: Cuba: The Bay of Pigs

1. Smith, *op. cit.,* p. 116
2. *Ibid.,* pp. 116–117
3. "Communist Threat to the U.S. Through the Caribbean," hearings before the Senate Internal Security subcommittee, August 30, 1960, Part 9; p. 687
4. *Ibid.,* p. 688
5. *Ibid.,* pp. 688–689
6. *Ibid.,* p. 699
7. Testimony before Senate Internal Security subcommittee, August 27, 1960; *loc. cit.,* p. 673
8. Smith, *op. cit.,* p. 230
9. Quoted by Clare Boothe Luce. "Our Global Double Bind," *Life,* October 5, 1962
10. Quoted in *Washington Report,* American Security Council, May 20, 1963
11. Quoted in Republican Congressional Committee newsletter, April 12, 1963; see also, *The Speeches of Senator John F. Kennedy, loc. cit.,* pp. 510–515, 679–681
12. Ross and Wise, *op. cit.,* p. 20
13. *U.S. News and World Report,* February 4, 1963
14. Mario Lazo, "Decision for Disaster," *Reader's Digest,* September, 1964
15. Ross and Wise, *op. cit.,* p. 20
16. Haynes Johnson, *The Bay of Pigs* (New York, 1964), p. 97
17. *U.S. News and World Report,* February 4, 1963
18. *Ibid.*
19. Fort Lauderdale, Fla., *News,* January 25, 1963

20. Fort Lauderdale, Fla., *News,* January 25, 1963
21. *U.S. News and World Report,* January 28, 1963
22. Johnson, *op. cit.,* p. 237
23. Lazo, *loc. cit.*
24. Johnson, *op. cit.,* p. 236
25. Milton S. Eisenhower, *The Wine Is Bitter* (New York, 1963), p. 281. Eisenhower's whole discussion of this episode, pp. 274–301, is highly instructive.
26. Quoted in Johnson, *op. cit.,* p. 236
27. *Ibid.,* p. 325

Chapter 25: Cuba: The Missile Crisis

1. Quoted in Elie Abel, *The Missile Crisis* (Philadelphia 1966), p. 11
2. James Daniel and John G. Hubbell, *Strike In the West: The Complete Story of the Cuban Crisis* (New York, 1963), p. 171
3. Roger Hilsman, "The Cuban Crisis: How Close We Were To War," *Look,* August 25, 1964
4. Daniel and Hubbell, *op. cit.,* pp. 15–16
5. *Ibid.,* p. 73
6. *Ibid.,* p. 91
7. See Sorensen, *op. cit.,* pp. 667-718; Schlesinger, *op. cit.,* pp. 794-841
8. *New York Times,* September 9, 1964
9. Quoted in Hilsman, *loc. cit.*
10. *New York Herald-Tribune,* August 17, 1964
11. Interview with the author, September 25, 1964
12. Fulton Lewis Jr., *The Indianapolis News,* February 4, 1963
13. Stewart Alsop and Charles Bartlett, "In Time of Crisis," *Saturday Evening Post,* December 8, 1962
14. Special Cuba Briefing, February 6, 1963; quoted by Congressman James Battin, *Congressional Record,* May 20, 1963
15. *Ibid.*
16. Statement issued by Congressman Bruce, February 4, 1963
17. *U.S. News and World Report,* February 11, 1963
18. Report of the Cuban Student Directorate, Miami, Fla., November 14, 1962
19. *Chicago Sun-Times,* February 7, 1963
20. Quoted by Battin, *loc. cit.*
21. *Ibid.*
22. *New York Herald-Tribune,* August 17, 1964
23. *New York Times,* November 8, 1964; interview in Brazilian newspaper *Tribuna,* quoted in *Free Cuba News,* Citizens Committee for a Free Cuba, Washingon, November 12, 1964
24. Interview with the author, September 25, 1964.
25. *Ibid.*
26. Battin, *loc. cit.*
27. *Ibid.*
28. "Cuba as a Base For Subversion In America," report of the Special Consultative Committee on Security of the Organization of American States; reproduced in the United States by the Senate Internal Security subcommittee; February 8, 1963; pp. 9, 22
29. *Chicago Tribune,* February 19, 1963

30. *Chicago Daily News,* February 19, 1963
31. *Ibid.*

Chapter 26: The Dominican Republic

1. Statement by President Johnson, May 3, 1965, text distributed by UPI.
2. *The Indianapolis News,* July 7, 1965
3. Quoted in speech by Senator Thomas Dodd, *Congressional Record,* September 16, 1965
4. *Ibid.*
5. *Ibid.*
6. "Full Story of Caribbean War: How Reds Plotted Takeover," *U.S. News and World Report,* May 1, 1965
7. *Ibid.*
8. Paul Bethel, "Dominican Intervention: The Myths," *National Review,* February 8, 1966
9. Jules DuBois, "Another Bay of Pigs In Dominican Republic?" *Chicago Tribune,* reprinted in *The Indianapolis News,* May 21, 1965
10. *Chicago Tribune,* September 17, 1965
11. Savannah (Ga.) *Morning News,* September 24, 1965
12. Testimony before the Senate Internal Security subcommittee, October 1, 1965; pp. 134–137
13. *Chicago Tribune,* November 17, 1965
14. *U.S. News and World Report,* September 27, 1965
15. *Ibid.*
16. *Ibid.*
17. *Congressional Record,* October 13, 1965, pp. 25954–25955
18. William S. Stokes, quoted by Senator Barry Goldwater, *Human Events,* November 9, 1963
19. Gutierrez, *op. cit.* See in particular, pp. 113–157, and 191–204
20. *La Verdad de Las Activitades Communistas en Venezuela,* tr. by Library of Congress, Nov. 27, 1950; statement by Rep. William Cramer, *Congressional Record,* February 7, 1963; see also Nathaniel Weyl, *Red Star Over Cuba* (New York, 1960), pp. 4–15
21. Weyl, *op. cit.,* p. 15
22. Romulo Betancourt, *Venezuela: Politica y Petroleo,* (Mexico, 1956), pp. 95–96
23. Edward Tomlinson, *Look Southward, Uncle* (New York, 1959), p. 195
24. Congressman William Cramer, *Congressional Record,* February 7, 1963 and October 13, 1962
25. Wessin testimony, *loc. cit.,* pp. 118–119
26. *Ibid.,* p. 115
27. *Free Cuba News,* June 23, 1965
28. *U.S. News and World Report,* May 10, 1965
29. Testimony of Juan Isidro Tapia Adames and Alfonso L. Tarabochia, before the Senate Internal Security subcommittee, December, 1965
30. *Free Cuba News, loc. cit.*
31. Schlesinger, *op. cit.,* p. 187
32. "Romulo Betancourt, A Tribute On His Visit to the United States, February 19–23, 1963," (Inter-American Association for Democracy and Freedom, New York, 1963), p. 18
33. *Ibid.,* p. 19

34. Schlesinger, *op. cit.*, p. 773
35. Ibid., pp. 186 *et seq.*
36. Johnson speech May 3, 1965, *loc. cit.*
37. *Ibid.*
38. Jules DuBois, "Dominican Pro-Red Troubles Blamed on U.S.," *loc. cit.*
39. *Ibid.*
40. *Free Cuba News, loc. cit.*
41. Robert S. Allen and Paul Scott, Savannah (Ga.) *Morning News, loc. cit.*
42. Tad Szulc, *Latin America* (New York, 1966), pp. 164–166.

Chapter 27: War In Katanga

1. "Eyewitness Story: City Doctors Back Tshombe," *The Indianapolis News,* January 4, 1963
2. Quoted in Ernest Van den Haag, *The War In Katanga* (New York, 1962), p. 14
3. "U.N. To Leave Congo Stronger," *Indianapolis Star,* June 29, 1964
4. Quoted by Michael Padev, *Phoenix Gazette,* December 22, 1961
5. State Department memorandum transmitted by Senator Vance Hartke, August 28, 1962
6. E. Primakov, "The Development of the Events in Congo," Moscow *New Times,* September 8, 1961
7. "The Real Facts About the Congo Crisis," *Congressional Record,* September 22, 1961
8. "The Crisis in the Congo," *Congressional Record,* September 8, 1961
9. "The Real Facts About the Congo Crisis," *loc. cit.*
10. *Ibid.*
11. "Prospects for Peace in the Congo," *Congressional Record,* January 25, 1962
12. Conor Cruise O'Brien, *To Katanga and Back* (New York, 1962), p. 264
13. *Ibid.,* pp. 266–267
14. *Ibid.,* p. 261
15. *Ibid.,* p. 264
16. "Aide Memoire," October 1, 1962; text released by American Committee for Aid to Katanga Freedom Fighters, New York, October 11, 1962
17. William R. Frye, "U.N. To Clamp Down on Secessionist Katanga," Dayton, Ohio, *Daily News,* November 30, 1962
18. "U.S. To Provide Jets For U.N. Push Against Katanga," *Indianapolis Times,* December 29, 1962
19. "2 Die In U.N. Army Mixup—Jadotville Taken Against Orders; Tshombe Flees," AP dispatch, *Indianapolis Star,* January 4, 1963
20. "Split In U.N. Is Reported On Katanga," AP dispatch, *Louisville Times,* January 5, 1963
21. *Ibid.*
22. *Indianapolis Star,* June 29, 1964
23. *U.S. News and World Report,* January 14, 1963
24. Michael Padev, "The U.S. Is Financing Murder in Katanga," *Phoenix Gazette,* December 29, 1961
25. "Missionary From Baltimore Lashes U.N. Katanga Policy," *Baltimore Sun,* October 14, 1961
26. "U.N. Troops Violate Churches, Hospitals," *The Tablet,* Brooklyn, N.Y.,

January 12, 1963
27. *Phoenix Gazette,* January 5, 1962
28. *National Review,* November 4, 1961
29. Ralph de Toledano, "Inside View of United Nations Congo Plunder," *The Indianapolis News,* June 17, 1963
30. *New York Times,* November 7, 1961
31. *New York Times,* November 13, 1961
32. Smith Hempstone, *Rebels, Mercenaries, and Dividends* (New York, 1962), pp. 176, 178
33. *Ibid.,* p. 185
34. *Ibid.,* pp. 188, 189, 192
35. Van den Haag, *op. cit.,* p. 29
36. *Ibid.,* p. 44
37. *Ibid.,* pp. 46, 45
38. *Time,* April 5, 1963

Chapter 28: How The Other Half Dies

1. Jules DuBois, *Danger Over Panama* (Indianapolis, 1964), p. 227
2. Hal Hendrix, "Canal Zone Treaty Coming Up?" *Indianapolis Times,* November 16, 1964
3. "What Really Happened," *The Spillway,* publication of the Panama Canal, January 20, 1964
4. Hendrix, *loc. cit.*
5. "Senate Must Ditch Proposed Panama Treaty," interview with Congressman Daniel Flood, Manion Forum radio broadcast, October 31, 1965
6. *Ibid.*
7. Statement issued by Congressman Flood, September 27, 1965
8. *Chicago Tribune,* September 29, 1965
9. Fulbright, *op. cit.,* p. 17
10. *Ibid.*
11. *Ibid.,* p. 24
12. *New York Times,* September 15, 1963
13. Senator Thomas Dodd, *Freedom and Foreign Policy* (New York, 1962), p. 200
14. *Ibid.,* p. 199
15. "Annual Report for the Year 1962," House Committee on Un-American Activities, January 2, 1963; p. 38
16. "Record Shows Guiana's Jagan Is A Communist," *The Indianapolis News,* September 27, 1962; "U.S. Communist Party Assistance to Foreign Communist Governments," hearings of the House Committee on Un-American Activities, November 14 and 15, 1962; p. 2025
17. Dodd, *op. cit.,* p. 199
18. *Ibid.,* p. 197
19. *Ibid.,* p. 198
20. *Ibid.,* pp. 205–206
21. Schlesinger, *op. cit.,* pp. 775–776
22. *The New Frontier of War,* p. 232
23. Dodd, *op. cit.,* pp. 271–272
24. *Ibid.,* pp. 272–273
25. *New York Times,* May 29, 1962

26. Richard D. Benson, "Indonesia After Gestapu," *National Review,* February 22, 1966
27. The quotations from Radio Havana are from Fulton Lewis Jr. syndicated column for April 1, 1962, King Features syndicate, New York; the quotation from Ray Colby is from *U.S. News and World Report,* August 31, 1964
28. Robert S. Allen and Paul Scott, "Aid To Ben Bella and Nasser Under Fire In Congress," *The Indianapolis News,* May 28, 1963
29. Robert S. Allen and Paul Scott, syndicated column for December 12, 1964, Hall Syndicate, New York.
30. *Ibid.,* June 22, 1964
31. *Ibid.,* July 6, 1965
32. Fulton Lewis Jr., "U.S. Foolishly Sends More Aid To Egypt's Nasser," *The Indianapolis News,* July 6, 1965

Chapter 29: The Double Standard

1. Quoted by Congressman William Bray, *Congressional Record,* February 7, 1964, p. 2440; see also "U.S. Is Denounced by Ghana Throng" *New York Times,* February 5, 1964; and "Ghana Students In United States Oppose U.S. Aid to Nkrumah," staff conferences of the Senate Internal Security subcommittee, 1964, pp. ix–xi
2. "Is U.S. Money Aiding Another Communist State?" hearings before the Senate Internal Security subcommittee, testimony of K.A. Busia; introduction by Senator Dodd, 1963; p. 1
3. *Ibid.*
4. *Ibid.,* p. 117
5. *Ibid.,* p. 3
6. "Africa Spy Network Bared," *Indianapolis Star,* June 10, 1966
7. Robert Morris, "Zanzibar Is The Cuba of Africa," *The Indianapolis News,* February 1, 1964
8. Elspeth Huxley, "Witches' Brew," *National Review,* March 10, 1964
9. *Ibid.*
10. "Zanzibar Regime Seizes U.S. Consul at Gunpoint," *New York Times,* January 14, 1964
11. Victor Lasky, *The Ugly Russian* (New York, 1965), p. 218
12. *Ibid.,* pp. 225–226
13. "Aid For Zanzibar's Reds?" *Oakland Tribune,* August 26, 1964
14. Eric K. Louw, *The Case For South Africa* (New York, 1963), p. 16
15. *The African Nettle,* Frank S. Meyer, ed. (New York, 1965), p. 176
16. "The Savage Logic," Richmond (Va.) *News-Leader,* August 9, 1962
17. "United States-South African Relations," hearings before the subcommittee on Africa of the House Foreign Affairs Committee, Part I, March, 1966; p. 154
18. Coyle, *op. cit.,* p. 185
19. "Congo Gives Base To Angolan Rebels For Troop Training," *New York Times,* August 21, 1962
20. Jacqueline Hallowell, "Angola and Mozambique," booklet printed by the New Bedford (Mass.) *Standard-Times,* 1962 p. 1
21. "Portugal In Africa," remarks and insertions by Congressman Hastings Keith, *Congressional Record,* March 13, and March 15, 1962

22. *New York World-Telegram and Sun,* July 27, 1961
23. *Washington Post,* July 19, 1961
24. *U.S. News and World Report,* July 9, 1962
25. "Is U.S. Money Aiding Another Communist State?" *loc. cit.,* p. 156
26. "Ghana's Vote," *Chicago Sun-Times,* February 14, 1964; see also, "Ghana Balloting Marked By Fraud," *New York Times,* February 3, 1964; and "Ghana Students In United States Oppose U.S. Aid to Nkrumah," *loc. cit.*
27. "Rhodesia: Pointing the Way to a Multiracial Africa?" remarks and insertions of Congressman John Ashbrook, *Congressional Record,* March 8, 1966
28. "Double Standard For U.N.? Action on Rhodesia, Not On Viet Nam," *U.S. News and World Report,* April 25, 1966

PART VI

Chapter 30: 'I Got My Job Through The New York Times'

1. Eugene Lyons, *Assignment In Utopia* (New York, 1937), p. 574
2. *Ibid.,* p. 572
3. *Ibid.,* pp. 575–576
4. *Ibid.,* p. 572
5. *Ibid.,* p. 573
6. *Ibid.*
7. See James J. Martin, *American Liberalism and World Politics* (New York, 1964), pp. 578 *et seq.*
8. Quoted by John T. Flynn, *While You Slept* (New York, 1953), p. 89
9. Quoted in Utley, *op. cit.,* p. 141
10. *Ibid.*
11. *Thunder Out Of China,* publisher's dustjacket
12. Toledano, *op. cit.,* p. 152
13. *Ibid.*
14. IPR Report, *loc. cit.,* pp. 138–139
15. IPR hearings, p. 682
16. *Ibid.,* p. 680
17. Toledano, *op. cit.,* p. 148
18. *Indianapolis Star,* June 7, 1965
19. *Newsweek,* December 10, 1962
20. *Ibid.*
21. *Ibid.*
22. Quoted in *Time,* July 27, 1959; the Matthews articles appeared in *New York Times* February 24, 25, and 26, 1957. For informed commentary on their impact and accuracy, see William F. Buckley Jr., *Rumbles Left and Right* (New York, 1963), pp. 60 *et seq.,* Weyl, *op. cit.,* pp. 133 *et seq.,* and Smith, *op. cit., passim* but esp. pp. 93–95. Also of interest in reflecting on Matthews' accuracy is the account of his fellow *Times* correspondent, R. Hart Phillips, in *The Cuban Dilemma* (New York, 1963)

23. Buckley, *op. cit.,* p. 62
24. *Ibid.*
25. Weyl, *op. cit.,* p. 135
26. Interview with the author, January 5, 1962
27. "Communist Threat to the United States Through The Caribbean," *loc. cit.,* p. 683
28. *Ibid.,* p. 685
29. *Ibid.,* p. 821
30. *Time,* July 27, 1959
31. *Return To Cuba,* Special Issue of the Hispanic American Report (Stanford, 1964), quoted in "An Answer to Mr. Herbert L. Matthews' 'Return To Cuba,'' "Association for the Reconstruction of the Cuban Economy (Miami, 1964)"
32. *New York Times,* July 29, 1959
33. *Life,* September, 15, 1961
34. *Ibid*
35. Stanley Millet, "Terror In Viet Nam," *Harper's,* September, 1962
36. Higgins, *op. cit.,* pp. 130–131
37. *Ibid.,* p. 354
38. *New York Times,* September 11, 1963
39. *Ibid.*

Chapter 31: To Russia, With Love

1. Nevil Shute, *On The Beach* (New York, 1958), pp. 68, 69
2. *Saturday Evening Post,* July 23, 1960
3. *Ibid.*
4. Eugene Burdick and Harvey Wheeler, *Fail-Safe* (New York, 1963), p. 7
5. *Ibid.,* p. 8
6. Hook, *op. cit.,* pp. 6, 8
7. On Fast's background, see Louis Budenz, *The Techniques of Communism* (Chicago, 1954), p. 320
8. Ralph Lapp, *The New Priesthood* (New York, 1965), p. 150
9. *Newsweek,* April 1, 1957
10. *Ibid.*
11. William Bradford Huie, *The Hiroshima Pilot* (New York, 1965), p. 14
12. *Ibid.,* pp. 226–227
13. *Ibid.,* p. 344
14. William Henry Chamberlin, *America's Second Crusade* (Chicago, 1950), p. 245
15. Hook, *op. cit.,* p. 24
16. O.F. Snelling, *007 James Bond: A Report* (New York, 1965), p. 110
17. John Le Carré, *Call For The Dead* (New York, 1964), p. 119
18. Hugh Kenner, "The Spy Comes Into The Drugstore," *National Review,* July 27, 1965

Index